THE MAKING OF THE INDIAN PRINCES

THE MAKING OF THE INDIAN PRINCES

EDWARD THOMPSON

GYAN

Published by

Gyan Publishing House
5, Ansari Road
Daryaganj, New Delhi-110002
Phone: 011-47034999, 9811692060
E-mail: books@gyanbooks.com

Distribution Network
gyanbooks.com
India, USA, Canada, UK, Australia

ISBN: 978-93-6920-060-3 (PB)

First Published, 1943

2nd Impression 2025

Printed at: Gyan Press, Delhi.

THE MAKING OF THE INDIAN PRINCES
Author: EDWARD THOMPSON

THE MAKING OF THE INDIAN PRINCES

THE MAKING OF THE INDIAN PRINCES

BY

EDWARD THOMPSON

FELLOW OF ORIEL COLLEGE, OXFORD
FORMER LEVERHULME RESEARCH FELLOW

CURZON PRESS

PREFACE

Now that India's right to independence has been acknowledged, the Princes' rights and status remain her outstanding constitutional problem. It cannot be decided by mere legal examination of their treaties with the Paramount Power. There exists, in addition, a body of practice and tradition. Also, there arises the question of the status and position of the parties to those treaties when they were made. This question only a knowledge of the events which shaped India's political framework can answer.

India's political framework was made in twenty years: in 1799–1819, between the death of Tipu Sultan and the elimination of the Peshwa. The period opens with the destruction of the Muslim kingdom of Mysore and ends with the disintegration of the Maratha Confederacy into a series of separate chieftaincies. These two conquests gave the British the control of India.

After Tipu's destruction the Marathas remained. When they were finally beaten down, Modern India was formed and its map in essentials drawn. The arrangement was to stay until the slow process of time and the coming of new systems of political thinking made it an anachronism, calling for Round Table Conferences, White Papers, and their sequel in constitutional legislation and political offers. India, as we knew it yesterday and the world has known it, was made in the space of these twenty years, first by the shattering of what Lord Wellesley styled 'the Mahratta Empire' and then, after a brief period of uncertain and faltering doctrine, by Lord Hastings' firm establishment of the States which had survived, each in the niche and status which was to be legally accepted as its own until our day. The Indian 'Prince' emerged in 1806, arising, like the Puranic Urvasi,[1] from the churning of the Ocean by the Gods and Demons, and received his position in India's polity in 1819.

In these twenty years were three major wars, the last major wars to be fought in India, except for the two Sikh wars, and one minor campaign. A detailed study of the first of these, that between the British and Tipu Sultan, lies outside my present purpose. The Muslim dynasty of Mysore was an excrescence, whose roots lay in

[1] The renowned courtesan and dancing nymph of Indra's heaven, who arose, like Venus, from the sea.

the personal qualities of two unusually vigorous alien rulers. It never challenged the overlordship of all India.

It was the second of these wars, the Second Anglo-Maratha War, that revealed the outlines of the India which was ultimately to escape absorption into the British system. Its result involved the subordination of 'the country powers' to the East India Company's Government, whose paramountcy now merely waited for the name. After 1819, only stupidity or hypocrisy or an excess of tactfulness could pretend that the East India Company was not the Paramount Power or that any of the Princes were its equals in status; the Third Anglo-Maratha War had made this clear.

Indeed, the rebound to an opposite opinion was so extreme that for close on forty years it seemed doubtful if the Princes would survive at all. The Paramount Power made no secret of its intention to annex their territories whenever a pretext could be found. The Mutiny caused a sharp revision of this attitude, and when it ended the Princes were ceremoniously re-established where 1819 had left them. The historian therefore finds himself compelled continually to return to twenty all-important years, to explain all the years which have followed.

'Personality' history is not now in vogue. A historian whose approach is through the medium of men rather than economic factors and trends is suspected of leanings to the Ruritanian school of history, a pleasant region halfway between history proper and the historical novel. The modern reader may therefore be deterred when he glances through these pages, to see an apparently multitudinous field of princes and princelings, chieftains and satraps and functionaries in the various secretariats. Historians of Modern India have been oppressed by the mass of detail unfamiliar to their readers, which they must handle and build into generalizations, and have not unnaturally been preoccupied with Governors-General and Commanders-in-Chief. In particular, Native India and its leaders have made only incidental appearances, their motives rarely understood or even regarded, their personalities left shadowy. Our writing of India's history is perhaps resented more than anything else we have done.

It has also resulted in error and misconception on our side. For us, over a century later, to accept the Princes as they are presented after that century—during which they have been a part of India yet separated from British India and in nearly all that concerned India as a whole almost passive agents—and to assume a modern attitude of over-simplification to a polity and constitution which were worked out by a succession of hammer-blows alternating with much wise and patient action, is to misunderstand India entirely. There is no other road to understanding the Princes and the problem their position and status now are, than by going through twenty significant years in detail, weighing the imponderables of personal forces as the men of that time had to weigh them.

To obtain this knowledge, one must have access to the diaries, minutes, reports, and records of the time, of which many have never yet been used. This brings me to the duty of acknowledgment of help that can rarely have been given so generously and by so many. Ten years ago, the Leverhulme Trustees by the award of a research fellowship enabled me to begin a study which was to take me far afield, into small dark rooms in remote places, where I found myself turning over bundles of mouldering letters of once-powerful men long dead, records tied up in *roomals* (handkerchiefs) and often still unsorted. The representatives of Lord Metcalfe put into my hands practically all that survived of his correspondence; for this kindness I am indebted to Miss Clive Bayley above all, and for much additional information. The India Office, and Dr. H. N. Randle, its librarian, gave free access to their own records. Lord Lothian, Secretary of the Rhodes Trust, cared about India and cared about history, and the Trustees twice gave me a grant to visit India in search of material. Friends like Sir Tej Bahadur Sapru told me historical details which they came across in law practice, some of them throwing light on men before my period, such as Warren Hastings. M. R. Jayakar put me in touch with men who held the key to Maratha traditions and manuscripts. Sir Akbar Hydari gave me the freedom of the Hyderabad records. Jawaharlal Nehru drew my attention to matters which an Englishman, left to himself, would be bound to overlook. Rai Saheb Sardesai left his remote home in the Western Ghats, to help me as no other student of Maratha history could. Lieutenant-Colonel Reginald Schomberg, D.S.O., C.I.E., my friend from days when we were both before Kut, introduced me to the Records Department of the Bibliothèque Nationale, Pondichéry. I have been allowed to examine records in Persian, Marathi, French, Urdu, Bengali, as well as my own tongue.

I wrote first my *Life of Lord Metcalfe*. I had known in a general way how remarkable and noble a man he was. But I had known far less than the reality, and I saw that I must go yet further and try to light up a whole period, a whole vanished and scarcely realized generation. The period 1799–1819 has not merely a political importance. It has a personal interest exceeding that of any other period in British-Indian relations.

No other period threw up so many men who were outstanding in gifts and character. Our nation has not begun to be aware of even their intellectual quality. Such a letter, for example, as the one Elphinstone (whose letters I have seen lying in scores, still awaiting study) wrote immediately after the Battle of Assaye should be famous. It came from the brain swiftly and was sent as it came, but no professional writer who ever lived could better it as literature in a single phrase. And Elphinstone habitually wrote on this level or very near it. Nor is there much wrong with the letters, written without any thought of their being 'literature', of Metcalfe and Malcolm (except that their handwriting is a sorrow to read, and Malcolm's in particular, especially in his later days, something which ought to be an offence against the law). They were wonderfully attractive men, vivid and eager and in the main tolerant and far-seeing. They have hardly had their equals in British history of any land or age.

Part of the reason for this intellectual quality was their experience. It was in this period, and most of all in the earlier of its two Maratha campaigns, that the British became 'acclimatized' in India. The psychological change and shift in their attitude was immense. Before this, their people had been adventurers. Now they were in India to stay. This compelled a revolution in thought, and not least in its subconscious levels.

Men to whom a change like this comes rarely themselves perceive it. But the historian has no right to look through his material so carelessly as to miss it. Perception of this change came to me, not in official despatches, but in the hurried and often confused letters of quite unimportant men, who had done little serious thinking in their lives but found themselves in the presence of a new world that forced thinking upon them. I have tried to make these men, and their leaders especially, living and distinct, and make no apology for citing freely incidents which might be regarded as trivial and beneath the dignity of history. In the process I learnt also how vivid and attractive were many of those Indian leaders who before had been little more than mere names of men who had gone down in defeat and hopeless resistance.

In conclusion, I return to acknowledgment of indebtedness. Most of all, I am in the debt of Mr. and Mrs. H. N. Spalding, who established a fellowship in Indian historical research, and to the Provost and Fellows of Oriel College, who accepted it and elected me to their number. Their steady kindness and interest can never be adequately acknowledged. I owe thanks, for facilities or advice, to the Rev. E. W. Thompson, M.A., who looked through a very early draft of this book: Mr. Dinkar Ganesh Bhide and Mr. Narayan Shivram Nadkarni, of the Bombay Records Office: Mr. D. B. Diskalkar and Mr. Bhusani, of the Parasnis Museum, Satara: the Officers of the Hyderabad State Records: Mr. H. G. Rawlinson, C.I.E.: Dr. T. G. P. Spear: Sir Patrick Cadell: and Sir William Foster, C.I.E.: the late Philip Morrell.

ORIEL COLLEGE, E. T.
OXFORD.

20 January 1943.

CONTENTS

PART I. THE EMERGENCE OF THE PRINCES

PART II. BRITISH PARAMOUNTCY

LIST OF MAPS

PART I
THE EMERGENCE OF THE PRINCES

I. INDIA AT THE END OF THE EIGHTEENTH CENTURY

The Marattahs possess, alone of all the people of Hindostan and Decan, a principle of national attachment, which is strongly impressed on the minds of all individuals of the nation, and would probably unite their chiefs, as in one common cause, if any great danger were to threaten the general state.—*Warren Hastings, in 1784.*

India contains no more than two great powers, British and Mahratta, and every other state acknowledges the influence of one or the other. Every inch that we recede will be occupied by them.—*Charles Metcalfe, in 1806.*

WARREN HASTINGS left India in 1784. On his voyage home he drew up an analysis of its political condition.[1]

The list of Powers which might be considered independent had shrunk from one cause or another, the East India Company having been the most effective dissolvent: 'it seems to have been the fixed policy of our nation in India to enfeeble every power in connection with it'. The Mogul Emperor, though hardly worthy to be reckoned among Powers of any sort or kind, he mentions because of the prestige attaching to his ancestors and in some degree to his person. The Nawabs of Oudh and the Carnatic, nominally servants of the Emperor, he notes as entirely dependent on the Company. Another nominal officer of the Emperor, the Nizam of Hyderabad, he sees in the position of a star destined to become a satellite but now the object of contention between rival heavenly bodies:

'His dominions are of small extent and scanty revenue; his military strength is represented to be most contemptible; nor was he at any period of his life distinguished for personal courage or the spirit of enterprise. On the contrary, it seems to have been his constant and ruling maxim to foment the incentives of war among his neighbours, to profit by their weakness and embarrassments, but to avoid being a party himself in any of their contests, and to submit even to humiliating sacrifices rather than subject himself to the chances of war.'[2]

There were also a number of small principalities, whose safety was in lying quietly under the shadow of some greater Power. Some of these, notably the Rajput states, all nominally dependents of the Emperor though actually fallen within the orbit of the Maratha chieftain Sindhia, were respectable from their antiquity.

[1] G. W. Forrest, *Selections from the State Papers of the Governors-General of India, Warren Hastings*, ii. 58. [2] *Ibid*, ii. 55.

They still survive, almost the only States with a title older than that of the British Government or with one not originally derived from an office under the Mogul Emperor.

The Punjab was unsettled. The Sikhs (as Hastings notes, a sect rather than a nation) were there struggling with Mussulman invaders and adventurers. Apart from this and other districts beyond the Company's present purview—such as Nepal, Sind, and Kutch—in India Hastings saw only two genuinely independent Powers, Tipu Sultan in the Mysore, and the Maratha Confederacy straddling across Central India and now reaching far into the north, controlling Delhi itself. It was certain that sooner or later war would come between these two Powers and the British.[1]

The Destruction of Tipu Sultan

The first of the wars which Hastings foresaw began when Tipu (29 December 1789) attacked the Company's ally, the Raja of Travancore. 'That mad barbarian Tippoo has forced us into a war with him.'[2] It ended, 1792, in Tipu's utter defeat. But the peace which followed this Third Mysore War was to be merely an armistice.

In the decade that ended the century, Tipu was in fitful communication with the French. Raging from his loss of a huge indemnity and of half his dominions, he felt blindly for allies, inside and outside India. This restlessness in no way differed from the normal behaviour, then or since, of warring or threatened States, but it was reprobated as proof of his ingrained faithlessness. His quarrel with the British was one of deep mutual hatred; the stories of his treatment of captives had rung through England.

Three wars only—the two World Wars and that against Napoleon—have been waged by the British with a conviction that defeat meant submergence. During the Napoleonic War the ruling oligarchy knew that the commerce which brought it wealth and financed the political arrangement which secured enjoyment of that wealth was threatened. When the Earl of Mornington reached India as Governor-General, May 1798, his class had worked itself into a frenzy of patriotism and exasperation against

[1] To the testimony of the Marathas' outstanding importance, which I cite from British sources, could be added that strewn *passim* in the French records at Pondichéry, especially the *Correspondance de Montigny avec Piveron de Morlat.* Morlat was sent as French agent to Poona in 1782; his duty was to counteract Malet, the British representative. The Marathas are styled 'la seule Puissance réelle dans l'Inde' (14 February 1787), a fact freely and often admitted.

[2] Lord Cornwallis, 15 April 1790: *Correspondence*, edited by Charles Ross.

Jacobinism (a term used as widely and loosely as such terms as 'Red', 'Left', and 'Communism' in recent years) and against Buonaparte. The latter was entangled in his Egyptian and Syrian adventure, which in retrospect appears a mere escapade but at the time was accepted as a serious attempt to break through to the growing British Empire in the East. Such a break-through was, as a matter of fact, part of Napoleon's larger hope. The new Governor-General came resolute to end the Company's quarrel with Mysore once for all. He regarded this as his contribution to Buonaparte's defeat.

Madras, long sunk in selfishness and corruption, and Bombay, an isolated and fragmentary property overshadowed by the power of the Marathas, he found hard to stir. But he infused his own excitement and enthusiasm into the British of Bengal. Calcutta subscribed and sent home, July 1798, £130,785 3*s.* 1½*d.*, a sum which included a small contribution by Indians.[1] There was immense, if passing, zeal to enrol as volunteers against invasion by the Corsican ogre, and plans were drawn up for the defence of the capital. Gentlemen turned out on Calcutta *maidan*,[2] complete with sidearms and musket, and attended by native servants carrying umbrellas, and bricks to put beneath Master's feet if Master had to drill in squashy places. The season was the monsoon, when the *maidan*, even now, can be very wet.

Tipu could hardly have escaped destruction by even the most circumspect humility. He gave a *casus belli* by inept negotiations with the French Governor of Mauritius,[3] which the latter boastfully published. These intrigues, with a not very important official, furnished an excuse for the war which Lord Mornington would have made in any case. It began in February 1799, and was over in three months. Seringapatam was stormed (May 4), and the Sultan's body was found in a pile of about five hundred crowded into a small space. The Governor-General's brother, Arthur Wellesley, as unshakably phlegmatic as Lord Mornington was excitable, standing in torchlight felt heart and pulse, and reported Tipu to be lifeless. His conquerors buried him with military honours, in which the elements joined, sweeping the island with a tempest of thunder and rain such as was hardly remembered in even that storm-ravaged region.[4]

[1] *India Office Records, Home Miscellaneous Series*, 481 (5), p. 80. Towards the loan presently raised for the Mysore War, the Governor-General himself subscribed Rs.120,000.

[2] An open space for recreation.

[3] Mornington to the Secret Committee, 30 October 1798.

[4] Seringapatam, an island in the river Kaveri, is notorious for electric storms.

A shrunken Mysore was placed under a Prince of the Hindu dynasty which Tipu's father, Haidar, had dislodged. The new Maharaja, a child,[1] showed a 'highly proper' decorum during the ceremony of his enthronement. His family, who had been discovered in abject poverty, behaved equally well, and acknowledged their grateful sense of dependence. 'We shall at all times', the two ladies of highest distinction told the Commissioners for the settlement, 'consider ourselves as under your protection and orders. . . . Our offspring can never forget an attachment to your government, on whose support we shall depend.' This language was rather more than the flowery recognition of favours received, which etiquette and custom prescribed. It underlined what was obvious; Mysore had become a puppet state. Its pacification was undertaken by a group of able soldiers, who afterwards left administration in the hands of Purnayya, a veteran Brahman politician, who governed it as Dewan.[2]

The French, all but ejected from India, had long watched despairingly from Pondichéry, conscious of their inability to help a state which they had encouraged into wars which destroyed it. To Cornwallis' campaign against Tipu, ten years earlier, they had given close and unremitting attention, and at its close exclaimed that at last both Nizam and Marathas must surely have their eyes opened, and begin to see how unwise they had been in warring against Mysore, thereby enfeebling the only Power 'qui puisse en imposer aux anglais'.[3]

Haidar and Tipu brought the East India Company nearer to ruin than any other Indian foes had brought it, and nearer than any subsequent foe was to bring it. But they were an episode only, lasting less than forty years. They took no root among the country powers.[4] With the Marathas, the greatest of these powers, Tipu's destruction left the Company fairly face to face.

[1] Three years old, according to Malcolm; five, according to Beatson.

[2] Chief civil officer.

[3] 27 February 1792: Pondichéry Records. It is interesting to note that, so far as my own uncompleted researches show, Warren Hastings is mentioned only once, in these very full records. Bengal was far away, and it was not until Cornwallis came in person to make war in South India that the French realized that the East India Company's actions were passing under a genuinely unified control.

[4] A common mode of reference to Indian states at this time.

II

THE MARATHAS

THE MARATHAS are a hardy nation from the Deccan and Western Ghats. Their homeland, Maharastra, lies between the 16th and 22nd degrees of north latitude, and stretches from the Satpura Hills to the Wainganga[1] and Wardha rivers, and to the borders of Goanese territory.

They became prominent in the later decades of the seventeenth century, under Shahji and his celebrated son Sivaji. The Rajputs had hitherto been the spearhead of Hindu resistance to the Mogul Empire. They now weakened, worn down by long and desperate fighting, and the Marathas took their place. Sivaji, founder of Maratha greatness, was a particularly devout Hindu and fought for Hinduism almost as much as for his own hand. For this reason, and because the Marathas were peasants, low in the caste scale, their Brahmans had exceptional power and influence. One main cause of the ascendancy which the Peshwas obtained was the fact that they were Brahmans and their persons sacred, whatever their misdeeds. This essential consideration is often overlooked.

With our recent historians, the Marathas' reputation is that of robbers pure and simple. It is true that this opinion can find support in the great authority of Sir Thomas Munro. 'The Mahratta Government, from its foundation, has been one of the most destructive that ever existed in India.'[2] But Munro's service was in Mysore and Madras, and he saw the Marathas solely as enemies; he never was where he could understand Northern India, an entirely different world from the South, and one which all through the centuries has had a different history and outlook. His exasperated witness was written in 1817, when for many years the Marathas had been the dregs of what they were. Munro himself was then marching against their last Peshwa, a man in whom no one has yet found any good quality, his memory still felt as a humiliation to the nation that he ruined.

Most of the distinguished men who dealt directly with the Marathas thought better of them. Hindu India cherishes their memory with pride, and they could not have conducted their

[1] The river made famous by Kipling's story, *Red Dog*.

[2] 28 November 1817.

protracted and successful fight against the Mogul Empire, without the support of the regions by whose resources they subsisted. We cannot

'deny to the Mahrattas, in the early part of their history, and before their extensive conquests had made their vast and mixed armies cease to be national, the merit of conducting their Cossack inroads into other countries with a consideration to the inhabitants, which had been deemed incompatible with that terrible and destructive species of war.'[1]

An officer who knew them exceptionally well, though he bears testimony to the desolation that they brought—'a Mahratta army are more indefatigable and destructive than myriads of locusts'—and speaks of the hardness of heart acquired from warfare,[2] which as in the case of Prussia had become their 'national industry', gives us also this attractive picture of their 'great simplicity of manners':

'Homer mentions princesses going in person to the fountains to wash their household linen. I can affirm having seen the daughter of a prince (able to bring an army into the field much larger than the whole Greek confederacy) making bread with her own hands, and otherwise employed in the ordinary business of domestic housewifery. I have seen one of the most powerful chiefs of the empire, after a day of action, assist in kindling a fire to keep himself warm during the night, and sitting on the ground on a spread saddle-cloth, dictating to his secretaries and otherwise discharging the political duties of his station. This primeval plainness operates upon the whole people. There is no distinction of sentiment to be discerned: the prince and his domestics think exactly in the same way, and express themselves in the same terms. There appears but one level of character, without any mixture of ardour or enthusiasm; a circumstance the more surprising, considering the great exploits they have achieved. But their simplicity of manners, uncorrupted by success, their courtesy to strangers, their unaffected politeness and easiness of access, must render them dear to every person that has had a commerce with them. Such a character, when contrasted with the insidiousness of the Brahman, and the haughtiness of the Mussulman, rises as superior to them, as candour and plainness are to duplicity and deceit, or real greatness to barbarous ostentation.'[3]

[1] Sir John Malcolm, *Central India*, i. 68–9.

[2] 'The Mahrattas are total strangers to charity, and possess an insensibility of heart with which other nations are unacquainted. The feelings get steeled by a repetition of distress, especially in a people whose ruling passion is avarice.' I would add that one thing which stands out in the literature that depicts India in the last forty years of the eighteenth century is the general hard-heartedness of Europeans and Indians. Misery was so common that men grew accustomed to it.

[3] *Illustrations of some Institutions of the Mahratta People*. By William Henry Tone, Esq., commanding a regiment of infantry in the service of the Peshwa. It is undated, but internal evidence places it in 1794 or 1795. It was addressed to an officer who was probably John Malcolm. Tone was a brother of Wolfe Tone.

India, usually under the necessity of selecting between two evils (except when no choice at all has been offered), has never been too critical of armed power operating in its midst. When Providence has seen fit to make your standard of comfort a wretched one, you accept chastening without complaint; if you must choose between King John and Robin Hood, Robin Hood seems saintly. Sivaji accordingly has been deified,[1] and not in Maharastra only.

Rise of the Maratha Chieftains

Sivaji's successors held their Court at Satara and were nominal heads of the Maratha Confederacy. But early in the eighteenth century they fell completely out of sight behind the Peshwa, who was originally Second Minister in Sivaji's *Astha Pradhān*, or Cabinet of Eight. The Eight all became hereditary ministers, and to-day the descendants of two are 'Princes'.[2] The Peshwa of Shahu, Sivaji's grandson, secured an outstanding authority, which his son, Baji Rao I, so strengthened that in 1727 he was granted full administrative powers. Henceforward the Maratha Government was in fact the Peshwa's Government, checked and qualified by the influence of the great semi-independent chieftains.

The Raja of Satara, the Confederacy's original and nominal overlord, 'from the mere force of prejudice' received 'some occasional attentions', scrupulously paid him. Enjoying 'the splendid misery of royalty and a prison', confined to his capital, on 'a very moderate allowance',[3] he yet formally invested every Peshwa with his *khelāt*.[4] No Peshwa could take the field without previously taking leave humbly of the Raja. The Satara district possessed a sacred perpetual peace, 'an exemption from military depredations of all kinds'. When any chieftain entered it he laid aside all marks of his own rank and his drums ceased to beat. Apart from this outward homage, which one of the four great chieftains, the Bhonsla Raja—who claimed to be himself, as Sivaji's descendant, the true Maratha head—hardly paid at all, the Raja of Satara did not matter in the least but was an empty pageant. The descendants of the *Astha Pradhān* ministers also, except for the Peshwa, sank into subordinate positions.

Four of the semi-independent military chieftains were of the first rank of importance: the Gaekwar, Sindhia, Holkar, and Bhonsla. They became associated respectively with Baroda, the

[1] His sword is worshipped in its own temple, at Satara.

[2] The Rajas of Aundh and Bhore.

[3] W. H. Tone.

[4] Sign of appointment, usually a shawl.

Ujjain-Gwalior[1] country, the Vindhya-Narbada country (Indore), and Nagpur-Berar. They were finally established in the third decade of the eighteenth century, but arose a full generation earlier. Their homage therefore went directly to the Peshwa, since in 1727 the Maratha Government became *de facto* the Peshwa's Government. The Gaekwar and Holkar and the Bhonsla were very loosely attached to the Confederacy, whose heart was Sindhia and the Peshwa. Gaekwars, Sindhias, and Holkars have survived into modern India as leading Princes—a title which in the eighteenth century they would have disclaimed with formal modesty.

A main source of Maratha strength was that from the first they were catholic in their political and military system and habits. They made use of the fighting qualities of other racial stocks in a manner to which only the Company, with its armies recruited from many castes, could in the late eighteenth century show anything comparable. The English, whose military commanders have been almost usually Scots or Irish and their Prime Ministers and great Cabinet officers often Scots or Jews, were the only enemy whose sinews of war were as elastic as theirs. Sivaji himself had freely employed Muhammadans, as Mahadaji Sindhia did later.

Warren Hastings, who understood most things Indian and possessed an unsleeping curiosity, knew all this. But it came as slow puzzling information to his successors. Lord Wellesley[2] seems to have been unaware of the Satara family's existence. He styles the Peshwa a 'sovereign' (which, theoretically, he emphatically was not; he was merely a Minister) and throughout his time in India he was under the impression that the Marathas were an 'Empire', with a 'Constitution' under which Sindhia, Holkar, Gaekwar, and Bhonsla held places like that of himself and his fellow hereditary peers under the British Constitution. It is true that the term 'Empire' was used by men better informed than Lord Wellesley, including Arthur Wellesley and Malcolm. But what to them was a term of convenience to him was an accurate description and in the light of his faith that this was so he acted throughout.[3]

During the latter part of the eighteenth century, Marathas and British had met in desultory fashion, both as friends and foes. The

[1] Gwalior, the Sindhia capital to-day, belonged to the Rana of Gohad until the last quarter of the eighteenth century.

[2] Lord Mornington was created Marquess Wellesley for his defeat of Tipu.

[3] Arthur Wellesley early saw his error. 'The greater experience I gain of Mahratta affairs, the more convinced I am that we have been mistaken entirely regarding the constitution of the Mahratta Empire' (20 June 1803).

former prowled very far from their home lands and Sivaji's brother Venkaji established a Maratha dynasty in Tanjore, near Madras. In the casualness of those earliest wars of the Company, a body of Marathas under an adventurer, Morari Rao, fought sometimes against the British, sometimes (as in Clive's Arcot campaign) on their side.

In 1772, when Warren Hastings lent the Nawab of Oudh a brigade to subjugate the Rohillas, it was well understood that the real menace, behind the Rohillas, was the Marathas. Two years later, in 1774, the Government of Bombay precipitated an iniquitous war with Sindhia and the Peshwa, and achieved thereby the miracle of bringing Hastings and his Council into temporary accord. The latter informed the Bombay Government that its action was 'impolitic, dangerous, unauthorized, and unjust', adjectives which were explained and elaborated.

The Gaekwar kept outside this war. So did the Bhonsla Raja, who was always 'somewhat aloof from the politics of Poona'[1] and throughout Clive's and Hastings' time cultivated with the Company friendly relations, which served the latter well. Holkar, too, can hardly be considered to have taken part in the campaign, which dragged on for several years. In January 1779, the Bombay Government surpassed itself in incompetence, an army surrendering at Wargaon, where its commander signed a convention which, Hastings said, 'almost made me sink with shame when I read it'. The convention, like that which Roman generals made at the Caudine Forks with a Samnite army, was repudiated, and the Marathas lost their advantage. Hastings, rising to perhaps the highest moment of even his vigorous clear-sighted career, in 1780 thrust out across Central India—into territory almost as legendary in its uncharted immensity as the kingdoms of Prester John or Kubla Khan—two soldiers, Popham and Goddard, who largely repaired the first disasters, though Goddard afterwards lapsed into carelessness that all but brought about a second Wargaon. Two years later (May 1782),[2] the war ended by the Treaty of Salbai.

This Treaty was important in more ways than one. The Company at last stood out among the Indian Powers, and negotiated on equal terms with one of the two other genuinely independent Powers. The war was recognized as having been on the whole a drawn contest, and it left a conviction on both sides that the sovereignty of India would ultimately be fought out between

[1] Colebrooke, Sir T. E., *Life of Elphinstone*, i. 111.

[2] The Treaty was not ratified by Nana Farnavis, the Peshwa's chief minister, until the following February.

them, with other Powers merely subsidiaries and subordinates. But for the present both were content with the situation and accepted it without rancour. They had been reasonably good-tempered foes, and Mahadaji Sindhia, who co-operated with Warren Hastings in bringing about a comprehensive and moderate settlement, liked and admired the British leader. He acted as the Peshwa's representative and also, independently, as guarantor of the treaty. This made him in effect almost a colleague of the Peshwa and left him the leading Maratha chief, a position for which his abilities well qualified him.

III

DECLINE OF MARATHA POWER

DESPITE HIS friendly feeling for Hastings, Mahadaji Sindhia proceeded to strengthen himself with European soldiers of fortune, especially as officers and artillerymen. Most of these were French, that nation being encouraged because of their secular hostility to the English, and also because the latter had the inconvenient habit of commanding their own people to leave a State whenever the Company found itself at war with that State. Their employers thus lost their services when most needed and when they were invaluable to the enemy as spies and intelligence agents. Following a heavy defeat by Sindhia in 1792, Tukoji Holkar, though he distrusted the Western manner of fighting and preferred the predatory Maratha fashion, mobile and sudden and free to pick its terrain, copied his rival in a small way, and began to enlist his own European troops and gunners.

Sindhia found a commander-in-chief in Count de Boigne, whose adventurous career had made him familiar with danger (according to tradition, he had held, among other appointments, the exacting one of lover to the Empress Catharine of Russia). De Boigne added a bayonet to the Maratha trooper's equipment of sword and target and matchlock, and under this wise leader Sindhia's armies overran the Rajput States. In 1789, they took Delhi from Ghulam Qadr, an Afghan, who in youth had been castrated by the Emperor and had taken his revenge later by blinding him and holding him captive. Sindhia, ordinarily a merciful man, inflicted a fearful punishment, and reinstated the helpless old Emperor. Shah Alam was treated with respectful kindness by his new protectors, whose elastic polity allowed of many nominal overlords at once. The authority they derived as his deputies and guardians gave a form of propriety to their far-ranging depredations, and they were a people who attached importance to forms.

The Peshwa was an ally of the Company in Cornwallis' war with Tipu (1790–2), and Maratha contingents rendered good service. But the nation then proceeded to destroy itself, so that Wellesley's attack in 1803 met a disorganized and weakened opposition. The last decade of the eighteenth century was one of constant clashing of Holkars and Sindhias, of civil dissensions monotonous in repetition and appalling in brutality.

The brutality stands out because, in comparison with the hideous cruelty of contemporaries, European as well as Asiatic, the Maratha record has been generally humane. Their governments, except when actively pillaging, were light; they had little purdah, and their social system as a rule dispensed with the barbaric funeral pomp of Rajput, Sikh, and Bengali, which immolated thousands of women annually.[1] But during the last decade of the eighteenth century, as one after another every respectable leader passed away, the nation lost its honourable characteristics, including its comparative humanity. On occasion, especially under the last Peshwa in Poona, Maratha executions vied in cold-blooded ferocity with the worst of other lands.

Mahadaji Sindhia died in 1794, and was succeeded by his grand-nephew Daulat Rao Sindhia, in every way his inferior. Daulat Rao in 1798 married a girl of great beauty, with whom he was infatuated, and fell completely under the influence of her father, Sarji Rao Ghatke, the evil genius of the Maratha nation.

The Sindhias' great rivals, the Holkars, less ostentatiously wicked, were also weaker in resources. Their celebrated Princess, Ahalya Bai, venerated in her life as nearly divine and after her death deified,[2] died in 1795, and her chief captain and minister, Tukoji Holkar, died two years later. The time's confusions quickly eliminated the elder of the latter's two legitimate sons. Two illegitimate sons, who were brothers, questioned the title of the remaining legitimate son, who was imbecile in mind and body and lived only to express a steadily developing viciousness, in which Ghatke and Sindhia encouraged him. The Holkars were soon reduced to the level of fugitive robber chiefs.

Meanwhile, the Peshwa's authority also sank to vanishing point. In 1795, Madhu Rao Narayan, whom Balaji Janardan Farnavis (Fadnis), best known as Nana Farnavis, the greatest Indian statesman of the later eighteenth century, kept in surveillance that was practically incarceration, either flung himself from a balcony or fell accidentally, to die of his hurts, 27 October. A puppet

[1] Malet, however, during his residence at Poona, lived beside a *sangam*, or junction of rivers, a site deemed particularly holy. Suttees outside his house were so frequent that they soon ceased to interest him: see his letter, 3 June 1789, printed in Sarkar and Sardesai, *Malet's Embassy*, 111. Nevertheless, it is true that the rite was dying out, and that even at the obsequies of Maratha rulers it was not common.

[2] Her temple occupies a commanding site on the crags at Maheswar, overlooking the Narbada River.

Peshwa who reigned from June to November of the next year was deposed after a brief period of confusion and intrigue and counter-intrigue, and Baji Rao II, cousin of the Peshwa who had died, was established by consent among the chieftains.[1] His father, Raghunath Rao, had been a protégé of the British and indeed the main cause of the First Anglo-Maratha War in Warren Hastings' time, which was brought about by his claim to the peshwaship. Baji Rao was distrusted from the first; the Maratha leaders, and Nana Farnavis most of all, always suspected him of readiness to accept a position of dependence under the Company. A youth of ingratiating presence but extreme timidity, he was crammed to the recesses of his personality with faithlessness and cowardice.

Henceforward the Maratha Confederacy was shaken by incessant quarrels and by civil war made lurid with sadistic executions. Dissatisfied with the ordinary methods of blowing from a gun and trampling by an elephant, Sarji Rao Ghatke invented such deaths as tying to red-hot cannons and festooning with rockets that carried the victim along in a whirl of explosions. As the century ended, Sindhia and Yeswant Rao Holkar, the abler of the two illegitimate Holkar brothers, marched and countermarched, fighting a series of battles, of which some of the fiercest took place when they were nominally at peace. The vast extent of territory which the Marathas occupied was swept with storm-winds, as if it were the playground of demons. China in our own day endured a similar misery under its warlords, whose frivolous contests led to the coming in of Japan.

Hyderabad and the Battle of Kharda

There was only one quiet interlude, when Nana Farnavis took advantage of the retraction and retrenchment enforced on the East India Company by the cost of Lord Cornwallis' campaign against Tipu. He accomplished the singular feat of bringing the Maratha chieftains together against the Company's protégé, the Nizam of Hyderabad. This was the last occasion when they all appeared under the Peshwa's authority.

Hyderabad, which to-day is recognized as in a class apart from the other Indian States, its ruler styled His Exalted Highness and Britain's Faithful Ally, attained this distinction entirely by the fact that it became very early a *tulchan* kingdom, straw-stuffed and held upright by the Company, except for a very brief period of

[1] For a good account of an extremely tangled story, see P. C. Gupta, *Baji Rao II and the East India Company, 1796–1818*, 1–20.

forgetfulness, when a whiff of hostility from the Marathas was allowed to blow it down. Unlike the Marathas, the State had neither racial nor religious cohesion. It was the creation of one able man, Asaf Jah, the Emperor's Wazir, who in 1724 withdrew to it as Subadar ('Overseer') of the Deccan and freed himself from all but nominal dependence on his master, in the same period as that in which the leading Maratha chiefs established themselves. He and his successors are generally styled Nizams, from his title Nizam-ul-mulk, 'Regulator of the State'. He died in 1748, and in the stormy days that followed Hyderabad was saved only by the coming of the British.

As the century neared its finish, the Nizam was very conscious that he was much the weakest of the four leading Powers of India —the others being Tipu, the Marathas, and the Company—and by long subservience had come to lean heavily on the British. Lord Cornwallis' successor, Sir John Shore, had neither the money nor the inclination for campaigns, though aware that the Nizam would have liked assistance in settling his differences with the Marathas. 'If I were disposed', he wrote,[1] 'to depart from justice and good faith, I could form alliances which would shake the Mahratta Empire to its very foundations.' He refused to depart from justice and good faith and to give assistance. It is customary to blame Shore for the defeat which overtook the Nizam, but this is to judge the former's actions through the eyes of Wellesley and of those who followed Wellesley.

For the Marathas were still in Shore's day what they ceased to be after 1803. They were genuinely independent. They held that the Nizam's relation to them was that of the Nawab Wazir of Oudh to the East India Company, that he was a protected dependent tributary chieftain. By treaty he had acknowledged their right to levy *chauth* and *deshmukh*[2] and to send their officers to collect these dues in his territory. Malet, in August 1794, wrote of his dominions as in a condition of 'dependence and thraldom' and of the Marathas' authority as being 'enforced by their officers under a variety of demonstrations throughout his country'.[3] Shore felt he had no choice but to stand strictly by the letter of treaties, by whomever made. The Nizam therefore appeared to him as a

[1] Letter to Charles Grant, 22 June 1796.

[2] *Chauth*, which was like the 'protection money' extorted by American blackmailers, was a quarter of the land revenue of a district which desired to be exempt from inroads. *Desmukh* was an additional tenth, sometimes added.

[3] J. N. Sarkar, *Poona Residency Correspondence*, iv. 118. I.O.R., H.M.S., 562: Sir Charles Malet, 16 September 1794.

defaulter who was trying to evade plain obligations. His record towards the Company had long been one of duplicity, and when he sent a desperate last-minute appeal his own State on merits seemed little entitled to help, as 'incorrigibly depraved, devoid of energy . . . consequently liable to sink into vassalage'.

The Nizam, disgruntled at his temporary desertion by his friends of the East India Company, followed Maratha example. He turned to the French and obtained his own Foreign Legion. But before his measures were matured Nana Farnavis in 1795 brought the long-standing dispute to the arbitrament of battle, which was boastfully accepted. Dancing girls sang the Nizam's expected triumph. Court buffoons were witty about it and his chief minister predicted that the Peshwa would be sent, with a cloth round his loins and a brass pot in his hand, to mutter incantations on the bank of the Ganges at Benares. There was one battle only, at Kharda, where his troops fled in dastardly fashion. The fight, apart from the pursuit, was won and lost as cheaply as Plassey. The victorious Peshwa went forward from it with downcast demeanour, which he explained as due to shame on both his enemy's account and his own people's, that the one should have yielded so contemptible a conquest and the other should consider it worth exulting over. The Nizam was mulcted of an indemnity, but was not treated harshly.

Helpless and humiliated, he was the destined dependent of whichever of the really great Indian Powers first troubled to demand his allegiance. The Marathas took little interest in him, and Tipu was too busy preparing for his own final struggle. It was therefore the British who reclaimed their strayed associate. Raymond, the much loved Commandant of the Nizam's French soldiery, died, and Lord Wellesley, recently arrived in India, at once (October 1798), as a preliminary to his attack on Tipu, seized the event as excuse and occasion for 'the expulsion of that nest of democrats' whom Raymond had gathered. The Nizam was half cajoled, half bullied, into disbanding his foreign auxiliaries. He was drawn back into alliance, and a treaty and a subsidiary force were clamped down on his State.

When the final war with Tipu began, four months later, Hyderabad was not a large State. But when war ended its boundaries were extended by the Nizam's acceptance of territory offered first to the Peshwa, on terms which he refused. They were extended again, another four years later, after the Second Anglo-Maratha war. Hyderabad to-day is as large as France, but no State can ever have combined such material importance with so undistinguished a record and so fictitious an independence, until comparatively recently.[1]

Its importance was trivial in the extreme, and its independence completely fictitious, in the half century before the Mutiny, and perhaps most of all in Lord Wellesley's time. No one deviated from an attitude of steady contempt for it. Though Hyderabad was the Company's nominal ally against the Marathas, as against Tipu, Arthur Wellesley considered that it was 'impossible for persons to have behaved in a more shuffling manner'.[2] The tergiversations of the Nizam's Government were a large part of the experience which led him to his conclusion, that events

'ought to be a lesson to us to beware not to involve ourselves in engagements either with, or in concert with, or on behalf of, people who have no faith, or no principle of honour or of honesty, or such as usually among us guide the conduct of gentlemen, unless duly and formally authorized by our government.'[3]

Baroda and the Gaekwar

Nana Farnavis' long unchallenged reputation as a statesman is being at last questioned by historians of his own nation. But it can hardly be questioned that he was right in his unswerving effort to give the Marathas a focus and head, and to make them a confederacy under the Peshwa and based on Poona. No one but the Nana could have secured the Gaekwar's assistance in the Kharda campaign. Since the Treaty of Salbai, in 1781, which closed a war in which the British had supported him against Sindhia, the Gaekwar's had been practically a protected State of the Company.[4]

The Gaekwar's subsequent relations with the British and with his own people for the sake of convenience can be briefly summarized here. After Kharda, he practically withdrew from the Maratha Confederacy. In 1799, when the Company annexed Surat, he

[1] I am commenting, of course, upon Hyderabad during the period when political India was in the making. Hyderabad to-day is a different matter.

[2] 26 January 1804: Owen, *A Selection from the Wellington Despatches*.

[3] 31 May: *Ibid*, 176. The Duke of Wellington very closely and frequently examined this question of whether he had to deal with gentlemen; it will be remembered that his comment on Napoleon's enigmatic character was that the latter was 'no gentleman'. The phrase and the attitude were entirely characteristic, and often repeated; they are of value, as revealing a certain standard of conduct, for himself and others. From this standard he would not willingly deviate, even when deviation was of advantage to his brother's government, and he did not like to sanction deviation by others.

[4] See the valuable contemporary 'Account of Affairs in Gujarat from 1782 to 25 June 1802': I.O.R., H.M.S., 241 (7), pp. 215–223.

was requested to make this acquisition more worth while, by handing over an adjacent district. He consented, but remarked that the Peshwa's sanction should be obtained. Both parties were aware that the Peshwa was in no case to refuse (which he would have done if free to do so). All he could do was to rebuke his straying and now all-but-emancipated vassal for concluding a separate treaty with the Company. The rebuke went unheeded; the Gaekwar was conducting a private war with the Peshwa's Governor of Ahmadabad, and hoped to get British help. He did not get it, but managed to succeed without it. In September 1800 he died, and Baroda was involved in civil war, which the British were asked to settle, both parties making the Bombay Government tempting offers.[1] The Bombay Government settled it accordingly, by another of the toy campaigns with battles costing two or three score casualties, which are so many in British-Indian history that they have deservedly dropped from sight. After one of these victories, in which between 5,000 and 6,000 men, of whom over 2,000 were Europeans, suffered 'the very considerable casualty list of 162'[2] (104 being Europeans) or something less than a thirtieth of their force, the General of the claimant whom the Company was supporting wrote with perhaps excessive enthusiasm (but it gives us the measure of the martial ardour which in nine cases out of ten was all that the British had to overcome): 'I was quite astonished to see the manner in which the English fought. I do not suppose anybody in the world can fight like them.'

The new Gaekwar, when the fighting was over and his enemies chased out of their fortresses, accepted a subsidiary force (25 June 1802), and one of the four great chieftains had been permanently detached from the Maratha confederacy. The British Resident, Major Walker, became practically ruler of Baroda, whose finances and administration were in ruins,[3] and the Gaekwar's dominions subsided into something strangely like peace. Henceforward, the troubles which for twenty years came thick and fast upon his brethren were probably interesting news items to him, but they were nothing more. The other Marathas continued to be like the sea, that is never at rest. But he himself had said good-bye to all that, and was *emeritus* from it.

Count de Boigne, the maker of Sindhia's army, retired in 1796, the year after Kharda. A French gentleman of pre-Revolution

[1] *Ibid*, esp. pp. 225 ff. and 253 ff.

[2] Sir Patrick Cadell, *History of the Bombay Army*, 137: a book based on a long family knowledge of India's forgotten wars.

[3] I.O.R., H.M.S., 242, pp. 443 ff.

type, he hated new-fangled ideas of liberty, fraternity, equality, and was well disposed to the Company, whose commission he had once held. He left Sindhia, as his last word, his reiterated warning that he would do well not to excite British jealousy, and that it would be better to disband his battalions than to fight. The Company showed de Boigne every courtesy in his journey from India to Europe, and arranged the transference of his vast fortune[1] to his native city, Chambéry, in Savoy. Here he lived with great distinction until his eightieth year, in 1830—a 'nabob' who dispensed lavish charity to his fellow-Savoyards. He was always ready to talk over Indian affairs with British visitors, and to express his poor opinion of his successors in Sindhia's higher command.

He was followed by General Perron, and the Ganges-Jumna doab, assigned for the upkeep of the French officers and their sepoys, was presently styled, by Lord Wellesley, Perron's 'independent state', and his 30,000 troops 'the national army' of that state.[2] Tipu's downfall, however, had already come as a knell to the dreams of recovering India, which France had cherished through three decades of failure and growing weakness. A handful of foreign mercenaries could make no difference to what destiny had settled.

[1] It is said to have amounted to two million sterling.

[2] To Secret Committee, 13 July 1804: Martin, iv. 137.

IV

LORD WELLESLEY AND THE PESHWA

Lord Wellesley on reaching India had found the Peshwa's authority 'reduced to a state of extreme weakness by the imbecility of his counsels, by the instability and treachery of his disposition, and by the prevalence of internal discord'. He set himself to obtain through him complete control of Maratha affairs.

For a while he was foiled. His intended agent

'deliberately preferred a situation of degradation and danger with nominal independence, to a more intimate connection with the British power, which could not be calculated to secure to the Peishwa the constant protection of our armies without at the same time establishing our ascendancy in the Mahratta empire.'[1]

In a torrent of exasperation Wellesley—whose language is a laval flow that never cools, fed by incessant renewal from the internal fires—ascribed to his opponent 'intricacy', 'perverse policy', 'treachery', 'low cunning', 'captious jealousy', 'the spirit of intrigue and duplicity inseparable from the Mahratta character'. With all this he contrasted his own 'just and reasonable', 'temperate' and 'moderate' proposals. He found the contrast maddening and the obstinacy which refused to fall in with his plans for a new order in India insupportable.

The Marathas had been distinguished among the ramshackle polities of India by a genuine patriotism which operated despite their dissensions. But their dissensions had now become too deep-seated for healing. In the warfare which followed with the British they were hopelessly outclassed in every phase, the diplomatic no less than the military.

Their carelessness as regards military intelligence was impossible to exaggerate, and was to increase a disparity which was immense already in equipment and organization. As Sardesai points out, while every British officer who toured their country used his eyes and afterwards his tongue and pen, and while a number of British could speak and understand Marathi, the Marathas 'knew nothing about England, about the British form of Government, about their settlements and factories . . . their character and inclinations, their

[1] N. B. Edmonstone, Secretary to Government, to Lieut.-Colonel Barry Close, Resident at Poona, 23 June 1802.

arms and armaments; perhaps even Nana Fadnis did not at all possess such details . . . the Marathas were woefully ignorant.'[1] Even Nana Farnavis 'was ignorant not only of the geography of the outside world, but even of India. The maps which he used in those days are extant and are fantastic, inaccurate and useless.'

As against this, the East India Company's Secretariat was served in the courts of Native India by a succession and galaxy of men such as even the British Empire has hardly ever possessed together at any other time. 'Their spy system was perfect.'[2] As a consequence, when war broke out in 1803, the Marathas, sprawling in their desultory fashion over half of India, had been tracked down over a score of years past, and their habits, their strength and weakness, scientifically docketed. Lord Wellesley's files contained information gathered as far back as 1779, in C. W. Malet's elaborate report[3] on the Sindhia and Holkar families and their history, when he was stationed at Surat. The same cool indefatigable observer, when attached to the Maratha camp before Kharda, had added, in March 1795, a fascinating analysis of his hosts' military methods or want of method. No one considered such reports to constitute espionage or any breach of hospitality. 'I consider it as the duty of every British subject in this country, however situated, to contribute to the utmost of his power, to the stock of general information.'[4]

Colonel William Palmer, who succeeded Malet as the Company's representative at Poona, was urged unceasingly to watch for the chance to establish British ascendancy over the Peshwa and through him over all the Marathas. Like Major Kirkpatrick, his colleague at the Nizam's court, Palmer was Indianized in habits and sympathies, and he carried out tactfully instructions which were couched in terms of excitement and exacerbation. Nevertheless, the Peshwa, though even his suspicious mind could hardly have guessed what close continuous studies of his conduct and intentions[5] were being passed to the Governor-General, felt like a wild beast of the jungle, when hunters are behind all bushes. Not the Peshwa alone, but Sindhia, the Bhonsla Raja, and Holkar, all ultimately behaved in a manner which put them at a complete political, as well as military, disadvantage and gave their

[1] *The Main Currents of Maratha History*, 213.

[2] Jadunath Sarkar, *Mahadji Sindhia and North Indian Affairs, 1785–1794*, iv.

[3] I.O.R., H.M.S., 242.

[4] W. H. Tone.

[5] See especially Palmer's letters from 7 December 1798 onward: I.O.R., H.M.S., 482.

adversary ample justification by his own standards of thinking to hold them up to indignation, as morally responsible for the outbreak of hostilities. To achieve this is a large part of what has always been considered statesmanship, in every age and land. It has rarely been achieved more triumphantly than in India, in the twenty years when Independence was lost. Maratha statecraft was casual and occasional, meeting the immediate demand with what appeared to be the best immediate answer, which was often an evasive one. These answers were taken up, explored, replied to, and filed by a Secretariat which had been stiffened into the sternest efficiency—a machine that lost account of nothing, but tabulated and kept and compared all that came into it, and drove remorselessly to its foreseen end. Sir Thomas Munro quoted with agreement and approval a remark made by the Maratha patriot Moro Pant Dikshit, to his friend Major Ford, in 1817, that 'no Native Power could, from its habits, conduct itself with such strict fidelity as we seemed to demand'.

It was the final campaign against Mysore which brought relations to their first crisis. When hostilities were about to break out, Lord Wellesley reminded the Peshwa of an agreement which bound the Company, the Nizam, and the Marathas in alliance, in the event of one of them being at war. The Peshwa procrastinated, and intrigued with Tipu;[1] his assistance never materialized until all fighting was over, when his troops took the field with superfluous alacrity and overran the north of Mysore. Wellesley was incensed; having a uniformly high esteem for his own sentiments, he was never at any pains to hide them, and was at none now. He nevertheless offered the Peshwa some of the territory of conquered Mysore—on terms which offended, so that the offer was not accepted, although the Governor-General had been at pains, according to his lights, to be entirely reasonable, hoping to find the Peshwa reasonable also, with his eyes not fixed on that gaudy toy, Independence. The Resident at Poona was instructed, 23 May 1799:

'Although the Peishwa's conduct . . . has been such as to forfeit every claim upon the faith or justice of the Company, I have determined to allow him a certain share in the division of the conquered territory, provided he shall conduct himself in a manner suitable to the nature of his own situation and of that of the Allies. . . .'[2]

[1] He was reported to have said that Tipu's death and defeat was like 'the loss of his right arm'. William Palmer to Lord Mornington, I.O.R., H.M.S., 574 (2).

[2] Martin, *The Despatches, etc. of the Marquess of Wellesley*, ii. 12.

Three weeks later, Palmer was told to notify the beneficiary

'that it is my intention under certain conditions, to make a considerable cession of territory to him, provided his conduct shall not in the interval have been such as to have rendered all friendly intercourse with him incompatible with the honour of the British Government. You will be careful in whatever communications you shall make on this subject to apprize the Peishwa that he has forfeited not only all claim to any portion of the conquered territory under the terms of the triple Alliance, but also under those of the declaration which I authorized you to make in my instructions of the 3rd of April. I wish, however, that the general tenor of your communications to the Peishwa should be of a conciliatory and amicable nature. . . .'[1]

The conditions attached were, that the Peshwa should accept a British force at Poona and employ no more Frenchmen; pledge himself to alliance if the French invaded India: and accept unconditionally the Company's arbitration of all disputes outstanding between him and the Nizam, and of all future disputes. In fine, that the Maratha confederacy should consent to abrogation of its independence and to inclusion in the British subsidiary system.

The Subsidiary System

The mischief which this system did to the States on which it was imposed, and its intensification of their people's sufferings, were clearly seen, frankly admitted, by the men who imposed it. With a new invincible force behind him, the most intolerable Prince was placed above the reach of complaint. Let the mildest of the Duke of Wellington's many comments be cited. Subsidiary troops, he wrote,

'are to oppose foreign invaders and great rebels, but are not to be the support of the little dirty amildary exactions. It is, besides, very disadvantageous and unjust to the character of the British nation, to make the British troops the means of carrying on all the violent and unpopular acts of these Native governments, such as, for instance, the resumption of the jaghires of the Mussulman chiefs in the Soubah's countries.'[2]

Sir Thomas Munro testified:

'There are many weighty objections to the employment of a subsidiary force. It has a natural tendency to render the government of every country in which it exists weak and oppressive; to extinguish all honourable spirit among the higher classes of society, and to degrade and impoverish the whole people. The usual remedy of a

[1] Martin, ii. 51 ff.

[2] To Major Shawe, 26 January 1804: Gurwood, *Despatches of the Duke of Wellington*, ii. 100–104. The Soubah is the Nizam.

bad government in India is a quiet revolution in the palace, or a violent one by rebellion, or foreign conquests. But the presence of a British force cuts off every chance of remedy, by supporting the prince on the throne against every foreign and domestic enemy. It renders him indolent, by teaching him to trust to strangers for his security; and cruel and avaricious, by showing him that he has nothing to fear from the hatred of his subjects. Wherever the subsidiary system is introduced, unless the reigning prince be a man of great abilities, the country will soon bear the marks of it in decaying villages and decreasing population.'

He considered that 'the simple and direct mode of conquest from without is more creditable both to our armies and to our national character, than that of dismemberment from within by the aid of a subsidiary force'. 'If the British Government is not favourable to the improvement of the Indian character, that of its control through a subsidiary force is still less so.' It was bound to bring war.

'Even if the prince himself were disposed to adhere rigidly to the alliance, there will always be some amongst his principal officers who will urge him to break it. As long as there remains in the country any high-minded independence, which seeks to throw off the control of strangers, such counsellors will be found. I have a better opinion of the natives of India than to think that this spirit will ever be completely extinguished; and I can therefore have no doubt that the subsidiary system must everywhere run its full course, and destroy every government which it undertakes to protect.'[1]

Of the corruption and tyranny that the system inevitably brought in its train, such witnesses as Metcalfe and Sutherland may be consulted *passim*.

For the Company, however, the system held immense advantages. By its means the Governor-General was present by proxy in every State that accepted it. Well-trained bodies of troops were dotted about in strategic and key positions. Their officers were exceptionally highly paid, and formed a notable addition to the Company's patronage. The whole cost fell on Native Governments which meanwhile sank into emasculation, relieved of the necessity to protect themselves, and with their rulers safeguarded against any danger arising from discontent. Finally, the system 'enabled the British to throw forward their military, considerably in advance of their political, frontier',[2] and kept 'the evils of war . . . at a distance from the sources of our wealth and our power'.[3]

1 Letter to the Governor-General, Lord Hastings, 12 August 1817; G. R. Gleig, *The Life of Munro*, ii. 460 ff.

2 P. E. Roberts, *India under Wellesley*, 36.

3 Arthur Wellesley: Lieut.-Colonel Gurwood, *Despatches of the Duke of Wellington*, ii. 613.

If war came, 'hostilities', Metcalfe noted in 1806, 'are carried far from our territories, and we still enjoy the advantages of a friendly country in our rear'.[1] We ourselves, in three continents, have learnt most painfully in recent years, how great are the conveniences of waging a campaign on others' soil and sparing our own; also, how effectively states can be disrupted from within.

[1] J. W. Kaye, *Selections from the Papers of Lord Metcalfe*, 3.

V

BRITISH AND MARATHA DIPLOMACY

NANA FARNAVIS foresaw his countrymen's subjection. He 'respected the English, admired their sincerity and the vigour of their government; but, as political enemies, no one regarded them with more jealousy and alarm'.[1] While he lived he warded off their suzerainty, without exasperating Lord Wellesley or losing the respect which the Governor-General accorded to him alone. His chief weapon was a disconcerting frankness. 'A man of strict veracity,'[2] he answered questions freely, and gave explanations which (Palmer points out repeatedly) tallied exactly with information received and checked up from other sources. 'Humane, frugal, and charitable,' he wore himself out in what he well knew was a vain effort to prevent the inevitable.[3] 'His whole time was regulated with the strictest order, and the business personally transacted by him almost exceeds credibility.'

The Governor-General's irritation was fiery, when under this wary guidance the Peshwa parried his proposals. He saw himself offering a pigmy eternal security, and honourable alliance with a giant. The response he characterized as 'vexatious and illusory discussion', 'temporizing and studied evasion'.

It was undoubtedly all this, and in fairness it must be noted that the British were not the only critics of the Marathas. Bussy complained (9 September 1783) that the French representative at Poona, while showing zeal and disinterestedness, had placed '*trop de créance aux protestations et au discours d'une peuple inconstante et perfide*'.[4] Their replies were no replies, or put forward to gain time or postpone a decision. It was a warring of different ethics and habits, and not of armies only. And when war came in 1803 (with the Peshwa nominally allied with the British) the Governor-General had this much excuse for his feeling of outraged blamelessness, that at one time or another every Maratha leader, including even Holkar, had sounded his agents on the chances of getting Company support.

[1] Grant Duff, *A History of the Mahrattas*, iii. 188.

[2] *Ibid.*

[3] For an excellent picture of his wisdom and firmness of character, in the days of his power, see *Malet's Embassy, 1786–1797*, edited by Sir Jadunath Sarkar and G. S. Sardesai.

[4] Pondichéry Records.

We can to-day see that neither side was as villainous as the partisans of either assume. Sir William Foster's words, of Sir Thomas Roe's attempts to get an agreement out of the Emperor Jahangir nearly two centuries before, are equally true of Wellesley's negotiations with the Marathas: a treaty on Western lines was 'an idea utterly alien' to their political system.[1] On the other hand, Wellesley never made the slightest effort to understand that system and to work with it. Unable to envisage any kind of state other than those known in Western Europe, complete with orderly and methodical chancellery and secretariat, he simply could not see how casual and desultory Maratha methods were. He declared frankly that he considered incorporation into the Company's dominions the greatest blessing it was possible to confer on the peoples of India. Failing this, he would have standardized India into something approaching English conditions; the Princes should be great hereditary territorial magnates, with detachments from the British army acting as their special police to suppress subversive ideas and persons. He saw some kind of 'Prince' in every chieftain who looked belligerent enough. He offered every such chieftain a place in the Company's family; his titles should bc confirmed, and his weapons taken over (on payment). H. St. G. Tucker, his Accountant-General, looking back on this period, wrote in 1814:

> 'As for subsidiary treaties, I am sick of the very term. Lord Wellesley was for firing off these treaties at every man with a blunderbuss.'[2]

Wellesley therefore misunderstood inquiries, which the Marathas meant as merely requests for a friendly 'accommodation' during temporary embarrassment, as solemn applications for a position which he was only too eager to force upon them. When Sindhia or the Peshwa found himself falling back, after some disastrous bout with Holkar—or when Holkar was fleeing to his Vindhya fastnesses—the warrior whose fortunes were at stake took more than a solely intellectual interest in the chances of borrowing a few companies of well-drilled sepoys. This was undoubtedly true. But he was certain to want afterwards, when the crisis was over, to dismiss these auxiliaries (if he had obtained them) with good will and gifts. He certainly did not want them except as a very present help in time of trouble. The political seesaw went up and down too swiftly for even a rout to be cause for despair.

[1] *The English Factories in India, 1618–1621*, viii.

[2] Kaye, *Life of Tucker*, 286.

'When the Devil was sick the Devil a monk would be.
When the Devil was well the Devil a monk was he!'

Moreover, for even this modified and temporary repentance the sickness had to be severe.[1] The Marathas had fought for generations to avoid submission to the Mogul Emperors; to Lord Wellesley it appeared strange that they should be unwilling to come under the mild regimentation of a Power that had come from Europe. But there it was. There was no searching of the heart of man, especially Asiastic man; it was full of deceit and desperately wicked and foolish. Nothing but necessity would make the Peshwa accept a subsidiary treaty and a Company's armed force. With increasing exasperation the Governor-General came to realize this.

Lord Wellesley's Dealings with Minor States

Not merely the Governor-General's tone, his actions frightened the Peshwa. In 1799, he annexed Surat and Tanjore, tiny principalities far apart. The suppression of Surat has called out a remarkable agreement of condemnation by historians, but is not of sufficient importance for more than mention here. Wellesley took it, on its Nawab's death, on the ground that in that part of India, and towards Surat in particular, the Company had stepped into the Mogul Empire's shoes, and inherited its right to dispose of dependent semi-regalities. Tanjore, an outpost which the Marathas had established during their wide wanderings, he took because it was perhaps the worst misgoverned of several states which European financiers had long pillaged. Also in 1799, Wellesley in a paroxysm of wrathful energy tried to force the Company's dependent during forty years, the Nawab of Oudh, to surrender his dominions, and all but succeeded. In 1801, he did extinguish the title and authority of the Nawab of the Carnatic, in whose name the Company had originally become one of India's martial powers, in 1747. The Marathas noted these happenings and the doctrine which justified them. As by a miracle, the Company had just failed to thrust an encircling arm along their north-eastern borders, in Oudh, and it was now in undisputed possession of all south India.

As for the menacing tone in which the Governor-General offered the Peshwa a slice of Mysore territory, it was the tone he habitually used with everyone, and it is unique, even in a record which includes Dalhousie and Curzon. He never caught even the

[1] See N. B. Edmonstone, Secretary to Government, to Lieut.-Colonel Barry Close, Resident at Poona, 23 June 1802.

most fleeting glimpse of any point of view but his own, which was always pikestaff plain and crystal-clear to him, so that to differ was to equivocate and to merit instant crushing. Wellesley lay down, slept, and awoke always the Governor-General, shaken from his dreams into a world of men and women calling for constant oversight and sharp correction. No novelist would dare to invent such a style of correspondence for one of his characters; he would be told that no person could ever be so humourlessly oppressed with his own towering importance and undeviating rectitude. Nevertheless, Lord Wellesley was. The Directors' recall of him is censured as injustice to a great man. The marvel is that, being human, they endured him so long.

By his own people, this manner was received variously. The very young, and the army generally, admired it intensely, and the Royal Tiger, as he styled himself, lived in a buzz of adulation, and was 'the glorious little man'.

Much of this adulation was sincere. We still feel strongly the prestige of rank. The early nineteenth century felt it much more. Men went to India in their teens, often at an age when they would now be still at their preparatory school. Boys flung out thus felt no inclination to criticize a nobleman of the vigorous decision and self-sufficing grandeur of Lord Wellesley. He made the times exciting and splendid. War, war, more war—against Tipu now, then against Dhundia Wagh and the Nairs, then against Sindhia and the Bhonsla, then against that rascal Holkar! 'Victory huddling on victory'—Periapatam, Malaveli, Seringapatam, Aligarh, Delhi, Laswari, Ahmadnagar, Assaye, Argaon, Gawilgarh, Dig, Farakhabad! How sick the French must be, and that little reptile Buonaparte most of all! Nelson had crowned the British name with glory at the Nile. But their own glorious little man was adding kingdoms like a boy gathering apples. He was directing campaigns which meant prize-money, new territories to be administered, new princes as dependents, triumph and everlasting fame. And those cheese-paring Directors grumbled about expense!

But as you study contemporary memoirs and letters you become aware of a reticence, and almost a sense of conspiracy, among the men who were ten years older than the schoolboys[1] who sur-

[1] Literally schoolboys, as attending Lord Wellesley's College at Fort William, Calcutta. Kaye remarks of Malcolm, 'He arrived in India, and was his own master before he was fourteen—an age at which the majority of boys of his station are drinking weak milk-and-water, and being whipped into Latin hexameters.'

rounded the glorious little man—the men who were in the late twenties and early thirties, and who did the actual conquering and administering. The Englishman of thirty in India is a veteran, even to-day. In the eighteenth century, he was almost an old man. John Malcolm had appeared for his ensign's commission when twelve years of age. 'Well, little man, and what would *you* do if you met Haidar Ali?' he was good-humouredly asked. 'I'd cut aff his heid', said the ferocious child; after the burst of laughter had subsided, he was told he would do. Three years later, Major Dallas in a Mysore mountain pass met two companies of sepoys marching behind a red-faced lad on a rough pony, and asked him for the commanding officer. 'I *am* the commanding officer', answered Malcolm. When Lord Wellesley reached India, Malcolm was twenty-nine, and more than half his life had been years of service. He, too, cursed the Directors' craze for economy, but not solely because it hampered the waging of glorious wars (though Malcolm could be enthusiastic enough about these). Wars were something which he and the men of his rank in the service waged themselves, and not by proxy; and war was not their only interest. Malcolm wanted money for other than martial uses only.

Away from Calcutta, on the Mysore front or wherever Company's troops were massing against the Marathas, were these men —Malcolm, Munro, Close, Webbe, Graeme Mercer, Arthur Wellesley himself—who knew from daily experience that conquest was not the matter of a few maps on a table and an excited walking to and fro and dictating orders and despatches. There were districts too starving or depopulated to furnish supplies on demand: there were anxieties about transport or rivers too swollen to cross. There were, they discovered, two sides to some questions. Sometimes the enemy or potential enemy had a case; sometimes, on personal acquaintance, he was not the boor or savage that he was previously reported. They sometimes thought a proposed war unjust, or at least an unduly hard measure.

But it was no use saying this to the glorious little man in his Council Chamber in far-off Calcutta. He had exploded on to Indian shores like a tempest, full of fury at the low manners and vulgarity of the society he found there. He described himself, in letters to his peers in England, as stalking solitary like a Bengal tiger, 'without even a friendly jackal to soothe the severity of my thoughts'. This promising beginning he kept up through a correspondence which for voluminousness is matched only by Warren Hastings'. What justification there was for its tone, in the general turpitude to which he testified, we can guess only; the Duke of

Wellington said there was hardly a good-tempered man in all India. But contemporaries were soon telling each other stories to illustrate their common terror;[1] and one and all, for the tiniest deviation from conduct which their master thought the right one, were overwhelmed with majestic scoldings. His Commander-in-Chief, a man far older than he, on occasion grovelled in abject abasement. One of his brothers, Henry, acted as the Governor-General's Private Secretary, and another, afterwards the celebrated Duke of Wellington, was advanced swiftly over the heads of senior officers, until he commanded the southern of the two great armies in the Maratha War of 1803. But they and the Governor-General never wavered into real friendliness; Henry and Arthur preserved intact a wary discretion. There clings to their relationship with one another and with other officers more than a little of the atmosphere of schoolboy friendships cemented under adversity and the overhanging threat of watchful Authority.

We must then be aware of two groups operating simultaneously. There was the Governor-General's immediate circle, to whom he was a good though stern master; typical of them was young Charles Metcalfe, in whose eyes Lord Wellesley could do no wrong, and whose gratitude for exceptional and consistent kindness is as clear as his perception that in sense of duty and public and private honour the Governor-General was outstanding. There were also the older men doing the actual fighting and administering, who remained rigidly reserved towards the Governor-General, while writing and talking freely amongst themselves, if in subdued tones. It is a very striking picture, and it has been twice repeated in India, though never with the completeness of contrast in Wellesley's time. Wellesley went through his term of office, learning nothing, and never suspecting the immense caution he enforced on those who might have enlightened him.

He had great qualities, and among them was a real and unwavering liberality, by the time's standards, of political thought. But our concern is with his political actions only.

[1] One of the lighter may be cited. Lord Wellesley, storming in to breakfast, found his egg not as fresh as he liked it. 'But that is not Your Lordship's egg!' wailed his servant. 'That is the chaplain's egg.' J. W. Kaye, *Life of Tucker*, 99.

VI

THE DEATH OF NANA FARNAVIS

Matters cannot last long as they are at Poonah: the Peshwah's Government must either fall to pieces or he must accept our support. If he should still be obstinate, out of his ruins some power may be formed whose authority it may not be difficult for us to secure and afterwards to enlarge to such a degree as we may think proper.—*Arthur Wellesley, 19 November 1799.*

While Nana Farnavis continued to deflect the Governor-General's invitations to bring the Marathas into the subsidiary system, nothing could be more fantastic than the picture presented by Madras or by the vassal States of Oudh and Hyderabad, a seething delirium of misery. In comparison, the regions where the Nana governed were an oasis of gentle security.

Yet even their bliss was strictly qualified; the fact that they were considered happy testifies to the lunatic disorder of the Indian scene. Malcolm, journeying from Poona to Bombay, in 1799, fell in with a small guard leading a young man whose hands were bound:

'I asked them who the prisoner was, and where they were going. The commander of the guard said they were going about a mile further, to a spot where a robbery and murder had recently been committed. "And when there," he added, "I shall cut this man's head off." "Is he the murderer?" I asked. "No," said the man, "nor does he, I believe, know anything about it. But he belongs to the country of the Siddee, from which the murderers, we know, came; and we have orders, whenever an occurrence of this nature happens, to proceed into that country and to seize and put to death the first male who has arrived at years of maturity, that we meet. This youth," he concluded, "was taken yesterday, and must suffer to-day." On my expressing astonishment and horror . . . he said that he only obeyed orders. "But," he continued, "I believe it is a very good plan. First, because it was adopted by Nanah Furnavese, who was a wise man; and secondly, because I am old enough to recollect when no year ever passed without twenty or thirty murders and robberies on this road, and all by gangs from the Siddee's country. Now they are quite rare; not above four or five within these twelve or fifteen years, which is the period this custom has been established."

'As we were conversing we reached the spot fixed for the execution. The guards halted and began to smoke their *hubble-bubbles*, or pipes. The prisoner's hands were untied, and he took a pipe along with them, with much apparent unconcern. Indeed, his whole conduct marked indifference to his fate. After he had smoked, his hands were tied behind his back as before; he was taken a few yards from the road, and desired to kneel. The executioner, who stood beside him, grasping a straight two-edged sword with both hands, called out to him, "Bend your head." The man did as desired, and by a most dextrous blow it was severed from his body. The trunk sprung upright, and fell backwards. A rope was then tied round the heels of the dead body, and it was hung up, on a low tree, for the terror of others. After this was done, the guard sat down, smoked another *hubble-bubble*, and then returned to the ghaut.'

By such methods—gamekeeper methods, suited to a country swarming with hawks and crows, and certainly not less humane than the methods of most countries of the world at that time —Nana Farnavis kept such semblance of civilization as prevented the utter disintegration of his threatened country. His authority seemed established; and, had he possessed a son and more physical courage, he might not only have temporarily stabilized the tottering Maratha power, he might have founded yet another anomalous dynasty. India might have seen the crazy political spectacle of the actual rule of a vast area being exercised by Farnavids, as humble deputies of helpless Peshwas, in their turn humble deputies of shadowy Rajas of Satara—while Gaekwars quietly cultivated their garden in Bombay's protecting vicinity, and Sindhias, with Bhonslas in their orbit, clashed with Holkars, all four continuing to pay ceremonial devoirs to Farnavid and Peshwa and Satara Raja and Mogul Emperor at Delhi.

His love of authority, however, undid him. The new Peshwa chafed, and in 1798 the Nana was imprisoned by Sindhia, with Baji Rao's concurrence; his relations and supporters were terrorized by cruel executions. Presently the confederates quarrelled and their reconciliation was cold and insincere. The Nana was released, after a heavy ransom had been extorted from him, and even persuaded to undertake the administration again. But his health and spirits were broken, his mind wandered into aimless talk, his time and remaining resources went to feed brahmans and beggars.[1] He died, closely guarded, March 1800. 'With him', said Colonel Palmer, in often-quoted words, 'departed all the wisdom and moderation of the Mahratta government.' That wisdom and moderation had not been very noticeable previously, and with the Nana's death the nation became marked out for sacrifice.

The Governor-General was eager to consummate the sacrifice immediately. Colonel Palmer's report covered the tortuous and

[1] *The last days of the Maratha Raj (1779–1818): Selections from the Peshwa Daftar*, edited by G. S. Sardesai, No. 41, letter 17. These documents are in Marathi.

troubled events at Poona, from 7 March 1800, and told of Sindhia's ambition to make the Peshwa 'a pageant', such as earlier Peshwas had made the Raja of Satara. Lord Wellesley eagerly pressed him to take advantage of Baji Rao's fears—in which, Palmer with iteration and reiteration had pointed out, rested the only chance of ever overcoming his deep and passionate repugnance to a connection with the British—to persuade him to conclude 'a Secret Treaty to compel Scindia to remove from the Deccan, the Company to engage to maintain his authority over the other acknowledged feudatories of the Maratta Empire.' This was a side-glance at Holkar also, who made no concealment of his contempt for the Peshwa and his desire to displace him by his cousin.

Events achieved what the Peshwa's free consent would have refused for ever, and brought the Marathas at last inside the net which had been swept and dragged around them with such pertinacity. The tangled story of civil dissension can be followed, by those willing to submit to a task of exceeding toil and trivial reward, in Grant Duff's earlier *History* or the recent one by Kincaid and Parasnis. Both books are insufferably tedious, for which their authors should not be blamed. It is unprofitable to recall all the occasions when Holkar pounced on Sindhia and ravaged Ujjain or Sindhia pounced back and ravaged Indore.

Some incidents, however, had importance.

In 1801, the Peshwa caught Yeswant Rao Holkar's brother and sentenced him to two hundred lashes and execution. He watched with delight from a balcony the wretched youth's pleadings and his trampling to death by an elephant (1 April). Cowed and depressed, at first Yeswant Rao Holkar wrote a very dutiful letter in minor key, admitting that Vithoji had given trouble and earned his fate. 'What has been done by the master the servants must consider as beneficial.'[1] He himself desired only to serve the Peshwa, as his ancestors had done.[2]

The mood passed quickly and other feelings replaced it. Yeswant Rao loved his brother, with the pity and passion which those brought up in misfortune and penury seem to feel, and Baji Rao's cruelty was never forgotten or forgiven;[3] Holkar's anger

[1] *Selections from the Peshwa Daftar*, 41, letter 30. It must be remembered that Holkar was of shepherd caste, whereas the Peshwa was a brahman. Even Yeswant Rao Holkar could not overcome the natural awe which these facts imposed.

[2] Up to her death, Ahalya Bai rendered annual accounts to the Peshwa; even she did not consider herself independent. G. S. Sardesai, *The Main Currents of Maratha History*, 55.

[3] I. Baillie Fraser, *Military Memoir of Lieut.-Colonel James Skinner*, C.B., i. 195.

'communicated an alarm to the conscious and cowardly mind of the Peshwa, which towards Holkar he could never afterwards conquer'.[1]

In June, Holkar, having separated two of Sindhia's detachments, forced one to surrender and cut the other to pieces. The British and Eurasian gunners died where they stood. Seven of the eleven European officers, who were most of them British, were killed, and three captured. These encounters strengthened Holkar in his belief that by traditional methods of warfare he could beat the new-fangled copied methods, even when Europeans were in command.

Another of Sindhia's detachments, however, checked him at Burhanpur, and in October defeated him disastrously in front of Indore, his capital, which Sarji Rao Ghatke pillaged and madly punished. The wells were choked with corpses of women suicides.

Sindhia and the Peshwa, happy in their opponent's apparent ruin, now proceeded to neglect alike measures of moderation and conciliation and of ordinary precaution. They were enjoying the lull before an earthquake.

Meanwhile the Governor-General was watching Maratha events, and the eyes which he used were the sharpest in India—those of Colonel Barry Close, in Arthur Wellesley's judgement 'the ablest man in the diplomatic line in India'. Close succeeded Palmer in 1801.

Close at Poona had an even abler assistant, the Honourable Mountstuart Elphinstone. This was the man on whose rocklike firmness, in the Third and final Anglo-Maratha War of 1817, the vacillating showy Peshwa was to be broken and the independence of the Maratha people finally lost. He was now (1801) at the outset of his great career; it is worth our while to form some impression of him.

He is twenty-one; handsome, excitable, eager, opinionated. His conceit arises from consciousness of possession of every advantage of person and family. An uncle is on the Board of Directors and he is linked by ties of blood with influential men in the British governing classes. He has a strong sense of family dignity, which he will never lose. Elphinstone is to die untitled, by his own choice. He congratulated common clay, in the person of John Malcolm, on attaining the dignity of knighthood, but at the climax of his own fame, when he had shattered the Peshwa, Elphinstone was infuriated to learn of his own narrow escape from a baronetcy, and wrote to his uncle, Lord Keith:

[1] Grant Duff, *History of the Mahrattas*, iii. 200.

'It would have annoyed and embarrassed me to have been obliged to accept a baronetcy, and thus to admit the superiority of an honour which I should have shared with half the aldermen in London, over that which I derive from my birth and which can never be held but by a gentleman.'[1]

In fact, in his admirable record there is little to put off the most fastidious, except a certain snobbish priggishness and in his early days a love of popularity. These faults went with a chill self-absorption, that perhaps did no one any harm but with posterity, as with his own age, wraps him round in semi-isolation and contrasts ill with the happy generous friendliness of Malcolm. Elphinstone thought little of *homo sapiens* and not much of even his most admired colleagues. He went through life largely indifferent to his fellows, even when they were his yoke-fellows. But many will feel that these were trivial flaws in a character so strong and compact.

Despite his high esteem for himself, Elphinstone was supremely capable of changing his opinions and of learning, and was fortunate in finding his first chief in a man who was himself outstandingly gifted. 'How communicative, candid, and sensible Colonel Close is!' he writes in his *Journal*. 'I do not give enough attention to becoming intimate with him.' Close had also exceptional wisdom and tolerance, qualities which Elphinstone's diary makes it plain were called for.

But the diary makes it no less plain than in the young man himself was present a gift of self-criticism that would presently amend his recklessness.

'Dined. I got out of humour, and talked violently and improperly of Lord Wellesley. I saw the impropriety all the while of attacking a person before another who said he considered himself intimately connected with him. I was led away by my ill-humour, which I attributed to my want of sleep last night. . . .

2 February. Went to Colonel Close's; talked with him about the Baroda negotiations. Lord Wellesley has not answered Mr. D.'s pressing letters for orders on that subject during the last nine months. What a careless devil! Shot with pistol, wrote journal, dined, disputed like an ass. Can't one help disputing? . . .

4 March. Dined. As I have left off wine for the improvement of my temper, I determined to make an experiment, and see how I should be affected by drink. I drank a good deal of claret—not enough to intoxicate me. It did well enough, and I did not dispute.

5 March. Had a pleasant conversation at breakfast. Afterwards I had some hot and violent disputes with Waring and Fussell. I was unreasonable and arrogant and supercilious. . . . How shocking it is to degrade oneself so! I have behaved thus twice since I came to

[1] 3 October 1818. Elphinstone was an 'Honourable'.

Poona, besides to-day. I have drunk very little wine since I came to Poona, except in water. I am now accustoming myself to drink my water plain. I shall now drink little or no wine. My principal reason for abstaining is that I may preserve my temper. Excess always makes me irritable. I must pay great attention to preserving my good humour, a contrary disposition in me generally proceeds from an opinion that I am slighted. What can be more contemptible?'

There were scores of young men in India, who were 'unreasonable and arrogant and supercilious'. But they were not carefully and closely feeling their moral pulse, and sifting and choosing from their environment those elements of it which they intended to allow to influence them.

Under such a master as Barry Close, Elphinstone learnt to press down the fires of his spirit, until they fused into a disciplined energy. At Poona, with the cool patience of their race, these two navigated the rapids, not allowing peril to disturb them one minute before it actually arrived. They engaged in the *holi*[1] pranks ('I liked the sly and graceful way in which the dancing-girls pelted us with balls of red powder in talc shell. When we were completely wetted and dirtied we had dancing again.') They galloped for miles, they stuck pig, shot tiger and gazelle and duck; their existence was a typical 'Bengal Lancer' existence of to-day or yesterday.

There were differences, however. There were no gramophones or radio, no illustrated papers, no memories or anticipations of musical comedy or film. Conversation therefore of necessity had a narrower range of themes than in the regimental mess of to-day; it had to satisfy itself with politics and philosophy and literature. Close, back from some trying interview with the Peshwa, relaxed into discussion of Burke ('he is in love with him') and read at length from the *Reflections on the French Revolution* ('the assertions seem to me as false as the language was beautiful'). They found in a fine phrase or book excitement, even ecstasy:

'Conversation turned on Pope's Homer. Some passages of Pope were mentioned which I, in silence, compared with the original. I always feel warmed and inspired by the mention of Homer; no other author gave me such pleasure in reading, or left such an impression. Colonel C. gave an account of Hyder's rise till late.'[2]

Ariosto, Hafiz, Lord Chesterfield, Horace, Spenser, Milton, Akbar, Babar, Firdausi—disputes as to whether nations have the right to remove kings for misconduct, as to the superiority of ancients or moderns—these were themes they found absorbing,

[1] The well-known festival in honour of Krishna, when red juice is flung about.

[2] i.e., Until late at night.

even when watching the death-day of empires. It is an astonishing picture. It differentiates them not merely from us to-day, it differentiates them still more widely from the austere heroes of the Mutiny period, who in national esteem have so eclipsed them. We note the absence of moral and religious tension, of concentration on the Bible as reading. We have escaped from the atmosphere and mentality of Joshua's camp before Jericho and are talking with Erasmus or Socrates or Falkland. Yet the men of 1800–1819, despite their coolness, tolerance, catholicity, and humanity, were every way as efficient and heroic as the men of 1857. It will make for understanding on our part, and for healing forgetfulness on the part of Indians, if both races can look on the carlier picture more.

VII

THE BATTLE OF POONA

As WE have seen, the Peshwa's sadistic savagery had driven into open hostility the most remarkable Maratha of his day.

Yeswant Rao Holkar's crimes ultimately made a formidable record. But at first skill and valour won more than forgiveness, they won deep admiration.

His life was one of unceasing struggle and peril, endured with the abounding high spirits for which he was renowned. The illegitimate son of a bondwoman, he experienced the murder of one brother by Sindhia and the public execution of another by the Peshwa. He took lightly even the loss of an eye by the bursting of a matchlock; jesting at the belief that a one-eyed man is wicked, he exclaimed that he had been bad enough before but would now surely be the *Guru* or high priest of roguery. He was generous as well as witty, and his wildness was pardoned as part of the eccentricity of genius; his followers smiled complacently when they saw him, dressed as a common *sowar* or horseman, riding mad races on a barebacked Maratha pony or seeking a night's oblivion of danger in the cherry and raspberry brandy for which his agents had scoured Bombay shops. He was of superior education as well as superior mental abilities, a skilled accountant and literate in Persian as well as Marathi.

No member of his race ever possessed the gift of guerilla warfare —that Maratha accomplishment by nature, from the times of Shahji and Sivaji to those of Tantia Tupi—in higher measure. His resources were always slight, but his energy and hopefulness boundless. When for the war that now followed he announced to his troopers that they must gather their own rewards, for he could pay them no longer, these conditions were accepted with enthusiasm. His reputation was such that, even when himself a fugitive from Sindhia's army, he had been continually strengthened by desertions from his pursuer. His personal courage was of the kind which soldiers most esteem, that of such leaders as Ney and Lannes, and he never lost his personal ascendancy until he lost his reason.

Such qualities have always counted in India. Malcolm, the most popular man on the British side—

'except Sir John Malcolm, I have heard of no one whom all parties agree in commending. His talents, his accessibility, his firmness, his conciliating manners, and admirable knowledge of the native language and character, are spoken of in the same terms by all—'[1] resembled Holkar in more ways than one. His kindliness made him a delight in a land where men settled into irritated and solemn middle age while in their twenties. A squeaky voice added drollery to his stories.[2] 'His overflowing spirits made him riotous, and he was generally known by the name of "Boy Malcolm"';[3] never troubled about his dignity, he joked and (what is more unusual) accepted jokes on equal terms with everyone, of whatever race or religion. Wherever he came, he must racket—must ride or shoot immediately, or play practical tricks; and he paid the inevitable price, in sometimes overdrawing on the bank of good will he possessed in unique degree. A touch of disrespect, even contempt, went along with the affection for him of wiser, more restrained (and much duller) men. This half-contempt continued beyond his own lifetime. Henry Lawrence, the most thoughtful man of the next generation, told Kaye, in 1854:

'I have always looked on Munro and Metcalfe as our best men. Perhaps I wrong Elphinstone, but I have never understood why he stands so high as he does, though, undoubtedly, he too is an able fellow. I hope you will turn out Malcolm a proper fellow, but I have been accustomed to consider him a clever fortunate humbug. He must have been more, or he would not have half the place he did with Wellesley, Wellington, Munro and other great men.'

Henry Lawrence is one of the very few whose opinions are always evidence. Something of his heavy hand of disparagement on Malcolm—not, I think, much—must be admitted as justified. There was an amateur touch, a reckless zest and impatience, which often marred Malcolm's achievement. His embassies largely failed, and his military strategy, as he showed in his one high command, at Mahidpur, 1817, was a headlong smack at the enemy (and hang casualties by the way).

But Malcolm did know a great deal, and that knowledge included men, even (and, indeed, especially) men of alien race and suffering humiliation. He had come out to India 'a careless, good-humoured fellow, illiterate' ('quite illiterate', the same witness, Graeme Mercer, told another correspondent), but curiosity luckily overcame this disability. He thrust himself enthusiastically into Persian studies and made himself a scholar, not in European

1 Heber in 1825. *Narrative of a Journey*, ii. 363–4.

2 J. Shipp, *Memoirs*, iii. 239.

3 Graeme Mercer, of their first acquaintance, in 1791.

studies, as Elphinstone and in high degree Metcalfe also were, but in Eastern matters. Without Malcolm's writings we should know far less about all kinds of out-of-the-way cults and practices and obscure history. Politically he did in Central India a work for which his name is still remembered, as no other's is, except perhaps Outram's. The traveller can test this for himself, if he will stray ever so little off the beaten tourist-track.

Malcolm's gifts were to be of use now, in a brief interlude just before the tempest broke. He averted the danger of Muslim hostility and based more securely than ever the legend of his indispensability whenever an Envoy Extraordinary was needed.

The trouble arose over the Persian Ambassador's death, and it was because of his Mission to Persia, in 1800, that Malcolm was asked to handle it.

His Mission had achieved very little, but his affability and lavish presents had won a personal success, his most effective arguments being enormous mirrors, that wildly excited the Shah. Nothing more of much importance resulted, and Malcolm, as almost always, rested too easily in the natural satisfaction which pleasant relationships gave him.

However, in 1802, Persia returned the compliment by sending a Mission to India. Its leader tried to calm a fracas at his doors, in Bombay, and was accidentally killed. This tragic finish of his errand shocked his hosts. Malcolm, the most distressed of all, wailed that 'in one moment the labor of three years' had been 'given to the winds', a conclusion which was to prove unduly pessimistic. The Governor-General sent him to Bombay immediately, to take all necessary measures,

> 'entrusted with powers that will enable me to alleviate in some degree private grief, and perhaps I may avert public misfortune. But I have little heart to undertake a work under such inauspicious circumstances.'

What followed brings out the variegated confusion of the Indian scene, and the fearlessness and ease with which men like Malcolm trusted themselves to it.

Malcolm embarked at Calcutta, 30 August 1802, sailed to Masulipatam, and thence journeyed overland, to Hyderabad, Poona, and ultimately Bombay. At Hyderabad, 'I found my native friends looking towards the rising storm'—that is, the Anglo-Maratha storm—'with great complacency'. At Poona, he assured the Peshwa that the Governor-General was thinking about him, 'and with that anxiety which the welfare of a prince excited, on whose conduct at this critical period the peace of India in a great measure depended.' The Peshwa received the assurance with unusual thoughtfulness and on the urgent question of a subsidiary alliance kept obstinate silence, so that Barry Close, standing beside Malcolm, could not hide his disappointment, murmuring in an aside, 'See how he winces at the least touch.'

Going on from Poona, Malcolm reached the Ghats late at night, in a profound slumber induced by a long palanquin ride in the hot sun. He was awakened by the flares of thirty or forty flambeaux, and a company of armed men on foot and horseback. A Maratha noble, hearing that Sindhia and Holkar were at war, had closed the pass as a precaution. He took Malcolm temporarily prisoner, from a confused notion that this fine bird might prove useful as a hostage if trouble presently came his way. Malcolm took this vicissitude calmly; he sent Close at Poona a note, to explain what had happened, gave his parole and went to sleep again. He rose early next morning and at once made friends with the entire Maratha village in which he found himself marooned. He entertained them and enjoyed himself thoroughly, so that ever afterwards he looked back on the two days he spent here with peculiar complacency.

On the second day, the delighted village entertained him back with an impromptu variety show. The only one of his new friends who understood some English, a former postal runner of the Company, took the chief part, as a European lady attired in 'a piece of old muslin made into a cap or bonnet, a common white cloth which was tied at the sleeves and waist to look like a gown, and bulged out on each side, with some sticks to make a hooped petticoat'. He walked slowly up and down (representing a minuet, Malcolm surmized), and then, singing '*La, la, la—Tol, lol de rol*', performed a country dance, 'and jumped and whisked about in every direction', a loudly applauded performance. The exultant artiste explained to Malcolm that the 'turn' represented a lifelong ambition. Ever since he had peeped in at the door of British social gatherings, thirty years previously, and 'seen these fine dances', he had wanted to teach them to his own people, 'but they have no sense, and cannot learn such things'. Next day, when orders arrived from Poona for his immediate release, Malcolm went on good-humouredly and almost reluctantly.

He found Bombay alarmed. The Governor, Jonathan Duncan, had been shaken by the fierceness with which the Persians expressed their anger. Malcolm, the Universal Ambassador, took the situation over, and by effulgent and efflorescent letters and a high assessment of the deceased's monetary value settled all trouble so effectively that Teheran was presently saying that 'the English might kill ten ambassadors if they would pay for them at the same rate'.[1]

The Persian tragedy, however, was at once forgotten, in news closer to British interests—the sudden descent of Holkar on Poona and the Peshwa's flight to the Company's protection.

Within a year of his disastrous defeat in 1801, Holkar swept up to Poona, spreading consternation. The Peshwa appealed to Close for help and promised to subsidize six sepoy battalions, to be stationed in his own territory, and to cede land producing six lakhs of revenue for their payment. Holkar attacked him and by his own personal recklessness scattered his troops and Sindhia's, winning a battle, 25 October 1802, that for a time seemed desperate. It took place near the British Residency, both sides being careful to respect the Union Jack which Colonel Close hoisted conspicuously. The Peshwa fled to the fort of Singarh.

Holkar, aware that the Peshwa had endeavoured to get Company support and would not hesitate to sign away independence as its price, the day after his victory invited Close to visit him. Close found him in a small tent, ankle-deep in mud. He had received a spear-thrust and a sabre-cut on his head, in his last forlorn charge up to Sindhia's guns, but spoke lightly of his hurts, was frank and courteous and 'expressed himself in the most friendly manner towards the Resident and the British Government'.[2]

It is interesting to note that, with a spasm of compunction for his 'rebellion', after his triumph Holkar sent the Peshwa food. But he followed him up and the Peshwa continued his flight until safe inside British territory, at Bassein.

[1] *Life of Malcolm*, i. 195.
[2] Grant Duff, iii. 209.

VIII

THE TREATY OF BASSEIN

Lord Wellesley and the Directors

ALL THROUGH 1802, the Governor-General's hostility was directed against what may be styled his Home Front. The Directors had outraged him by peremptory orders to reduce his military forces, by interference in patronage and personal matters, by a want of confidence generally. They had offered him, he told them, 10 January 1802, 'the most direct, marked and disgusting personal indignity which could be devised', by reducing the allowances granted to Colonel Wellesley by the Madras Government, 'for the purpose of defraying the charges of his arduous and extensive command in Mysore'—'a most offensive instance of the conduct of the Court'.

'Probably that excellent officer (whose high and noble spirit of integrity can only be equalled by his valour and military skill)[1] will spurn the indignity offered to himself and to his family by this act of unwarrantable suspicion, and will resign in disgust the command which he has exercised with such distinguished honour and advantage to his country and with the affection and admiration of the whole civil and military service on the coast, of the reigning family of Mysore, of the unfortunate family and nobility of the late Sultan, and of every class of our subjects in that country.'

The Directors' behaviour had the effect of bringing the two famous brothers to one of their extremely rare moods of common opinion; Arthur Wellesley commented with severity on 'the corrupt and vulgar interference of Leadenhall street. . . . All these measures are aimed directly at Lord Wellesley, and he cannot remain in the government, and no *gentleman* can succeed to him, if means are not taken to prevent them in future.'[2] The Directors, he pointed out, had flooded Madras with people formerly dismissed from India for good reason, 'persons sent home for their crimes'. They had displaced Mr. Webbe, 'the implacable, indefatigable, and irresistible foe of the corrupt system of intrigue and peculation which had long pervaded the service at Fort St. George[3] . . . the declared and ardent enemy of every author and abettor of corruption in that service.' Mr. Webbe had been Lord

[1] This was prophetic. Colonel Wellesley had not yet shown these qualities

[2] 20 April 1802, to John Malcolm: Owen, *Wellington Despatches*, 516–518.

[3] That Arthur Wellesley, however angry, was justified is made clear, abundantly and *passim*, in the correspondence of the chief author of the trouble,

Wellesley's nominee (by the appointment of the Governor, Lord Clive, who was completely subservient) to the post of Chief Secretary to the Madras Government. The Directors had been guilty of other interferences also.

The Governor-General therefore asked to be allowed to go in 1803.

The Peshwa's defeat and helplessness, however, and his offer to accept a subsidiary force if restored, changed the position. Wellesley abandoned all thought of resignation, and wrote (24 December 1802) of a 'conjuncture of affairs which appears to present the most advantageous opportunity that has ever occurred of improving the British interests in that quarter . . . on sound and durable foundations'.

The Secret Committee of the Honourable Court of Directors were informed also that Holkar's power 'possessed no solid foundation in the justice of his cause, in popular opinion or in the extent of political or military resource'. At a farewell interview Close told this upstart, who 'directly and earnestly appealed for his advice in the present situation of affairs', that 'it was indispensably necessary that both parties should consent to refer their differences to the mediation of the British Government'. Close then went to Bassein, and with the Peshwa (whose power was so solidly established on those foundations in which Holkar's was deficient) concluded a Treaty (31 December 1802)[2] which brought him into the Company's family of subject Princes.

over a period of nearly twenty years. Dundas writes, 20 June 1784, acknowledging the Duchess of Buccleuch's helpfulness in sending in her list of recommendations for posts in India, 'weeks before the India Act was passed' (Holden Furber, *Henry Dundas, First Viscount Melville, 1742–1811*, 31): 'as the influence you are naturally supposed to have over me will of course bring upon you many applications . . . one of the most essential parts of my duty must be to check the Government of India in the exercise of its unmeasured and unprincipled patronage. Every Department of the Administration of India both at home and abroad is at present overstocked with unnecessary servants, who, of course, having no lawful occupation, must subsist upon the plunder of the Company and the peculation of the natives of India.' It was Madras that received most of this influx, who were chiefly Scots. On 23 March 1787, Dundas told the newly appointed Governor, Sir Archibald Campbell, 'It is said . . . that the County of Argyle will be depopulated by the emigration of Campbells to be provided for by you at Madras.' Contemporary lampoons besought 'his highness' to appoint someone to India who was English.

[2] Ratified by the Governor-General, 11 February 1803.

Position of the Maratha Leaders

Holkar's rise was mere 'rebellion' and 'menaced usurpation', in the opinion of the Governor-General, who moreover considered his 'illegitimacy' of great importance. Sindhia's position, however, puzzled him. The last Sindhia (who, incidentally, had been illegitimate, like Yeswant Rao Holkar—but of this Wellesley was ignorant) had been guarantor of the Treaty of Salbai, and freely recognized by Warren Hastings as a Prince in his own right (although in feigned humility he himself used the title of *patel*—village headman—only); and the Peshwa's power was obviously insignificant, nearly all of it being Sindhia's. Wellesley therefore thought Sindhia's explicit adherence to the Treaty of Bassein essential, and pressed on him repeated invitations 'to partake the benefits of the defensive alliance'. But this 'unprincipled chieftain', true to 'the perfidy and violence' of his character, which had 'aggravated the pressure of the Peishwa's affairs and virtually annihilated his authority',[1] while expressing gratification at the overtures began to withdraw himself apart from his 'sovereign'. It was a discouraging response.

The Peshwa's reinstatement was immediately undertaken by Arthur Wellesley, now a Major-General. He had no enthusiasm for his protégé and was under no illusions as to the probable upshot of the Treaty of Bassein. 'There can be no doubt but that the establishment of our influence at Poonah will be highly disagreeable to the majority of the Mahratta chiefs'; it would 'interfere materially with the interests of some and the objects of ambition of all'. War he held to be utterly unnecessary, even from the viewpoint of British interests, which were better served by leaving that tumultuous nation to their own dissensions. The Company's new ally was 'a cipher, bearing the name of Peshwah, without a particle of power'. Its other associate, the Nizam, was equally worthless as a friend. 'One bad consequence of these subsidiary treaties is that they entirely annihilate the military power of the governments with which we contract them, and their reliance for their defence is exclusively upon us.' 'If the allies had come out of Poonah with me, there would be no war.'

'In my opinion, we ought to withdraw from Poonah, and leave some chance that the principal chiefs may have the power of the state in their hands; we ought to keep up our connexion with the Peshwah, so as that he might not be trampled upon; at the same time, we ought to increase our influence over the chiefs of the

[1] N. B. Edmonstone to Close, 23 June 1802.

Empire, in order that it may preponderate in all possible cases in which the state should be called upon to decide.'[1]

As to the Marathas' supposed military menace, Arthur Wellesley thought little of it, and most of those officers who had been in close touch with the Country Powers would have agreed with him, and with Thomas Munro, who had written, half-a-dozen years earlier:[2]

'Experience has shown, that augmentation of territories does not augment the force of the Mahrattas; it only serves to render the different chiefs more independent of the Poonah government, and to lessen the union of the confederacy. With more territory, they are not half so formidable as they were fifty years ago; but Tippoo is, what none of them are, complete master of his army and of his country.'

Contemptuous of the supposed Maratha menace, Munro added: 'Mussulmans, from the spirit of conquest mixed with their religion, are much more disposed than Hindoos to spread among their armies all the advantages of foreign discoveries. Whenever the Nizam adopts them, he will become the most powerful prince in India, for he has now in his dominions great numbers of excellent horse and brave men, who want nothing but discipline. He and Tippoo, with regular armies, would be far more dangerous neighbours than the Mahrattas. Their system would be conquest, that of the Mahrattas only plunder. Ours ought therefore to be to let the Mahrattas strip the Nizam of as much of his dominions as they please, and to join them on the first favourable occasion to reduce Tippoo entirely. When this was effected, it may be said, they would turn their whole force against us; but the interests of their leaders are so various that we should never find much difficulty in creating a division among them; and, admitting the worst, that we did not succeed, their united force would be able to make no impression on us. I have seen enough of their warfare to know that they could do little in action, and that their mode of laying waste the country would be more destructive to themselves than to us, and would never effectually stop our operations. It would not hinder us from making ourselves masters of all the Malabar coast, nor from re-establishing the Rajahs of Oudipore and Jaipore, and many other princes who are impatient to recover their independence. They would soon get tired of the war, and resume their old disputes about the Peshwah and his minister.'

General Wellesley's Advance on Poona

Arthur Wellesley from first to last preserved a tolerant perception of the Marathas' difficulties.

[1] To Malcolm, 20 June 1803: Gurwood, i. 514 ff. 'The Empire' of course, means the Maratha Confederacy.

[2] 30 September 1796: letter to his father, Gleig, *Life of Munro* (one volume, second edition, 1849), 108–109.

'Habits of industry are out of the question; they must plunder for subsistence, or be destroyed, or starve, or be taken into the service of some of the allied powers. As we have now narrowed the scene so much, we must not expect that our own territories will be entirely free from their depredations. In fact, if they are to meet the Company's troops in all countries, they have no choice excepting the richest and best cultivated, and those in which they are likely to meet the smallest number of these formidable troops.'[1]

He forgave on a generous scale the pillage they inflictcd on others.

However, he had his orders, and in obedience to these he took the fugitive Peshwa home (Holkar, whose time in Poona was spent mainly in a drinking bout, peacefully withdrawing), through a country devastated by incessant civil war. There was not a stick left standing within one hundred and fifty miles of Poona. Forage and grain were all devoured, houses had been pulled down for firewood, the land was empty. 'Excepting in one village, I have not seen a human creature since I quitted the neighbourhood of Meritch.'[2]

When he left Poona, a little later, to seek contact with Sindhia's southern armies the wilderness was continuous. 'All signs of cultivation ceased.'[3] The starving survivors

'might be seen hovering round their dismantled dwellings in different degrees of exhaustion, from the first cravings of hunger to the later and more passive dejection of long privation. But still, amidst all this wretchedness, there was nothing of violence in their despair. The victims seemed to await the approach of death with patience and resignation, if not with apathy.'

'This patience under suffering' appalled the spectator from happier lands. 'The courage of the Hindoo is of a passive nature, while that of the European is active; the former being inert, has only its own weight to give it power; the latter has activity to increase its momentum.' 'The moon had just risen, and showed me a group of famished wretches seated under the walls of the village', surrounded by their own dead. It was useless to ask of such shadows the way. In the half-lustre,

'the dark bloodless countenances . . . assumed a hue perfectly unearthly . . . their sunken eyes, hollow stomachs, and emaciated frames, spoke the extremity of wretchedness. . . . As I approached, packs of jackals, preying on the wasted bodies of the latter even before the eyes of the helpless survivors, ran howling away at the sound of my horse's feet—their instinct teaching them that I was a different kind of being from those scarce living wretches, whom they

[1] To Major Shawe, 26 February 1804: Gurwood, 1067–8.

[2] To the Governor-General, 21 April 1803 (Owen, 224).

[3] J. Blakiston, *Twelve Years' Military Adventures in Three Quarters of the Globe*, i. 145–9.

viewed more with greediness than fear—while the vulture, rising reluctantly from his bloody banquet, flapped his broad wings in anger, and joined the wild chorus with discordant cries. The moon's pale light shed a suitably mournful tint over such a scene.'[1]

Malcolm accompanied General Wellesley, and presently wrote to Edmonstone (12 May) that the Peshwa was in his capital again. 'A decided and spirited support' was being given to his authority. It might at times, he thought, prove necessary 'to address him in very plain and decided language', but if he could be kept to his engagements 'we may smile at the ill-assorted union of the northern chiefs, against whose efforts it is nevertheless our duty to take every possible precaution.'[2]

There was abundant reason for precaution, and for close watchfulness. The Peshwa's restoration 'was not the restoration of the old régime . . . Sindhia would dominate no longer, nor would Holkar march again to Poona, but . . . he had lost his hold on the army and the foreign policy of his State. . . . He had secured what he wanted, freedom from his own chieftains, but at what price he had yet to discover.'[3] The price was a misery to him for the next seventeen years, and at last this misery drove him to his last desperate and entirely hopeless attempt to escape from his protectors, and to the ending of the office which his ancestors had made second only to that of the Mogul Emperor.

For the war which now followed, responsibility lies on all the antagonists. The Company's Government had determined to settle what was none of its business. The Peshwa meant to keep his position, at whatever cost to his nation. Lastly, Sindhia, when terrified of Holkar, had made the mistake of asking the Company to help him, and had not the sense to see that he could not play fast and loose with a Power like the British, as with the shifting inconsequent chieftains of his own land.

Holkar, hating all the other parties, kept out of the quarrel's opening stages, and indeed was hardly invited to enter it. Only Sindhia's and the Bhonsla Raja's formal adherence to the Treaty of Bassein were considered important by the Governor-General.

[1] Blakiston. [2] *Life of Malcolm*, i. 219.
[3] Gupta, *Baji Rao II and the East India Company*, 50.

IX

COLLINS AND METCALFE AT POONA

THE MARATHAS, once a great nation and despite their marauding habits a lifestream making for health in the body of a land sick with cruelties and the bigotry of superstition and religion, had reached their lowest point of character. Moreover, they had declined from their former championship of a Hindu population persecuted and oppressed and had reduced to subjection the ancient Rajput states. As its arms progressed victoriously up country, the Company became aware of allies, feeble but eager, behind the enemy's lines. India would be well rid of what had become solely devastating inundations. The Marathas were about to be given boundaries and pent within them.

Yet the Governor-General's amazement, when he found that these boundaries were not going to be accepted without a struggle, was in keeping with the austere naïvety of his character. He did not want war; he would be satisfied if Sindhia dismissed his Frenchmen and ceded the Ganges and Jumna valleys and the Bhonsla Raja ceded Orissa, and if both of them accepted the Company's suzerainty and right to settle all disputes between the Marathas and the Nizam. These convenient arrangements would link up the Company's dominions by means of broad bands of territory between Bengal and South India and Bengal and Delhi (which would automatically fall under British protection). Acceptance of them seemed a simple matter, and no one dared enlighten him that his interference in Maratha affairs was 'openly aggressive'.[1] Close and Elphinstone, the main instruments of this interference, confided to each other their dislike of much of what they had to put through. But Wellesley, convinced of his own integrity and of Maratha perfidy, shut his eyes deliberately to the fact that the most abounding perfidy was that of his own protégé, the Peshwa. Holkar, the supposed brigand, was recklessly valiant, generous to his followers, and admired by even those he pillaged, and his 'right' was good enough by current standards. As for Sindhia, by the time peace was finally made in 1804, between him and the leading British officers considerable friendliness was established. But from first to last no one ever had any feeling but contempt for

[1] Colebrooke, *Life of Elphinstone*, i. 39.

the Peshwa, whom the Governor-General reinstated at Poona, with a guard of Company's troops and the status of absolute ruler over all the Marathas, who thereby officially became a subsidiary and dependent nation. The chieftains of every degree lost by the fiat of an outside Power that independence among themselves which they had always possessed.

THE WAR'S POLITICAL IMPLICATIONS

Of the Afghan War of 1839, Kaye observes, 'In India every war is more or less popular. The constitution of Anglo-Indian society renders it almost impossible that it should be otherwise'.[1] In 1803, the prospect seemed the more joyous, because war would enable the British exiled in the East to contribute their own remote additional smack at the French. 'You surely cannot have a scoundrel in England', wrote Malcolm, 5 September 1803, 'with whom the war with Buonaparte is not popular. . . . The Marquis is in high health and in high spirits at the prospect of rooting out Monsieur Perron and his blessed brethren.' The Company's allies were equally delighted. The Nizam's Court, harassed by heavy regular payments for the subsidiary force, was exultant that those 'Mahratta gentlemen' were to be 'taught a lesson', and incidentally pay their instructors handsomely. 'The autumn of 1803 was a season . . . of glorious excitement',[2] of intense gleeful anticipation.

For a while longer, the Governor-General continued to believe what he chose to believe. He had settled Maratha affairs on a just and acceptable basis, and would get rid, without bloodshed, of 'that brigand establishment',[3] 'the French state erected by M. Perron on the banks of the Jumna'. This state was a scarecrow of his own imagination—a set of broken men anxious only to collect and, when the time came, convey their money safely to Europe, which was possible only by the Company's assistance and protection. These facts Arthur Wellesley, in his laconic pregnant fashion, noted coolly, to Malcolm, not to his own brother:[4]

'The more I see of the Mahrattas, the more convinced I am that they never could have any alliance with the French. The French, on their arrival, would want equipments, which would cost money, or money to procure them; and there is not a Mahratta in the whole country, from the Peshwah down to the lowest horseman, who has a shilling, or who would not require assistance from them. . . . The greater experience I gain of Mahratta affairs, the more convinced I

[1] *History of the Afghan War*, i. 375. [2] Kaye, *Life of Malcolm*, i. 235.

[3] Lord Wellesley to Lord Hobart, 20 November 1803.

[4] 20 June 1803.

am that we have been mistaken entirely regarding the constitution of the Mahratta Empire. In fact, the Peshwa never has had exclusive power in the state: it is true, that all treaties have been negotiated under his authority, and have been concluded in his name; but the chiefs of the Empire have consented to them and the want of this consent, on the part of any one of them, in this case, or of power in the head of the Empire, independent of these chiefs, is the difficulty of this case at the present moment.'

His dislike of doing what he considered injustice made him resent one part of his duties especially. Many of the principal *jagirdars*, or landowners, in the districts near Poona, had become, with good reason, recalcitrants to the Peshwa's authority. The Peshwa demanded that British power should bring them to heel again, and the Governor-General apparently acquiesced in this demand as part of what the Company had undertaken to carry out.

Charles Metcalfe

The British Resident at Sindhia's camp at Ujjain was Colonel John Collins, from his overbearing manner nicknamed 'King Collins'—a grotesque manikin who moved everywhere complete with zenana and batteries of artillery. It proved important in Indian history, that for a few months of the summer of 1802 he was assisted by Charles Metcalfe, the star pupil of the Governor-General's new College at Fort William. It was during this experience that a distaste for native courts, a dislike of native princes and their ways, and in especial a detestation of the Maratha people, came to Metcalfe. It never left him.

Metcalfe was one of the loneliest men who ever went to India, and his natural introspection was deepened by the fact that he arrived desperately in love, his passion unreturned. He lived and died officially unmarried,[1] his intimate secrets sealed in his own heart. He was unfitted for social exercises or enjoyments and hated the rough camp life which he shared with Collins. Collins, for his part, may be pardoned for not foreseeing what was hidden under an exterior and practice homely and unathletic to a humiliating degree.

The habit of Metcalfe's life was almost as studious as Elphinstone's, but his mind was not lit up by the imaginative brightness of genius or variegated by swift and eager delight in physical activity. Our ancestors kept journals, and Metcalfe's at Eton,

[1] He had three sons, but the whole story is obscure. See my *Life of Lord Metcalfe*, 101.

when a boy of fifteen, is crammed with a record of steady heavy reading that makes one wonder if he ever knew any leisure. 'Took a solitary walk' is the one variant occasionally sprinkled through the tale of study and discussion. Here is an entirely normal entry:

'Whole school-day. Read Homer. Virgil. Concluded Bryant's Dissertation.[1] Began Tyrwhitt's,[1] tending to prove that they were written by Chatterton. Took a solitary walk, and employed myself in making a few verses to Solitude. Drank tea with Neville. Retranslated part of my translation of Rousseau. Read Ariosto, &c.'

On the way out to India, the drawn-out voyaging of those days included a week of sightseeing in St. Helena, where Metcalfe's *Journal* shows the man as he remained throughout life. He confronted this show of things with absolute integrity—yet not in itself, in the open-air unthinking manner of John Malcolm, but through the glasses of his own ideas and reading. These always threw a mist of induced emotions over whatever he saw.

'From this ridge you look down on an immense abyss, which from its depth and steepness is called Eternity; and, indeed, any despairing lover might in one instant, without any trouble or noise, put an end to his existence in one step; the appearance cannot be better described than by making use of the allegorical term, "Beauty in the lap of Horror".'

Nor was there anything in the appearance of this studious young man to attract esteem. Malcolm was a handsome giant, Elphinstone a comely spirited boy. Metcalfe was short and undistinguished, his plainness of feature a constant mortification. He wrote to J. W. Sherer, 20 June 1802, 'Let mankind say what they will, a pretty face is an excellent introduction, and before now I have had to regret the bad effects of an ugly phiz—particularly with the ladies'. After distinctions had fallen fast and early upon him, his plainness added to the affection felt for him; Lord Minto in 1809, when Metcalfe was twenty-four, in a burst of enthusiasm testified, 'he really is the ugliest and most agreeable clever person—except Lady Glenbervie—in Europe or Asia!' Such tributes, however, though gratifying, and doubly so from a Governor-General, give a strictly qualified pleasure when the recipient is young. It was long before Metcalfe overcame his awkwardness in the midst of a society whose tone was recklessly adventurous and athletic and martial, conscious of physical prowess and well-being.

But Metcalfe, even more than Malcolm, almost more than

[1] He was much occupied with the Rowley Poems; Bryant and Tyrwhitt discuss their authenticity.

Elphinstone, was to be a 'man of destiny'. His fate seemed prefigured by such trivial incidents as sometimes appear to set out a man's representative quality. He reached India on the first day of the new century, and when he left it, after thirty-seven years of service unbroken by a single visit to any other land, having made a deeper mark on British policy than any other man of his time, he had covered more than a generation, during which the whole political face of the sub-continent had been revolutionized. He had been present through every minute of these happenings.

He reached India richly endowed with advantages outside himself. His 'highly respectable father' (as Lord Wellesley styled him) had amassed a fortune in the spacious earlier days and was now an East India Company Director. In consequence, India abounded with Metcalfe's relations; his *Journal* shows that in almost every important settlement he could flush at least an aunt or godfather.

In this opening year of his career, 1801, Metcalfe, not yet sixteen, symbolically became the first student of the College which Lord Wellesley had established for civil servants at Fort William, to supersede the old method of turning them loose in uneducated infancy. Wellesley was in sore trouble with the Directors, who resented his wars and expensiveness and his habitual contempt for them, and Metcalfe's father was one of his few supporters. The 'glorious little man' therefore treated the boy with exceptional graciousness, his attentions to him being 'on every occasion, marked and flattering'.

After six months of College and Indian experience, Metcalfe contributed to a students' symposium on the best method of getting to understand an Oriental people. He thought the most helpful guidance came from linguistic studies.

'The general character and peculiar genius of a people may be collected from their language. From the openness and boldness of the expression in our own, we discern evident marks of that nobleness of mind and freedom of spirit, which dignify the Briton.'

Contrariwise, 'in every sentence' of Oriental speech 'appear that humility and slavish submission, or that haughtiness and despotic insolence, which have ever been the characteristics of Asiaticks'.[1]

The Founder of the College was impressed by these reflections, and saw the statesman in the forming. This essay 'was one of the ten best sent in to the Lord', and Mr. Metcalfe was told by the Lord in person that 'he considered my progress greater than that of any other' student. Metcalfe might be—as he sorrowfully

[1] *Essays on the best means of acquiring a knowledge of the manners and customs of the natives of India:* by the Students of the College of Fort William in Bengal, 1802.

admitted, constantly was—the ugly duckling of Calcutta society, 'out of my element' on hog-spearing parties and at balls and routs and cross-country gallops. But he was well on his way to swanhood though, in his ignorance of this, he begged his father to recall him, and to get him some clerkship in London. 'I find', he told his *Journal*, 5 October 1801,

'how much inferior the most excruciating bodily torment is to mental agony—the result of reflection and too much sensibility. I cannot exist in absence of my family . . . I am, however, willing to believe that the sufferings I at present labor under will be shortly removed, and that it hath pleased Almighty Providence to ordain me this time of penance that I may learn Humility, Patience, and Obedience to His Divine will. How awful is the thunder of the Lord, which, growling o'er our heads, proclaims His power—how mighty is His vengeance—how dreadful His wrath! Who shall oppose it? Man, remember the fall of our Great Ancestor. He sinned, and mark his punishment.'

Metcalfe was reading too much Rousseau. Also, too much Old Testament. Things were not really as bad as they seemed. In Calcutta he had acquired that essential to success, a 'gang' of his own; the most brilliant and ambitious of the younger writers formed a fraternity which they styled 'the Howe Boys',[1] all of whom were destined to positions of influence and high emolument.

Metcalfe's highly respectable father was delighted when he learnt that his son was being sent to assist

'my old friend Jack Collins—the situation of all others which accords most with my wishes, and I hope this letter will find you happily situated with the man who of all others in India is most interested in the welfare of my son. You are now in the high road to diplomatic fame . . . your attention will be called officially to the general politics of India.'

The Howe Boys, equally delighted, gave him a farewell dinner and rousing send-off. Everything seemed set for immediate success.

But the Jack Collins of his father's rosy memories from days when the Metcalfe fortune was being picked up out of Bengal's disorder and revolutions was now 'King Collins', a colonel well over forty years of age, with more than thirty years' experience of India. He was not the person to welcome assistance from anyone, except of the most obsequious sort.

The boy of seventeen, fresh from intensive study of introspective authors and with his carefully kept commonplace books and

[1] Kaye, half a century later, confessed himself unable to recover the name's full significance. It indicated 'the possession of manly attributes of all kinds'. It was, of course, taken from Lord Howe, hero of 'The Glorious First of June' (1794); like the Wellesleys and Metcalfe, an Etonian.

diaries, had opinions, and thought them worth airing. This impression Collins quickly corrected. Metcalfe wrote to his fellow Howe Boy, J. W. Sherer, 20 June 1802: 'his conduct towards me has been such that I have not words to express my contempt of it . . . it is only from hearing particular anecdotes that you would be able to judge of his extraordinary character. To say the best of him, he is a man whom one ought immediately to quit.' Metcalfe quitted him very soon indeed; and, a few months after their brief partnership had been dissolved, he noted sadly in his *Journal*:

'We are often reproached for what we are taught to do. To differ in opinion from men of greater age and experience is looked upon, in a young man, as a great presumption. Yet are boys at school and college taught and compelled to criticize the best and most celebrated authors that the world has known and to argue on all subjects, even in favor of an untenable proposition.'

The best and most celebrated authors, however, are dead when we are encouraged to criticize them; and few of them, even in life, were Anglo-Indian colonels accustomed to decades of trembling subservience. The contrast between Metcalfe's early experience and Elphinstone's good fortune is almost an explanation of the contrast between their moods in later years; Elphinstone was as buoyant as Metcalfe was pessimistic and low-keyed in tone and expectation. It is not easy to overestimate the importance of the part played in the career of every man who has served in India, by the first chief to whom he is sent for district training and work.

Metcalfe returned to Calcutta, and tried to drown his wretchedness in the study of Arabic and such 'extras' as Lucan's *Pharsalia*, Volney's *Travels in Egypt and Syria*, and the *Carmen in Pisonem*. King Collins for some time wrote him cordial letters overflowing with assurances that he was bound to succeed, and adding, 'Remember, I am your banker, as well as your sincere friend.' The friendliness was not reciprocated. Metcalfe wrote (16 June 1807), when he heard of his former chief's death,

'I felt a stronger spirit of resentment against him than I have ever felt towards any other man. He has reached that goal at which all enmities subside; mine are at an end. I sincerely forgive him for the wrong he did to me; and I trust that God will forgive me if I ever wronged him.'

In his resentment Metcalfe included Maratha affairs as well. They were always distasteful to him, as recalling wretched memories.

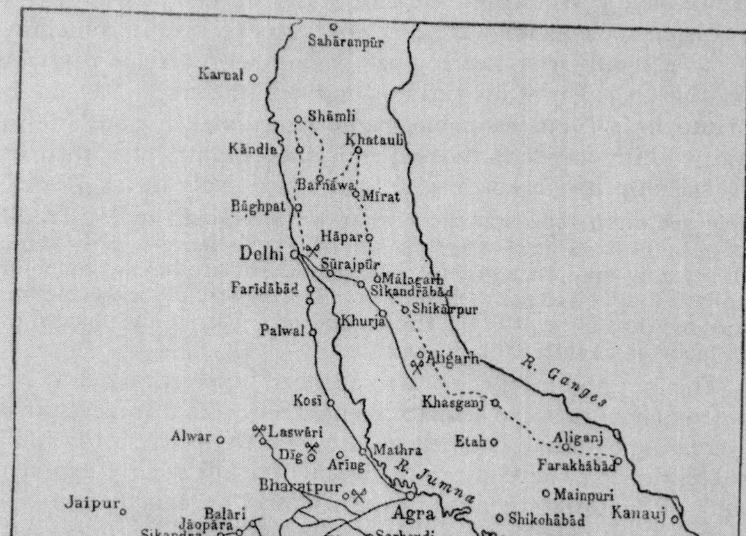

MAP
TO ILLUSTRATE
LORD LAKE'S CAMPAIGNS
1803 - 1805

X

OUTBREAK OF WAR

THAT COLLINS was quite unconscious that he had aroused in his young colleague a feeling of hatred gives us the measure of his obtuseness. He was equally obtuse as regards Sindhia. 'Collins (whom he detested) thought Sindhia had a great personal regard for him.'[1] He was pertinacious ('I exerted every mode of persuasion that I was master of') in trying to force on Sindhia acknowledgment and acceptance of the Treaty of Bassein, and was as blind as with his own countrymen to faults of deportment and their effect.

Sindhia and the Bhonsla Raja, aware of the Company's warlike preparations, were planning to consult together and probably to join forces. Sindhia answered (28 May) Collins' peremptoriness with studied negligence; the Resident must wait until he and the Bhonsla Raja had talked matters over, and then he would be informed if it was peace or war. 'These words he delivered with much seeming composure.' Since his predecessor had acted with Warren Hastings, after the First Anglo-Maratha War, as guarantor of the settlement, Sindhia certainly felt that he was entitled to be consulted before being presented with the accomplished fact of a radical change in Maratha status and the chiefs' relations among themselves and with the British.

Sindhia scored another point over the exasperated Resident, when he and his ministers ignored the Treaty of Bassein: they 'made no remarks' on it, and did not even ask for a copy of it. It was no concern of theirs, they implied, what promises the Peshwa chose to make to a foreign power. The Peshwa meanwhile, double-dealing always, was having his own secret negotiations with Sindhia, which were not by any means identical with his ostensible efforts to bring him into his own concordat with the Company.

The Bhonsla Raja was included in the war which followed, mainly because of actions exceptionally ill thought out for even a member of this exceptionally casual and shiftless family. In Warren Hastings' time, the Bhonslas had been very useful to the Company; they sat loose to the Maratha confederacy, partly

[1] Elphinstone, 23 April 1808.

because they had settled down into definite territorial status far more than the wandering Sindhias and Holkars, partly because their possessions lay at a great distance from Poona and close to Bengal, partly because they themselves claimed the ceremonial supremacy which the Marathas gave to the Rajas of Satara. They were easily detached therefore, and for twenty years had been vaguely swinging in the Company's general orbit; possessing no strong feelings or ambitions, they were willing to discuss projects and plans with anyone and everyone, while incapable of any genuine alliance.

The Peshwa's acceptance of the Treaty of Bassein, however, put the Raja in the class of powers whose independence was threatened. He had written to the Nizam (of all people!) a letter expressing his resentment, and he now moved his army towards Sindhia's. But he so little made up his mind that Sindhia presently found himself fighting almost singly. Then, after Arthur Wellesley's lightning victory at Assaye, the Bhonsla Raja, scuttling back to his own territory, was overtaken and crushed at Argaon, which can only by courtesy be styled a battle.

Lord Wellesley Decides on War

On 27 June, the Governor-General, pained by Sindhia's 'insolent and hostile declaration to Colonel Collins' and the 'recent proofs of determined hostility and arrogant ambition' that he had noticed in him and the Bhonsla Raja, instructed Major-General Wellesley—whom Lord Clive, the Governor of Madras, had (as directed) appointed to command the southern army—to drive the erring chiefs inside 'their respective territories' and to take all other measures that would afford full satisfaction and security. Sindhia's language to Colonel Collins amounted 'to a positive act of aggression upon every received principle of the law of nations'. Yet the Governor-General still believed that the offender would probably do as he was told and that there would be no fighting.

The belief, however, quickly vanished; and, as excitement rose, the hope (or fear) of a peaceful settlement vanished also. Despatches flew from him, and his mind worked like a never-resting shuttle. He dictated instructions, which were sent flying out over India, to the Company's scattered representatives at every Court. Night succeeded to a day passed in unremitting labours.

'But still by the bright lamp-light the young writers resolutely plied their pens, as hour after hour the Governor-General continued to dictate the despatches, upon which the fate of principalities depended. . . . And still, as Adam, Bayley, Jenkins, Metcalfe, Cole,

Monckton, and others wrote and wrote . . . he told them ever and anon that their work would soon be done, and that there was a table spread for them in the banquet-room, at which they might presently drink success to the campaign. Though it was now the exhausting month of August, and rest and food were denied to them throughout many long hours, there was not one of them who flagged at his desk. Sustained by their youthful enthusiasm, they continued at their work till past midnight; then, weary, hungry, and athirst, they were conducted to the table which had been spread sumptuously for their entertainment. It was a festival not soon to be forgotten. A special message from Lord Wellesley instructed them to give full vent to their hilarity—to use his cellar as though it was their own, and not to think that they were bound to be quiet because they were in Government House.'[1]

The War's Objectives

Lord Wellesley listed the aims of the campaign as four in number: to seize all Sindhia's lands between the Ganges and Jumna, to obtain the person of the Emperor, to form alliances with the Rajput and other states beyond the Jumna (thereby excluding Sindhia from northern Hindusthan), and to extend the Company's territory by occupying Bundelkhand.

The item which concerns possession of the Emperor's person became of great political importance later, and is of some importance in a controversy which lingers still, though only ignorance could have ever permitted it to arise.[2] There can be no question that Lord Wellesley regarded the Emperor, however indigent and powerless, as the fountain of legitimate political right, and highly coveted his support, as 'giving greater stability and strength'[3] to the Company's dominion. He resented angrily M. Perron's control of 'that rich possession . . . the person of the unfortunate Shah Alum' and 'consequently . . . the authority of that wretched Prince'.[4] This rich possession M. Perron 'could transfer . . . as well as his property of whatever kind it may be, to a French adventurer or officer willing to make such a purchase'. It was therefore marked for seizure, and listed among Lake's first objectives.

The Governor-General did not, however, want his intentions to be generally known; his sense of delicacy made him prefer that

[1] Kaye, *Life of Metcalfe*, i. 100–101.

[2] The alleged offence of rebellion against the East India Company, for which the last unhappy Mogul was tried in 1859, condemned, and sent into exile.

[3] Cunninghame to Ellis, 24 September 1831: I.O.R., H.M.S., 708.

[4] Wellesley to the Directors, 13 July 1804: *Intercepted Despatches* (London, 1805), iv. See also Martin, iv. 138. The despatches were taken off the *Hope*, an East Indiaman.

they should be kept secret. A French privateer was so inconsiderate as to capture despatches relating to the Emperor, written with even franker diction that the Governor-General ordinarily used; when the French Government had the impertinence to publish them in the *Moniteur*, the disclosure was felt to be just the kind of ungentlemanly thing that Frenchmen did. Much sarcasm was packed into italics, after the manner of the age: 'the robbery of Ambassadors and Couriers exclusively *adorns* the page of French history, and *decks* the annals of the illustrious dynasty of the fourth race!'[1] The British Government answered this action with the somewhat empty gesture of publication in London also.

Declaration of War

Collins handed Sindhia General Wellesley's laconic ultimatum, whose statements, as we have seen, the writer did not believe: 'I offered you peace on terms of equality, and honourable to all parties. You have chosen war, and are responsible for all consequences.'[2] He left his camp, 3 August 1803.

On 8 August, Wellesley summoned the Ahmadnagar commandant to surrender. He refused, so the fort was assaulted, and on the 11th it submitted. There were 1,200 men, mostly Arabs,[3] in the garrison.

The fortress had not been taken by assault, so by the laws of war if rigidly practised it was not liable to plunder. Two sepoys who overlooked this technicality were at once hanged, one either side of the gateway: 'a measure which, it must be confessed, created some disgust at the moment, but which, at the outset of a campaign, was perhaps a necessary example for the sake of discipline, and a proper vindication of the British character for justice and good faith'.[4] It was at any rate, a clear expression of the character of their terrible commander, and a warning to the troops of the peril under which they lived. That peril they were never allowed to forget.

At Aurangabad, Arthur Wellesley was received by King Collins in the regal fashion which he had used for so long that it was now the normal manner of his life, taken unthinkingly for granted. A brigade of native gunners, attached to the Envoy's escort, greeted the British general with a salute of field pieces.

'In front of a noble suite of tents, which might have served for the

[1] *Intercepted Despatches*, 9.

[2] Gurwood, *Despatches of the Duke of Wellington*, i. 617.

[3] That is, Muhammadan mercenaries.

[4] *Blakiston*, i. 141.

Great Mogul, we were received by an insignificant, little, old-looking man, dressed in an old-fashioned military coat, white breeches, sky-blue silk stockings, and large glaring buckles to his shoes, having his highly powdered wig, from which depended a pig-tail of no ordinary dimensions, surmounted by a small round black silk hat, ornamented with a single black ostrich feather, looking altogether not unlike a monkey dressed up for Bartholomew fair. There was, however, a fire in his small black eye, shooting out from beneath a large, shaggy, pent-house brow, which more than counterbalanced the ridicule that his first appearance naturally excited.'

As they came out of Collins' tent presently, he was overheard to say to Wellesley, 'I tell you, General, as to their cavalry, you may ride over them wherever you meet them; but their infantry and guns will astonish you.'[1]

The Company sent out four separate armies, of which two fought minor campaigns. Against these, in every quarter Sindhia managed to muster about 37,000 infantry, 41,500 horse, and 422 guns,[2] and the Bhonsla Raja an uncertain but considerably lesser number of troops of sorts.

General Lake, the Commander-in-Chief, directed personally the Army of the Jumna and Ganges Doab,[3] consisting of 10,500 men, another 3,500 being detached to overrun Bundelkhand. He had three European cavalry regiments, one European infantry regiment, and 200 European gunners. General Wellesley in the south moved from the Nizam's dominions into the country between the Godavari and Tapti rivers. He had 2,000 Europeans and 7,000 sepoys. He called up the Hyderabad subsidiary force, which gave him another 8,000 men, and collected more sepoys, bringing his army altogether to 21,000 men.

The Minor Campaigns

Colonel Murray, under Arthur Wellesley's general direction, overran Gujarat, where Sindhia had only scattered posts. Baroach was stormed, 29 August, as the climax of a week's operations costing from start to finish 79 casualties; and the few remaining garrisons surrendered with practically no fighting. Colonel Campbell, with 600 Europeans and 4,300 sepoys, overran Orissa, a dependency of the Bhonsla Raja, with equal ease a little

[1] *Ibid*, i. 144.

[2] Blacker, 29. Blacker gives the Bhonsla Raja 30,000 horse, 8,000 infantry; they were of poor quality compared with Sindhia's. According to the same authority, Holkar, who was not in the war's first campaign, had 31,000 horse, 13,000 infantry, and 200 guns.

[3] A 'Mesopotamia', the territory between two rivers.

later (September and October), meeting with no ordered opposition. The province of Cuttack was added to the Company's possessions, and British officers, their work finished thus expeditiously, were at liberty to duck-shoot on the Chilka Lake, and to explore the 'sterile sandy waste, the mournful cast of which is heightened by the hollow roaring of the sea and the sight of innumerable skeletons that whiten the cheerless plain'—bones of pilgrims who had died on their way to Juggernaut's shrine.

This war proved immensely important as marking an expansion of the British spirit, now for the first time widely diffused abroad. Hitherto, the Company's centres had been in South India and Bengal and the tiny enclave round Bombay; and the glories of Muslim India and the inhuman strangeness of the remoter shrines of Hindu India had remained largely legendary. Travellers had seen them, but travellers only, men busied in unusual occasions rather than ordinary ones. Readers of my own generation will understand, if they remember what such names as 'Baghdad' and 'Lebanon' meant before the First World War, when they stood for places well off the general beat of British enterprise. To those of us who saw them, it was strange to realize that we were actually walking in the City of the Arabian Nights or on the hills from which Solomon got his cedars and the Psalmist and the Shulamite so much of their imagery. In the memoirs of this Anglo-Maratha war, it is startlingly vivid to look across more than a hundred years to soldiers of our race trying to tell how they felt when they first went in groups to view the Taj or to examine the grimly notorious shrine of Juggernaut—that uncouth temple where an incomprehensible people reverenced 'ugliness as the personification of the divine attributes'[1] and Brahmanism seemed to flaunt its difference from all other religions of the modern world.

[1] Thorn, *Memoir of the War in India*, 263.

XI

BRITISH AND MARATHA MILITARY TACTICS

THE 1803 campaign inaugurated the long period of what C. E. Montague has styled 'gymkhana wars'. It was the type and epitome of colonial campaigns of the next hundred years, a norm from which only the Gurkha, Afghan, and Sikh campaigns seriously deviated. An Isandlwana or the cutting up of isolated levies in the Sudan have been regrettable incidents, but they hardly ruffled even the edges of a strength as invincible as some engine pitted against flesh and blood. They could quickly be set right, for the equivalents of panzers and *Luftwaffe* were then ours: as a Victorian poet observed:

> 'Whatever happens, we have got
> The maxim gun, which they have not.'

One reason for British negligence of all Indian affairs has been our perception of the fact that most of our triumphs in India have been of pinchbeck quality. In our inmost mind we decline to argue the point of precedence between Assaye and Albuera, or the Mutiny (despite the lavish squandering of V.C.s which contemporary hysteria demanded) and the Crimea. With yet sterner wars in our record since, Indian wars are scarcely likely again to seem of first importance. No people have more rigorous standards than we have, when we come at last to sober judgment of our achievements, and it is by no means unjustified (though unfortunate) that this stigma of second-rateness hangs over our thought of everything Indian. We begin to see the price exacted, though late, by the tale of easy victories and by the kind of cantonment and station life which they encouraged, during decades when European countries were building up severely professional armies.

The holiday spirit of these wars (that is, for one side) is illustrated by innumerable incidents, of which one will serve, from the bloodiest of its battles, that of Assaye. Saiyid Hussain, leading *havildar* of the Fourth Cavalry, dashed into a body of enemy horsemen and took their standard, whereupon Floyer, his own commanding officer, brought him and the standard to General Wellesley, who felt the occasion called for a display of 'that eloquent and correct knowledge in the native language for which you were celebrated.'[1] He patted him on the back, exclaiming, '*Acha havildar! jemadar*' ('Good havildar! jemadar'). A *jemadar* the havildar instantaneously became therefore, and his subsequent career, which brought him medals, pensions, and a palanquin from Government, contained no honour that he esteemed equal to Wellesley's pat on the back. In 1819, when all the Maratha wars were over and the Peshwa deposed, Malcolm gave an Assaye dinner, for which he wrote what Kaye generously calls 'one of the most spirited of his poetical compositions'—a poem notable even in the galaxy of Anglo-Indian verse (which includes Metcalfe's advice to a friend who was thinking of committing adultery[2] and the even more remarkable, and numerous, effusions of Herbert Edwardes). The *havildar* who had been smitten into jemadarship told Malcolm that he felt a personal share in the Victor of Waterloo's deeds, 'as your increasing fame gave increasing value to the notice you had once taken of him'; and he followed Malcolm's dinner by one of his own, concluding with a nautch for the British officers. The reason for these proceedings was made clear by an illuminated head of Wellesley Saheb Bahadur, above Persian characters that 'announced to those who had not seen the light of your countenance in the original, for whom the picture was intended'. *Wellesley* Saheb, the *jemadar* (now a *subadar*) insisted, refusing to use the name Duke of Wellington; 'he said (and I think very justly) that was your European name, but your Indian name was Wellesley Bahadur'. Finally, the local untouchables held their own corroboree, a drunken sweeper explaining to Malcolm: 'We all get drunk for Wellington name'. Not many battles cause so much joy, sixteen years afterwards.

Yet these one-sided wars had results, as most of the enormous slaughters of recent days had not, and results which have lasted to our own day. Moreover, this Anglo-Maratha campaign was far and away the most considerable of all the gymkhana wars which it began, and it entailed at its start some stiff fighting.

British and Maratha Discipline

Both armies on the march presented the appearance of vast and sprawling disorder. They took along with them a dependent host, of grain-sellers, shopkeepers, courtesans, whose encampments sprang up immediately, whenever they halted, into the semblance of cities, with tents and streets of booths.

A careful observer, however, would note that the British kept

[1] Malcolm to the Duke of Wellington. [2] See my *Metcalfe*, 258.

both artillery and cavalry extricated, even in the babel and confusion of a camp. The sword-arm could swiftly be in action if any surprise were attempted. In the Maratha camp, the only part that carried 'the appearance of regularity' was the mushroom fair that sprang up,

'the Bazar which generally forms a very long and broad Street to the Tent of the Chief and of any chief of any consequence, whereas the rest of the camp is so straggled and destitute of all order, that it is a most difficult thing to get through the crowds of Camels, Bullocks, Horses, &c., to the Interior of the Camp, which subjects them to the utmost confusion in case of an alarm. . . . I have even seen the Artillery Park so stationed as to be surrounded and to be rendered totally useless but by the sacrifice of their own people.'[1]

That sacrifice had hitherto rarely been extorted, for the swarms of irregular cavalry scouring the country for forage and provisions had been able to give warning of the approach of any army as disorderly as their own. But it was extorted disastrously in the wars with the British, perhaps because Maratha scouts dared not go as far afield as usual.

The difference was almost heightened when the armies were on the march. By the British, transport and followers were kept always inside a well guarded and rigidly disciplined square of fighting men, with an efficient cavalry or patrols thrown out on the flanks and pickets. In contrast, the Marathas, for all their supposed adoption of Western methods, had merely lost old advantages without gaining new ones. They had ceased to be guerillas flitting over a terrain where orderly armies lay stranded. They straggled like some peasant uprising, and were similarly doomed to be slaughtered by professional technique:

'In Jones's "History" march means one or more columns of troops and ordnance moving along roads, perhaps between two hedges: in the Mahratta history, horse, foot, and dragoons inundating the face of the earth for many miles on every side, here and there a few horse with a flag and a drum, mixed with a loose and straggling mass of camels, elephants, bullocks, nautch-girls, fakeers, and buffoons; troops and followers, lancemen and matchlockmen, bunyans and mootasuddies.'[2]

The impersonal efficiency of the Marathas' adversaries was exemplified in Arthur Wellesley, Commander of the Company's Southern Army. In the literature of their class his despatches and

[1] Secret Report of Sir Charles Malet, March 1795: *I.O.R.*, *H.M.S.*, 242, p. 31. The abundance of goods offered in these improvised streets of shops greatly impressed the British, from the days when Morari Rao and his free companies were allied with Clive, in the Company's earliest wars in South India.

[2] Elphinstone to Grant, 20 April 1822: *Life of Elphinstone*, ii. 137.

letters are by themselves, attaining absolute irreducible brevity and absence of emotion. All details are seen to, all matters taken into consideration. Everything—transport, bridging material, the shooting or hanging or flogging of offenders, the provision of food or bullocks or native porters—is 'ticked off' in the clearest and most laconic style on record, unclouded by a moment's weakness of feeling or hesitation.

Against minds as cool as this, educated to service first, all thoughts of gain being postponed until victory had been secured—against the stern terrible discipline of the British Army, which makes the memoirs of the period revolting to read but no more excited those who inflicted it than pheasant-shooting excites our gossip-writers of to-day—the Marathas could oppose only half a confederacy. The Peshwa, its supposed head, was their enemy's unwilling colleague; Holkar, their ablest general, was a sulky onlooker. Their fine show of artillery and foreign officers and gunners, their imitation of Western methods (so alien to the Maratha way of fighting), gave them but a bogus efficiency and, as Sir Thomas Munro noted, were but a means of 'dressing them out for the sacrifice'. Their cannon made them unwieldy and immobile, and took from them the immemorial Maratha freedom of choice of battlefield. They were pinned down where these precious arms were stationed and held there as on an anvil until battered to pieces. When they sought to superimpose on medieval methods the elaborate weight of a modern army, their finances were practically non-existent, their commisariat was still a matter of chance supplies picked up by their scouring cavalry:

'Not only is half the Grain and Forage allowed to the Horses embezzled, but Horses are changed, reported Dead, and every species of the most flagitious Peculation practised with Impunity. . . . Insomuch that I have sometimes been inclined to think that the Government must have some mode of reimbursing itself for these palpable Dilapidations by withholding the Pay due to its Troops.'[1]

To make the picture exact, the rough justice which this shrewd observer surmises must be remembered as being strength as well as weakness. The Maratha trooper, when his pay was in arrears, for good reason did not resent it as the sepoy did.

The Marathas still possessed two advantages which might prove of value, if the fighting were ever stripped of its modern style and reduced to elementals. Their wants, for man and beast, were of the slightest. Their lowly caste permitted a wide range of food: for example, every animal food except beef. Ceremonies were few,

[1] Malet.

ablutions of a ritual nature were hardly required at all; the soldier could sit down straight away, after marching or fighting, and dress and cook and eat. Only one luxury accompanied the army, the courtesan (and it is on record that the women who accompanied the Pindaris, the Marathas' irregular auxiliaries, fought and pillaged more pitilessly than the men). The British, on the other hand, wasted a vast proportion of their strength to provide a standard of living which by war's exiguous and primitive needs was luxurious, and in the case of officers always as luxurious as circumstances allowed. They had often elaborate camps, with mausoleums fitted up with drawing-rooms and marquees where balls could be held. The higher officers brought wives and daughters. There were hunting and pig-sticking parties.

Secondly, the Marathas had, and still have, the most genuine democracy in India. It has kept them, even in the century of subjection since their downfall, from ever sinking to the servility of some nations, or to others' wrath of helpless bitterness. As Elphinstone noted, after the wars had finished, the state of affairs reported from Bengal seemed horrifying in his part of the land, where the poorest peasant as a matter of course sat down in the British official's presence, and expected as well as gave respect. In the Maratha fighting forces, we are told, every horseman 'looks upon himself as Company for his Chieftain and always sits down with him'.[1] At certain times, and in certain kinds of warfare, brotherhood has had its value. The Anzacs made no pretence of believing that a gulf of social and intellectual inequality yawned between their officers and men, yet in battle they showed a terrible efficiency not always found in units rigorously knit with cords of deference and discipline.

[1] *Ibid.*

XII

LAKE OPENS HIS CAMPAIGN

LAKE CAMPED near Kanauj, on the Ganges, a little above the twenty-seventh degree of latitude, in a region of splendid ruins, tombs and palaces plunged in luxuriant jungle. Here officers and their families picnicked in tents made comfortable with glass doors and brick fireplaces.

The days were spent in hunting. The General distinguished himself by pistolling a huge tiger, as it was about to spring on a sportsman who had speared it. The nights were dedicated to revels, in 'a spacious ball-room' (formerly, probably, part of a palace), 'fitted up for the purpose' and accommodating 'an elegant assemblage of youth and beauty, grace and hilarity, softening the cares of life and removing every apprehension of danger'. Lake was the father of four lovely daughters, who presided over the festivities. 'The finest wines of every clime, from the exhilarating Sheeraz of Persia to the ruby Carbonelle and humble Port, abounded'.[1]

The district had been recently taken from the Nawab of Oudh, in payment of arrears of debt. Rich in itself, it was of great strategic value also, advancing the Company's frontier to where a wedge could be driven between Sindhia's Frenchmen and the rest of the Maratha forces.

Since the Battle of Cuddalore, 1783, when half of Haidar Ali's army was French, the Company's sepoys had not encountered a European foe. It was well understood by the British that Sindhia's Frenchmen, who had worked so hard to bring about war ('which held out such an alluring prospect of a rapacious desire and the gratification of national vanity'),[2] were overjoyed at its outbreak. But the outward behaviour of this volatile people does not invariably correspond to their feelings; and did not now. Lake entered

[1] Thorn, 81. Madeira and wine from the Cape were the common drinks. Whisky was unknown.

[2] *Ibid*, 63. The meaning of the sentence is blurred, but that is characteristic of Thorn when he feels the subject calls for dignified or poetic language. It is characteristic also of the literature of the period, that when an author has set down the word 'rapacious' or 'rapacity' his general satisfaction that he has said the right thing makes him indifferent to what other words accompany this all-important one. 'Rapacity' is what he means; and if he has said 'rapacity' the rest is leather and prunella.

Sindhia's territory, 29 August, at four in the morning, near Aligarh, and after a skirmish General Perron removed his forces, leaving with the fort's Commandant, Colonel Pedron, instructions to fight to the last. 'I hope in a few days to send back the English general as fast or faster than he came. . . . The eyes of millions are fixed upon you. Remember' (he exhorted him) 'that you are a Frenchman.' But this—as Leslie Stephen observes, of a similar exhortation to Portuguese troops told off, during the Peninsular War, to attack a crack enemy regiment particularly well posted—proved to be not a very inspiriting recollection. Insusceptible to napoleonics, Pedron at once opened negotiations for surrender. His second-in-command, Baji Rao, a Maratha, placed him under arrest, and Lake had to assault. Colonel Monson led the stormers, and Aligarh fell on 4 September, at a cost of 260 men. The defenders lost far more—2,000 in killed alone, it was said, the moat being clogged with corpses.

James Skinner, the ablest soldier of mixed blood that ever fought in India, had left Sindhia's service a few days previously. He stood beside Lake, watching while the 'handful of heroes ran like lions' at one embattled gate after another, to blow it in and rush ever forward. Lake exultantly asked him what he thought 'of European fighting', and was assured that no fort in Hindusthan[1] could stand against it. In his memoirs Skinner declares that 'the courage displayed by the 76th surpassed all I had ever seen, and every idea I had formed of soldiering'.[2] Lake spurred his horse to the outer gate, where the majority of the victors' few dead lay crowded. 'It is the fate of good soldiers!' he cried, bursting into tears. He galloped back, and gave the place up to a plunder as vigorous as the assault.

The troops ferreted out an immense loot, over which they fought afresh. Skinner, playing a detached part, an unemployed spectator as yet, watched two sepoys trying to rob a British soldier carrying a bag of money. The soldier tore it open and pretended to scatter its contents, which the sepoys stooped to gather, whereupon he shot one and bayoneted the other. Then, taking off his jacket, he made a new bag by knotting the sleeves: recovered his gains: reloaded his musket: and offered Skinner fifty dollars to convoy him safe to camp, which he did. Baji Rao was killed in the storming, and Pedron, an elderly man in a green jacket with gold lace and epaulettes, was brought in a prisoner. Two hundred and eighty-one guns of various kinds were taken.

[1] That part of India which lies between the rivers Satlej and Narbada.

[2] Baillie Fraser, i. 267 ff.

Sindhia's British Officers

Many of Sindhia's ablest officers were British; still more were Eurasians, sons of British fathers. If they should be captured fighting against the Company they would be hanged as traitors. The Eurasians, especially, were in a pitiable dilemma. Though often inheriting the European's best martial qualities, since Lord Cornwallis' time they were refused admission into the Company's regular services, except as subordinates and menials. They had no choice but between penury or service to some Indian prince.

This Anglo-Maratha war, however, was lit up with much humanity and even nobleness; it is one of the few wars that both sides can study without feelings of shame. The Governor-General, calling in all Sindhia's British nationals, promised them something better than beggary, offering them the same rank and pay (as irregulars, not as King's or Company's officers) as they possessed already. Sindhia had the generous unwisdom to let them go. Some of them repaid him by making it a condition of their new service that it should not be against him. Others were less honourable. One furnished the Company with a detailed account of his troops and their composition and artillery. Another, an Irishman, Lucan, was so zealously helpful that his work was tactlessly stressed in public despatches, to his own grim undoing later. When the first fighting took place, at Aligarh, Lucan, who had just arrived, volunteered to lead the stormers 'and point out the road through the fort, which he effected in such a manner as to gain the particular thanks of the commander-in-chief and the public acknowledgments of the government'.[1] Skinner, who had come over from Sindhia at the same time, felt the slur which this officious treachery put on Lucan's late comrades and states the same facts differently:

> 'I am sorry to add, that the gate by which these gallant fellows entered was pointed out to them by Lieutenant Lucan, an Irishman, and an officer in the Mahratta service, who received for the job 24,000 rupees, and a commission in H.M.'s 76th.'[2]

Skinner's Horse

Enemy cavalry who had surrendered and were being formed into a corps of Company irregulars saw James Skinner riding with Lake. His valour was legendary and his name had long been twisted into that of the great Alexander, 'Sikander'. 'Give

[1] Thorn, *Memoir of the War in India*, 99.

[2] Baillie Fraser, *Military Memoirs of James Skinner*, i. 271.

us Sikander Saheb', the new corps begged, when asked to suggest their officer. Skinner's Horse was formed accordingly, the premier cavalry regiment of the Indian Army.

Skinner, like many of these despised Eurasian soldiers of fortune, was chivalrous as well as valiant. The Marathas had been good masters and good comrades, and he stipulated that his men should not be asked to serve against Sindhia. Lake consented. They therefore took no part in the further harassing of Sindhia, though they fought with distinction against Holkar later. Indeed, without their services the British would have put up a very ineffective show against that redoubtable outlaw.

Bishop Heber, who came across Skinner's Horse in 1824, found them 'the most showy and picturesque cavaliers I have seen since I was in the south of Russia'—the Cossacks of India:

'They had turbans of dark red shawl, long yellow caftans with dark red cummerbunds, and trowsers of the same colour. The commander of the party had a long spear with a small yellow pennon, the others had each a long matchlock-gun which they carried on the right shoulder with the match ready lighted. They had all, likewise, pistols, swords, and shields, and their caftans and turbans so strongly quilted, as to secure them against most sabre-cuts. Their horses were very tolerable in size and appearance, but hot and vicious, and the whole cavalcade had an appearance remarkably wild and Oriental. They are reckoned, by all the English in this part of the country, the most useful and trusty, as well as the boldest body of men in India, and during the wars both of Lord Lake and Lord Hastings their services and those of their chief were most distinguished.'[1]

Their Colonel, Sikander Saheb, was 'a good and modest, as well as a brave man'.

General Lake

When he heard of it, General Wellesley was deeply impressed by the capture of Aligarh without escalade. But these headlong seizures of massive fortresses in the end cost the British dear. Both Lake and Wellesley came to think that the only strategy called for in a commander was to hurl men at guns and walls. Within two years of these absurdly easy conquests Lake threw away lives and prestige vainly, at Bharatpur; and in the Peninsular War Wellesley bought Badajoz with a pile of dead. I do not believe that either would have fought these bloody actions in the way he did, if it had not been for the contempt for strong defences induced by Aligarh, Ahmadnagar, Agra, Gawilgarh, and the other mighty bastions so trivially yielded in the Maratha War.

[1] *Narrative of a Journey*, etc., ii. 283.

Lake was the best type of English traditional general, active and affable and bluff, the fox-hunter on parade. 'It mattered not at what time of the morning the army commenced its march, there was Lord Lake in full uniform, buttoned to the chin, powdered and peruqued.' He rose at two a.m. to dress, the result of good ways acquired in Lincolnshire, where the bucks, Lord Yarborough told Malcolm, were at immense pains to ride out properly attired, so as to leave 'a genteel corpse' if they broke their necks.[1] War to Lake was merely fox-hunting on a grand scale and its tactics were exactly similar. You found your quarry, then you rode hard at him, with all the pack you had. This was generalship, as he had always understood it. Kind and generous to his men, he kept them always soldiers, and allowed none of the mawkish civilian pursuits. In season and out of season he exhorted everyone:

'Damn your writing!
Mind your fighting!'

verses of his own composition, and the only poem he was ever known to quote.[2]

Lake knew already all that he was ever going to know. But his young colleague in the south, a major-general of practically no fighting experience, was learning his art as he went along. The British have reason to feel grateful to India, and to the Marathas in particular, for providing Arthur Wellesley with so much instruction so cheaply.

Aligarh had hardly fallen, when Sindhia's commander-in-chief, Perron, appeared in Lake's camp. He had been ousted by intrigue. The Company escorted him down country with ostentatious respect, and most of the other French officers in Maratha employment, whose value had been immensely overassessed by the Governor-General, followed him as quickly and as soon as they could.

Nor were they all French. Perron, short of European subalterns, had been 'under the necessity of inviting Swiss, Germans, and even Portuguese, to join his battalions'.[3] They were accepted, as stopgaps only, until such time as better men could be obtained from France (which was now difficult, the Company so closely watched India's ports). They knew this, and few of them were really eager to risk their lives. The fall of a renowned fortress, the

[1] *Life of Malcolm*, i. 343.

[2] See Metcalfe's letter to Sherer, 14 March 1806 (Kaye, *Life of Metcalfe*, i. 203): 'There is not a book in this army. The Commander-in-Chief does not patronize literature.'

[3] *Brief Remarks on the Mahratta War, etc.* (1804), 18.

scurrying of rats from the sinking ship of Sindhia's fortunes, were spectacles that rallied to the British side a number of minor chieftains and spread defeatism through the enemy's ranks.

XIII

THE BATTLE OF DELHI AND THE FALL OF AGRA

The Battle of Delhi

The Battle of Delhi was fought, 11 September, in a position which historians (following Thorn) state to have been six miles short of the city. It is twice that distance, and the Jumna intervenes.[1]

Lake's army, starting at three a.m., marched eighteen miles in eight hours and were settling into camp when Maratha horsemen annoyed them. Lake led a reconnaissance in person and drove them back, to discover the main enemy body posted on rising ground flanked by marshes, with cavalry behind. He sent back orders to his artillery and infantry to advance immediately, he and his own cavalry meanwhile drawing and holding the Maratha fire. Two horses were shot under him, and the apparent hesitation of the British during this time of waiting gave the enemy a false exultation of victory. His infantry arrived, and the cavalry feigned a retreat, which enticed the Marathas out of their entrenchments, to be confronted by the entire British army. Lake himself, in the attack which followed, led the renowned 76th regiment, with two major-generals and all his staff in the front of the charge, while his cannon were rushed up to short range. The Marathas fled, and the cavalry drove them into the Jumna, where the galloper guns disposed of 'prodigious numbers of them'.[2] Others were chased into ravines, and slaughtered there. The victory was complete, 68 cannon and 61 tumbrils laden with ammunition being accounted for at a cost of 461 casualties.

It was an astonishing feat, to march for eight hours, pitch camp, and then fight an improvised battle. The Governor-General's gratitude to Lake was extreme, and his letter of thanks was written under stress of abounding emotion:

'Much as I feel indebted to the merits of your army, justice, universal consent of all parties, and the plain evidence of indisputable fact concur to point my principal attention to your matchless energy, ability, and valour. You have formed the army to this illustrious and extraordinary achievement, and to your personal exertion must be

[1] See *The Journal of Army Historical Research*, January 1932. [2] Thorn, 113.

attributed the promptitude, skill, and irresistible intrepidity which marked our operations on that memorable day. The result must be the utter extinction of the last vestige of French influence in India, the defeat of the ambitious and rapacious views of the Mahratta confederates, and a speedy peace with ample indemnity and security to the allies. You are entitled to the highest honours and rewards which your country and your king can bestow. . . . My private gratitude cannot be expressed, nor is it possible to form a hope of discharging such a debt according to my estimation of its extent. My life, however protracted, could not furnish the means of satisfying my sentiments on this occasion; but whatever can be expected from the most cordial, firm, and zealous respect, affection and attachment, must ever be commanded by you from me, and from every person connected with me.'

Lord Wellesley, as Kaye remarks in his *Life of Tucker*, 'came out to India to conquer Provinces and perplex the Revenue'. With his finances sunk in debt after the war with Tipu, he was aware of growing anger in the Directorate in London. His only chance was to present his masters with swift and overwhelming victory, so that criticism would be silent against the plaudits of his admirers. Lake had given him such victory, the boon which of all he most desired, and relief and sense of indebtedness make his letters to this subordinate unique. They overflow with an excitement that often seems out of control.

In his delight, Wellesley did more than merely write emotional etters of thanks. In the fall of Delhi, which followed automatically on this victory, over half a million rupees were taken, which the Governor-General, 'deeming it to be the duty of the government to anticipate the sanction of his Majesty and of the honourable the Court of Directors', authorized Lake to distribute immediately. Honorary colours were presented to the regiments that had taken part in the fighting.

In Delhi, the blind and aged Emperor, to whom Warren Hastings had written in terms of more than oriental humility and extravagance, was found waiting under a small tattered canopy, trembling to know what would be his fate at the hands of these new conquerors to whom Providence had transferred his person. His helplessness and misery touched them, and these were alleviated, so far as their extremity permitted of alleviation. In return he bestowed on Lake the title of 'The Sword of the State, the Hero of the Land, the Lord of the Age, and the Victorious in War', explaining that this was the second highest honour he could bestow. He apologized for not bestowing the highest of all, but it had already been given to his other distinguished servant Sindhia. Lake accepted the explanation and was proud of his title. He honourably refused to take from the Emperor's penury a large sum of money in addition.

The Begum Sumroo

Of the numerous petty chieftains who hurried in to make their peace, the Begum Sumroo attracted the most notice. She was relict (widow or mistress) of Walter Reinhardt, a German adventurer who came to India as a carpenter in the French navy. His companions nicknamed him *Sombre*, from his appearance and temperament, and on Indian tongues this became *Sumroo*. After various changes and desertions, he was in the service of Mir Qasim, Nawab of Bengal, when the rupture between that prince and the Company came in 1763, and he personally supervised the Patna massacre of the British (October 1763). His wife, a Kashmiri dancing girl, survived his death (a violent one) in 1778 and by help of the prowess of that remarkable man George Thomas[1] established herself as a semi-independent princess in Sindhia's train.

The Begum appeared at Lake's headquarters just after he had dined, when the commander-in-chief, 'a little elevated',[2] embraced her, 'to the utter dismay of her attendants'. 'It is the salute of a padre to his daughter', the lady explained, with excellent presence of mind. She was a Christian, as Sumroo had been, and the explanation was seen to be the right one. She was greatly petted by her new friends, in whose company she was often to be seen riding on horseback or in a howdah. She still possessed considerable remains of former beauty, which had vanished when Bishop Heber saw her in 1825 and found her 'a very little queer-looking old woman, with brilliant wicked-looking eyes'. Heber is the authority for one of the best known of Anglo-Indian tales of horror, of how she buried alive a slave-girl who had excited her jealousy, and sat smoking her hookah over the grave. I am afraid it is true.

The Begum was confirmed in the possession of her lands, though her troops, who were with Sindhia confronting Arthur Wellesley, fought on after her defection and were the only infantry who left the field of Assaye in good order.

[1] A sailor who made himself for a time an independent raja, and offered to conquer the Punjab for the Company. See *The Foreigner*, an interesting reconstruction of his career in fiction, by John Travers (Mrs. Eva Bell).

[2] Baillie Fraser, i. 293.

The Fall of Agra

Leaving Colonel David Ochterlony in command at Delhi, Lake marched against Agra. Its foreign officers being unwilling to make a resistance, the garrison imprisoned them. The siege began 10 October, and a week later was successful, 8,000 men surrendering, with 164 guns and quantities of stores and ammunition. Those who have seen Agra Fort must be astonished to recall its surrender by an armed host, after scarcely even nominal defence.

It is easy to understand why war used to be so popular. The military seized 24 lakhs of rupees in Agra and precipitately shared them out, a deed which filled their Commander with terror. Lake was a veteran of the Seven Years' and American Revolutionary Wars, and in his sixtieth year; but he shook when he thought of the possibility of the Governor-General's anger. His own share he dared not touch as yet, and wrote abjectly:

> 'If I am wrong, or have acted contrary to your wishes, I shall be most miserable. . . . I hate all money concerns, and sincerely wish I had nothing to do with this.'[1]

Wellesley, however, continued in his mood of joyful affability and exaltation. He was now able to tell Lake of his own brother's 'noble and splendid victory' at Assaye, and told him to cease grieving over 'the necessary loss of gallant British blood, which must attend such extraordinary efforts of valour'[2] as the world was now witnessing. He himself was 'persuaded that many lives have been saved by the early sacrifice of a few brave men'.

> 'If the successes of your operations stood alone, they would astonish all Asia; but, combined with the blows struck in every other quarter, it is impossible to convey to you an adequate idea of the splendour of your fame in this part of the world. With all the sanguine temper of my mind, I declare that I could not have hoped for a completion of my plans at once so rapid and so secure. I must now send you fresh instructions, as you have reached the limits of all my first ideas.'

It was all right about the money, he added. The letter 'quite overpowered' its recipient, and left him 'with a most grateful and feeling heart totally devoid of utterance'. Its 'kindness has completely debilitated me, and made me shed so many tears of joy', Lake's nerves were 'quite unstrung' by it.

When the British first advanced, large sections of the populace fled in terror, not only, or even mainly, of the brutal and licentious soldiery, but of that dreaded engine, their legal system, the High Court of Calcutta. This was understood to be a man-devouring monster, without sense or pity. When it was realized that the

[1] Martin, iii. 414. [2] *Ibid*, 419.

creature had not yet left its usual haunts the people returned. Presently they were acknowledging the unprecedented fact of a victorious army passing through territories without wasting them with fire or destroying their civilian inhabitants. Lake attached importance to this, as being of even military value. We need not idealize the Company and its conquests. But it brought two things which India had hardly ever known, discipline and patriotism. No general, however successful, thought of setting up for himself, a fact which filled its enemies with amazement. Sindhia and Holkar and Peshwa fought each for his own hand, and were helpless against the co-ordinated efforts of their opponents.

One result of Lake's victories was that the Raja of Bharatpur on 9 October came into the Company's alliance and sent a body of horsemen to co-operate with the British. Bharatpur's example was quickly followed by Alwar, Jaipur, and Jodhpur.

XIV

THE BATTLE OF LASWARI

THE MARATHAS rallied at Laswari, thirty miles north-west of Agra, where Lake came upon them at sunrise, 1 November. They were strongly posted and had cut a reservoir's banks, to flood the approaches. Without waiting for his infantry, whom he had left toiling far behind, Lake flung his cavalry at the enemy's artillery position, a nest of cannon chained together behind a breastwork strengthened with a zareba of transport wagons, the whole masked by elephant-grass. The gunners held their fire until the cavalry were within twenty yards; and they fought with such desperation that after the battle Lake enlisted their survivors in the Company's service—which most of them were quite willing to enter, so entirely had Indian armies become mercenary. Only on the British side, as a rule, was there the stiffening which patriotism gives.

Lake did what was the equivalent in the First World War of attacking without artillery preparation, and the cavalry failed to oust the enemy. The infantry, marching up like Blucher's army at Waterloo, arrived about eleven o'clock, breathless and dusty. The Marathas faltered, and opened negotiations, being given an hour, which both sides used to strengthen themselves. It was nearly noon (of all hours for a frontal attack!) when Lake guided the infantry into their last mile, of which they managed to traverse most unseen, by using nullas and luxuriant grasses. On emergence they were met with a terrific fire, which ravaged the devoted 76th Regiment in particular. Lake's charger was killed, and his son, Major Lake, dismounting to offer his own, was struck down. Lake could not pause for even his wounded son but had to gallop off to bring up the 12th and 16th Native Infantry to assist the 76th. An attack made by Maratha cavalry on the flank was feeble and the battle began to fade out from Laswari. It gathered vigour in the village of Malpur, where resistance continued until four in the afternoon, when Maratha ruin was complete. The British had lost heavily, over 800 dead and wounded, but their opponents' losses were immense, believed to be close on 7,000 killed alone. Lake when his troops cheered him responded with a deeply felt gesture. He 'took off his hat and thanked them, but told them to despise

Death, as those brave fellows had done', pointing to the enemy gunners who had died at their posts.

Seventy-one cannon were captured and immense stores of ammunition, in addition to an unascertainable amount blown up during the battle. The ground presently became so offensive with its rotting thousands that the victors had to march away from it. As Sindhia had meanwhile lost the battle of Assaye to Arthur Wellesley, his power lay prostrate, and the armies which his predecessor and he had made through so many years were shattered beyond repair.

Lake's despatches, a complete contrast to his colleague's in the southern campaign, are so drenched with the emotion of the events they describe that it is easier to recreate the Laswari battle than almost any other in our annals. He had taken a terrific risk, and it had been a near thing; his own son was severely wounded, and at the crisis of the battle his father had seen him apparently dying and had had to leave him. The incident naturally stirred men's imaginations; the Governor-General in far-off Calcutta found himself trembling as he read of it. There is a human and spectacular quality about Laswari that sets it apart—the infantry straining up while the sun beats almost perpendicularly down: the nullas drowned in waving tall grasses: the Maratha gunners dying in the deadly lairs which they had woven before their guns, with their foes massed in slaughter in their front: the English commander's struggle between anguish and duty. Lake's sentences describing the day huddle tempestuously and incoherently over each other:[1]

'I never was in so severe a business in my life or any thing like it, and pray to God I never may be in such a situation again; their army is better appointed than ours, no expense is spared whatever, they have three times the number of men to a gun than we have, their bullocks, of which they have many more than we have, are of a very superior sort, all their men's knapsacks and baggage are carried on camels, by which means they can march double the distance; we have taken all their bazar, baggage, and every thing belonging to them, an amazing number of them were killed, indeed the victory has been decisive. The action of yesterday has convinced me how impossible it is to do any thing without British troops, and of them there ought to be a very great proportion. The returns of yesterday will, I fear, prove the necessity of what I say too fully . . . the wound of my dear son rendered me totally unfit for any thing, but I thank God his wound is less severe than I at first believed, when I first saw him upon receiving it it almost unmanned me, but the alarming crisis when it happened obliged me to quit him, and look to the

[1] Martin, iii. 445 ff. and 456 ff.

troops, who at that time wanted every assistance I could give them. . . . I think, without exception, yesterday was the most anxious day I ever experienced, for had we been beaten by these brigades, the consequences attending such a defeat must have been most fatal. These fellows fought like devils, or rather heroes. . . .'

Lord Wellesley's reply moves with an equal passion of excitement:

'The action is one of the most brilliant of which I have ever read the relation. Your personal exertions in it surpass all praise, all example, and all honour and glory acquired by any Commander of an army, whose actions have reached my knowledge. . . . The dreadful and distracting event of your son's wound in your presence in the heat of action, and in the most urgent and critical moment of your own public duty, was such a trial as heaven has seldom given to human fortitude. . . . No scene equal to this trial ever was presented to my imagination, nor do I believe it is to be paralleled in all history. . . . I declare to you solemnly, that your resolution under such a blow, your instant return to the attack of the enemy, and the alacrity and ardour with which you prosecuted the glorious victory of that day, constituted such a variety of extraordinary and affecting circumstances, that I could not command strength of mind to read your letter in public. . . .'

'Lake is a glorious old fellow', wrote Elphinstone excitedly, to a friend. 'All people here praise his letter extremely. I was struck with it at first, because the compliments to the killed are well brought in. . . . Write me which campaign you think most of, ours or his.'[1]

[1] 10 December 1803.

XV

GENERAL WELLESLEY'S VICTORIES

THE STORM of Ahmadnagar was followed by some minor operations. Then the Battle of Assaye was fought, 23 September.

The Company's forces engaged are usually stated to have been about 4,500. This leaves out the lascars and pioneers, who suffered severely, and 6,000 is about the right number. Against these, the Marathas had some 10,000 infantry, largely under French command; and also a horde of cavalry and infantry, of the kind generally styled irregular, ready to skirr away on the hint of danger. The Bhonsla Raja provided many of these. He himself was the first to flee, and can hardly be said to have been present at all. Arthur Wellesley's testimony is that the behaviour of all the enemy cavalry, from first to last, was 'most dastardly'. The Maratha infantry were offered up as sacrifices.

The victory was criticized at the time as needlessly costly, and may have been. Arthur Wellesley had notoriously won his high command because he was the Governor-General's brother, and for no other reason, and there was as yet no glamour about his name. He had won no battles, except against a fugitive brigand,[1] and had seen little service. It was well known that in the operations before Seringapatam he had slept when under orders to conduct a storm, a greater dereliction from duty than many for which he executed men without hesitation; and that only General Baird's magnanimity (this, and no doubt his connection with the Governor-General) had prevented him from being broken, as any less influential officer would have been,[2] and had given him the chance to rehabilitate himself.

As in Lake's battles, so at Assaye, little time was spent on artillery preparation. Since every Englishman was eager to expedite 'the great and glorious work of destroying the last nests of French scoundrels in India',[3] thereby saving 'our great and flourishing possessions from the claws of that rapacious tyrant, the First Consul',[4] everyone who could, civilians included, took a hand in

[1] Dhundia Wagh, after the Mysore War.

[2] For the incident see Blakiston, i. 79 ff.

[3] Malcolm to the Hon. Henry Wellesley, 5 September 1803: *Life of Malcolm*, i. 231. [4] Lake to the Governor-General, 14 November: Martin, iii. 455.

the fun. Elphinstone, when the battle started, was lolling in his palanquin. 'But, seeing that something was going to happen', he tumbled out and mounted his horse ('for I had no notion there would be anything worth seeing with the infantry'). It was a case of 'There are the enemy! Everyone at them!'

The Marathas were stationed along the further bank of a stream that was hardly anywhere passable to guns. The ground in their front was broken up by nullas, and very unfit for cavalry charges, which were the deciding factor in these Indian battles. They flung these advantages away, allowing Wellesley to take his guns across the only ford, while they merely fell back on a second position, backed by another stream—a deathtrap if they were defeated.

Wellesley's guns, having crossed the stream, opened fire at 400 yards' distance. Losing heavily in men and bullocks, they were immobilized, so the General ordered them to be left where they were, while his troops went for the enemy 'bald-headed'. He himself at first led the helterskelter battle, and was almost into Maratha headquarters before he realized it:

'Somebody said, "Sir! that is the enemy's line." The General said, "Is it? Ha, damme, so it is!" (you know his manner) and turned. . . . The 74th (I am assured and convinced) was unable to stop the enemy; and I know that the sepoys were huddled in masses, and that attempts which I saw made to form them failed; when "the genius and fortune of the Republic" brought the cavalry on to the right. They charged the enemy, drove them with great slaughter into the Joee Nulla, and so saved the 74th . . . the cavalry, which had then crossed the nulla, charged up its bank, making a dreadful slaughter but affording a most delightful spectacle to us, who were halted on the side nearest the field of battle, unable to cross on account of our guns. . . . The General was going to attack a body of the enemy (from their left, I believe), who, when we had passed them, went and spiked our artillery and seized our guns, and recovered some of their own, and turned them all against our rear, which annoyed us a good deal. When the General was returning to the guns there was a heavy fire, and he had his horse killed under him . . . the General passed the night, not in "the pride, pomp and circumstance of glorious war" but on the ground, close to an officer whose leg was shot off, and within five yards of a dead officer. I got some curry and bloody water, which did not show at night, and lay down and slept without catching cold.'[1]

Assaye was Elphinstone's first experience of war. He settled down to read Shakespeare right through, while waiting for a

[1] *Life of Elphinstone*, i. 65. Blakiston tells how the troops rushed into the stream, as soon as the battle was over, to drink the water, though it was tinged with blood and full of corpses.

second battle; and interested himself in examining the stricken field, to see if there were many European dead. The romantic revival was well under way, though Keats and Shelley were not yet writing and Wordsworth and Coleridge were hardly known except as eccentrics. All these young men were intensely serious, and most of them took literature as an absorbing study. But Elphinstone was alone in the imaginative style which he could give to his most ordinary letters. Exploring the scene of the fight, this is what he saw:

'There was a Roman Emperor who said he liked the smell of a dead enemy. If he did he was singular in his taste. We are horribly perfumed with such a smell as he liked, but I would rather smell a living enemy. I went yesterday evening to the field of battle. It was a dark, cloudy evening. I rode by myself, and saw *plurima mortis imago*. Some of the dead are withered, their features still remaining, but their faces blackened to the colour of coal, others still swollen and blistered. The Persian I mentioned was perfect everywhere, and had his great quilted coat on; but his face had fallen or been eaten off, and his naked skull stared out like the hermit's of the wood of Joppa (in the *Castle of Otranto*). Kites and adjutants, larger than the Calcutta ones, were feeding on the bodies, and dogs were feasting in some places, and in others howling all over the plain. I saw a black dog tearing, in a furious way, great pieces of flesh from a dead man, looking fiercely, and not regarding me. I thought the group horrible and sublime.'

Arthur Wellesley took his triumph phlegmatically, sending Malcolm a characteristically businesslike note, which lighted into a sparkle of enthusiasm only in the statement that 'we have got more than ninety guns, seventy of which are the finest brass ordnance I have ever seen'. Henry Wellesley bore similar testimony. 'Scindiah's infantry were far better than Tippoo's, his artillery excellent, and his ordnance so well equipped, that it answers for our Service. We could never use Tippoo's.'[1] The postscript to General Wellesley's letter contained the only hint of the personal part its writer had played:

'The bay horse was shot under me, and Diomed was kicked, so that I am not now sufficiently mounted. Will you let me have the grey Arab? I must also request you to get for me two good saddles and bridles.'

Arthur Wellesley sent Munro also a description of the battle,[2] in which he showed full awareness of criticisms that might be brought (in fact, were already being brought) against him as tactician and strategist. Its simplicity and detachment are of a

[1] Henry Wellesley, 3 October 1803: Gurwood, *Despatches of the Duke of Wellington*, i. 755.

[2] 1 November 1803; *Life of Munro*, i. 347 ff.

most unusual quality, and justify that respect which his achievement always keeps. He seems to have understood from the first perfectly and exactly what he could do, and much of his success was because of this fact, that he had himself and his abilities, his resources and the abilities of those who served him, completely in hand. This may not be genius, but it pulls a man through to victory; 'knowing his own talent as he knew it—and he knew it as a runner knows his pace, or a cricketer his best hit—he was certainly right'.[1]

Munro, who received the letter, understood the facts no less, and was prepared to give the victorious general credit, without rising into excitement about his conquest. 'You are quite an enthusiast with respect to General Lake', he wrote to his brother.

'General Wellesley had, however, great difficulties to encounter, a greater body of infantry and artillery, a much more formidable cavalry, and all animated by the presence of their sovereign; not dispirited by the desertion of their officers, like the northern army. If there was anything wrong at Assye, it was in giving battle; but in the conduct of the action, everything was right. General Wellesley gave every part of his army its full share; left no part of it unemployed; but supported, sometimes with cavalry, sometimes with infantry, every point that was pressed, at the very moment that it was most necessary.

I allow them both great credit; but, after all, I see nothing very extraordinary in the success of the war. I never doubted that the result would be what it has been.'

Such was the famous Battle of Assaye, a swift exchange of blows, ending in a complete British triumph. It is always reckoned a severe battle, which the victors' losses sufficiently show that it was. Their casualties were over 2,000, including auxiliaries, and the proportion of dead to wounded was unusually heavy, in the ratio of four to eleven. The Maratha losses were beyond computation, but were estimated at 1,200 killed and 5,000 wounded. Sindhia was finished, and the Marathas lost all but honour. That, at least, they preserved. 'Their infantry is the best I have ever seen in India, excepting our own; and they and their equipment far surpass Tippoo's. I assure you that their fire was so heavy, that I much doubted at one time whether I should be able to prevail upon our troops to advance; and all agree that the battle was the fiercest that has ever been seen in India. Our troops behaved admirably; the sepoys astonished me.'[2] As the same witness observed, when his Indian career was ending, 'There is no man who has a higher opinion, or ought to have a higher opinion, of the sepoys than I

[1] W. E. Henley, Introduction to *The Collected Poems of T. E. Brown.*

[2] Arthur Wellesley to Malcolm, 28 September 1803: Gurwood.

have. I have tried them on many serious occasions, and they never failed me, and always conducted themselves well.'[1]

The victors' heavy losses were due to frontal rushing of positions held by men who fought without hope. The defeated struggled valiantly, yet cannot be said to have distinguished themselves otherwise, when we consider their advantages. Why the Maratha chieftains ever allowed themselves to drift into war, when they were going to wage it in so haphazard and piecemeal a fashion, it seems impossible to understand. They fought in so divided and hesitant a manner that their opponents hardly needed to do any thinking or planning. It was just a question of clearing up detachments in detail by a bullheaded dash. 'The conduct of Asiatics is frequently so capricious that it cannot be foreseen by any reasonable estimate of their interests.'[2]

The truth is, they expected to be beaten, knowing that they had already been soundly beaten in Hindusthan. There can be no doubt that one reason why they lost a dingdong battle, to inferior numbers who had to assault over rough country, was their awareness of Lake's resounding victories.

On 11 November, General Wellesley received Sindhia's *vakil*. An armistice was half arranged, twelve days later, but neither side regarded it pedantically. The principal stipulation, which was where the respective armies were to remain, was ignored by both sides. Wellesley followed the Bhonsla Raja, who was retreating towards his own territory with the only considerable enemy force remaining, one that was melting away rapidly. Sindhia continued to keep near his confederate, all the time sending *vakils* to entreat the British not to attack the latter. These entreaties were ignored, and on 28 November, six miles from the village of Argaon, Wellesley found himself in touch with his quarry.

His men were weary, after a gruellingly hot march, and he had decided to encamp, when mounted patrols located his prey, drawn up before Argaon. It was about 2 p.m.[3] when Wellesley mounted a village tower and saw them, about three miles to his front, halted 'without showing any disposition to retire. On the contrary, it seemed as if they wished to offer us battle, or, at least, to take to themselves the credit of having done so. This was a piece of braggadocio which the General could not stand.'[4] 'Although

[1] To Josiah Webbe in 1805: Owen, 458.

[2] Grant Duff, *History of the Mahrattas*, ii. 421.

[3] According to Blakiston. The action, of course, could not begin without some necessary delay; even so, Blakiston is probably an hour or two out in his memory.

[4] Blakiston, i. 195.

late in the day, I immediately determined to attack this army.'[1] Immediately attacked it was, accordingly, and destroyed.

Inevitably, when desperate men are cornered, they put up rough episodes, and there were enough of these—particularly when Sindhia's cavalry 'with a large body of Persian troops'[2] joined in concentrating on the 74th and 78th regiments—to entitle Argaon to the name of battle. But the victors' total casualties amounted to 346 only; no British officer was killed, and very few wounded. It was a complete clean-up, so far as time permitted. 'Unfortunately, sufficient daylight did not remain to do all that I could have wished, but the cavalry continued their pursuit by moonlight, and all the troops were under arms till a late hour in the night.'[3] Elephants, camels, baggage, guns, muskets, made up an unwieldy accumulation of booty.

Like its predecessors (but even more so), Argaon realized the Irishman's traditional ideal of a fight. There was nothing private or professional about it; anyone who could get hold of a horse or a pistol joined in. Elphinstone, who had not managed to get into a cavalry charge at Assaye, managed it now, and testifies that he found it only mildly exciting:[4]

'I felt quite unconcerned, never winced, nor cared how near the shot came about the worst time; and all the time I was at pains to see how the people looked, and every gentleman seemed at ease as much as if he were riding a-hunting.'

Such of the enemy as he encountered were pacific, and he was too much of a knight to treat them with harshness:

'I stopped to load my pistols. I saw nobody afterwards but people on foot, whom I did not think it proper to touch. Indeed, there is nothing very gallant in attacking routed and terrified horse, who have not presence of mind either to run or to fight.'

After Argaon, the only considerable operation was the siege of Gawilgarh, invested December 6th and stormed on the 15th, with the loss of a little over a hundred men, a ridiculously slight butcher's bill for such a fortress. Elphinstone took part in this also, though warned that his civilian clothes rendered him liable to pay for his martial excursions by being taken for a deserter. For the defenders the storming was a bloody business (out of a garrison of 8,000, none escaped but those who dropped down the walls, their enemies having closed the gates), but for the attackers it was a merely noisy affair:

1 *Despatch*, 30 November 1803: Martin, iii. 474.

2 Thorn, 301. These were Mussulman irregulars: 'supposed to be Pathans,' says General Wellesley.

3 *Despatch*. 4 *Life of Elphinstone*, i. 89.

'Scaling ladders were brought, got up the hill, and applied to the second wall. The enemy fled from their works; we rushed over the wall, and the fort was ours. I forgot to mention that at the first breach all ran where they liked, without order; it was the same here.'

General Wellesley saw to it that the adventurous civilian received a captain's prize-money and gratuity and the Governor-General's approbation; and told him he had mistaken his vocation and should have been a soldier.

XVI

THE MAKING OF THE TREATIES

IT WAS a lasting grief to Malcolm that he had missed the battles; he joined General Wellesley the day after Gawilgarh fell, to take charge of the political business. To the grave young Major-General, whose mess was awed and solemn with heavy sense of responsibility, he brought a plentiful supply of beer and wines to ameliorate what he called their starving condition, and came scattering 'a brisk explosion of jokes'. As the Raja of Nagpur remarked, on the eve of his own ruin, thirteen years later, 'Malcolm Saheb makes fun of everything'.

Everyone now was grateful for this quality, whose disabilities were not yet apparent. Indian visitors he received with an ease and understanding which no one else showed them, so that their faces lit up when with him, and the misery of humiliation and helplessness vanished. Malcolm's eager dashing spirit, moving on stormy waters always, brought everywhere the lightening of its own generous happiness. He has remained a legend, long after the memory of graver men has faded from the land. There is a club at Mahabaleswar, the hill-station which he founded in the Ghats, where (native belief has it) nightly the ghost of Malcolm Saheb used to appear until recently, with a simultaneous flying open of all doors and windows and a shout, 'Boy! peg *lao*!'[1] 'Why did the windows fly open?' I have asked. 'Why, because he wanted the cool air, of course!' This particular haunting was said to be exorcised every dusk by bringing two pegs and two cigars, along with a moderate amount of soda-water; pegs and cigars would next morning be found to have been consumed.

Malcolm, tall and handsome, was the typical soldier-sportsman-statesman of the time and of all time. In a campaign he was always skirmishing on the army's fringes, for the chance of a shot at a tiger or a spell of pig-sticking. One of a Scots farmer's large family, he was without social or racial prejudices and accepted with equal frankness men and women of every sort, the Maratha free companion (whom others styled brigand) and the Raja's courtesan no less than General Wellesley. So far as Arthur Wellesley ever had a personal friend, it was Malcolm in these years, when a

[1] 'Bring a peg' (of whisky).

diffidence and grace of comradeship, the more noticeable from contrast with his official stiffness towards his brother the Governor-General, make 'the Iron Duke' not altogether like the figure which has taken eternal place in our national memory.

Malcolm is an example of what a man can do with his mind if he confronts experience without prejudice and lets facts make their ungrudged impression. His writings are wise and tolerant, and illumined by wider knowledge of what Indians really thought than either Metcalfe or Elphinstone ever attained. His adventures were not on the Indian field only; he was sent on two missions to Persia. His last years of service were clouded and ineffective; the times had changed, and he was as out of date as Sir Philip Sidney would have been in one of our British inter-war Cabinets of this century. But during the first twenty years of the nineteenth century it was the ambition of every imaginative young civilian or soldier to serve under John Malcolm, the acknowledged King of 'Politicals'.

Always magnanimously on the lookout for the exceptional man, Malcolm immediately took over Elphinstone. The two spent the day of his arrival (16 December) negotiating with the Bhonsla *vakil*, and during the following night Elphinstone supervised the *munshis* who copied the treaty in his tent. 'I woke every now and then, and looked over them.' Next day, in a long personal talk, Malcolm went straight to the business of bringing this brilliant fellow-Scot into his work of remaking Native India. General Wellesley, whom the Governor-General had given two great pieces of patronage, the Sindhia and Bhonsla Residencies, wanted to offer the latter to Elphinstone. Malcolm pressed him to take it. At first styled merely Secretary (to a Resident who would arrive later for a brief term), he would be Resident in all but name and would soon have the title as well as the fact. Elphinstone, flattered and delighted, puzzled him by hanging back from his destiny, for a reason which he kept from Malcolm, 'almost ashamed' of it. The reason would have gone to the Iron Duke's warmly susceptible heart, had he dared to mention it. He revealed it only to his one confidential correspondent, in a letter '*Not for the Profane*': 'I begin to long for idleness, society, and ladies'. He 'dreaded' to be stationed in Nagpur, where he would be almost solitary.

But Elphinstone's outstanding abilities had undone him. When the Bhonsla Raja signed, on Christmas Eve, 1803, a treaty giving away the best part of his dominions (though he rigidly refused to accept a subsidiary force), Elphinstone was appointed his Resident. With extreme reluctance, he joined the Raja's camp, on the 30th, and one of the greatest careers ever lived by anyone in India had begun.

Elphinstone was not long with the Bhonsla Raja, whose court he left three years later, in January 1807. But the peculiar difficulties of a Resident were never better shown than in his experience, which involved duties that he resented while accepting their necessity. The Raja, 'an old, fat, black, mean fellow of fifty, very heavy-looking and sad in his appearance, but quiet and civil in his manners',[1] maintained a sullen reserve. He could not forgive himself for his folly in throwing away his family's long neutrality and joining a losing cause, or forgive the British for having stripped him of his best territories.

General Wellesley, 'though he dislikes the system of subsidiary forces', thought the Raja should have such a force. The Raja thought otherwise, and Elphinstone predicted, rightly, that he would continue to refuse one until 'something firm is settled about Holkar'. Meanwhile, his conquerors were like a schoolmaster watching a boy who has been punished and is expected to do something that will justify further castigation.

His Resident's main duty, therefore, was to act as his spy, bribing his ministers, as the Spanish Ambassador at the court of our own James I bribed the Cecils and Howards. Yeswant Rao Ramchandra, the minister who had negotiated the treaty of peace, offered his services and General Wellesley recommended him to the Governor-General for a pension of Rs.6,000 for this assistance. Elphinstone felt that it was essential to have a constant stream of intimate information, and that he should know whatever the agents of Sindhia and Holkar were proposing; and in this gloomy taciturn court he could obtain this only by methods whose discovery would be very inconvenient.

> 'I do not like the ways in which intelligence is obtained. I hate anything that is secret and indirect, and abhor to do what I should be unwilling to avow. If the Raja discovered that I was inquiring into the situation of his armies and the intrigues of his Court, what should I say? I should avow it, and tell him that he had once brought down a dangerous war on us in the middle of a profound peace, that afterwards we should want prudence and attention to the welfare of our country if we neglected to watch him.'

This espionage, which all Politicals maintained, was responsible for much of the suspicion which when Indian chiefs revealed it was a source of pain to the British Government. The best men were more than a little ashamed of the system. Colonel Sutherland,

[1] Letter to Strachey, 12 January 1804 (*Life*, i. 121).

summing up, a whole generation later, deplored these 'secret news-writers, and those spies and intelligence establishments, the employment of which is so repugnant to the feelings of an Englishman, but which most persons in power have thought it necessary to maintain.'[1]

We must return to Sindhia's peace treaty, which proved more troublesome than the Bhonsla Raja's. His first *vakils* were considered insufficiently accredited, so were sent back. On 23 December, his chief minister, Wattel Pant, appeared, a gentleman of 'sour, supercilious, inflexible countenance, in which no penetration could ever discern a glimpse of feeling'. Malcolm promptly nicknamed him 'Old Brag', from the qualifications such a face gave him for the game of *brag*, a forerunner of poker. Many years later, after Waterloo had been fought, Malcolm, on leave in England, called on the Duke of Wellington, and they chatted about the leading men of France. What was Talleyrand like? Why, the Duke answered, he was like Old Brag, only not so clever.

General Wellesley associated Elphinstone[2] with himself and Malcolm in the discussions. The Treaty of Sarji Argengaon was drawn up, 30 December, and Malcolm set off for Sindhia's camp, to get it signed. By the terms, Sindhia was ejected from the Ganges-Jumna *doab* and from his Deccan possessions, and his hold on Rajputana was considerably loosened. As some offset to these losses, what remained was guaranteed to him independently of the Peshwa. He thus became a Prince in full status.

The Bhonsla Raja having refused to accept a subsidiary force, Malcolm expected Sindhia also to refuse one, or at least to hold out against having it stationed inside his territory.[3] It is astonishing that he gave way, and probably he would have done this for no one but Malcolm. But an Irishman, Mr. Pepper, deserves to be associated with Malcolm in his success. On the day when the British mission were presented to Sindhia (12 January 1804) a terrific hailstorm hurled on the tent roof, making a sombre music to his thoughts, as he sat gloomily impassive through the ceremonial. Suddenly there was a ripping of canvas, a 'torrent' cascaded through the gap, and 'a hideous yell of "Oh, Jasus!"' went up. Mr. Pepper had received a hundredweight or two of ice-cold water. Sindhia burst into joyous appreciation, and the heavy

[1] J. Sutherland, *Relations subsisting between the British Government in India and the Different Native States*, 12.

[2] Elphinstone was out of the later stages, as he left for Nagpur, 28 December.

[3] It was ultimately stationed outside his frontier, but near it.

Durbar 'degenerated into *a Malcolm riot*'.[1] Maratha officers rushed out to gather hailstones, which Sindhia and his ministers pressed on their visitors. All fell to eating them, 'and the scene more resembled a school at the moment when the boys have got to play than an Eastern Durbar'. Good humour lived on, even though negotiations dragged; and on 28 February, Malcolm, having completed his task, got into an old coat and hat to celebrate his achievement by joining in the *holi* festivities quite in the old larky manner of Warren Hastings' days:

'Scindiah is furnished with an engine of great power by which he can play upon a fellow fifty yards distance. He has, besides, a magazine of syringes, so I expect to be well squirted.'[2]

Well squirted he was, but the sport did him no good. 'The cursed hooley play' gave him a sharp attack of fever.[3]

Trouble was renewed later, between Sindhia and the British, and came close to a second outbreak of war. But in this further quarrel Malcolm took the Maratha chieftain's side. What happened is really part of the war with Holkar, and will be related in its place.

[1] Arthur Wellesley's account to the Governor-General (*Despatches*, ii. 701), based on Malcolm's letter to him.

[2] Malcolm to Arthur Wellesley (*Life*, i. 246). [3] Malcolm to Major Shawe.

XVII

DIFFICULTIES FOLLOWING THE CONCLUSION OF PEACE

The system of moderation and conciliation by which, whether it be right or wrong, I made the treaties of peace, and which has been so highly approved and extolled, is now given up. Our enemies are much disgusted, and complain loudly of our conduct and want of faith. . . . However, the Governor General is sincere in his notions upon these subjects. He considers his decisions to be strictly correct.—*Arthur Wellesley, 13 May 1804.*

WHEN THE Treaty of Bassein was made, Colonel Close had wished to bring Holkar, as well as Sindhia and the Bhonsla Raja, into that settlement. The Peshwa, however, refused the slightest concession to an enemy so dreaded, and insisted that Holkar was a 'rebel'. He intended to get him hanged by the British, distrusting a man he had wronged so greatly. The Governor-General adopted the same attitude. Lake was instructed (4 June 1804): 'at a proper season you will issue a proclamation signifying your intention to treat all such persons [Holkar, Amir Khan, and their associates] as common robbers and felons.'[1]

Holkar, sulky, conceited, irresolute, watched with satisfaction Sindhia's downfall. Despite the Governor-General's intentions for his future, so long as he kept to territory which the British Government considered to be his personal estates, he was safe enough. But he suddenly took fright at the completeness of Sindhia's defeat, and entered on a course of action so foolish that it is reasonable to suspect that the insanity of his last years was already working.

During the campaigning, he moved up and down Malwa restlessly, 'levying enormous contributions from friend and foe'.[2] He requested Lake to retire on Agra, as his 'near approach to his victorious army appeared likely to produce unpleasant circumstances' (whatever that meant). He wrote letters, sometimes humble, sometimes arrogant. He gave no definite *casus belli*, but every provocation short of that.

After Agra fell, he gave a deeply resented provocation. Sindhia's loss of the fortress had been largely due to the poltroonery of its foreign officers. One, Major Brownrigg, had come over with five battalions; then the commandant, Colonel Hessing, whom his own

[1] Martin, iv. 82. [2] Grant Duff, iii. 270.

men had put under arrest, persuaded them to surrender, and managed to carry off several lakhs of Sindhia's money for himself. These adventurers, whose gains were mostly invested in Company funds, scuttled off at the first chance, rather than imperil them. The British Government made a fuss of them, and loudly published their desertion and subsequent services, as it had done with Stuart and Lucan. Holkar thereupon summoned his own foreign officers, and gave them the choice between promising to stick by him, even if it came to war with the British, and death. The choice was really between execution by him or by a British provost-marshal. Three Eurasian officers, Vickars, Todd, and Ryan, refused to pledge themselves, and were beheaded. They were charged, perhaps unjustly, with correspondence between one of their number and General Lake. This 'atrocious transaction',[1] a flagrant example 'of the spirit of arrogance which Jeswant Rao Holkar assumed upon all occasions',[2] angered no one more than the Governor-General. Vickars had served with particular distinction, having been *pars magna* in his master's defeat of Sindhia and the Peshwa at the Battle of Poona. Chivalry had left the war, which was destined to grow yet crueller.

Sindhia was raging against the peace he had accepted. By what he regarded as an act of bullying dishonesty, Gwalior was taken from him. To-day all India thinks of Gwalior as inextricably linked with the Sindhia name. But it was Mahadaji Sindhia who first captured it, in Warren Hastings' time, from a petty chieftain, the Rana of Gohad. Mahadaji lost it to the British, and Hastings restored it in 1780 to the Rana, who proved unable to hold it. In 1784, Sindhia recaptured it and incorporated the Rana's territory with his own. Hastings, since the Rana had been treacherous towards the Company and he and Sindhia had formed a mutual kindness, was well content that the Maratha should keep it. Sindhia obtained also a legal sanction for his conquest, by the Emperor's grant, and this (however strange it may seem to those whose notion of the Marathas is taken over simply from the accounts of foreign historians) seems to have invested the place with sentimental value.

In 1803, when war broke out, Gwalior was in the domains of Ambaji Inglia, one of Daulat Rao Sindhia's leading nobles. Ambaji, whose name is prominent in the events of the first decade of the nineteenth century (nearly always in connection with intrigues of more or less turpitude), was himself plotting to attain independent status, and in October 1803 he entered into disloyal

[1] Martin, iv. 11. [2] *Ibid*, iv. 100–101: 15 June 1804.

correspondence with the British, to whom he promised the fortress. The British, whose part in the complicated and intricate dishonesty of these proceedings was that they were negotiating with his master, on 16 December concluded a separate treaty with Ambaji and established him as a 'Prince', with a territory of his own. Ambaji, however, cheated them also, by secretly ordering the Commandant of Gwalior not to surrender his charge, and a force sent to take quiet possession of it found themselves excluded. The Governor-General thereupon wrote General Lake (24 January 1804) an infuriated letter: 'I authorize and direct your Excellency . . . to make an example of the Commandant of Gwalior by a public execution', 'for the purpose of deterring native Commanders from similar acts of wanton obstinacy'—unless it should be found that Ambaji was responsible, in which case 'all negotiation or treaty' should be rejected with 'the author of this atrocious treachery'. Gwalior was invested accordingly, and fell, 5 February, without bloodshed. It was established that Ambaji was responsible, and the Commandant's neck was saved.

Malcolm, who had concluded the treaty of peace with Sindhia, was satisfied that it had been done on the understanding that the latter should receive back Gwalior, which had belonged to him when war broke out. He wrote to General Wellesley:

'As to the fort of Gwalior, I am persuaded one of the chief causes of the peace was to save it; and such is the importance they attach to that place, that I sincerely believe our having insisted upon its surrender would have protracted the conclusion of the peace. I wish to God that demand had been made, and that you had either obtained it, or left it by a specific article in the possession of this Government. . . . All that remains of Mahratta power in India is indissolubly associated in men's minds with thoughts of this famous fortress.'[1]

He told his friend: 'There is one evil . . . which I dread more than the Marquis's displeasure—the loss of my own esteem, which I must have incurred had I acted contrary to what I have done on this occasion. I wish to God you would contrive to let me escape from this scene with honour and without reproach.'[2]

General Wellesley sympathized with him, and had already written:

'If Gwalior belonged to Scindiah, it must be given up; and I acknowledge that, whether it did or not, I should be inclined to give it to him. I declare that when I view the treaty of peace and the consequences, I am afraid it will be imagined that the moderation of the British Government has a strong resemblance to the ambition of other Governments.'

[1] *Life of Malcolm*, i. 263. [2] *Ibid*, i. 267 ff.

Malcolm fought hard for Sindhia, feeling justice and his own honour involved. He wrote (30 March 1804) to Graeme Mercer, one of the many men who once played in India a part that can be equalled only from the records of Ancient Rome and yet have completely fallen out of memory:

'if we determine a case of disputable nature in our own favor because we have power, we shall give a blow to our faith that will, in my opinion, be more injurious to our interests than the loss of fifty provinces. What has taken us through this last war with such unexampled success? First, no doubt, the gallantry of our armies; but, secondly—and hardly secondly—our reputation for good faith. These people do not understand the laws of nations, and it is impossible to make them comprehend a thousand refinements which are understood and practised in Europe. They will never be reconciled to the idea that a treaty should be negotiated upon one principle and fulfilled upon another.'

He argued that there must be regular native governments, to prevent the country from being overrun with robbers and to give adventurous spirits employment. The safety and tranquillity of India depended on this. Nor would there be a better neighbour than Sindhia, 'if we act with a liberal and conciliating policy towards him'.

General Wellesley concurred. 'I would sacrifice Gwalior or every frontier of India ten times over, in order to preserve our credit for scrupulous good faith, and the advantages and honour we gained by the late war and the peace; and we must not fritter them away in arguments drawn from overstrained principles of the laws of nations, which are not understood in this country.' 'What brought me through many difficulties in the war, and the negotiations of peace? The British good faith, and nothing else.' Arthur Wellesley even went so far as to write to his brother, Henry Wellesley (13 May 1804):

'Scindiah's government, although it has concluded the defensive alliance, is not satisfied with us; and the misfortune is that, between ourselves, I think we are in the wrong. The difference relates to the fort of Gwalior, which Scindiah thinks ought to belong to him, and the Governor General will not give it up. I differ in opinion with the Governor General both as to the right and policy of keeping the fort: I have delivered my opinion to him regarding the latter, but have said nothing upon the former, as the question turns upon a nice point of the law of nations, which the Governor General has argued with his usual ingenuity; but I acknowledge I differ from him entirely. . . .

The Rajah of Berar . . . is equally dissatisfied . . . with the manner in which the treaty of peace has been carried into execution. The Nizam's government have pressed upon him most powerfully, and I think that the Governor General has not treated him with liberality. . . .

In fact, my dear Henry, we want at Calcutta some person who will speak his mind to the Governor General. Since you and Malcolm have left him, there is nobody about him with capacity to understand these subjects, who has nerves to discuss them with him, and to oppose his sentiments when he is wrong. There cannot be a stronger proof of this want than the fact that Malcolm and I, and General Lake, and Mercer, and Webbe, were of opinion that we had lost Gwalior with the treaty of peace.'[1]

To Webbe he added (23 May 1804): 'The Governor General may write what he pleases at Calcutta; we must conciliate the natives, or we shall not be able to do his business; and all his treaties, without conciliation and an endeavour to convince the Native powers that we have views besides our own interests, are so much waste paper.'[2]

As Arthur Wellesley noted, the Governor-General was not a man whom anyone could instruct or persuade. His advisers (if one may use such a term of anyone near Lord Wellesley) largely sympathized with Malcolm. But when the latter wrote to one of them, Edmonstone, 'God knows, throughout the whole of this troubled scene my attention has been exclusively directed to one object—the promotion of the public interests', the Indian All-Highest underscored the last two words, and appended the marginal comment: 'Mr. Malcolm's duty is to obey my orders and to enforce my instructions. *I* will look after the *public* interests.' He regarded Malcolm's claim to personal opinions as highly offensive and presumptuous, and wrote him letters which Arthur Wellesley called (6 June 1804) 'quite shocking. You did not deserve such treatment, positively, and I am not astonished at its having distressed you.' The Governor-General's personal secretary, Major Merrick Shawe, dropped him a hint of the political causes underlying Lord Wellesley's fury:

'Whatever your motives may have been, your conduct has certainly placed Lord Wellesley in a very embarrassing situation, and, when that is the case, God knows that he is always inclined to vent his feelings freely against those who have occasioned him difficulty and trouble. Your having shown a great disposition to admit the justice of Scindiah's right to Gwalior and Gohud is likely, Lord Wellesley thinks, to give his enemies in Leadenhall Street room to found an accusation against Lord Wellesley of injustice and rapacity, in marching upon and retaining these possessions contrary to the opinion of the Resident'.

Even a volcano subsides after eruption; and at last, on 14 June, the Governor-General, who always wrote with his sceptre, sent Malcolm his forgiveness. It was peppered with the heightened

[1] Owen, 395–7. [2] *Ibid*, 399.

language he habitually employed—'acrimonious', 'irritating', 'vexatious', 'arrogant'. But was nevertheless recognizable, and unmistakably, as Lord Wellesley straining every nerve to be courteous and affable, and Malcolm, relieved, responded in the abject fashion which the Governor-General exacted:

'The extraordinary kindness with which your Lordship has condescended to explain the causes which led to your displeasure at part of my conduct . . . has filled my mind with sentiments of the warmest gratitude and most devoted attachment . . . the whole tenor of my future conduct shall be regulated in the strictest conformity to your desire; and I shall be proud in every opportunity I may hereafter have of showing that I am not unworthy of the favor and condescension with which I have been treated.'

'Condescension' is a word which Lord Wellesley must have heard a thousand times from his cringing inferiors, grateful for a word of pardon after they had committed the crime of being in the right and of disputing for that right. It is a flashlight on the snobbery of our people that men like Lake and Malcolm, masters of authority over many thousands, so constantly played the part of Mr. Collins towards Lady Catherine de Burgh when the thought of Lord Wellesley entered their minds.

Sindhia lost Gwalior accordingly, and between him and the Company peace existed only in name, and barely in that. The Governor-General nevertheless felt a deep pleasure in his personal triumph, which had not been one over Sindhia only. 'Scindiah's advisers and friends will be disappointed, they will not move me as easily as they have shaken Major Malcolm.'[1] To the Directors he wrote self-approvingly:

'Your honourable Court will observe with satisfaction, that the peace is founded upon principles of exemplary faith and equity towards our allies, of moderation and lenity towards our vanquished enemies, and of just regard for the general prosperity of this quarter of the globe.'[2]

That summary dissolves under analysis. We have seen what the vanquished enemies thought. As for the allies, the Berars were to be ceded 'to his Highness the Soubahdar' (the Nizam), who received also a considerable part of what is now the northern territory of Hyderabad State; he gained, if not tangibly, at any rate in release from vexation, by Sindhia and Bhonsla abandoning all claims to monetary payments, &c., including claims for the past. The Nizam nevertheless betrayed only a modicum of that gratitude which he doubtless felt; he and the Peshwa, the other beneficiary, seemed to feel that they had been co-partners in the kind

[1] 30 April 1804: Martin, iv. 63. [2] 14 March 1804: *Ibid*, iv. 37.

of banquet described in *Alice in Wonderland*, when the owl and the panther shared a pie together. The Peshwa, the Governor-General pointed out, was entitled to nothing, on a strict interpretation of his rights. However, he was to be given Ahmadnagar city and considerable surrounding territory. Raging at Sindhia's escape from its suzerainty, 'the court of Poonah on this occasion manifested a spirit of cavil and of inordinate pretension, wholly unbecoming the relative situation of his Highness the Peishwa, and unsuitable to the nature of the obligations imposed upon his Highness by the arduous exertions of the British Government for the re-establishment of his authority'.[1] For a long time the Peshwa even refused to sign the treaties of peace and partition.

[1] Lord Wellesley: Martin, iv. 98.

XVIII

YESWANT RAO HOLKAR

MEANWHILE, HOLKAR'S conduct, though foolish, was not altogether unprovoked. The Governor-General, holding it his business to settle everyone else's business on the lines that to him seemed right, made it clear that he regarded Holkar as marked out for chastisement when a convenient season came, for his conduct towards the Peshwa and Kasi Rao Holkar, his own father's legitimate son:

'The authority exercised by Jeswunt Rao Holkar, in the name of Khundeh Rao, over the possessions of the Holkar family, is manifestly an usurpation of the rights of Cashi Rao Holkar, the legitimate heir and successor of Tuckojee Holkar. Consistently therefore with the principles of justice, no arrangement can be proposed between the British Government and Jeswunt Rao Holkar, involving a sanction of the exclusion of Cashi Rao Holkar from his hereditary dominions.

Under the sanction of his Highness the Peishwa's authority, the British Government would be justified in adopting measures for the limitation of Jeswunt Rao Holkar's power, and for the restoration of Cashi Rao Holkar's rights, either by force or compromise; and the spirit of our engagements with his Highness the Peishwa might be considered to impose on the British Government an obligation to comply with a requisition on the part of his Highness for that purpose under the public protection of the British Government. The Peishwa may not be anxious for the reduction of Holkar's power, or for the restoration of Cashi Rao Holkar to his hereditary rights. But it may be expected that his Highness would readily concur in a proposition for the restoration of Cashi Rao, and for the punishment of Jeswunt Rao Holkar.'[1]

There is a great deal more of this, and Wellesley repeatedly returned to the argument, always in the same manner. He was prepared to go to any lengths to clamp down on Indian states his own British notions of 'legitimate' rights and to extirpate what he considered 'usurpation'. Kasi Rao was 'imbecile both in mind and body',[2] 'an infamous blackguard, despised by everybody, full of prejudices, hatred, and revenge, and without one adherent or even a follower.'[3] The Holkar family rejected him utterly, Arthur Wellesley

[1] Lord Wellesley to General Lake, 9 January 1804 (Martin, iv. 4 ff.).
[2] Grant Duff, iii. 148. [3] Arthur Wellesley.

pointed out, and to support him would 'disgust Scindiah's government'. He had been 'concerned in his brother's murder', and General Wellesley was opposed to taking up the cause of 'usurpation founded on murder'.

Frederick the Great considered a certain quarrel as not worth the bones of a single Pomeranian grenadier; the Governor-General might reasonably have considered Kasi Rao Holkar's restoration not worth an Indian sepoy's, and might have left the Holkar 'rights' to sort themselves out. But, as ever, he was obstinately blind and deaf to anything but his own opinions; and, as ever, he saw their carrying out in the light of a duty:

> 'The enterprizing spirit, military character, and ambitious views of Jeswunt Rao Holkar render the reduction of his power a desirable object with reference to the complete establishment of tranquillity in India. The restoration of Cashi Rao Holkar to his hereditary rights by the aid, and under the protection of the British power, would be highly creditable to the justice and honour of the British Government, and advantageous to its interests. It might be expected that Cashi Rao would readily acquiesce in any arrangement which might be deemed advisable for the security of our interests as the condition of his restoration. Indebted to our power for the recovery of his rights, and depending on our support for their preservation, his interest would be permanently consolidated with that of the British Government. His restoration would obtain the concurrence and applause of every state in India, and would afford to the Peishwa an additional proof of our sincere disposition to respect the rights of the Mahratta feudatories, and to fulfil the obligations of our public faith.'

An angel asked William Blake, 'Does a firm belief that a thing is so make it so?' Wellesley's letters and despatches are the perfect example of a mind persuading itself that the path of interest is the path of duty. They are, however, sincere; he succeeded in fooling himself. But he did not for one minute succeed in fooling his brother or any other public servant outside his own sycophantic entourage.

The Governor-General, however, as he reluctantly recognized, was having such trouble with the Directors in England and had got the finances into such embarrassment, that 'an immediate attempt to restore' Kasi Rao was out of the question. Castlereagh wrote to him warningly (9 September 1803—received, 29 February 1804) of 'two points . . . not admitting of the smallest doubt',

> 'that there is but one feeling and opinion in his Majesty's councils, that the Government of India can in no hands be so advantageously placed as in your Lordship's . . . that there prevails in all minds the most anxious disposition to give your Government a cordial and honourable support . . . I am very sorry I cannot perceive a corres-

ponding disposition in the Court of Directors . . . it would be only exposing your Lordship's name, at least to most unmerited coldness, were I to call upon the Court to concur with the King's Government in *urging you* to continue in the Government of India. . . . Mr. Addington and I were of opinion that we could not in justice to your Lordship *claim* at your hands so great a sacrifice as that of continuing to administer so arduous a trust.'[1]

This was an unmistakable intimation that his resignation would be a relief.

He no longer wished to resign. The Marathas were still incompletely subdued, and he meant to see this matter through. With unwonted coolness he took stock of his resources, and measured them against his temptations. One of the latter was afforded by the Maharaja of Nepal, who had abdicated in 1801 and come to live at Benares. He was anxious to return with British help. Wellesley considered the opportunity to obtain over Nepal the control which at one time he was eager to obtain over every Indian state; he rejected it, for reasons entirely wise and honourable. The Maharaja's abdication had been voluntary, so no question of injustice in his present position seemed to arise; and at this time the Governor-General was fussing even more than usual about just rights and, above all, hereditary rights (the most just of all), giving much time and attention to the Rana of Gohad and other chieftains submerged under the Maratha inundation of earlier days. He even wrote his Commander-in-Chief, General Lake, a letter, 20 February 1804, which shows an uneasy consciousness of the strength of Sindhia's claim to Gwalior.[2]

He decided to bring first to the issue 'the just rights' of Kasi Rao Holkar. Would Yeswant Rao Holkar acquiesce quietly in his own displacement? To some good judges it seemed unlikely, though Lord Wellesley seems to have more than half expected that he would. Wellesley decided on a game of subtlety, which for success depended on extreme trustfulness and simplicity in his antagonist —qualities which neither admirer nor detractor had ever ascribed to Yeswant Rao Holkar. Wellesley advised Lake (17 January 1804) that 'A pacific conduct towards Jeswunt Rao Holkar in the present moment will not preclude the future restoration of Cashi Rao Holkar. . . . It will be necessary, however, to regulate our proceedings with respect to Jeswunt Rao Holkar in such a manner as to avoid any acknowledgment or confirmation of the legitimacy of his dominion.' With these reservations in his mind, Lake was to inform the latter that 'the British Government will be disposed

[1] Martin, iv. 29 ff.

[2] See especially sections 6 and 7.

to arbitrate the differences' between him and his half-brother, 'and to adjust the claims of the several branches of the family on the principles of equity and justice'. This was kind, and it seemed all that could be done.

Yeswant Rao Holkar, had he been wise, would have merely rejected the offer, while agreeing to abstain from pressing claims for *chauth* and *deshmukh* against territories now taken into the Company's sphere. All he had to do was to keep the peace during his enemy's time, whose sands were now obviously running out.

He could not bring himself to do this. To Sindhia, smarting from loss of Gwalior and the sense of being robbed of the fruits of submission, he sent a *vakil* proposing alliance and renewal of the war. Sindhia promptly acquainted the British of these overtures; he was not yet prepared to forget his quarrel with Holkar. Holkar next, replying to the Company's offer to arrange his affairs for him, sent Lake, in March 1804, a number of proposals which were rejected as extravagant, as indeed they were; he was enjoying the luxury of bargaining. He asked for Hariana and Bundelkhand, and districts in the Ganges-Jumna doab, as well as what he now actually occupied; also, that his right to levy *chauth* on other districts should be recognized. He was ranging up and down, distressing Lake beyond measure ('I never was so plagued as I am with this devil; he just, nay hardly, keeps within the letter of the law, by which means our army is remaining in the field at an enormous expense'). Possessing an impish sense of humour, Holkar stressed 'the long-existing unanimity between me and the English Company', and suggested that acquiescence in his terms would 'be fruitful of benefit and advantage', and with a shrug dismissed the alternative:

> 'My country and property are upon the saddle of my horse, and, please God, to whatever side the reins of the horses of my brave warriors may be turned, the whole of the country in that direction shall come into my possession.'

Lake replied temperately and with dignity.

At last, on 16 April, the Governor-General authorized his generals to attack him, a prospect which Holkar accepted cheerfully. Holding a poor opinion of Sindhia's beaten armies, he meant to flit through the wild Central Indian country in the old Maratha style. He would not give formal battle, with batteries that would be lost after their gunners had been slaughtered. He would choose his field—would appear at a difficult ford as dusk was falling, or at the narrow end of some mountain pass. General Wellesley, aware of this antagonist's character and abilities, urged the advisability of having in all Indian campaigns, and most of all against Marathas, some of the country's people on your side. Lake, agreeing, thought that Sindhia ought to undertake the settling of Holkar for the Company. 'Sure I am that the only mode of meeting this reptile would be some decisive measure on the part of Scindiah.' This was pointed out to Sindhia, who did not dispute it, but showed no enthusiasm for the role allotted to him. He was compelled to provide a body of horse; he did it grudgingly.

Holkar's best allies, had he known it, were time and the growing opposition to Lord Wellesley in London. The latter continued to treat the Directors with scorn. In letters to fellow-peers, including Lord Melville, he referred to them usually as 'that most loathsome den of the India House', 'that den of rapacity'. It was a period of violent writing, when many strong-smiting words were heavily worked. None was more used than 'rapacity', an especial favourite with the Governor-General, who looked round the globe and saw it everywhere triumphant except in Calcutta. Warren Hastings, who admired his conquests and envied him his unfettered power, said, 'If I was in his confidence I would tell him that civility costs nothing'.

The Chairman of the Directors was Charles Grant, a man disposed to give way to no one; he had spent eighteen years in India in the Company's service, and shared to the full the retired Anglo-Indian's conviction that he knew everything there was to know about India, and that nothing had changed since his time. A friend of Wilberforce, he was deeply religious and humanitarian, and to him war was not glory but bloodshed and pillage. Parliament had forbidden territorial extensions,[1] yet Wellesley was prepared to add India to the Company's possessions, to the utmost extent which funds and credit would allow. And, doing this, he did it with a scornful self-sufficiency which was galling. Grant's correspondence continually makes such complaints as 'Not a line has been received from Bengal', at a time when the public knew that some fresh war had been proclaimed or mighty strongholds stormed and great battles won. He wrote to Jonathan Duncan, Governor of Bombay, 1 June 1804:

> 'I believe that Ministers are astounded at what has happened. . . . The Court of Directors, with a very few exceptions, most seriously disapprove and lament it, as both morally and prudentially wrong in its principle, and full of danger in its consequences. The treaty of Bassein was laboured, in order to give us an ascendency in the Peshwa's Government; it set a British head over the members of the

[1] Act 24, George III, Cap. 25. See Auber, Peter, *Analysis of the Constitution of the East India Company*, vi. 60.

Mahratta Empire; it, therefore, violated essentially the constitution of that Empire, and the right of its separate members, as well as the treaty of Salbye. It was the true cause of the war. It was a scheme of ambition and aggrandisement, contrary, therefore, to the law of 1784, and in its principle unjustifiable. The professed object was peace, but it immediately produced war. . . . The formidable power of the Mahrattas and their French force have been mentioned as causes of alarm to us; their disciplined infantry and artillery proved their bane. Had they adhered to their predatory war with horses it might have proved fatal to us, and as to the sovereignty of Perron, of which we have heard, it seems he preferred to it the condition and security of a private station under our protection.'[1]

This quotation shows that Grant had the ability, always exceptional, to recognize far-reaching changes when they were actually happening. He was aware that one swift crowded campaign had transformed the whole political face of India and in a few weeks had swept away for ever arrangements and alignments which had lasted for centuries. To George Udny, a Member of the Governor-General's Council, he wrote (1 June) sentences that must have infuriated Lord Wellesley, as they were quite possibly meant to do:

'if we have without necessity followed a line of policy at all likely to provoke war, especially if that policy were in itself unjust, then is the war unjust, and we are chargeable with all the guilt of it—the bloodshed, miseries, and devastation which it has occasioned. I desire to be thankful that I have not to reckon with myself for any part of these enormous evils. Near the warm sun of superior power, dazzled with many specious and plausible reasonings, delivered with great mastery of language, and combined with very sagacious political management, I might have too easily yielded. . . . In reality, what was this policy, but getting an ascendency in every cabinet in Hindostan? How were we to cultivate the arts of peace, if perpetually engaged in the politics and disputes of all the Durbars of India?'

He scoffed at the alleged French menace which had been overthrown; the Company's Generals had dealt with it with absurd ease. And, indeed, he was right when he pointed out (16 September 1805) that Wellesley had gone far towards ruining the Company, especially in England, calling up again 'all the concealed enmity which our past transactions have excited', ravaging its finances and wasting European lives. Castlereagh, President of the Board of Control, was as dissatisfied as Grant, with Wellesley's self-sufficient methods and attitude.

[1] Henry Morris, *The Life of Charles Grant*, 256.

XIX

FIRST STAGES OF THE WAR WITH HOLKAR

The disturbances occasioned by Jeswunt Rao Holkar and his adherents, have proved a vexatious and painful interruption of tranquillity.—*Lord Wellesley to the Court of Directors, March 1805.*

General Wellesley ordered Colonel Murray to conquer Holkar's possessions in Gujarat, while Lake detached Colonel Monson to drive him south. Holkar fell back rapidly, crossed the Chambal, and was soon out of contact. He lost fortresses, but his officer Amir Khan, a Pathan adventurer who now becomes very prominent, made some amends for this by stirring up trouble for the British in their recently subdued province of Bundelkhand, where two companies of sepoys and fifty artillerymen with their guns were cut off (22 May 1804) 'by mere vagrant banditti'.

The season was the height of summer, and the British suffered intensely, marching through the choking swirl of immense dust-devils such as assailed our march across the Mesopotamian desert to Baghdad in 1917, or in Libya more recently. These

'were only the precursors of the still more tremendous demon of the storm—the typhoon, which, like chaos, came on the wings of the tempest, rolling before it immense torrents of burning sand, giving such a density to the atmosphere that the sun, which appeared at first as red as blood, was afterwards, by the gradual increase of the opacity, totally eclipsed. Night, with tenfold terror, now darkened the horizon, the awfulness of which was heightened by the howlings of the tempest, resembling the roar of thunder. This scene of horror lasted about half an hour, during which the affrighted multitude lay prostrate on the ground, as if anticipating the dissolution of the world.'[1]

Showers usually followed. Then would emerge almost naked men and women ranging the country to recover cloths which the storm had whisked far away, and bullocks it had stampeded, while the British had terrified horses to recover.

Monson moved south, to protect Rajput princes who were begging for support, and to join Colonel Murray, who was supposed to be advancing from Gujarat. Monson presently found himself in unknown mountainous country in Central India, and heard

[1] Thorn, W., *Memoirs of the War in India conducted by General Lord Lake and Major-General Sir Arthur Wellesley*, 348–9.

that Murray had suddenly grown afraid of Holkar and fallen back. So, on 8 July, he also, having 'advanced without reason . . . retreated in the same manner',[1] sending his baggage on ahead.

The monsoon was at its height, the country was bogged and heavy. Disasters began with the capture of Lieutenant Lucan, whose services had been consistently distinguished and who was above all men obnoxious to the Marathas. Lucan was wounded, and soon after died. Skinner says he was tortured to death, Thorn inclines to believe that he merely died of his wounds. Other reports were that he was poisoned; Grant Duff, who later made special inquiries, heard that he died of a bowel complaint. The emphasis laid on his helpfulness and the knowledge of Maratha resentment of this helpfulness made his fate a matter of peculiar interest to his contemporaries.

It was of interest to his enemies also, and tradition ascribed it to the direct prowess of Holkar himself, singling out, like Saladin after Kurn Hattin, the most hated of all his opponents:

'The Muharaj at Lucan flew,
As swoops a Falcon on its prey,
His water-tempered blade he drew,
And streams of gushing blood found way.

The broken host took fright and flight,
Death was among them freely dealt,
Sepoys and soldiers, black and white,
The sword's keen edge in plenty felt.

A raging Lion, Juswunt Rao,
Came upon Lucan, brave and bold,
And striking at his head one blow
His head upon the green sward roll'd.

The army saw their leader's fate,
And forthwith in confusion turn'd—
Such the reward of those, whose hate
Like Lucan's against Hulkur burn'd'.[2]

Monson made a stand at the Mokandara pass, where Holkar demanded his surrender, which was refused. Monson shook off an attack, 11 July, and next day pressed on again, through torrential rains. On the 21st, crossing a swollen stream, he lost many men by drowning. His sepoys suffered a worse horror yet. Their wives and children, in the disorderly manner of the period, had accompanied them, and the river divided them from their protectors; Bhils massacred them. Monson struggled on, beset by a mosquito-host of foes, losing men continually. Presently he had to abandon every

[1] Arthur Wellesley.

[2] Acworth, H. A., *Ballads of the Marathas*, 216–17.

gun, and finally his troops broke under the slaughter of Holkar's artillery, a disorderly remnant fleeing into Agra, 31 August.

This was the worst defeat the British ever suffered in India, and the tragic story is made more revolting by the bitterness and ungenerosity of the warfare. Holkar mutilated and defaced captured sepoys who refused to serve him, and those who in their extremity gave way were put to death by the British at a later stage, when they tried to return.[1] Monson was said to have a bad name with the sepoys, and to be unable to get on with them.[2] Nevertheless they fought bravely, under circumstances cruel beyond precedent.

The Governor-General behaved towards his unsuccessful General with magnanimity. When it was believed that Monson was dead, he wrote of his 'poor friend':

'Whatever may have been his fate, or whatever the result of his misfortunes to my own fame, I will endeavour to shield his character from obloquy, nor will I attempt the mean purpose of sacrificing his reputation to save mine. His former services and his zeal entitle him to indulgence; and, however I may lament or suffer for his errors, I will not reproach his memory if he be lost, or his character, if he survive.'

The Governor-General's conquest and pacification seemed to fall into the melting-pot. Holkar swept triumphantly up to Muttra, which the British abandoned. He then (8–14 October) tried to rush Delhi and obtain possession of the Emperor. Ochterlony's sepoys put up a defence which, though long ago completely forgotten, was 'one of the greatest and most important actions that have been performed'.[3] Harassed and worn incessantly and exceedingly, they successfully kept a city ten miles in circumference. Holkar showed, as previously, a cruelty to prisoners that had formerly been absent from the contests of British and Marathas, and this steadied many wavering chieftains. Nevertheless, defections occurred, the most flagrant and resented being that of the Raja of Bharatpur.

Lake, who had hoped his work was done, wearily took up the task of following his elusive enemy. He found it one perplexing almost to madness.

'This monster will of course be driven out of Hindostan, and where he is to go I know not. . . . It is most provoking that this fellow should escape, but really so many untoward circumstances have happened that I am quite wretched. If Colonel Murray, or any one

[1] Shipp, i. 143. Shipp queerly writes of Monson's 'masterly retreat'.

[2] This is unacceptable. Monson was a notoriously kind-hearted commander, who so loathed the use of the lash that he rarely sanctioned it.

[3] Metcalfe to Sherer, 14 March 1806.

else who may be in command, would but come forward at all, this monster could not escape.'[1]

He added a P.S. 'The Bhurtpore Rajah has behaved like a villain, and deserves chastisement; a very short time would take his forts.'

But mere exasperation by itself was helpless. It seemed almost a miracle when, on 13 November 1804, Holkar's infantry were brought to battle before the Raja of Bharatpur's fortress of Dig. The 76th Regiment were again the heroes of a hard day, which cost 643 casualties. The Marathas lost two thousand killed and drowned, and 87 guns, including six eighteen-pounders formerly presented to them by Lord Cornwallis, as part of the spoils of victory over Tipu, in 1792. What gave Monson, who actually won the battle (the commander, General Fraser, receiving a wound of which he died a few days later), greatest pleasure of all was the recovery of guns and transport lost in his retreat. Monson, equal to anything that required merely courage, was equal to nothing that required the least cerebration, however; and after his victory he fell back on Muttra for supplies, when he 'might have spared a battalion or two to have fetched them'.[2] Given chance after chance, whenever in independent authority he made his superiors throw up their hands in despair.

Holkar, who had been separated from his infantry and was conducting his own retreat, was surprised by Lake in person at Farakhabad, four days after the Battle of Dig. 'The moon was up, and the night mild and pleasant'; the Marathas, drugged with cold and fatigue, wrapped in thick blankets, did not hear their pursuers until round after round of grape was bursting among them. 'It awakened some but sealed many in an everlasting sleep.'[3] Massacre followed, and the Company's cavalry cut the tired and terrified troops to pieces.

Holkar, who had heard of his Dig misfortune the evening previous to this dawn, while watching a nautch, had kept his news to himself, and the troubled night he spent in consequence of it enabled him to be one of the few who escaped. His men, unable to get to their jaded ponies, swarmed up into mango-trees that covered the plain, and there tried to conceal themselves or continue the unequal contest with matchlocks. They were all discovered and pistolled, and tumbled lifeless to the ground. Lake, marching on steadily, found the countryside strewn with dead, and villages filled with wounded who had crept into shelter. The

[1] 19 October 1804: to Lord Wellesley.
[2] Lake to the Governor-General, 19 November 1804 (Martin, iv. 245).
[3] Thorn, 391.

popular imagination was terror-struck by the speed of his arrival, which had fairly beaten the guerillas at their own game.

Lake every day realized now more fully how menacing the situation had been. 'The people in all parts have assisted Holkar' (for whose head a reward was offered)[1] 'and have been perfectly ready to rise (in some parts they did show themselves openly) had he not been so closely pressed.'[2] Every chief was sympathetic to his cause; Sikhs, Rohillas, the Begum Sumroo, even the Muslim leaders and princes of Delhi and the surrounding regions, were plotting to join in one concerted effort to expel the British.

Dig and Farakhabad made a temporary scattering of these clouds. But they looked to be gathering again when Lake received Monson's announcement that he intended to march back to his stores. 'It is somewhat extraordinary', Lake wrote, vexed and bewildered, to the Governor-General,

> 'that a man brave as a lion should have no judgment or reflection. In all my letters to him during the command he had formerly, have I uniformly recommended it to him to reflect and consider before he acts. It really grieves me to see a man I esteem, after gaining credit in the extreme throw it away in such a manner immediately.'

Fortunately, Monson's retreat was arrested before he reached Agra.

Dig itself was stormed, at midnight on Christmas Eve, when the moon, 'rising at half-past twelve, shed a very seasonable light', and enabled the British to win a complete victory, at bloody loss to the enemy but with only 43 killed and 184 wounded themselves. The Maratha gunners, with their usual devotion, stayed to the last and were bayoneted. Much grain and ammunition, 100 guns, and £20,000 worth of specie were taken.

We have seen Malcolm playing *holi* with Sindhia, and Elphinstone at Assaye and Argaon joining in the courtly pastime of a cavalry chase. In the storm of Dig, the other member of 'the Big Three' who were to mould India's destiny during the next twenty years won his own military laurels.

After the unhappy episode of association with King Collins, Metcalfe had returned to obscurity in Calcutta. But the Governor-General liked him too well to leave him there, and knew the value of his father's support, in a Directorate which was turning increasingly hostile. He sent Metcalfe to Lake, 23 August 1804, as Political Officer, a journey that proved adventurous and perilous. Thieves attacked Metcalfe's palanquin, and left him with two fingers

[1] Lake to Wellesley, 18 November (Martin, iv. 242).
[2] Shipp, i. 183.

shortened and wounds in breast and head. He recovered in the care of relations at Cawnpur, and reached Lake's camp in October.

A boy not yet twenty, he was a civilian sent to soldiers at a time when the jealousy of the services was even exceptionally fierce. Few men can have ever undertaken a difficult job more cruelly disabled for it—to be chief liaison officer between the military power and civilian officials taking up duty in newly conquered districts—to negotiate with native princes—to advise when treaties were drawn up—to be in high authority, while all the time snubbed and cold-shouldered as a mere clerk. Everyone else was riding and pig-sticking and shooting, and to him field sports were a torture. 'There is not a soul here whose pursuits are like mine, and my want of vivacity is generally pitied.'[1] 'The brisk Arab and the open plain were nothing to him';[2] he preferred the palanquin or slow-moving elephant. It is on record that twenty years later, when Sir Charles Metcalfe was Member of the Governor-General's Council, one of Calcutta's minor amusements was to peer at His Honour taking cautious exercise on a vast somnolent cob, flanked by walking syces, inside his own compound at Alipur. However, because you are not all the time excitedly thinking about killing, it does not follow that you have a coward's heart.[3] Metcalfe took desperate measures, the only ones that could have been effective. He volunteered to accompany the storming party at Dig, and was ever after Lake's 'little stormer'. His 'spirited conduct' was mentioned in despatches, and he had passed once for all the gulf that yawns between soldier and civilian.

[1] Metcalfe to Sherer, 14 March 1806. [2] Kaye, *Life of Metcalfe*, i. 42.

[3] Sir Thomas Munro cared as little about 'sport' as did Metcalfe. One of his tenets was that animals have rights and had not been created merely to give us pleasure by their slaughter. He went out of his way to assure them a place of their own in the world. See his *Life*, i. 298.

XX

THE SIEGE OF BHARATPUR

I think that no success could indemnify us for continuing this ruinous war one moment longer than the first occasion that may present itself for our getting out of it without dishonor; and there is no acquisition which we can obtain by it that would not be productive of the greatest inconvenience to us. We are apparently now waging war against two chieftains who have neither territory nor army to lose. Our prospects, surely, of advantage or losses are not equally balanced. Our treasury is now completely emptied; we can send home no investment; and I am reduced to the necessity of taking the very disagreeable step of stopping the treasure destined by the Court of Directors for China, in order to have a chance of being able to get rid of a part of our irregular forces. I consider our possession of the person of Shah Allum and the town of Delhi as events truly unfortunate, and unless I should be able to persuade his Majesty to move further to the eastward, we can only secure him from the danger of being carried off by the maintenance of a large army in the field, which will be an expense that our funds cannot bear. I deprecate the effects of the almost universal frenzy which has seized some of the heads (which I thought the soundest in the country) for conquest and victory, as opposite to the interests as it is to the laws of our country.—*Lord Cornwallis, 14 August 1805, to Malcolm.*

LAKE'S 'LIGHT-HEARTED'[1] army encamped before the Raja of Bharatpur's capital, 2 January 1805. Holkar, anxious to help his ally, hovered on their outskirts.

Bharatpur held a large and desperate garrison, who when the British in their opening assault displayed incompetence overcame their own fears, and thereafter showed unusual enterprise. They deepened the moat at the point where they guessed the main attack would come; and threw out in front of the fortress ambushes, to harass the enemy's advance with a flank fire. All breaches were quickly repaired and strengthened with stockades.

Here Lake threw away his fame.

On 9 January, at seven in the evening, he sent forward three columns, across a moat whose water was breast-high. They were repulsed, with a loss of over 450 men. Lake decided that a reconnaissance of the ground was advisable before launching a second assault.

The reconnaissance was made by Indian troopers. They pretended to be deserters fleeing from pursuers (who fired blank cartridges). In the broken terrain two of the horses fell, and their riders begged the fort's defenders to show them the gate by which they might escape the British. It was pointed out, and under cover

[1] Pearse, *Lake*, 355. In 1826, Metcalfe was told by an Indian spectator that the Company's soldiers in their heedlessness had looked from the walls 'like marriage processions'.

of coming to it the troopers made a hurried examination; and then raced back, through a now genuine fire from the indignant garrison.

These brave men reported a practicable breach, which was attempted, 21 January, by stormers who carried ladders specially prepared to serve also as helps to cross the moat. They found the defence had dammed the latter and swept into it an augmented mass of water, which made it unfordable. A few swam over, but the rest were merely a target, and lost 600 men before they could extricate themselves. The united cavalry of Holkar, Amir Khan, and the Bharatpur Raja now appeared, and the besiegers became themselves besieged, although by an inept enemy, who always gave way before attacks.

Lake, making the best of a bad job, published a General Order congratulating his men on their gallantry,[1] and served out extra *batta*.[2] His staff concentrated on the production of coracles on the ancient British model.[3] This inland navy included also a huge portable raft, buoyed up with oilskin casks.

Before the third attack was ready, Holkar's closest associate, Amir Khan, made a diversion.

The alliance of these two free companions had begun as that of equals, with a written promise to share all loot exactly; and, although the Maratha's superior abilities and fearlessness made him soon the prince and the other his dependent, Holkar always 'distinguished the Patan from his other leaders', leaving him sole and absolute authority in his own forces. This authority, however, was qualified by the continual turbulence of his following, who were desperate from want of pay. On one occasion, they beat their commander, and half strangled him with his own turban.

Amir Khan was not considered brave, whereas Holkar was reckless, and most of all when threatened most, so that he was regarded with admiration, as well as with a resigned perception that Providence intended well to him. Amir Khan was detested and despised, and was 'clownish and rude in appearance and address; mean in person; of dark Hindoo-like complexion; poorly

[1] The Bengal European Regiment obtained their nickname of 'The Dirty Shirts' on 6 February 1805, when Lake told them that their dirty shirts were a credit to their wearers.

[2] Additional allowance.

[3] In Indian official military archives there must be some formula for making these. They were again made for the crossing of the Nahr el-Falik, in Palestine, in the summer of 1918—made but never used, since in September, when the crossing took place in Allenby's advance, the Falik contained only six inches of water.

and dirtily dressed, and his language low and coarse'.[1] This unflattering account (which might be buttressed with others like it) nevertheless needs this qualification, that he was unfailingly loyal to Yeswant Rao Holkar, whose grim sense of humour he shared. Their association was cause of much misery to India; but they could endure suffering as well as make it.

It should be added that Amir Khan's manner of life was as frugal as his master's. 'The flour of his bread he mixed up on horseback, and collected the wood to dress it with the butt end of his spear, then dropping fire into it from the match of his gun, he toasted the cakes with the same spear, and so ate his meal, always ready for the enemy.'[2] After his own fashion he was also pious; devotion, as we well know, has no necessary connection with ethics. To Holkar's proposal, 'to abide the severest tests of the touchstone of experience, so that our names may go down to posterity with credit on the record of time', Amir Khan replied: 'How true it is that he who gives in the service of God receives a hundredfold! I have no love for goods or gold, but out of regard for you and yielding to your persuasion I have been several times warned from the invisible world that high destinies await me. I consent to give the horse of my ambition the reins in the field of high enterprise.'[3] The invisible world's predictions came true. Amir Khan ended his life as an orthodox 'Prince', created by the British Nawab of Tonk, which his successors rule to-day. But perhaps this mystical strain of fervour was a later perception of the court historian who recorded his deeds while his patron was still living.

Amir Khan now (February 1805) enlarged the war's area by an incursion into Rohilkhand, whither a Company's cavalry force followed him. A stormy little campaign ensued, chequered for both sides. Amir Khan was ultimately reduced to great distress, mainly because of the work of Skinner's troopers, under their gallant and skilful leader. At Afzalgarh, he was fairly caught, and his remnants of an army smashed by British artillery.

The whole Maratha War may now seem too trivial to deserve extended notice. But this was a turning-point in the history of the British in India. It was now that they became 'naturalized', where hitherto they had been hardly settled (and that near the seaboard only). We can trace their 'education', almost from week to week, under the guidance of those instructors, Sindhia's half-breed

[1] Baillie Fraser, i. 70.

[2] Busawan Lal, *Memoirs of the Pathan Soldier of Fortune the Nuwab Ameer-ood-Doulah Mohummud Ameer Khan*, 33.

[3] *Ibid*, 98.

ex-officers. There is an unsuspected quicksand at a river crossing, and a gun is sinking; the nearest elephant, drawing back with dreadful trumpetings, finds firm ground, and twists his trunk about the gun and pulls it and his carriage to shore. The watching artillerymen are assured that they can (and will be wise to) trust 'the beast with the hand'.[1] On the further river's bank are steep wet slippery places; several camels, overloaded for such a terrain, splay out and wreck themselves, and have to be shot. The British transport personnel note that the camel is meant for sandy soils only, and that they would have done well to accept this before disaster emphasized it. Pushing ever north-west, the invaders find themselves awed by the breath-taking loveliness of the Kumaon Himalaya. Though they did not know this, they were at the place where that wondrous range has always most impressed Indian imagination, rising sentinel-fashion and abruptly, almost as if there were no brushwood of intervening foothills. Kalidasa has preserved this sense of watching deity at India's frontiers, in his great stanza about the snowy summits shining day and night, like the bright eternal laughter of Siva.[2] Even to-day the traveller gets it, though he sees it from the dining-car of his train. It made a tremendous impression on the British who saw it in 1805. They began to cease to be mere adventurers. The land revealed itself as something too majestic to be only pillaged.

Having dispersed Amir Khan's foray, the British returned to their siege. It was now that their loss of prestige was painfully driven home to them. On the eve of the third assault, at dawn of 19 February the besieged, with unheard-of temerity, sallied out and destroyed a just-constructed battery. Next day, they anticipated the British assault by making a much larger sortie, and ran, stabbing and shooting, along the parapets of trenches crowded with the waiting stormers. Defeatism seized the latter, who canvassed the chances of their enemy having mined the approaches under cover of this outbreak. The third assault proved the most deadly hitherto, and 900 men were killed and wounded (20 February).[3] The European spearhead refused to follow their officers,[4] the 76th Regiment for the first time declining to be slaughtered. It was a dismal affair, with the gallantry and losses almost all on the sepoys' side.

[1] *Hastinmriga*, 'the deer [in the oldest English sense of that word] with the hand'. The phrase preserves the first freshness of astonishment with which the Aryan invaders of India saw the animal.

[2] *The Cloud-Messenger*.

[3] Forty-nine British and 113 sepoys were killed; 176 British and 556 sepoys were wounded.

[4] Pearse, 380.

Lake, who had exhausted his strategy, tried personal appeal, upbraiding his men 'in terms of affectionate regret, rather than stern severity',[1] and offering them yet another chance to win back reputation. Every one of the European infantry volunteered in response. A forlorn hope (now a phrase of rhetoric, but then a grimly technical and severely descriptive term) was formed, which Lieutenant Templeton, one of the 76th's few surviving officers—he had been out of the third assault, by reason of a wound received in the second one—volunteered to lead. The main assault was entrusted to that much-tried warrior, Colonel Monson.

Both attacks failed utterly. The besieged, aware that this fourth resistance, if successful, would save them, flung on the stormers masses of timber, flaming oil-drenched cotton bales, and home-made devastating bombs. Templeton placed the colours on the wall's summit, but was killed there. Monson, after two hours of fighting, having lost nearly a thousand men,[2] had to withdraw. The siege subsided into a blockade, having cost, up to the evening of 21 February, 103 officers and 3,100 men.

From first to last it had been a most lamentable business. Bharatpur could have been easily taken in the first assault, if the British commander had thought it worth while to study the confused terrain before launching his troops on what proved to be difficult exploration work rather than fighting. The enemy, who were then thinking only of escape, recovered heart; the town's entire population took a hand in subsequent operations. The British, unused to reverses, in each following attempt had the terrifying experience of having to march over their dead comrades, whose cries and groans, as they lay out of reach of help, had previously haunted them. The besiegers were reduced to great straits, and flour was sold at sixteen rupees a seer.[3]

[1] Thorn, 455.

[2] Sixty-nine British and fifty-six sepoys killed: 410 British and 452 sepoys wounded.

[3] *Selections from the Peshwa Daftar*, 41, letter 37.

XXI

BHARATPUR AND INDIAN AND BRITISH REACTIONS

BY INDIAN opinion, the British defeats were considered Holkar's victory, the Raja being merely his ally. The sensation they caused is vividly preserved in newswriters' reports. A phrase which for nearly a century abounds in Maratha references to our people occurs repeatedly. The British were 'those who go by water'. What (it is asked indignantly) are they doing in the heart of India? 'The fish ought to keep to the water.'

The Peshwa, who moved restlessly from before Holkar's incursions and advances, was more than a little watchful of Sindhia.[1] Sindhia's own reactions were interesting. Holkar's exhibition of the efficacy of Maratha tactics had deeply impressed him, sullen under what he regarded as the theft of Gwalior and the wanton rehabilitation, at his expense, of Gohad, the principality his own predecessor had long ago extinguished. Exultant newswriters told of British disasters, and reported that three high officers had been taken prisoner. Distressed by British demands on him, and intensely excited, Sindhia burned to join up with Holkar, and Jenkins had immense difficulty in holding him back.[2] On 18 October 1804, he drew up a long letter[3] to the Governor-General which the bearer (under instructions) held back until four months later, when the final collapse of the operations against Bharatpur encouraged him to present it. 'The prosperity of the garden of friendship' being the object of his 'anxious solicitude', Sindhia pointed out that the garden was suffering from trampling feet, and drew His Excellency's attention to what he asserted was the usual practice of 'Princes and chiefs of high rank and power' when they had made engagements. 'It is incumbent on both parties to observe' such engagements. Holkar had devastated large tracts of his territory: his advice and warnings had been ignored: he had been refused pecuniary help: he had been sometimes left to bear the brunt of the common enemy's anger. He reasserted his claim to Gwalior, and said that the Company ought to help his ravaged finances, since his and their interests were now identical. He made charges against British officers, and spoke contemptuously of his

[1] *Selections from the Peshwa Daftar*, 41, *passim*, especially letters 37 and 38.
[2] *Ibid.*
[3] Martin, iv. 281 ff.

Resident, Josiah Webbe, a very sick man, who died 9 November 1804. He showed frankly that he thought little of British ability or integrity:

'As the war with Holkar, in consequence of the officers of your Excellency's troops thinking too lightly of it, has now run to a great length, and my territory has been exposed to the last degree of devastation, and as Mr. Webbe neither fulfils the obligations of treaty or of friendship, nor returns any answers to my plans of operation. . . .'

Sindhia's treatment of Webbe was bad enough. But Webbe's successor, Richard Jenkins, who was not yet twenty, was received with such gross disrespect that he asked for his passports, and despite various delays, owing to Sindhia's reluctance to go so far as open war again, he left the Maratha camp, 23 January 1805. Sindhia sent a messenger after him, begging him to return, and promising to be guided by him. Jenkins consented, but while he was in durbar with Sindhia his baggage was plundered by Pindaris, and two of his officers and some of his sepoys wounded. Sindhia expressed horror, but did nothing; Jenkins was kept as a practical prisoner, exposed to daily insults. On 23 March, Sindhia announced to his Resident that he intended to march to Bharatpur, to mediate a peace between the warring parties—a statement which produced from the Governor-General a protest which for once we may call tame and inadequate:

'To proceed at the head of an army to the seat of hostilities, for the purpose of interposing his unsolicited mediation, was an act not only inconsistent with the nature of his engagement, but insulting to the honour and highly dangerous to the interests of the British government.'[1]

Wellesley, however, replied formally to Sindhia's letter of complaint, written in the previous October, and with such sternness that the complainant was cowed, and promised reparation for the outrage on Jenkins' camp. Sindhia declared that all that had happened was that 'the acting resident was agreeably to usage delayed until a successor arrived'.[2]

Sindhia nevertheless kept in close touch with Holkar and Amir Khan, who not unnaturally asked for some practical proof of his sympathy. They needed money badly, so Sindhia, remembering the treachery over Gwalior of Ambaji Inglia, 'who professes to be my friend', gave them permission to plunder the latter, on condition that he received half the proceeds. Ambaji was accord-

[1] *Ibid*, iv. 494 ff.

[2] J. Sutherland, *Sketches of the Relations subsisting between the Government in India, and The Different Native States*, 151.

ingly seized, and tortured into surrendering a large number of lakhs. Sindhia felt pleased, having killed two difficult birds with one stone. But the party that profited most was the Company, for Ambaji became an inveterate enemy of Holkar and Amir Khan, and the new Maratha confederacy, which was all but formed and might have been more dangerous than the old one of which the Peshwa was the head, passed into the region of might-have-been.[1]

In his letter to Sindhia, the Governor-General stood on the strict letter of the Treaty, which (like the Versailles Treaty, and most other treaties ever made) had been a 'dictated' one:

> 'Your Highness is bound to employ your utmost exertions in conjunction with the British power in the prosecution of joint war. No obligation however is imposed upon the British power to afford to your Highness pecuniary aid for that purpose.'

The British were 'therefore entitled to expect' the utmost that Sindhia could do, whereas their side of the bargain was 'entirely optional'. There never was a harder scrutineer of his own case than Lord Wellesley. One concession only was made, and that not so much in friendship to Sindhia as in penal visitation of another prince, who was fighting shy of entering into engagements with the Company; the Raja of Jodhpur was handed over to his Maratha overlord, from whom he had temporarily escaped. 'Your Highness will act according to your pleasure towards that Raja.' For the rest, his Highness was told that if he compelled the British to renew the war, 'every exertion of the British arms' would again be made.

> 'for the necessary and salutary purpose of imposing a due restraint upon the violence, treachery, and ambition of a state, whose perverted counsels have manifested an utter contempt of every obligation of justice, faith, gratitude, and honour.'

The young (who among the British in India were in an overwhelming majority, while hardly one was old, as we consider age) thought with Metcalfe that the only self-respecting course was to 'breathe the spirit of an insulted and mighty power', refusing discussion until every foe was beaten into helplessness. But a wholesale Maratha war had passed beyond the Company's depleted strength. Sir Arthur Wellesley, on the eve of departure for Europe,[2] wrote, 'Take my word for it, we are not now in a state to attempt the conquest of Malwah—an operation which, under other circumstances, would be a mere joke'. Emeritus from all these troubles, he solaced himself with remarking to his friends that he

[1] Henry Beveridge, *History of India* ii. 800.

[2] He sailed, 9 March 1805.

had foreseen what would happen if the Maratha confederacy—useful from its very quality of ramshackle elasticity—were broken up, and that he did not think the Commander-in-Chief or he himself had conducted the war as well through their deputies as they had done in person.

In the mood for relaxation, General Wellesley looked up Nana Farnavis' widow, who was attracting a lot of admiration from the British by rumours of her beauty. He reported that the girl of seventeen was 'very fair and very handsome, and well deserving to be the object of a treaty'.[1] That treaty (i.e. guaranteed pension) he obtained for her—he was never indifferent to good looks in a woman—and offered her his escort back to Poona, which she refused. But his letters she kept, and showed them long afterwards to Lady Falkland, who noted her curiously. 'She is very old, but still traces of great beauty are visible, the features small and delicate, and her eyes large and bright for her age'.[2]

Among others who visited her in her springtide was Lord Valentia. When her brother asked him to be a friend to Nana Farnavis' wife, the Englishman answered boldly that he knew nothing of the speaker's sister, but knew only a curtain, which did not greatly interest him or seem an object for befriending. The attendants laughed, and the purdah dropped, revealing 'really a very pretty girl, fair, round-faced, with beautiful eyes'.[3]

A charming distressed Maratha girl might take up Arthur Wellesley's time. The Governor-General had sterner distractions. He woke up to the necessity of sending Sindhia someone who had at any rate passed well beyond his teens, who understood Indians and was respected as understanding them—Graeme Mercer or Malcolm. Malcolm's going was ultimately decided on, to the alarm of the ferocious young; it is one of many signs that the official attitude was now fast hardening, that even Elphinstone wrote that Malcolm

'will do admirably to conciliate Sindia, after he has been sufficiently punished; but as he is apt to take likings and attachments to natives, and seems to have one to Sindia, I hope he will not have to negotiate with him till he has lost 10,000 men and 150 guns.'[4]

Elphinstone's own difficulties with the Bhonsla Raja were being

[1] 18 May 1804: to Colonel Barry Close.

[2] *Chow-Chow*, 135.

[3] Viscount Valentia, *Voyages and Travels to India, Ceylon, The Red Sea, Abyssinia, Egypt*. ii. 158.

[4] Yet Elphinstone could see Sindhia's side when he chose. 'While he behaved well he was bullied; when he did everything but murder our ambassador he was treated with kindness and respect' (27 September 1805).

exacerbated, the Governor-General having chosen this time of all times—when the Raja in his bitterness once even threatened to try to recover part of his forfeited territory forcibly—to press again the subsidiary alliance. Holkar's tide of temporary luck (it was pointed out) was ebbing; presently his discarded followers would be roaming wildly in search of subsistence, and Nagpur would undoubtedly invite pillage, unless a Company's force protected it. The argument was strong, but other arguments proved stronger. 'The unhappy prince was not prepared to pay the price which was exacted from all sovereigns who recognized our supremacy, and the negotiation came to an end.'[1]

The leader of the Nagpur war party, the Raja's brother, to show that there was no personal animus against the Resident sent him a present of greyhounds, Elphinstone being a vigorous sportsman. Even this civility did not lull suspicion to rest. The recipient looked the gift-horse closely in the mouth, and analysed its qualities:

'viz. (1) one pup, that died mad this morning; (2) one dog of the coat and colour of a bear and nature of a jackass; (3) one dog without a tail—he might as well have sent one without a head; and (4) one very good bitch, all arrayed in cloth of gold.'

Meanwhile, this astonishing man continued to rise long before daybreak, to read the Greek tragedians,[2] and to write to his friend Strachey in the Governor-General's office long letters which pass easily from political disquisitions, expressed with cool prescience, to excellent comparisons of Horace and Hafiz. If the crisis ever came, as we know it did come, twelve years later, it would find at the heart of the storm a man whose equanimity was unshakable for even a moment.

Bharatpur was yielded finally as a by-product of the rout of Holkar and Amir Khan. The siege had sunk into a mere blockade, when the Raja took advantage of the news of Lake's elevation to the peerage, in March, to send him congratulations and to ask for peace. His *vakils* arrived accordingly, 10 March, and his sincerity was deepened when his ally Holkar's camp was beaten up twice

[1] Colebrooke, *Life of Elphinstone*, i. 129.

[2] A typical entry is that of April 1808: 'We [Jenkins and Elphinstone] rise at four and read Sophocles, generally about 200 lines, till it is time to ride. We sometimes read on our return, which takes place about seven. After breakfast, business generally prevents our beginning Xenophon, which is our forenoon's lesson, till eleven; we then read twenty or thirty pages, eat a sandwich, and read separately—I Tacitus and the books on the French Revolution—till two; then we read Grotius till evening. I feel extremely the want of method, but am at a loss how to remedy this very serious defect.'

(29 March and 2 April). Holkar, his fortunes manifestly falling, fled across the Chambal with the remnants of an army. The Raja of Bharatpur obtained peace on easy terms, paying immediately three out of twenty lakhs indemnity, and promising to engage no Europeans without the Company's sanction. Dig was not to be restored to him until he had given proof of his change of heart.

Before handling the Sindhia nettle, Malcolm had to visit Lake, who was marooned, rather than camped, in Central India, on the banks of the Chambal, where Holkar and Sindhia were now in contact. Lake had a sprawling horde of no less than 300,000 men, the vast majority being camp-followers. There is no wonder that Marathas call this period 'the time of terror'. Even in their moods of peace, these immense armies were spreading hungry pythons.

Lord Wellesley went home, in August 1805, while Holkar was still at large. He was recalled, as so often happens, for his merits as much as for his faults. He had shown a disposition to interfere with Hindu religious customs—had put down the sacrifice of children at Saugor Island at the mouth of the Hugli, and had been inclined to consider the prohibition of widow-burning. He had been willing to throw India open to missionary effort. Much worse, he had opposed the Company's short-sighted grip on their monopoly. India's foreign trade was far beyond their own shipping, and the tonnage allotted to private enterprise[1] was ridiculously inadequate to deal with the surplus. As a result, the Company kept their own countrymen out of all this flourishing business, while French, Dutch, Americans, Malays, and Arabs under their protection crowded into it. They were enriching Europe at the expense of their own people.

Lord Wellesley fell, then, to a combination of enemies. The monopolists, the pacifists, those who were frightened of debts and new commitments, those who disapproved of his friendliness towards missionaries and his desire to see India move towards civilization, those whom his manners had offended, were all against him.

His attitude in this matter of shipping was entirely characteristic of his mind, which was in many respects essentially a liberated one. His despatches, almost invariably excited and imperious, often wildly arrogant, naturally prejudice the reader of to-day. But it is unfair, in judging the men of bygone ages, to look only at their words and actions in one short excerpt of their lives, especially one that was crowded with passionate and tempestuous activity. Wellesley saw only the case that he wished to see: he judged solely

[1] By the Act of 1793, 3,000 tons only. Wellesley wished to increase this.

by the opinions which he brought with him to a country whose utter disparity from his own, in every fashion and degree, he never seems to have suspected: his enemies were very far from being the black ungrateful aggressors that he thought them, but were often very bewildered and childish fugitives, wondering at the vivacity and ardour of his reproaches and pursuit of them. But he was right in thinking that the Company had no choice but to advance to paramountcy, or else to leave the appalling chaos of India to get yet fiercer and wilder, until their own position there became precarious. He was justified in the poor opinion he formed of the Company's aims, which were merely mercantile and mercenary, and of most of their personnel. His enthusiasm fired that of the new young generation, who served him gladly and to whom he was increasingly a kind and most encouraging master; and he set a new standard of service and disinterestedness.

He was both too proud and too just to shift on to subordinates the blame when affairs went wrong; he stood by them if they had been honest, however blundering and inadequate. His character held a fine magnanimity, very unlike the inhuman coldness of his brother. In every cause which later generations have accepted as a clear choice between barbarism and civilization, Richard Wellesley was for the latter, and Arthur Wellesley was for the continuance of the former—whether it was flogging in the army (often, as in the Peninsular campaign, flogging to death), negro slavery, or Catholic emancipation. In his after-career, Richard Wellesley was consistently 'Liberal', in the best sense of that now unpopular word; and his brother's success seemed to him marred by an inability to place himself on the side which was morally right.[1]

The last months of Lord Wellesley's rule went draggingly by. Now at last thoroughly realizing that his grandiose dream had escaped him, he marked time till his successor came.

[1] As he amusingly revealed by an incident in his old age. 'Little Gore, come here, and I'll tell you something!' The boy thus beckoned came up; and Lord Wellesley, frowning, then said, 'My brother the Duke of Wellington is a very stupid man, a very stupid man.' As Mr. Philip Morrell, who had this story from Bishop Gore (son of the 'little Gore' who had been enlightened), remarked to me, the fact that Lord Wellesley felt impelled to confide in a small boy shows how resentfully he had brooded over the matter.

XXII

ARRIVAL OF LORD CORNWALLIS

THE BRITISH GOVERNMENT in England have often been criticized because that successor was a man who had already served in India and was now old and ailing. But the Governor-Generalship had become a problem. Wellesley himself had made it at last a first-rate position, not lightly to be filled by anyone who could push his claims on the Directors and the Board of Control.

Some people were slow to realize this change. A Mr. Charles Crauford, for example, who had recently married the Dowager Duchess of Newcastle, wrote to Dundas, drawing attention to the fact that, as stepfather to the young Duke, who was a minor, he controlled at least seven parliamentary seats, the largest number in the gift of one man. 'I am perfectly ready to place the whole of this influence at the service of the present administration. On the other hand I am sure you will not think it unreasonable that I should look to something considerable for my family.' He added, 'without further preface', that his terms were that 'the head of my family, my eldest brother, Sir James Crauford', should succeed Lord Wellesley as Governor-General of India. To which Dundas answered politely enough, making it plain that he would be glad of the offered support, yet with something of a snub. 'I am sorry you should have had the trouble of entering unnecessarily into a detail of particulars which it is impossible for me to take into consideration with the view in which you state them.'[1]

Lord Cornwallis was appointed accordingly, almost as an acknowledged stopgap. He reached Calcutta, 30 July, and began with the not too tactful observation that he found 'a general frenzy for conquest and victory even in those heads which I had believed to be the soundest'—a remark which stirred Metcalfe to indignation. 'He agrees that the wisdom or necessity of a particular course of policy, which he is pleased deliberately to term a frenzy, is strongly impressed upon those heads which he had believed to be the soundest.' Respect for their judgment 'would have led common characters' to look into the reasons for such a prevailing conviction, from a suspicion that

[1] Letters dated 5 and 8 March 1800: quoted from Melville MSS., Lot 750, Holden Furber, *Henry Dundas*, 141.

'such a universal effect might have some good cause which it would be right to search for. But this man has a head so very sound that the only thought that arises in his mind is that there is not a sound head in India. He proves either that he is no judge of heads, or that he disagrees with the soundest heads.'

His 'manner and substance of speech', after the advantage of exactly one month on Indian soil, were 'precisely the same as they were on the first day of his arrival. There is some immoveable notion in his head.'[1]

There was. He wrote home to the Directors that he had found the Company at war with Holkar and hardly at peace with Sindhia; and to all protests in India Lord Cornwallis replied that the financial position was too desperate for any measures except immediate peace, which he proceeded to work for, not always wisely or with due consideration for British honour. For example, he waived Sindhia's treatment of Jenkins, without further argument promising at once to restore Gwalior.

The proposals for peace caused dismay at the Front, where war had become exceedingly pleasant. Holkar was definitely a fugitive, whose camps were broken up from time to time by *daurs*—lightning rushes at daybreak, followed by an exhilarating chase; and the Army had left the Chambal, where food supplies were precarious and inadequate, and was enjoying itself in the old Mogul cities of the upper Jumna, the officers billeted in those superb tombs which all the world now admires:

'These dwellings of the silent dead were now the habitations of active and lively beings, who, without offering any offence to the *manes* of the original occupants, indulged themselves in various festivities during this dreary season. Though the upper rooms and galleries did not overlook gardens diffusing the fragrance of Eden, watered by numerous streams and resounding the choral notes of the songsters of the groves, they were enlivened by the presence of many beauties, whose fascinating powers might have inspired an Anchorite with cheerfulness, and made the most rigid Mussulman forget the houries of Paradise.'[2]

Lake, however, had to obey orders. But he obeyed them with an economy of compliance and with discretion, holding back the Governor-General's proposals and telling Sindhia that until he released Jenkins he had no chance of getting a settlement. Sindhia released Jenkins accordingly, and agreed to dismiss Ghatke and to accept as adviser in his place the supposedly more honest Ambaji Inglia. Holkar, seeing his prospects of drawing in

[1] Letter to J. W. Sherer, 31 August 1805.

[2] Thorn, 475.

Sindhia vanish, in September crossed over the Satlej into the Punjab, hoping to rouse the Sikhs.

Lord Cornwallis was now seen to be dying; he had become incapable of business. He died, 5 October, and was succeeded by his Senior Member of Council, Sir George Barlow, as acting Governor-General. Lake thereupon took control of the Sindhia negotiations, which Malcolm put through. The Treaty of Sarji Argengaon remained in force, but was modified (22 November)[1] in many respects. Sindhia promised never to readmit Sarji Rao Ghatke to his councils; he received back suzerainty over Gwalior and Gohad, and the Chambal was agreed upon as the boundary between his state and British India; a pension of four lakhs was settled on him, and his wife and daughter were given *jagirs*[2] in Company's territory. Most important of all, the Rajput states were practically divided into spheres of influence. Sindhia renounced all claim to tribute from Bundi or any other state north of the Chambal or east of Kotah; the British promised to enter into no treaties with Jodhpur, Kotah and other chiefs in Malwa, or with Marwar and Mewar, and not to interfere between them and the Marathas. These were such terms as Sindhia could never have hoped for from Lord Wellesley, and they give us the measure of the damage which Holkar had inflicted. Sindhia was well content. He was still better pleased when Sir George Barlow in 1806 voluntarily and unnecessarily withdrew protection from even those states to which it had been pledged. By that time peace had been made with Holkar also, and the withdrawal operated towards him as well.

This action was particularly unjust to Jaipur and Bundi, states that had 'maintained the alliance with honour and generosity' and 'performed such essential service' as to have become 'obnoxious both to Sindhia and Holkar'.[3] Bundi's 'integrity and attachment had been displayed in a very marked manner',[4] during Monson's retreat. Their betrayal opened up a chapter in British-Indian history which is painful reading.

The action, which Barlow carried to further lengths than a patriotic and resolute man on the spot need have done, was inspired by a conviction, born out of years of warfare, that the Maratha heart was deceitful, and above all things desperately wicked. No truce could be made or kept with it; it must therefore be given some space where its criminality might rage unchecked. As the Secret Committee remarked in 1809, when Metcalfe, under

[1] Ratified, Christmas Day, 1805. [2] Estates.

[3] Grant Duff, *A History of the Mahrattas*, iii. 311.

[4] Thorn, 496.

Minto's direction, reversed the withdrawal, Sindhia and Holkar were 'irreclaimably addicted to predatory incursions into the territories of the petty states'.[1] The Rajput states were therefore deliberately tossed to them, as flesh to tigers, and formally notified of their desertion. The cis-Satlej Sikh states were not so notified, but the same system was acted upon in their case also.

We have been anticipating events. Holkar and Amir Khan, wisely writing off their hopes of Sindhia, in the autumn of 1805 fled before Lake. It is said that the hunted fox, when not too hard pressed, will pause to pick up a stray chicken. The two confederates came upon the Raja of Patiala and his Rani, who maintained through these years a squabble of lyric intensity. 'God has assuredly sent us these two pigeons to pluck', observed Holkar piously. 'Do you espouse the cause of the one, while I take up with the other.'[2] They delayed accordingly, until they had furnished themselves from the foolish pair.

Hitherto the relations of British and Sikhs had been slight. The members of Surman's embassy to the Great Mogul, nearly a century earlier, had with pity and admiration watched the Sikhs pass through Delhi as prisoners, to the cruel deaths which they endured with such fortitude. Warren Hastings had thought of them as a possible danger to his puppet Nawab of Oudh. At the Battle of Delhi, it is said that Sindhia was helped by an army of 5,000 Sikhs, who afterwards dispersed. Their help must have been nominal in the extreme—a gesture put out to vindicate the time's admirable impartiality, rather than a genuine arm of succour. The same impartiality had been shown at almost the same time, by the 'occasional services'[3] of isolated Sikh chieftains to the Company. In 1804, Sikh detachments helped a British force in straits, at Shamli, near Saharanpur.[4] On the whole, the Sikhs had been friendly disposed to the Company, and inclined to look critically upon the Marathas.

Lake followed up the fugitives; and Metcalfe, with the advanced detachment, opened up that correspondence which always spread fanwise, like a preliminary skirmish between outposts, before Indian armies. The Raja of Patiala was informed that Major-General Dowdeswell had heard of his many good qualities, and was suffering anxiety on account of a report that so fine a character had slipped into action adverse to his interests, by joining Holkar. 'It is not consistent with your famed wisdom to associate

[1] India Office Records, Home Misc. series. [2] Amir Khan, *Memoirs*, 276.
[3] J. D. Cunningham, *A History of the Sikhs*, 128.
[4] *Ibid*, 128.

yourself with such a man.' The prowess and terror of the British arms were tactfully but plainly brought to his notice, and he was asked to choose between the Company's vengeance or 'great kindness'. The Raja hastened to reply that this letter had given him delight. 'The case is, that since the bright sun of British rule has enlightened the countries of Hindostan, I have sincerely and faithfully fulfilled the duties of submission and attachment to the Government.' He admitted that he had suffered a visitation from Holkar, that 'wretch whose profession and livelihood is plunder'. 'From necessity I submitted to one or two conferences', and had to seem to be friendly. 'I have no asylum but in the British Government, to which I shall ever look up.' He looked forward to their troops' arrival.

Presently the British Commander-in-Chief reached Patiala, whose Raja went through his favourite symbolical action of surrendering the keys of his citadel. Lake, however, was not at present collecting kingdoms. He pushed on, crossed the Satlej, and invaded the Punjab.

Its most important chief, the celebrated Ranjit Singh, was in mid-career of his great work of welding together a Sikh empire,[1] and he watched with painful interest a campaign taking place on his territory, without the formality of his leave. There is a tradition that he went disguised into Lake's camp, like Alfred spying on the Danes. One way or another, he formed opinions which were largely responsible for the fact that, so long as he lived, there was peace between the Sikhs and the Company. On the approach of the British, he called a council of war, which decided to wait on events, trusting that God would be good and would influence both armies of invaders to exercise their valour solely amongst themselves.

Ranjit Singh longed to get rid of both belligerents. Lake, aware of this, halted on the Beas (which the classically minded, conscious that they were warring in Alexander's footsteps, preferred to style the Hyphasis), to receive Holkar's envoys. The necessary Malcolm, leaving Sindhia, had accompanied the Commander-in-Chief, and on 14 December 1805 an arrangement was come to, whereby the Marathas were to be allowed to return quietly to what was now to be recognized as Holkar's principality.

On 7 January 1806, Metcalfe by invitation visited the enemy's camp, and peace was made. Holkar and his chiefs were undisguisedly joyful, and 'the One-Eyed' (as the former was nicknamed) was courteous and pleasant, with 'not at all the appearance of the

[1] The British at this time style him merely 'Sirdar'.

savage that we knew him to be'. 'The jewels on his neck were invaluably rich', and he played with a small lap-dog. Metcalfe was greatly pleased when he found out afterwards that, without realizing it at the time, he had managed to snub Amir Khan, who was 'blackguard in his looks' and tried to show off his fierceness. 'I consider his behaviour to have been affectation. He had the impudence to ask from me my name, which must have been known to him.'

Holkar had been ejected far from his territory, like a stone slung by a giant. 'Among a confederacy of robber princes, he was the most of a robber and the least of a prince', and his condition was now desperate. He must have thought the victors mad when, on condition of his abandoning all claims to the land north of the Chambal, they restored their conquests south of the Tapti and Godavari rivers, as well as Indore. Barlow later voluntarily added Tonk Rampura, a concession which Holkar celebrated with artillery salutes and the remark that the British were 'great rascals and not to be trusted'. He bargained hard now, when he was in fact helpless, and the stickiest part of the negotiations related to Jaipur, which he insisted was his tributary. Malcolm, aware that he intended to punish the state for helping the British, was rigid, and won his point. It therefore seemed particularly uncalled-for, when Barlow without solicitation sent the Maratha chiefs 'Declaratory Articles', handing back their freedom of action towards Jaipur and Bundi. 'It is, I suppose', Metcalfe noted, 'the first time that a Government has found fault with its negotiators for getting too much.' Malcolm wrote, with deep feeling, 'This is the first measure of the kind, that the English have ever taken in India, and I trust in God it will be the last.' The rigorous retraction which followed so swiftly on the prodigal extension of the Company's power left in a state of devastation and wretchedness the regions where British arms had recently been exerted.

Holkar promised to march back peaceably, without pillaging on the way, and by a specified route; and to employ no Europeans in future without the Company's permission. Part of these conditions he promptly fulfilled; that is, he returned to the territory so unexpectedly given back to him, though he did not pedantically stand upon the order of his going, either as to the prescribed route or the engagement to refrain from plundering. 'He is at present', Metcalfe wrote, 14 March 1806, 'engaged in plundering the Sikhs. Be it said to his credit, that he plunders most those who befriended him. . . . This is a happy state of Peace.' His colleague Amir Khan, disappointed in his hope of being himself also recognized as a territorial prince, proceeded in the same general direction, with the menacing observation that 'a fly could annoy an elephant', as the British should learn.

XXIII

CONSIDERATIONS OF THE PEACE

THE GENERAL conclusion of peace, and still more the terms on which the settlement of Northern India was made, were furiously denounced at the time; and British historians have never yet had a good word to say for them. Metcalfe's judgment may be cited, for many reasons: not only because, young as he was (where most were far from being even middle-aged), his intellect was unusually clear and controlled, but also because he rarely talked at random, and had already formed the habit of drawing up reasoned and elaborate examinations of questions of public importance. No words sufficed for his distrust and scorn of Barlow.

It was easy to feel scorn for Barlow, a cold and stiff-mannered official, whose personality was repulsive in its lowness of emotional temperature. His mind was set in departmental grooves; he

> 'had immense respect for the written law, the dignity of office, and the gradations of authority; he never encroached on the privilege or prerogative of others, and never yielded an iota of his own.'[1]

He had been so long the hand (and little else) by which supreme authority acted that his own judgment had almost died. Nor had his ideas, while they still existed, ever been marked by any originality or nobility. 'The two principal objects', he had minuted, as far back as 1793, 'which the Government ought to have in view in all its arrangements are to ensure its political safety and to render the possession of the country as advantageous as possible to the East India Company and the British Nation.' These sentiments perhaps most men of his time would have passed as unexceptionable, but they were rejected by Sir William Jones, who wrote marginally, 'I have presumed to alter the first words. Surely the *principal* object of every Government is the happiness of the governed'.

Barlow's administration has rarely had any defence made of it. His character has fared somewhat better. He had integrity and sense of duty; and his very coldness, as Lord Minto (who had the task of superseding him, under unpleasant circumstances) gratefully observed, brought along with it this negative merit, that he did not seem to resent slights or wrongs to himself.

[1] Kaye, *Life of Malcolm*, i. 367.

In his exasperation now, 'Something more than cold approbation', Metcalfe cried,

'is required to foster great minds. . . . Men who perform great actions want to be admired, and are not content with being approved. . . . Men will not serve zealously unless their government is zealous to do them honor. I venture to pronounce that this administration will be coldly served. Lord Wellesley, from the fire of patriotism which blazed in his own breast, emitted sparks which animated the breasts of all who came within the reach of his notice.

Our present Governor is too cold in his character to give any warmth to others; and this characteristic of his private life seems to be a feature of his public administration.'[1]

Cold, cold, cold, he keeps repeating, with a wildness of vexation whenever he thinks of the Governor-General. The rare exceptional spirit, he admits, will pour itself out, praise or no praise; 'but general arguments are applied to the generality, and these do certainly require the stimulants of Hope and Ambition.'

It is very hard to champion Barlow against such a prosecutor. Even when he stated his case himself (and in some ways it was a strong one) he did it with a tepid and sluggish flow of sentence and diction, that seems inhuman. Timidity was in all his thought; and the apologia, from sheer lack of backbone, fails to reach dignity. 'I wish his Lordship', he told Lake, replying to the latter's protests,

'to understand that I offer these sentiments only as my opinion, and by no means as a decision against the correctness of his Lordship's judgment, which may be right. But as I am personally and exclusively responsible to the East India Company and to my country for the terms of the pacification, I am persuaded that his Lordship's candor and liberality will satisfy him that I have only discharged my duty to the public and to myself by adhering to my own opinion. If I had adopted his Lordship's sentiments in opposition to my own opinion, and if an early interruption of the peace were to follow, his Lordship will be sensible that my urging that I had conformed to his advice in preference to being guided by my own judgment, would be no justification whatever of my conduct.'

This rectitude—firmly planted on undeniable fact though it is—turns in too much upon itself. Chill egoism, rather than selfless devotion to public duty, sustains it.

'My father informs me', Metcalfe wrote (28 September 1805), 'that he lost the situation of Deputy-Chairman this year because the majority of the Directors did not choose to join the active friend of Lord Wellesley to Mr. Grant, his inveterate enemy. . . . I am very happy at it.' For his father, early in 1806, he wrote his first important political analysis. I call it important, for anything which proceeded from this mind—so precise and sensitive in

[1] *Selections from the Papers of Lord Metcalfe,* 1 ff.

its selection of the essential, and of the phrasing to express thinking that to an exceptional degree was exact and scrupulously just—is that. Metcalfe and Warren Hastings are by themselves, among the political thinkers which the history of Britain in India has produced. But the paper is hardly mature. Barlow had abandoned the attempt to frame a settlement that went into the innumerable detail of the Indian situation, and in seeking for a broad and ready simplification had fixed upon the Jumna as the Company's border.[1] Metcalfe, who had accompanied an army that had swept hundreds of miles beyond this border, begins with an outburst of vexation—understandable, when we remember the inhuman immobility with which Barlow had taken his stand, at a period when the British ranks were full of men of generous and rushing feeling. To every argument, Metcalfe complains, Barlow answers that the Jumna boundary 'is a fundamental principle of my administration, and to this all other considerations must yield'. Metcalfe cries out angrily:

'If the Jumna was a river of such depth as to form a boundary, some reason might be supposed for making a boundary of it. But the fact is, it is everywhere fordable in all months excepting those during which, in common with it, every rivulet swelled by the rains is impassable. The lands to the west are as fertile, the people under good government would be as quiet, and the states with whom we have alliances are as good as elsewhere. What object is it which shall make one bank of such a stream the object of dread and aversion, when the other is everything desirable? . . . Sir George Barlow, in his closet, looking at a map, sees a black line marking the course of a river; he draws his pencil along this line, and says, "Thus far shalt thou go, and no farther"; and this forms a fundamental principle. I can fancy no other cause for his astonishing determination to keep nothing that he can get rid of on one side of the imaginary line. But he may as well set his chair on the sands of the sea, and order the waves to stop; for the influence of Britain will roll in spite of him beyond the Jumna.'[2]

If that sounding rhetoric is examined, however, even from this statement it emerges that Barlow had a case. The Jumna as a frontier represented a tremendous increase of territory and responsibility, gained after an exhausting and prolonged war. Rivers *do* form a boundary readily seen and accepted, as nothing else except the actual sea does. A mountain range is more open to argument; an artificial line offers more temptations to aggression. Even if the Jumna is, as Metcalfe says (and as he might have said of practically every river of Central India), fordable except in the

[1] With a trifling modification.

[2] *Selections from the Papers of Lord Metcalfe*, 1 ff.

rains, the river-bed remains, a line plain to the eyes. Barlow was not seeking a fortified frontier, a natural bulwark which no enemy could storm—but a boundary which would have in it the seeds of peace, not those of future argument.

The Minute (for so it may be called, though drawn up for private study only) contains a good deal more of mere patriotic eloquence; and much of it was abundantly answered, and over and over again, by Metcalfe himself in his later years. His scorn of 'the determined spirit of penury which is evident in this administration' would have been noted grimly, a quarter of a century afterwards, by Sir Charles Metcalfe the rigorous foe of expenditure on imperial ends—the statesman whose horror of debt was almost pathological—the man who asserted, and kept on asserting, that the people of India were shamefully overtaxed, by a Government ignorant of their poverty and careless of their needs. The insistence of the indignant young man of twenty-one, that human nature was entitled to look for reward, and that 'when a man's conscience tells him that he has worked hard and merited well, he expects reward', would have seemed merely tiresome to the ungrudging servant of duty that this young man became.

We can also know, not guess only, what would have been Metcalfe's maturer judgment on such posturings as this, strewn throughout this earlier statement:

'I have heard much of the vicious consequences of the spirit of ambition and aggrandisement which has sullied our character; I have heard, I say, much of this, but have seen nothing either of the vicious consequences, or imaginary causes. That our power, reputation, glory, have been aggrandised, I cannot deny. They have been proudly and nobly aggrandised. I have also heard much of a charming notion of keeping our place in India and our tranquillity by a new system of generosity, moderation, and innocence.'

'From our pacific, mild, moderate, amiable character', he writes to Sherer (12 February 1806), 'Holkar may play as many tricks as he pleases, and we shall have the generous magnanimity of overlooking them.'

Turn history's pages, to when the dreams of empire were again fiercely stirring, now to stretch beyond the Indus and if possible into Central Asia. We know what happened to those dreams, in the retreat from Kabul. That was under Lord Auckland. But it was in the government of his predecessor, Lord William Bentinck, that men began to meddle with those frontiers which the Company, by solemn treaty with Ranjit Singh, had engaged to leave scrupulously alone. Lord William went up country, in 1831, to meet the Sikh leader, and while thus engaged listened to the advice of men eager for glory and increase of territory. No Governor-General ever received a franker or more desperate letter from a subordinate, than the protest sent him by Metcalfe, left behind in Calcutta to act in his superior's absence:

'I see that no one is proof against the temptation of extension. It seems to be contrary to our nature to remain quietly contented with what we have got. . . . It is wonderful how we invariably confirm and justify by our conduct the jealousies and suspicions with which we are viewed. . . . We are too overbearing to be thwarted, and thus we advance crushing the independence of every state that we come near. We profess moderation, and nevertheless show by our continual restlessness, that there is no safety in our neighbourhood.'[1]

It is hard to see how that judgment of his own people differs from his 1806 condemnation of the Marathas: 'To meet their ambition and enterprise with the language of peace, would be to preach to the roaring ocean to be still'.

The Case for Sir Thomas Barlow

Barlow never marshalled his own justification except so as to arouse contempt. His defence, however, may be indicated under four heads, which serve also as a justification for the settlement of India which was made in accordance with instructions from London.

Taking first the abandonment of the Rajput states to Holkar and Sindhia, this in itself was as disgraceful as Metcalfe styled it, a 'shocking business',[2] 'these *horrible* designs'.[3] Here his political instincts did not mislead him; and he could not refrain from repetition and underlining of the unethical nature of this aspect of the peace. 'I would wish to see our government feelingly alive to points of honor, and less tenacious of argumentative right.'

'One shocking proposition is, that we shall derive security from the dissensions of our neighbours; and a still more shocking system is founded upon it, which is intended, and must tend, to revive in Hindostan, in the Mahratta Empire, and on every quarter of our extensive frontier, all those quarrels, wars, and disturbances and depredations which are now nearly entirely crushed.'[4]

'The Governor-General, in some of his despatches, distinctly says that he contemplates in the discord of the native powers an additional source of strength; and, if I am not mistaken, some of his plans go directly, and *are designed* to foment discord among those states. To foment discord seems to me barbarous, unwarrantable, and

[1] Letter, 9 October 1831 (hitherto unpublished: from Mr. Philip Morrell's collection of Bentinck papers).

[2] Letter to Sherer, 12 February 1806.

[3] Letter to Sherer, 18 December, 1805. [4] *Ibid.*

monstrous; and even to contemplate in it any source of strength is unworthy of our preeminent station. Such a policy at best can only be suited to petty estates. Applied to our empire in India it is extremely filthy. Lord Wellesley's desire was to unite the tranquillity of all the powers of India with our own. How fair, how beautiful, how virtuous, does this system seem; how tenfold fair, beautiful, and virtuous when compared with the other ugly, nasty, abominable one!'[1]

But this policy of profiting by the heathen's silly habit of raging together (and of encouraging that raging whenever it showed signs of dying down) was accepted by others besides Barlow. Elphinstone's blithely unethical advice[2] to a Committee of the House of Commons, in 1832, represents views formed in this earlier period. Lord Wellesley himself had begun the process of deliberate sacrifice of the Rajput states; and that placidly non-moral person, his brother, writing from England, told Malcolm (31 July 1806) that in his opinion the Maratha lions might with propriety have been tossed a few Christians of their own, instead of being so roughly chased away by British armies. He had thought, in 1804, 'that the Rajpoots ought to have been subjected to the control of Scindiah's Government, as the only mode of re-establishing it in the state in which it must exist, if it is to exist at all'—though he adds that he is not 'sufficiently acquainted with all that has passed between the Rajpoots and our Government' since Monson's defeat, to be able to judge if the former should be handed over to Sindhia now.[3] While regretting 'that it has been necessary to allow Holkar to exist and to be at large', Arthur Wellesley warned his correspondent that 'men in power in England think very little' of India 'and I really believe that in the opinion of the majority of people in this country, it would have been better to cede the whole of Oude'—which for thirty years had been helplessly an apanage of the Company—'to Holkar, than to continue the war with him'. He himself—on the general question of these Native States—always thought that these disorderly princelings served a purpose. He had fought the war, when it came, in his phlegmatic deliberate terrible fashion, and had smashed Sindhia and the Bhonsla utterly. But he never pretended that he thought it either necessary or right, and almost up to the moment of its outbreak told his own intimates that the Company would be wise to see to its own affairs, using the Marathas as a cesspit into which undesirables might be tumbled, and as a means of awing the Nizam:

'There may be some who imagine that the best thing that could

[1] *Selections from the Papers of Lord Metcalfe*, 7.

[2] Quoted in this book, p. 271.

[3] *Life of Malcolm*, i. 534 ff.

happen to us would be to see the Mahratta government crumble to pieces, and upon its ruins the establishment of a number of petty states. With those who think thus I differ entirely. Not only we should not be able to insure the tranquillity of our own frontiers, and could not expect to keep out our enemy, but we should weaken the only balance remaining against the power of the Nizam. This, it is true, is contemptible at present, but in the hands of able men might be turned to our disadvantage . . . we ought to have such a balance as would always keep the Nizam's state in order. With this view the Mahratta power, as it stood prior to Lord Cornwallis's war, ought to be preserved if possible, and we ought with equal care to avoid its entire destruction and the junction in one body of all the members of the Mahratta empire.'

Barlow interfered only when the Company's interests demanded it. Thus, when the Nizam (not unnaturally thinking that the British, withdrawing from Rajput and Maratha affairs, might withdraw from his also) was discovered to be restive under his alliance, he was sharply called to order and the intrigue scotched. Similarly, Barlow refused to weaken the Treaty of Bassein and was against abandoning it, holding that the connection with the Peshwa was essential to British safety. But Central India was given over to rapine, as outside the sphere of British interests.

The second consideration that may be urged in Barlow's defence is the new conscience stirring at home, which it is usual in derision to style the Exeter Hall spirit. This spirit was to force abolition of the slave trade and ultimately of slavery itself: to humanize the penal code: and to compel in India the prohibition of human sacrifice, suttee, and thuggee. It was now hostile to Lord Wellesley's wars.

Thirdly, Lord Wellesley's habitual disobedience and insolence to the Court of Directors made his employers determine to pull their servants back to obedience and unambitious ways. Lord Cornwallis told Sir George Barlow, 6 January 1805, that 'Lord Wellesley's neglect and contemptuous treatment of the Court of Directors' was 'exceedingly embarrassing to the King's Government'.

Finally, the Company's finances were ravaged to an extent that looked like inescapable ruin. (How they were later repaired is a question into which few who are sensitive about our national record would care to look too closely.) Wellesley's own Accountant-General has put it on record that the war with Tipu, which preceded that with the Marathas, began with a debt of £7,500,000. The deficit on the year 1797–8 alone was 33 lakhs of rupees. At the end of October 1805, the Paymaster to Lord Lake's army had sent in no accounts to the Military Audit-General since September

1804, although 'during the last six months the Army and the Paymaster have been quietly settled in cantonments'. In other words, finance had been abandoned in despair. Auxiliaries and regulars alike were in arrears of pay, regions were devastated. Peace was necessary, and it came; and the Indian Government settled down—by retrenchment, by pressure upon such dependents as the Nawab of Oudh, and by the export of opium ('I approve of the opium monopoly, because it enables us to draw a large revenue from a foreign country', wrote Tucker,[1] 4 October 1806)—to restore the land which had been reduced to misery.

[1] H. St. G. Tucker, *Review of Indian Finance*, cited by Kaye in *Life of Tucker* 86.

XXIV

THE WAR'S RESULTS

But what good came of it at last? Quoth little Peterkin.—*Robert Southey,* The Battle of Blenheim.

A strange and unknown and volcanic force made its way through the soft and yielding strata of Indian society and crystallized them into their present form.—*Sir Lepel Griffin,* Ranjit Singh, 14.

So ENDED the Second Anglo-Maratha War. Its importance lay not in any territorial acquisitions, but in political and psychological changes.

The 'Princes', as we know them, were disentangled from India's confused polity. The Indian Prince, far from being, as most suppose, an impressive survival from antiquity, as such entitled to the veneration called forth by the spectacle of never-challenged right, is the creation of Lord Wellesley, in his half-dozen years of daemonic activity. It required a subsequent war and settlement, a dozen years later, to determine the Princes' rights and status. But the Order, as we know it, was now established.

The Company withdrew officially behind the Jumna. But it could not withdraw in fact. The shadow of its irresistible strength hung over Native India as a constant challenge and possible menace. 'Sovereigns you are and as such must act', cried Metcalfe. Sindhia had obtained what he desired, recognition of right to territories held by original grant from the Peshwa. But British protection and faith were pledged to 'upwards of a hundred persons', including *jagirdars* (estate holders), west of the Jumna.

The Peshwa's own position was now that of a definite princeling, only rather more dependent than most. His administration remained unchanged from the Duke of Wellington's description of it. 'The only principle' of his 'government at present (excepting, indeed, jealousy of my influence)' was a 'system of revenge', joined to resentment towards the Power that had circumscribed his limits and given him his status. It was not possible for the Company to draw a cordon round its possessions, and give leave for anarchy to revel outside, while forbidding it to wash against its barriers and over them.

'Our policy and our arms', observed Arthur Wellesley, 'have

reduced all the powers in India to the state of mere ciphers.'[1] Bengal, 'the paradise of nations',[2]

'enjoys the advantage of a civil government, and requires its military force only for its protection against foreign enemies. All the other barbarous establishments called governments, without excepting even that of Fort St. George, have no power beyond that of the sword. Take from them the exercise of that power, and they have no other; and can collect no revenue, can give no protection, and can exercise no government. The Native governments, I mean those of the Nizam and the Peshwah, are fifty times worse than ours in this respect. They do not choose to keep armies themselves, their territories are overrun by a race of armed men, who are ready to enlist with any body who will lead them to plunder.'

This state of things was bound to be brought to a sharp conclusion, sooner or later, and this must be done by the same Power that had precipitated it. Twelve years of sheer misery lay before northern and central India—during which men asked themselves increasingly, and asked the Company's Residents, if there were no controlling authority over all this anarchy.

'This truth of old was sorrow's friend:
Things at the worst must surely mend.
The difficulty's then to know
How long oppression's clock can go.'

The Mogul Emperor

At the head of all the Princes now told to hold their place, and plunder within their alleged confines, had been the Mogul Emperor, to whom Nizam and Marathas and Rajputs all rendered nominal allegiance. After his rescue or capture (whichever way we regard it) by Lake, he was given reason to consider himself still the acknowledged suzerain of the sub-continent, including the Company and their possessions. In his case, what was considered the indignity of a formal treaty was waived. 'The Governor-General does not deem it advisable to enter into any written engagement whatever with His Majesty; nor is it His Excellency's intention to solicit any concession.'[3] Nevertheless, the Resident at Delhi gave him a paper next year, legalizing the terms of his relationship with the British. He had survived the tempests and was still in a place apart, beyond and above the warring and plotting mob of Rajas and Nawabs.[4] He was 'the King' (by his

[1] 27 December 1804: to Major Shawe.

[2] Wellington's own quotation marks, possibly sardonic.

[3] Declaration of November 1804. See Edmonstone's letter to Ochterlony, 16 November: *I.O.R., H.M.S.*, 708, pp. 53 ff.

[4] For fuller details, see my *Metcalfe*, chap. ix.

new title), and 'His Majesty', where the others were merely Highnesses. By Wellesley's settlement, he kept all that the heart of Majesty might wish, so far as sounding titles and the pomp of outward deference went. But all that he was given of actual authority (and the giving must be considered generosity) was a tiny kingdom round Delhi, in whose administration he was not to interfere, though Muhammadan courts were instituted and revenues collected in his name, and officers appointed by him, in agreement with the British Resident.

This, in the opinion of many, was far too much. Colonel David Ochterlony wrote to Edmonstone,[1] 30 November 1804, 'earnestly requesting, from a knowledge of the disposition and temper of his Majesty and his probable successor', that the Emperor should be pensioned off, with fixed stipend. Any lands assigned to him would 'be unproductive of the real value', would 'flatter the pride' of His Majesty and 'open a path to grants which would in a short time' deprive him of all territory, for his bounty had been consistently 'weak, ill-placed, and indiscriminate'. The Resident's controlling power could not prevent oppression outside Delhi, 'and exorbitant taxation' inside it. His probable successor opened up even more alarming prospects, being 'imbecility personified, and under the guidance of a woman of low extraction . . . weak, proud, and in the highest degree avaricious and rapacious'.

Ochterlony, besides being one of the small band of British who combined in equal degree genuine sympathy with and insight into Indian feeling with the common sense of their own race, was fully justified in this advice, by what had happened in Madras during the appalling alliance between the Nawab of Arcot and dishonest officials. But Barlow had a quality which has been overlooked, that of choosing representatives who, whatever their other shortcomings, were perfectly adapted to carry out his plans. He had been so long in India, and, above all, so long at the Central Government, that he knew to a nicety the characters of all the men available. Ochterlony was sent away from Delhi, and in his place was appointed as Resident Archibald Seton. Seton, himself hard-working to an almost insane degree, and humble and self-effacing, entered enthusiastically into Barlow's (which, in fairness it must be remembered, was also Wellesley's) desire to pay every possible attention 'to the feelings of his Majesty'. In a short time, he had built up again in Delhi expectations that were troublesome to the Supreme Government throughout the next half-century.

[1] That is, in reality to the Governor-General. Edmonstone, of all his servants, notoriously was closest to Lord Wellesley's mind.

The Princes

By the 1806 settlement, the Peshwa, the other main prop of Indian eighteenth century politics, now ceased to be anyone's suzerain. The Nizam and the four great Maratha chiefs all now entered into direct and individual subordination to the Company, and the Maratha confederacy was a matter of history only. Even Holkar, after two years of chase and flight, was as rigidly pinned down as Sindhia; and both were—for the first time—'Princes'. The Jumna, as we have seen, was the boundary between the Princes and the foreign substance now so firmly wedged into India's body politic and territorial. Beyond the Jumna, such minor chieftains as the cis-Satlej Sikh rulers of Patiala, Faridkote, and Jind, who had made a technical appearance on (or near) the battlefield of Delhi as Sindhia's vassals, now were dismissed again —after their brief sojourn under the shadow of the Company's power—into whatever uncovenanted mercies they could find in the no man's land between the Marathas and Ranjit Singh in the Punjab. We shall hear of them again, as also of the 'King of Delhi'. But for the present Barlow—under instructions—had made a peace; whose transitory and deceptive character he further emphasized by throwing to the outer wolves one or two more minor princes, beyond those whose bodies he had engaged to deliver up.

XXV

THE PSYCHOLOGICAL CHANGE IN THE CONQUERORS

THE PSYCHOLOGICAL revolution caused by the war has been indicated. It deserves a further word.

The British are notoriously phlegmatic, and their reputation for stolidity, one presumes, must not be gainsaid. *Securus judicat orbis terrarum.* Yet, as they found themselves masters where mighty names, such as Babar and Akbar, had preceded them, they felt themselves stirred. When they followed Holkar across the Satlej, the ever-present thought was that they were marching where Alexander had come, more than two milleniums before them. They were watering their horses in Hydaspes and Hyphasis! They were now definitely the lords of India, and their mercantile character an anachronism. Nothing could stand against them; it was merely a question of a little time, until their ravaged finances had recovered and new means had somewhere emerged, and while they were waiting these Indian states would be steadily and inevitably weakening yet further. The kingdom and the power and the glory were theirs.

The victors, then, in that remote region of majestic streams and in sight of the world's grandest mountains, stood still for a moment, astounded and awed by sense of their place in a great pageant and procession of life and history. Where 'Alexander erected twelve massy altars as the memorial of the pride of conquest, there the power of a hyperborean nation, whom he would have designated as barbarous, had, after the lapse of many ages, made the same river witness to the settlement of an honourable union'.[1]

Such sentiments may seem to our own epoch childishly fanciful. But they played a part in determining men's actions, more than a century ago, as they played a part also in Palestine and Mesopotamia, less than a generation ago. It was now that the sense of their Indian destiny took hold of men—not, as formerly, of an occasional man only, a Warren Hastings or a Thomas Munro—but of the generality who did the rank-and-file work of fighting and administering. Before this war there had always been a

[1] Thorn, 499.

reasonable chance that the British might relinquish India, as the Portuguese and Dutch and French had done. After it, there was none, unless all India could be welded into one tumult and passion of resistance, which was impossible. Something of this realization, that nations had again reached a place where their destinies were settled for a great while to come, was in the minds of the Sikhs also, whose outwardly friendly *sirdars* watched the military evolutions performed on the Punjab plains, for their delight (and instruction). It is noted by the war's historian that when these evolutions were over and Holkar's treaty signed, and no further excuse remained for continuing in the Land of the Five Rivers, 'our departure was very satisfactory to the Seiks'.

Beyond question, it must have been. There had been an inroad of all-conquering Martians; they had gone away again for a season, and the land's natural inhabitants might sink back to their own ways and find comfort in their own festivals, with thankfulness to the gods who had shown them so great destruction yet had preserved them. Ranjit and his people celebrated the Holi, 'unembarrassed by the presence' of the invaders, 'with joy and rejoicings commensurate to the fears they had entertained'.[1] Ranjit himself paraded on an elephant, in company with his favourite courtesan, drunk in public sight; and his excesses brought on a disease which for four months confined him to his house. His followers breathed more freely, and hoped they might be able to forget the peril that had so lately walked within their borders.

> 'History, not wanted yet,
> Leaned on her elbow, watching Time, whose course,
> Eventful, should supply her with a theme.'

[1] Henry T. Prinsep, *Origin of the Sikh Power in the Punjab*, 46.

PART II
BRITISH PARAMOUNTCY

XXVI. MUTINIES. THE CHAOS OF CENTRAL INDIA

THE VELLORE MUTINY

SIR GEORGE BARLOW, Acting Governor-General, had reason to think his appointment would be confirmed. But the British Ministry, determined to recover patronage from the Directors' hands, in 1807 appointed Lord Minto, and sent Barlow to Madras as Governor. He might have returned to Calcutta as Governor-General later; but did not, because of two mutinies in his Presidency, which alarmed the Directors. Since he was still in Bengal when the first occurred, he escaped blame for it. But the second took place while he was Governor of Madras, and it finished his chances.

The earlier mutiny was at Vellore, where Tipu's numerous family resided. They were assumed to have been cognisant of it, and may have been. But their countenance (if they gave it) was not the cause of the outbreak, which was because the authorities were completely out of touch with Indian opinion—a fact which Munro, Arthur Wellesley, and others had long lamented. Since it was crushed immediately, amid a fury of indignation, the fault was in no degree remedied.

The mutiny was caused by Sir John Cradock, the Madras Commander-in-Chief, who issued new regulations to stiffen the sepoys' appearance of efficiency. They were required to wear a hatlike turban, to cut their moustaches in a prescribed fashion, to clean-shave their chins, and to give up earrings and caste marks. These regulations were taken as signs of the Government's intention to convert its troops compulsorily to Christianity, which 'popular opinion in India . . . is wont to regard rather as an impure mode of life, associated with the wearing of hats, the eating of beef and pork, the drinking of spirits, and the neglect of personal purity, than as a system of lofty theological doctrine'.[1] No one willingly consents to be made into something more objectionable than Providence intended him to be, and in May 1805 a company stationed at Vellore 'firmly but respectfully' rejected the new headgear on religious grounds. Beveridge (writing three-quarters of a

[1] *Oxford History of India*, 610.

century ago, when England was much exercised over albs and surplices and chasubles) observes: 'when it is considered how much commotion the subject of man millinery has produced, and is producing, in one of the most enlightened churches of Christendom, it is impossible to deride the honest scruples of the childish and ignorant sepoy'.[1]

It did not, however, prove impossible at the time, and nineteen of the protestants were court-martialled by the Madras authorities. Two received 900 lashes each. The rest were sentenced to 500 lashes, but pardoned on promise to submit to the thing they abominated. A Hindu and a Mussulman were officially consulted; they reported that the changes did not imperil their respective religions, so the matter was regarded as finished. Hence the angry sense of betrayal felt when, on 10 July 1806, the 1,500 sepoys at Vellore attacked the 370 Europeans there, massacred more than a hundred, and besieged the rest in the fort above the main gateway.

The news reached Arcot, sixteen miles away, by six o'clock of the same morning. Two hours later, Colonel Gillespie raced up with European and Indian cavalry. He passed through the two outer gates, which the mutineers had left open, and the beleaguered men above the third gate swung him up by a rope.[2] Presently his galloper guns arrived, and blew in the gate. Vellore was recovered within a quarter of an hour, the rebels putting up a very poor resistance. Four hundred of them were killed, including over a hundred taken prisoner and lined up against a wall and shot with canister. More orderly executions and other punishments followed by course of law. They did not go so far as to include the Muslim Princes, whom Gillespie considered guilty, by what may be styled *prima-facie* evidence:

'If a man is to judge by physiognomy, the Prince Moiz-ud-Din's countenance most decidedly convicts him. I visited him early this morning: he and his family had been the whole night at prayers, a thing very unusual'.[3]

However, Tipu's family were removed to Madras, and ultimately to Calcutta. Lord William Bentinck, the Governor of Madras, and Sir John Cradock were recalled to England.

The new turban had caused trouble in Hyderabad also. But the commander of the subsidiary force waived its use, pending the result of representations to headquarters, and disaffection vanished.

[1] *History of India*, ii. 814.

[2] Often said to have been improvized of belts. Gillespie's own account shows that this was not so.

[3] British Museum MSS. See, for Gillespie's misunderstanding of what was merely a marriage feast, Eric Wareham, *The Bravest Soldier*, 119.

BARLOW'S FINANCIAL POLICY

Exigencies, as well as his own temperament, were to blame for some of the shortcomings of Barlow's administration. When Lord Cornwallis took over from Lord Wellesley, the pay of Lake's army was in five months' arrears; the new irregulars, recruited largely from Maratha deserters, were also unpaid—they must have wondered why they were not allowed to collect their own emoluments, as when they were in Sindhia's or Holkar's service. Cornwallis, and then Barlow, turned most of them adrift, 'men who lived only by the sword' and must live by it now. In the European services also, Barlow, having no choice to do otherwise, drove the work of retrenchment on, urging Madras and Bombay to imitate Bengal, and 'to establish a system of the most rigid economy through every branch of their civil and military expenditure' and 'to abrogate all such charges as were not indispensable to the good government and security of the provinces under their control'. He managed to set the revenue on a sound basis, and if his term of office had not been so brief the surplus due to his efforts would have come in his time.

But he surrounded his name with a cloud of contempt and hatred which has lasted to our own day. The successive wars, with their prize-money and absence of regular audits, had induced a feeling of expansiveness, as in men who in dreams have seen the coffers of Paradise lie open and unguarded. Tucker wrote to Barlow of 'ten or a dozen of the public servants' who 'support something approaching to a royal state'. To cut down such splendour seemed to the men who enjoyed it a dangerous blow at British prestige, which (as they pointed out) weighed far more with them than their own interests and comfort. From every cantonment, a howl went up.

> 'It was not only in Lord Lake's camp that the utmost indignation was excited, and the bitterest enmity provoked. There was hardly a native Court, with a Residency or a Commissionership attached to it, in which a group of political officers did not tremble for the security of their old gains, whilst the lavish expenditure in which they had been wont unquestioned to indulge was now regarded by Government as profligacy, and denounced a crime. From one end of the country to the other, sinecurists and monopolists were smitten with dismay.'[1]

Even Charles Metcalfe[2] wrote angrily to his friend Sherer

[1] Kaye, *Life of H. St. G. Tucker*, 197.

[2] But he was very young (four days short of twenty-one). A fortnight later, Metcalfe admitted 'that the principle laid down for the retrenchments is good. As for individual feelings, they must suffer.'

(26 January 1806) about 'the furious zeal for reduction . . . without any steps to make a recompense'.

Lord Minto's Arrival

Lord Minto reached Calcutta, 3 July 1807. As Sir Gilbert Elliot, he had been one of the managers appointed by the House of Commons to conduct the impeachment of Warren Hastings, and India was an old interest of his. He proved an admirable Governor-General, quiet and friendly, a change from both the excitable Wellesley and the frozen Barlow. His private letters are witty and observant, strangely modern in tone. On the whole, he obeyed the Directors' orders to refrain from interference with native states. But a certain amount of interference took place, and its trend was inevitably towards their ultimate complete subordination, which obviously could not be far off.

In 1807, in Bundelkhand, which Amir Khan intermittently infested, the British learnt that India contained codes of honour as fantastic as those of Regency London, though in different kind. Lakshman Daua, a chieftain of free companies, who thought that, like other successful adventurers, in the general pacification he should be allowed to keep what he had conquered, was ejected from his fort of Ajagarh. Disappearing for a time, he turned up at Calcutta, with a request that he might be either restored or else blown from a gun. Neither request was granted. Meanwhile, his father-in-law, a supposedly quiet old man, had been given charge of his family, kept as hostages in Ajagarh. He carried out this duty by putting all to death (by request, their own), and then sat down, sword in hand, before their apartments, to await the inevitable investigations. When these came, he completed his trust by killing himself. This spirited action was strongly approved by other chieftains, and Colonel Martindale, who had taken Ajagarh, had to conduct a difficult warfare in Bundelkhand for some years. It died down finally by compromise. In 1809, Gopal Singh, a leader whose capture had proved impossible, was quieted by being made a respectable territorial chief. In 1812, Kalinjer, another fortress, was attacked unsuccessfully, but its possessor surrendered on terms. The Raja of Rewa was then brought into the British system, and made to promise to keep peace with his neighbours.

In three widely separate regions—Travancore, Rajputana, and the Punjab—the Company's actions had rather more important results.

Travancore, an old ally in the Mysore wars, was in great misery, 'shockingly misgoverned',[1] 'among the most scandalously misgoverned of Indian states'.[2] An earlier treaty, that of 1795, had pressed leniently on the Prince, whose territories were guaranteed in return for his obligation to help with what troops he could provide, if the Company needed them. In 1805, a new treaty, which the Raja continued to assert was forced upon him, changed this for an obligation to pay for a subsidiary force of four battalions. The tribute fell into arrears, and the Raja and his Resident entered on a long wrangle as to whether he could afford the subsidiary troops. It was clear to the Company that his own troops were a wanton extravagance, and should be disbanded, a prospect which the troops themselves disliked. The Raja, agreeing with them, entered into negotiations with the neighbouring state of Cochin, and made warlike preparations. When the Madras Government got ready an expeditionary force to quell him, he pretended to repent. But, a little after midnight, 28 December 1808, the Resident was attacked in his house. He escaped by hiding himself, and afterwards managed to reach a British ship. Thirty European soldiers on another ship, one of several that were bringing reinforcements to the Residency, were lured ashore and drowned, tied in pairs back to back, an atrocity which moves Thornton to his often-quoted conclusion, that it

> 'would almost seem to justify the opinion avowed by some Europeans who have enjoyed the best means of judging of the state of Travancore, that in turpitude and moral degradation its people transcend every nation upon the face of the earth.'[3]

A short war followed, in which both Cochin and Travancore were quickly conquered. The Dewan of Travancore, the moving spirit of the troubles, was repudiated by the Raja, and committed suicide in a temple; his brother was hanged. The whole episode is a queer anticipation of the Manipur one of 1891.

Thornton, who takes a thoroughly gloomy view of the people of India during this period, observes that 'it appears that the Mahratta character is true to nothing but its own inherent depravity'. And, certainly, in this last decade of independence the Maratha chieftains present a picture equally fantastic and repelling. Holkar, returned from his long and devious flight before the British armies, decided to meet his financial difficulties in the way that the Paramount Power always recommended, by discharging 20,000 of his horsemen. They disapproved, and disapproval was heightened by the circumstance that their pay was in arrears.

[1] *Oxford History of India*, 615. [2] Thornton, *History of India*, iv. 118.
[3] *Ibid*, iv. 122.

Accordingly, they placed him in *dharna*, the time-honoured Indian method of 'going on strike', later to be made familiar by Mr. Gandhi. To free himself, Holkar gave them his nephew as a hostage, whereupon the fasting pretorians made the nephew the state's ruler. Holkar, however, still had the infantry with him; and he managed to pacify the cavalry, by exacting their pay from the Raja of Jaipur, one of its allies whom the Company had cast to the wolves. His mind was made up to run no further risks, and both his nephew and his half-brother Kasi Rao Holkar (whose rights had so exercised Lord Wellesley) were now eliminated.

In the remorse that followed, the dark insanity which had always lurked in Holkar's brain began to range unchecked. He made preparations for a new and vaster war against the British, while keeping himself madly excited with brandy.[1] His brain's fever was aggravated by fierce labour at his own cannon foundries, where in three or four months this Peter the Great *manqué*—as, in his energy and command of men and his habits of personal manual effort and interest in arms and their making, we may term him—cast over two hundred brass guns. In 1808, it became necessary to put him under restraint, and for three years he lived tied up with ropes and fed on milk, until he died, 20 October 1811.

Holkar's State was meanwhile administered, in so far as such a word can be used of what was a ceaselessly seething turmoil, by a regency exercised by Amir Khan and Yeswant Rao's favourite mistress, Tulasi Bai,[2] a woman profligate and vindictive but of great beauty and physical activity. 'She rode (an essential quality in a Mahratta lady) with grace, and was always when on horseback attended by a large party of the females of the first families.'[3] Meanwhile, Amir Khan, when not assisting her inside the Indore sphere of influence, was by no means idle.

It is almost meiosis to style this celebrated man a freebooter, though this was his official reputation. No man, even in Central India, ever had so long a run for his money (or the money he collected from other people, who happened to be insufficiently furnished with guns). Nominally Holkar's dependent (in so far as he possessed any fixity in the Central Indian nightmare), Amir Khan, as Sir Alfred Lyall remarks, 'lived at free quarters for twenty years', raiding widely and continuously, at the head of an

[1] Cherry and raspberry brandy were his favourite drinks. 'The shops of Bombay were drained of these and other strong liquors for his supply': Malcolm, *Central India*, i. 246.

[2] She was about twenty-four when Yeswant Rao Holkar died.

[3] Malcolm.

army which at its height, in 1809, by his own account consisted of 40,000 horse and 24,000 Pindaris, strengthened with artillery.[1] They wandered wherever rumour told of property inadequately guarded. Amir Khan joined Muhammad Khan in 1809 in far-reaching depredations, and offered the Pindaris a settlement on Bundelkhand territory, which would establish them as a threat to the British dominions there.[2]

A year later, Richardson, the Agent to the Governor-General in Bundelkhand, became seriously alarmed.[3] The Company could not allow another Moslem power to rise in Hindusthan on the ruins of the Mogul power, and anyone able to lay hands on revenues could make himself a power. Amir Khan had behind him 'the enthusiasm of a sanguinary and bigoted religion'; the Company should be at pains to destroy any ambitious Mussulman, to 'step in with vigor to nip the evil in the bud'. If tactfully approached, the Marathas might be persuaded to join in hunting him down; Jaipur would help, and Holkar's and Amir Khan's own troops could be persuaded to desert. Only Ranjit Singh might—conceivably—offer him aid. It was a pity that there was no British Agent at Lahore. If war broke out with Amir Khan, it would be well to send one.

Amir Khan's excursions and incursions were seasonable, in the word's rigid sense. Though supported by 'the enthusiasm of a sanguinary and bigoted religion', he was in no way bigoted in his choice of prey. For six months of the year, while the Narbada flowed as a defence to the Nizam, he busied himself in Bundelkhand or other northerly districts. The river fell by the end of October or, at latest, the middle of November, and grew fordable; then, as the flocks of cold weather migrants appeared in the skies, Amir Khan would arrive on the Hyderabad fields. His position was always precarious, but he was not without experience of vicissitude and when things became threatening could look round the Central Indian horizon and see possible allies or points of refuge. There was the Bhonsla Raja, for example. Past history seemed to show that only fear kept him to his engagements with the British Government.[4]

As to Sindhia, he was fully occupied, trying to get rid of turbulent nobles and to meet his debts. His only certain resources

[1] Lyall (*Asiatic Studies*, 192) reduces this figure to 30,000 horse. The number must have varied much and frequently.

[2] *I.O.R., H.M.S.*, 519 (1).

[3] *Ibid*, 519 (1 and 2): 27 June 1810.

[4] *Ibid*, 519 (1).

were his and his family's allowances from the Company. In 1809, he had the good fortune to get rid of Ghatke, who (with Barlow's consent) had been readmitted to his councils. Ghatke at last menaced even Sindhia, who called for help, and in the ensuing struggle a noble transfixed Ghatke with his spear 'and thus rid the world of a being, than whom few worse have ever disgraced humanity'.[1] Sindhia lived always a prey to remorse for the crimes he had countenanced under Ghatke's influence.

In 1810, luck was again kind to him. The death of the suaver but hardly less scoundrelly Ambaji Inglia offered an opportunity, which Sindhia immediately seized, of reducing what had been a practically independent state inside his own dominions. He overran Ambaji's semi-principality of Gohad and established his permanent headquarters at Gwalior, which became the Sindhia capital. He thereby laid to rest a grievance which had rankled ever since Lord Wellesley deprived him of this fortress—as he considered (Malcolm and Arthur Wellesley concurring), by sharp practice and the use of superior power. Though Cornwallis had nominally restored it to him, it had been in possession of his too-powerful vassal.

Sindhia and Holkar no doubt behaved badly. But these chieftains—now that their area of loot was circumscribed and since they dared not disband their forces—had no choice but to quarter the latter out in their own lands, which were soon bled white. There remained then only the expedient of taking famine outside, and glutting it on the Rajput States which the Company had ostentatiously deserted. Udaipur was so continuously devastated that, in 1817, of its 50,000 houses not 3,000 were occupied, the rest having been abandoned and their rafters removed for fuel.

Other states were pillaged even worse. But Udaipur's wretchedness seemed pre-eminent, since it was lit up by the sacrifice of the famous girl-princess, Krishna Kumari, in 1807. Her story has stirred Indian imagination as poignantly as anything in Sanskrit legend. It was noticed by the British at the time, and in a manner that deserves a moment's examination.

Barlow's happy expression of his anticipation, when he withdrew from Central India, that Sindhia and Holkar would now busily weaken each other, has been censured as unworthy of the head of a civilized administration. But political cynicism, only occasionally cloaked under pompous talk of lofty purpose, had taken possession of the period; in spirits like Malcolm and Tod you are aware of a deep feeling of helplessness and humiliation.

[1] Grant Duff, iii. 324.

There was a conflict of States, Jaipur and Jodhpur, for the hand of the Udaipur princess, Krishna Kumari, and it was argued that her father, the Maharana, had entered into contradictory arrangements. In Calcutta this was a topic for jocosity, so far from Central India's misery was the capital of British power. The Accountant-General wrote playfully:

'The Rajpoot Rajahs are about to take up arms for the purpose of deciding their claims to the fair hand of the Princess of Oudipoor; and as Scindiah feels deeply interested in the question, and Holkar is supposed to be not altogether indifferent to the young lady's fate, hopes may be entertained that she will make a very desirable diversion in our favor. The gallantry of our Alexanders, however, if they were left to themselves, would, I believe, induce them to take a very active part in resolving this connubial difficulty.'[1]

Krishna Kumari herself settled the difficulty by drinking poison (a solution suggested by Amir Khan), which she did with a courage and composure beyond all praise. 'Women', was Prinsep's pitiless comment, reflecting the amused carelessness of British Calcutta, 'should die young and by violent means, if they desire the reputation of their beauty to live with posterity. . . . Her story deserves well to be commemorated in a Melo-drama.' On the whole, the usual judgment that Sir George Barlow's administration touched the lowest depth of meanness in the British record in India is not unfair.

In January 1809, Amir Khan ventured outside the area where rapine was admittedly in order. He took a chance in the Bhonsla Raja's territories, nominally on behalf of the now incapacitated Holkar, and demanded the restoration of jewels of which his master had been pillaged at an earlier period of his tempestuous career, at a time when he had taken refuge in Berar. The Bhonsla Raja had no subsidiary alliance, having steadfastly refused one, and by the strict letter of the British engagements should have been left to make what defence he could. Lord Minto, however, with characteristic common sense and refreshing honesty wasting no words over his high aims and intentions, acted, with inconsistency indeed, but rightly. He wrote to Holkar to ask if Amir Khan were really acting by his orders. Holkar's minister disavowed the freebooter; and he wrote to Amir Khan, directing him to leave Berar. The Raja, aided by British forces, managed to eject the invaders. Lord Minto then urged on him the acceptance of a subsidiary force, which again he was unwilling to have, though afraid to refuse openly. In the end, he escaped it.

By degrees, the unspeakable wretchedness of Central India

[1] Kaye, *Life of Tucker*, 196. *Kumari* means Princess.

became known in British India and became a source of shame. It grew obvious that there could be but one end, a taking over of responsibility by the Power whose might had shattered such defences as the people had once possessed, and left them exposed to the Amir Khans, Inglias, and Ghatkes.

This period, then, saw the Nizam and Peshwa—by natural process, and almost without overt action—reduced to further subordination, and Cochin and Travancore warred down after a brief rebellion. It saw the Rajput states ravaged by their own dissensions, and by Amir Khan and the Marathas, who in their confined range marched and pillaged, like the Devil in the *Apocalypse*, when he knew his time was short. They were bounded eastward by the Company, and north-westward by the powerful Sikh state which Ranjit Singh had established in the Punjab.

There were signs also that the Company would presently reach out its hands to Sind, that southern lock on the Land of the Five Rivers and on its chief river, the Indus, in especial. In 1809, Lord Minto concluded a Treaty of 'eternal friendship' with its Amirs, and 'the Government of Sindh' promised that it would not 'allow the establishment of the tribe of the French in Sindh'—a promise unnecessary and irrelevant. The tribe of the French were much occupied with troubles in countries very far from Sind.

In 1808, the year previous to the Sind Treaty, the coming paramountcy cast its shadow before, and threw out a veto that bound even Ranjit Singh himself.

XXVII

THE COMPANY'S EMBASSIES

The Growth of Ranjit Singh's Power

At the conclusion of the protracted war with Yeswant Rao Holkar, when British armies in pursuit of him entered the Punjab the small Sikh states on the southern bank of the Satlej—Nabha, Jind, Patiala, Faridkote—had come under Company suzerainty. They did this in the vaguest manner possible, neither paying tribute nor obtaining any promise of protection.

Presently the British withdrew, and Ranjit proceeded to establish himself firmly along the Satlej's northern bank. In 1806, Nabha and Patiala quarrelled. Ranjit sent a courteous note to the British Resident in Delhi (whose Assistant happened to be Charles Metcalfe, now a veteran of twenty-one): he crossed the river, and made both parties accept his settlement of their differences. Next year, in the course of the secular squabble between the Rani and Raja of Patiala[1] the lady invited his arbitrament. Ranjit came and gave it, and went back with rewards of a valuable diamond necklace and a celebrated gun which he had long coveted. Guns and horses were Ranjit's passions, though the ferocity with which he pursued them has been much exaggerated.

Ranjit was a type of man new to the Company's servants and not repeated since. He was a conqueror who disliked bloodshed, and in his administration he was infinitely more merciful than any European state. 'Never perhaps was so large an empire founded by one man with so little criminality.'[2] 'His triumphs', wrote even Metcalfe, 'seem in general to be bloodless. . . . Where he sees an inclination to oppose, he appears to act with caution, and not to be too eager in attacking.[3] Where he thinks the instant and complete subjection of a chief or place doubtful, he is willing to temporize; content with a small acknowledgment of his superiority as a beginning, he leaves the completion of his plan to another time.' Henry Fane, next to Ochterlony the ablest soldier among Ranjit's British contemporaries, wrote: 'As evidence of being a really good

[1] See p. 128 of this book. [2] Prinsep.

[3] This was not due to lack of physical courage. He was 'extremely brave, a quality rather rare among Eastern princes' (Jacquemont, *Letters from India*, 173).

man may be cited the fact of his having never put a man to death for even the most heinous crime.' Osborne, who visited him nearly thirty years later, in Lord Auckland's governor-generalship, bore the same testimony. 'Except in actual open warfare he has never been known to take life, though his own has been attempted more than once, and his reign will be found freer from any striking acts of cruelty and oppression than those of many more civilized monarchs.'[1] I believe that Metcalfe's own astonishing record, a few years later,[2] although it was a continuation of Seton's practice in Delhi before him, was largely due to the fact that he learnt, during his sojourn with Ranjit Singh, that a government could be strong without incessant executions such as happened in Metcalfe's own land.

Ranjit's faults were of other kinds: his notorious pederasty,[3] to which physical necessity early persuaded him and which increased with age,[4] his scant regard for good faith or his word. His intellectual curiosity was great[5] but never at one stay. 'His conversation', said Jacquemont, 'is like a nightmare.' But Europeans found him easy to work with. Though 'remarkably shrewd in seeing through dubious adventurers and getting rid of them', Ranjit trusted those he decided to employ. 'When M. Allard has reason to complain of him, he is not afraid to treat him coldly for a month or two, and so manages to make him revoke the measure which has justly annoyed or affronted him.'

[1] *The Court and Camp of Runjeet Singh*, 94–5. Prinsep says the same: 'He has never taken life, even under circumstances of aggravated offence.' Ranjit occasionally inflicted mutilation but (by contemporary standards) not seriously. He did not as a rule go so far as to maim: at least, I have not come across any instance of his doing this. On 18 July 1815, for example, he ordered the ears and noses of fifteen thieves to be cut off (*Events at the Court of Ranjit Singh, 1810–1817:* translated from papers in the Alienation Office, Poona: edited by H. L. O. Garrett and G. L. Chopra).

[2] 'The Governor of a territory 150 miles long and the same broad, almost without control, from the distance of the Supreme Government, with the power of life and death in my own hands (I thank God that having this power for eight years I never inflicted death but once, and that was for a vile unprovoked assassination).' Charles Metcalfe, 24 June 1820: Edward Thompson, *Life of Lord Metcalfe*, 124.

[3] Jacquemont, *Letters from India*, 173. 'He is a shameless rogue who flaunts his vices with as little embarrassment as Henri III used to do in our country.'

[4] *Ibid*, 171 and *passim*. See also Osborne, and any contemporary witness, also *passim*.

[5] Jacquemont found him 'almost the first inquisitive Indian I have seen, but his curiosity makes up for the apathy of his whole nation'.

Captain Matthews in Lahore

In the spring of 1808, a Captain Matthews, incapacitated from service by loss of a leg and therefore on half pay, travelled in the Punjab for pleasure and camped eighteen miles east of Amritsar. A friendly person, he wrote enthusiastically that he found it

'impossible to fancy myself in a foreign Country, the Inhabitants are so very attentive, and seem to look upon me as their Deliverer. . . . I do think the Siques and Singhs the very best people in Hindustan, approaching much nearer to the European Character than any of the other Classes. I am constantly applied to for Wine, and had I brought a hundred Dozens I could have got rid of it by according to their wishes.'

Nothing, Captain Matthews thought, could have been jollier. The Singhs

'bear a great similarity of Character to British Sailors, spending their money as fast as they get it in the pleasures of Women and Wine. The Concourse of fine Women who go to bathe at the Temple in a morning is prodigious, they are far superior in Symetry of Person and beauty of Countenance to those of any part of India I have seen.'

British prestige stood high, and did not depend solely on the islanders' capacity to enjoy strong drink; the Singhs were aware that the English had other activities. The name of Lord Lake was better known than that of Alexander, 'whose fame they have as totally forgotten as if he had never come'. The people had never ceased to recall their astonishment when they found their persons and property were safe, during the British incursion in pursuit of Holkar.

There were drawbacks in this popularity, of course. 'The natives here think Europeans know everything',[1] and the blind and aged, as well as the merely sick, flocked to him for healing. Captain Matthews visited the Golden Temple, and distributed (in a very small circle) Rs.200, whereupon the priests told him eloquently what a satisfactory character he was, and how deeply they esteemed such a nation as he represented.

Ranjit Singh, too, was friendly, but with reservations and watchfulness. At first he thought that Matthews must be a spy or agent—and he was right to this extent, that Matthews, like every other officer visiting a strange territory, was expected to send back reports to his Government, and did so. Ranjit wrote to the Indian Government, proposing a treaty of friendship, to be concluded through his visitor.[2] The enemies of either were to be expelled by

[1] Letters to Captain G. F. Fagan, Acting Adjutant-General, 3 and 4 May (*I.O.R.*, *H.M.S.*, 592, 4).

[2] Letter received by Indian Government, 6 July 1808.

the other party, and refused asylum. He was informed, in language unfairly slighting to Matthews, that the latter was a person of no importance, useless for active service, and travelling for mere pleasure. This at once reacted against Matthews, who was presently told that if he had been a gentleman he would have brought letters and presents from the Governor-General. He was obviously an adventurer, out to get a job from the Maharaja, and should be made to sit on the floor, instead of being accommodated with a chair! This unkindness troubled him.

In his expansiveness, Matthews talked to everyone. Ranjit was having trouble with his mother-in-law and one of her daughters, who were intriguing to overthrow him and tried to get Matthews' help. Another item of news sent back by the latter was the extent of disaffection among the subordinate Sikh leaders. He reported also that some of Ranjit's following were urging him to make war on the Company, a project which Holkar too was pressing on him.

Matthews presently returned to British India. Events now began to move faster. Ranjit, who had, he thought, sufficiently established his title to suzerainty of the country between the Satlej and the Jumna, followed this up by a letter asking the Governor-General why a British force was being collected on the Jumna. 'The country on this side of the Jumna, except the stations occupied by the British, is subject to my authority. Let it remain so.'[1]

Charles Metcalfe's Mission

The States fast falling under Ranjit's influence continued to intrigue with both parties; they reminded the Governor-General that they had some claim to be considered the Company's feudatories. Metcalfe was accordingly sent to Lahore, to effect as comprehensive a settlement as possible, 20 June 1808.

His main task was part of a scheme which, a century and more later, we may feel entitled to style grandiose. The Treaty of Tilsit had frightened the British Government. 'The unscrupulous ambition of the great French usurper and the territorial cupidity of the Russian autocrat'[2] were leagued together, and that chief bogy of Indian foreign policy, the dread of Russia, had entered politics, where it was to exercise so disastrous and unnecessary an influence right down to our own times. Minto planned to frustrate this alliance, by a solid block of linked kingdoms between British India

[1] The Chiefs of Jind and Kaital were actually in attendance on Ranjit when official tidings of Metcalfe's coming Mission reached him.

[2] Kaye, *Metcalfe*, i. 239.

and Europe—the Punjab, Afghanistan, Persia. Metcalfe listed, as his 'Main object', 'Counteraction of the designs of the French'. The destiny of the cis-Satlej Sikh States figured amidst a medley of subsidiary objects. Malcolm was again in Teheran, Elphinstone was to go to 'the King of Cabul'. He himself was to be their liaison between Central and Western Asia and British India.[1]

Metcalfe's mind took fire. His boyish dreams were coming to fulfilment! He saw himself sending his own emissaries out into half-legendary regions, and 'baffling the gigantic intrigues of Napoleon and Alexander throughout the whole expanse'[2] of half a continent.

His actual duties proved to be more circumscribed, and infinitely tedious. He found himself negotiating with a will-o'-the-wisp—a will-o'-the-wisp courteous, but full of evasiveness. There were hints of mockery and menace in the quags over which the solemn Englishman was led. Metcalfe complained that Ranjit Singh declined to be categorical. The truth was (as he himself had the frankness to admit, when challenged with it) that it was the Company who were mysterious to the point of provoking dread of their designs. It was all very well to keep on stressing Ranjit Singh's ineradicable jealousy and suspicion. But here was a Mission, forced upon him before he could even say whether it was welcome or not. At its head was a tremendously serious young man who insisted that he had come with earth-shaking news, yet to every request that his important news should be made known quickly continued to ingeminate, 'Not now! not now!' At last this portentously guarded secret was allowed to emerge, and turned out to be a warning that the Governor-General had 'authentic tidings' that a man called Napoleon Buonaparte was going to swallow up Persia, Afghanistan, and then the Sikhs and the Punjab. It is no wonder that when they heard this precious announcement the bearded *sirdars* looked carefully at Metcalfe, and looked carefully at him again—and yet again. He did not *seem* mad, but only too sanely balanced. Then there must be something dark and dreadful behind this Mission, which had been sent all this distance ostensibly to chat about goblins.

Moreover, the question of the Cis-Satlej Sikh chieftains was kept at first in a very subordinate place. Since British historians state otherwise, Metcalfe's own testimony must be cited. 'When I went on that mission it was not in contemplation to protect

[1] For Metcalfe's Mission, see *I.O.R.*, *H.M.S.*, especially folios 511 and 592–5.

[2] Kaye, *Metcalfe*, i. 252.

the chiefs between the Sutlej and the Jumna.'[1] When some of the Cis-Satlej chiefs had sent embassies to Delhi, in 1808, asking to be taken under protection, the reply to them had been that the British Government itself would judge what was necessary, if and when circumstances arose, but was under no obligations to do anything. In consequence, these chiefs had compulsorily all entered into some kind of negotiations with Ranjit Singh and had passed more distinctly under his shadow than under that of the Company. He had made not infrequent incursions across the Satlej, and was admittedly in possession of part of its left bank. He had reason when, at a later stage of the discussions, he asked Metcalfe by what right the British, after deliberately withdrawing protection, now claimed to exercise it. Ranjit 'admitted that at the termination of the Mahratta war, if we had planted a post at Loodhiana, he should have acknowledged our right to do so as the successors of the Mahratta power; but he denied our right to revive at pleasure an obsolete claim, which he had satisfied himself, from our conduct, we had entirely relinquished'.[2]

The chiefs themselves were largely responsible for their difficulties. 'The greater number have become companions of his Harem in order to acquire influence sufficient to ward off his blows from their own territories. . . . They do not scruple to turn his arms against others. Indeed, he first came in because some of them asked his aid against others.'[3]

At first, then, Lord Minto and his Council had not made up their minds about these minor Sikh states. They admitted that British honour was 'in some degree' engaged. The question was: Was it so far engaged that honour should outweigh expediency?

Perhaps it would not have outweighed it. But presently expediency itself came over to the side of honour. It became clear that Ranjit Singh was utterly unimpressed by the French bogy, and the Company themselves learnt from Europe that this bogy—for the time being, at any rate—seemed to have dematerialized. The problem for both parties became simplified, into one of what each could get out of the other.

The home authorities, who grew afraid of finding that they had sent out another annexationist Wellesley, examined very closely

[1] Letter to Richard Jenkins, 3 November 1814.

[2] Kaye, *Selections from Metcalfe's Papers*, 14.

[3] *Ibid*, 20. See also *I.O.R.*, *H.M.S.*, 593. They had frequently acknowledged Ranjit's supremacy, in the usual manner: by gifts. Ochterlony himself admitted (Cunningham, *History of the Sikhs*, 144) that his proclamation in 1809, taking the Cis-Satlej states under British suzerainty, was based on a misunderstanding of their true status.

the reports sent to them, and remarked that the proposal to extend protection over the Cis-Satlej states was a distinct departure from the policy laid down under Barlow. In this opinion the Indian Government had to concur. It *was* a reversal, and Minto so intended it. So, since Ranjit's alliance against the French was obviously going to be worth very little, if accompanied by a rankling grievance for having lost loot on which he had set his heart (and, to a great extent, his actual hands)—and since the French menace now seemed somewhat ridiculous—the Governor-General[1] resolved to take a stand upon the question of the Cis-Satlej states. Metcalfe was so informed. In return, it was recognized that Ranjit must be allowed to compensate himself out of the Afghans (with whom, as represented by the ruler of Kabul, the Company was just now trying to conclude exactly the same kind of treaty) and smaller Mussulman chiefs on his western borders, and out of his Gurkha neighbours in the north-west Himalaya. Things were sorting themselves out, between these three nations who were all alike busied in 'looking for an empire'[2] —the British, the Sikhs, and the Gurkhas.

Metcalfe's difficulties, meanwhile, were no less physical than psychological and political. Ranjit Singh not merely declined to be more categorical than his opponents, he declined to be even localized. He moved from place to place, while Metcalfe followed. He fled to favourite dancing girls,[3] and plunged into deep debauches. He demanded why he must surrender places he had conquered, he grew 'care-worn and thoughtful'. They discussed Holkar, whom Ranjit Singh called 'a pukka rascal' (*haramzada*), to which Metcalfe made the correct reply, 'that when we were at war with him we used to call him a great rascal, but as we were now at peace we always spoke of him with the respect due to a friendly chief'. Ranjit enjoyed this; he seems to have liked the young grave Envoy. Finally, in an interview which the Envoy indicated was meant to be his farewell, Metcalfe gave the stern warning that the Company were determined to take under protection the Cis-Satlej States. Then occurred the famous incident, when Metcalfe saw Ranjit, 'with surprising levity', prancing his courtyard on his favourite horse. The action really indicated the tremendous tension that held him. (Metcalfe did not guess this,

[1] Very strongly influenced by N. B. Edmonstone, 'the ubiquitous Edmonstone'.

[2] Cunningham's phrase (*History of the Sikhs*).

[3] He was so much under the influence of one of them, Marar, that he even struck coins in her name.

but) Ranjit had practically decided to accept war. Metcalfe understood suddenly, when the latter's Minister (his master still engaged in equestrian self-exorcism) presented a reply, which asked why the Company wanted 'a small post on the Sutlej? Surely such a demonstration would not deter the French from advancing!' Metcalfe waived the question of the French, and demanded an immediate answer on the Cis-Satlej states, remaining while Ranjit dismounted and entered into a long council discussion. The upshot was that Metcalfe was informed that the Raja had agreed to his demands.

The Envoy might have been expected to be pleased. But the British, aware of their strength and already forgetful of certain disquieting episodes in the last stages of the Maratha war, were impatient with these Indian royalties, and any hesitation to yield prompt compliance to demands that were put out nominally as requests from one sovereign power to another was treated as impertinence. Metcalfe wrote indignantly:

> 'And so the demands that I had presented, respecting which I had not been able for a fortnight to procure the least answer, were now treated as if they were mere trifles with which there was not the smallest difficulty in complying!'

Hardly so, however, as he was to find. Affairs dragged on, until in January 1809 Colonel David Ochterlony advanced to the Satlej with a detachment that was the vanguard of an army following under General Leger. Neither side was ready to fight, and there was further delay. In February, Metcalfe's Mussulman sepoys offended the Sikhs by parading their Mohurrum *tazia* near the Golden Temple, at Amritsar; and on the 25th, a band of *Akalis*—the 'Immortals', Sikh enthusiasts—attacked his camp and were routed. The incident was decisive. Ranjit, who appeared in person towards the close of the skirmish, was impressed by the efficiency of Metcalfe's escort. He sent troops to protect the Mission; and sent with them his infantry and artillery commanders, and made a special request that Metcalfe would 'cause them to plunder and destroy any village that had behaved in a disrespectful manner'.[1] With great difficulty (as he then believed) Metcalfe dissuaded these officers from so drastic a rebuke. 'They informed me that they had positive orders to plunder the villages, and put to death the inhabitants.' All this, of course, was merely Ranjit's fun, as Metcalfe himself, when he knew Ranjit better, certainly realized. It has, however, been taken at face value by many writers, who have not had Metcalfe's excuse for so taking it at the time.

[1] Kaye, *Life of Metcalfe*, i. 278.

Meanwhile the French were having trouble in Europe. Metcalfe was able therefore to tell Ranjit that there was now no need for a definite treaty between him and the Company, whereupon—to his chagrin—this unaccountable Raja 'did not express the disappointment which I had expected'. But the Governor-General changed his mind again; and the treaty, a very short and simple one, was made, 25 April 1809—under threat of war, Ochterlony being now encamped on the Satlej.

Ranjit Singh lost the Phulkian[1] states, but was allowed to keep such left bank territory as he had acquired on the river before Metcalfe's coming. The treaty provided for perpetual friendship, which as a matter of fact was kept for over thirty-six years. The Cis-Satlej Sikh chiefs were taken over on extremely easy terms, paying no tribute and being left in entire freedom as to internal affairs, required only to help to preserve their own independence, if ever threatened. The home authorities reviewed the proceedings, and gave them their complete if tepid approval. And Ranjit Singh turned his energies northward, to the conquest of Multan (1818), Kashmir (1819), and Peshawar (1823).

One factor that greatly impeded Metcalfe's mission, and deepened that distrust which he found so inexcusable and strange in Ranjit Singh, was his charge to prepare the way for Elphinstone's mission to Kabul. This had necessarily to move across Ranjit's territory, and the Sikh feared that this was the first approach towards annexation of the Punjab, or, at the very least, abrogation of his independence. He feared, too, that the mission would be spying out his resources. In this he was not so unreasonable as has been represented; Metcalfe had been expressly ordered to gather all the information he could, particularly all of military value—and he was a man whose habit was to exceed what was demanded of him, and he did so (emphatically) in this instance.

The British Government learnt, for example, that Ranjit kept all artillery in his own hands (thereby anticipating the British custom after the Mutiny of 1857), and had 40 guns and 100 camel guns on swivels: that he had 6,000 cavalry, 1,500 regular infantry, and 5,000 irregular infantry—might, perhaps, have some 15,000 troops of all sorts, at his utmost strength: that his subordinate chiefs had another 15,000. The Punjab was run on a feudal basis, and Ranjit was therefore free from the cost and bother of a civil government, and was always able to take his place at the head of

[1] Nabha, Patiala, Jind, Sirhind.

his army. 'It is almost incredible, yet it is asserted, that he has scarcely any regular revenue from his Country.'[1]

There was a great deal more of similar useful information. Ranjit can hardly have been ignorant of his visitor's assiduous inquiries, or of the fact that their results were being transmitted to Calcutta. It appeared to him that the Company asked a very great deal—a promise to bear the brunt of a French invasion in which he did not believe but which was represented as something very tremendous and terrible, non-interference south of the Satlej, passage across his lands for a second mission to his prime enemies at Kabul—and in return offered exceedingly little.

Elphinstone's Mission

The British Government intended that Elphinstone should go to Afghanistan, whether with Ranjit's consent and Kabul's consent or against them. He set out, October 1808, but never reached Kabul. As things turned out, this was as well. For Napoleon's sky had again clouded; his armies were caught in the Peninsular campaign and also in renewed hostilities with Austria. The Company therefore economized on the presents they sent, and Elphinstone's embassy proved a sombre comedy, more amusing to-day than he found it at the time.

Moving first through Rajput territory, Elphinstone was mistaken for Amir Khan returning at the head of his brigands. The villagers ran to their thorn hedges, with torches and matchlocks. The Sikhs suspected darkly that the Company was plotting to obtain an Afghan alliance against them, to partition the Punjab. Elphinstone got no further than Peshawar, which was then Afghan soil. He found it hard to persuade the Afghans that his distant Government had gone to all this trouble, because of an enemy so remote as Napoleon, who in these valleys seemed almost mythical! If not mythical, then how terrible and wonderful he must be! They listened sceptically to the Envoy's insistence that the British were really able to look after themselves, and were not begging Kabul for 'protection'.

The Kabul Government asked for aid to suppress the Amir's brother, who was in rebellion. When Elphinstone said he could not promise this, frank surprise was expressed as to why he had come, asking alliance and with nothing to offer in return. The most imaginative and intellectually alert man that ever went to

[1] 8 November 1808. Metcalfe's Mission is treated at length in my *Life of Lord Metcalfe*, pp. 73–102.

India, he understood the situation perfectly, and realized that his Government had merely made fools of themselves. 'It is still dark and gloomy', runs a characteristic entry in his journal, 'and I have been in low spirits all day . . . and fearing no credit will be got or much good done here.' He reported that the Amir was 'incredibly poor' and 'very weak', and controlled only Kabul and Peshawar, with 'a kind of authority over the hills, very short of entire command'. While he waited, the Amir was driven from his kingdom, and the rest of his life was spent as a pensioner of the British in India, except for his exceedingly brief recovery of his rule in the iniquitous war of 1839, which ended in his death and the expulsion of his British allies.

Malcolm's Second Mission to Persia

In his second mission to Persia, Brigadier-General John Malcolm, the senior member of 'the Big Three' of Northern and Central India, slightly preceded his compeers, in 1808. At the very time when Metcalfe set out, he was hanging about in Bushire, and part of Metcalfe's very complicated instructions was to establish a cipher correspondence with him, by means of secret agents, through the Punjab and Afghanistan.

Malcolm, the most popular man in India, was excellent in personal relationships but had moods when he was dictatorial. His mission was a complete failure. Persia was feeling that after his former mission she had been rather excessively left alone by Britain; and now she was being attacked by Russia. In this time of much wooing, a French Embassy promised the intercession of Napoleon, Russia's new ally, and Persia was persuaded to lean in that direction. Malcolm lost his head before what he exaggerated into a crisis, and left in anger, to form schemes for an armed expedition to seize and fortify some island in the Persian Gulf.

The schemes came to nothing. Moreover, the London authorities chose to send an Ambassador of their own, Sir Harford Jones. The British Ministry and the Directors distrusted Malcolm, who was not a King's officer but only a Company's officer and had risen in irregulár and almost disobedient fashion. His lavish expenditure on his former mission was a valid reason for some distrust. The Persians were puzzled by the coming of Jones and his rival mission, which in defence explained that Malcolm's mission had been a very inadequately authorized affair. Lord Minto from India repudiated Jones' mission, which obtained a treaty of not the best kind. This Minto grudgingly accepted. The whole business, from first to last, was not an example of diplomacy at its most efficient.

The best results of the Persian and Afghan missions were two excellent books, by Malcolm and Elphinstone. The former's is written with all its author's lively catholicity of interest, and the latter's abounds in the vivid and imaginative prose of which Elphinstone, alone of British-Indian authors, held the secret.

XXVIII

DOMESTIC TROUBLES AND COLONIAL EXPEDITIONS

The White Mutiny

The main thrust of Minto's administration, though it suppressed internal disorders and pushed the Princes steadily down into subordination, was outside India. Even Metcalfe's Punjab expedition illustrates this, for the Punjab was regarded as being what in many respects it is, part of Central Asia rather than India proper.

Meanwhile, inside India the Company was threatened by what was the only real peril, disaffection in its British personnel. General Macdowall, the Madras Commander-in-Chief, had not been made a Member of Council and felt aggrieved. Presently orders from London compelled the Governor, Sir George Barlow, to abolish an expensive perquisite by which officers who commanded native regiments were allowed the same amount for tent contracts in both war and peace and whether tents were provided or not. A man 'very sparingly endowed with temper and judgment', the Commander-in-Chief fomented senior officers' rage, which rose to fantastic heights. Meetings, amid wild applause, drank seditious toasts and prepared armed rebellion. Masulipatam and Hyderabad were the two most excited centres. The rank and file of the one European regiment in the Presidency, which was stationed at Masulipatam, were drawn into the revolt, and arrested their colonel, bringing in an outside officer to take his place.

Malcolm, himself a Company's officer, sympathized with the bitter feeling that had grown up through many years of subordination to King's officers. He was sent to Masulipatam, to take over the regimental command. Arriving just in time to prevent the mutineers from marching to join their fellow-mutineers at other stations, he found himself among men excited to the point of lunacy, and humoured them by seeming to fall in with their double-edged toasts. One way and another, he secured what he felt entitled to consider a kind of order, and felt he might venture on the introduction of discipline again.

A punishment parade, 14 July 1809, gave him his chance to address the whole regiment publicly. As the ghastly spectacle of floggings was about to commence, 'in that impressive moment, when even the sturdiest heart begins to sicken', Malcolm forgave the condemned, and took occasion to explain that the rumours that the regiment was to be disbanded were false. Even so, he failed in the end, and had to return to Madras, to urge that only a complete climb-down on the Government's part could prevent a general rising. His prestige was badly shaken, and the Madras Council recorded a severe and damaging Minute on his conduct.

At Seringapatam, the revolt came to fighting. The officers seized the treasury and the fort, and two native battalions that were so ill-advised as to march to their assistance were scattered by cavalry, and lost 200 killed and wounded. The self-established garrison in Seringapatam cannonaded the troops sent to effect their submission. But presently the mutineers everywhere gave in, realizing that they were outweighted. The affair died down, after few and grotesquely slight punishments.

The Duke of Wellington wrote from Badajoz to Malcolm (3 December 1809), that nothing could be 'more absurd' than the pretext for what had happened. He made it clear, however, that even his own notorious severity did not prevent him from being willing to take a lenient view of mutiny when the mutineers were European high officers. 'I who have arrived pretty nearly at the top of the tree should be the last man to give up any point of right or military etiquette.' Still, these mutineers, he thought, had gone beyond all reason.

The War in Java

What more than anything else quieted these discontents was the Company's embarkation on vast exploits outside India, bringing exciting occupation and the emoluments that accompanied war. The Mauritius islands were taken in 1809 and 1810; in 1810, the Moluccas; in 1811, Java. Lord Minto in person accompanied the last-mentioned expedition, to make the political arrangements.

The storming of Fort Cornelis, near Batavia, was led by General Rollo Gillespie, the hero of Vellore, who held in his generation a position unique between Clive and the Mutiny names. Britain came into possession of an immense new empire, of which practically nothing was retained for more than a few years, only Mauritius (but not Bourbon) and a few adjacent islets being kept at the general peace in 1815.

The fighting in the East Indies was severe and full of interesting incidents. None of our wars was more picturesque than this one, which has so completely gone from national memory. The British gained glimpses, not only of strange new rich tropical regions, but of Eastern governments that, even after long experience of Indian states, seemed astonishing. For example, at Bali a chief sent the Governor-General a propitiatory present of slaves—five boys between eight and thirteen years, 'all fine, spunky-looking boys',[1] and two girls four or five years old, dressed in their best apparel. Colonel Taylor, a lively person, happened to notice in the corner of the room two spears,

'and of necessity he began tossing and brandishing them about, and at length the scabbards were pulled off the bright blades at the ends of the weapons. The moment this happened the poor boys all huddled together, and the youngest left the rest and came with his little hands joined together, in the most supplicating manner, and with the most imploring face, walking from one of us to the other, and evidently begging for his life, though he did not utter a word, nor even cried; but he appeared terrified. It was like one who had little hope of obtaining his request, and who had been accustomed to consider the thing he feared as a sort of natural doom that was to be expected. It was with some difficulty, even after the spears were removed, that the children were reassured. They certainly thought that they had been dressed out to be sacrificed or put to death for some cause or other, and when they saw the naked points of the spears they thought their time was come. This is the less surprising, as there is every reason to believe that each of them had seen his father put to death by a number of spears, which is a common mode of execution. Next day they were all very merry and happy. . . . The girls will puzzle me most. I have some thought of baking them in a pie against the Queen's birthday.'

Minto found slavery 'established in all these countries to a shocking extent'. The children of slaves continued slaves, and both the Dutch and English Company had multitudes of these. Slavery for debt was common; and for a large debt it overtook the whole family. Wives and children of criminals, after witnessing their executions, were scattered as slaves, as in Warren Hastings' regulations against dacoity, forty years earlier.

Minto went to Malacca, and gave an object-lesson in disapproval of Dutch former colonial methods of justice.

'Finding some instruments of torture still preserved, although they have been long disused, I had the cross upon which criminals were *broken*, and another wooden instrument that had served as a sort of rack, burnt under the windows of a room from which executions are seen by the magistrates, where I and the magistrates were assembled for the purpose; and at the same time various iron articles for screwing thumbs, wrists, and ankles, and other contrivances of that

[1] *Lord Minto in India* (*Life and Letters . . . from 1807 to 1814*), edited by his great-niece the Countess of Minto, 291.

diabolical sort, were carried out in a boat by the executioner into the roads, and sunk in deep water, never to rise or screw poor people's bones and joints again.'

Java gained four years of enlightened administration by the great Sir Stamford Raffles. It went back to the Dutch in 1815.

XXIX

THE MOGUL EMPEROR AND DELHI

METCALFE WAS twenty-one when he was appointed Assistant to the Resident at Delhi. It gives us the measure of the spacious grandeur that had fallen to the British, that his first biographer speaks of this post with scorn, as inadequate to a man of Metcalfe's qualities and experience. Metcalfe himself thought highly of these; when a temporary emergency next year made it necessary for him to serve as Collector of the populous and important station of Saharanpur for one month, he wrote to Sherer in Calcutta:

'You will be able to conceive that my disgust and annoyance is not small in being sent on the insignificant duty of acting as Collector in the absence of Guthrie from his station . . . it may be repeated whenever the convenience of sending me from Delhi to act for any Collector in the vicinity may suggest itself to the wise head of an unaccommodating Secretary.'

The blind old Emperor died, December 1806, and was succeeded by a gentleman whom Metcalfe derisively styled 'the illustrious Ukbar'. He had been born a prisoner, and in later life was compelled to 'exhibit as a dancing boy before Golam Quadir'.[1] He was described by Ochterlony as 'imbecility personified . . . and in the highest degree avaricious and rapacious'. His horde of dependents kept him desperately poor; his monthly stipend of a lakh of rupees a month[2] was quickly eaten up—this, at least, must be remembered in justification of what seemed his avarice and rapacity.

In Delhi, Resident and Assistant pulled together tolerably, but not unanimously. The former, Alexander Seton, stirred Metcalfe to affection and exasperation in almost equal degree. Deeply humble, industrious to the point of eccentricity, he refused to degrade his fine young Assistant by letting him perform 'mean occupations' such as burdened his own day. He seldom came 'either to breakfast or dinner. He rises before the day, and labors until the middle of the night. He does not move out; he takes no exercise,

[1] Major George Cunningham to Henry Ellis, Member of the Board of Control, 24 September 1831. See *I.O.R.*, *H.M.S.*, 708 (3).

[2] In 1809. Wellesley had granted the King Rs.90,000 a month, and in addition seven *nazars* or ceremonial gifts of Rs.10,000 on festivals. The Heir Apparent had his own allowance of Rs.30,000 a month.

and apparently no food'. To the Emperor, who was meant to be nothing but a pageant and puppet, he showed such an exaggerated respect that it raised 'ideas of imperial power and sway, which ought to be put to sleep for ever'.

Metcalfe, young and decided, was the modern age, grimly realist in that epoch of tumbling dynasties. Let the Emperor have his £200,000 pension, and play at being monarch inside his rambling mansion. But let him know that he was merely an amusing anachronism.

'Let us treat him with the respect due to his rank and situation; let us make him comfortable in respect to circumstances, and give him all the means, as far as possible, of being happy; but unless we mean to establish his power, let us not encourage him to dream of it. Let us meet his first attempts to display Imperial authority with immediate check; and let him see the mark beyond which our respect and obedience to the shadow of a King will not proceed.'

It often made him 'wonder, and at the same time time almost made me mad, to see a most worthy excellent man'—that is, Seton—'blind to such gross absurdity, and a dupe to wild and romantic feelings'.

Something could have been urged on Seton's side; and Metcalfe, wiser than when he served under King Collins, did not let private disapproval wreck their personal relationship. Before this became strained, he was paid the tremendous compliment of being sent on his mission to Ranjit Singh. How much British-Indian history has depended on the temperament of its actors will be realized if we imagine what would have happened if Seton, instead of his masterful young Assistant, had gone to Lahore.

After his successful mission, Metcalfe was specially summoned to the Governor-General. He reached Calcutta, June 1809, to find Lord Minto preoccupied with the Madras officers' mutiny, and about to sail for the southern Presidency. Metcalfe was told to accompany him as temporary Deputy-Secretary, and obtained a pleasant and prolonged holiday. When he returned, in May 1810, he was sent to Gwalior, as Sindhia's Resident. He held this post for only three-quarters of a year; he went to it with loathing, performed its duties dispiritedly, and ever after referred to it with distaste. It may have been that the memory of early bitterness was ineradicable. However, his penance was ended in February 1811, by a characteristically rollicking letter from the Governor-General ('Most sincerely and affectionately yours') telling him that Seton was probably going to the Governorship of Prince of Wales' Island (Penang), in connection with the approaching campaign against Java.

'In that event, I shall with (or without) your consent, name you to the Residency of Delhi. . . . If you ask my reasons for so extraordinary a choice, I can only say that, notwithstanding your entire ignorance of everything connected with the business of Delhi—a city which, I believe, you never saw; and with Cis and Trans-Sutlejean affairs, of which you can have only read; and notwithstanding your equal deficiency in all other more general qualifications, I cannot find a better name in the list of the Company's servants; and hope, therefore, for your indulgence on this occasion.'

Metcalfe had many reasons to welcome this great appointment. Our predecessors were franker than ourselves about their zest for financial profit; Metcalfe, a normal Company's man in this, happily noted that he could now save £100 a month. Despite his generosity, he did this easily, and his hopes presently rose to saving £3,000 a year. Henceforward, by the mere steady fulfilment of duty a fortune accumulated. In return, he did more than any other man to set the course of India's future.

His work was unending, and of every imaginable kind. Though only twenty-six, he held semi-regal state, supported by what was styled a 'Family'—the numerous officers of the Residency, with their wives and children. He had his troubles with these; but they were trifles to those he endured from the King's family. The latter found their 'tribute' of £200,000 inadequate, and they fought over the late King's savings, and intrigued to recover wealth and sovereignty. The young bloods often oiled their naked persons, and rushed into the female apartments with drawn swords, to pillage the inmates. Rumours of murders committed inside 'the labyrinthine recesses' of the Palace reached the Resident. In addition, he had responsibility for the whole of the administration.

With what unique combination of efficiency and mercy he did his work is not realized. He observed with pride, 'Capital punishment was almost wholly abstained from, and that without any bad effect. Corporal punishment was discouraged, and finally abolished'. He put down widow-burning and slavery and rejected the King's demand that the slave trade, that profitable business, should continue inside the Palace. He urged a land settlement of the kind that was afterwards adopted, and pressed to be allowed to push forward irrigation.

Yet this supremely interesting man was by nature strongly conservative; it was only in Calcutta that he could ever have been regarded (as he was) as dangerously radical. Mr. Philip Morrell generously brought to my notice a letter in the unpublished correspondence of Lord William Bentinck, which illuminatingly brings out both Metcalfe's natural caution and also—what a study of Indian conditions abundantly brings out, at every period—how very far Liberalism in British circles in India lags behind Liberalism in England. The letter was written to Sir Charles Grant, President of the Board of Control, from Ootacamund, 14 April 1834:

'If it should happen that you decide upon appointing a separate Governor for Fort William, I believe Sir Charles would prefer the latter to Agra and I should say that he is better fitted for the latter than the former, as well in consideration of the merits of his character, which are great and numerous, as of the imperfections also, which though few in number have their inconvenience. The business of the Lower Presidency is infinitely more extensive and varied than that of Agra, and therefore requiring in a greater degree the great experience and knowledge of Sir Charles. For the same reason he would be a most useful addition to the Council of India as Governor of the subordinate Presidency, and in the Governor General's absence nobody is so fit to perform his duties. He is besides highly honourable, generous, hospitable and kind and a great favourite with all and therefore well adapted to the large and mixed society of Calcutta. The Presidency of Agra is as it were a new country. The revenue settlements have still to be made, and there is much wanting in the way of improvement. Sir Charles has peculiar notions as well in respect to revenue from land as to our judicial system. He is moreover not favourable to improvements. He objects to them partly on the score of expense and partly upon the principle "as the commerce has [been] handled heretofore, so it may continue hereafter". He sets no value upon a good road. I ascribe this to his long absence from England and to his having in consequence more the feeling of the old Indian than the modern European improver. I think also, at Agra as at Madras and Bombay, a person not in the service would make the better Governor. Sir C. with all the material independence belonging to him is still more or less fettered, without knowing it, with the service feeling. He would be most inflexible and upright with a case actually brought before him, but he would not go out of his way to reform abuse, or to find fault with a public officer. He is one of the best natured men I ever saw and one of the most delicate minded. It is from extreme kindness that he is disposed to extend to young men who are his favourites virtues that they have not and to promote them accordingly.'

This passage brings out also the outstanding detachment and real Liberalism of Lord William Bentinck, by far the most underrated of all Indian Governors-General.

Yet Metcalfe, a man sent out from home in almost childhood, in the intense loneliness of his position and the integrity and courage of his mind developed ideas far in advance of his time, and almost equal to those of Munro and Elphinstone, though inferior in breadth and insight to Bentinck's own. After the age of these great servants of the Indian Government there descended on official opinion such a frost of complacency and distrust, that if such men as these had returned to India they would have been regarded as dangerous subversives. Metcalfe even urged, for years before as Acting Governor-General he effected it, the liberation of the press, which we can still find plausible arguments for dreading. He urged also the throwing open of India, without restriction, to the settlement of unofficial Englishmen.

XXX

METCALFE AND CENTRAL INDIA

EVEN MORE exacting than Metcalfe's duties as administrator and arbiter of quarrels in Delhi were those of his position as the Paramount Power's representative. When he succeeded Seton he fell heir to a sea of troubles. The dreadful sufferings of the Rajput States, Amir Khan's favourite prey, have been related by Tod in his classic book. But affairs were little better in Sindhia's and Holkar's dominions. Metcalfe reported that Yeswant Rao Holkar's death had made no difference. He laconically added that he intended to make a visit of condolence to the deceased Prince's *vakils*, next day but one, and that preparations were going forward to place on the *gadi* ('seat of office') Malhar Rao Holkar, a boy four years old, son of another concubine but adopted by Tulasi Bai, who now ruled in his name.[1]

Under such governors, it was only a matter of time before its own internal disorders precipitated Indore on disaster. Meanwhile, these disorders exercised themselves internally, in civil war. The baby Maharaja survived only because his most formidable competitor, a cousin of Yeswant Rao Holkar, raided into the Nizam's and the Peshwa's dominions, and was routed in both, by the British subsidiary forces.

However, Jaipur's tribute to Holkar (and Amir Khan) had been at last fixed at 17 lakhs, and Amir Khan had marched out of Jaipur territory.

There were countless other disagreements among the protected Princes, who saw no reason why they should not settle these by war. Most restive of all was the still unchastened Raja of Bharatpur, whose repulse of Lake's repeated attacks had given him unique prestige all over India. Metcalfe's immense influence with Government came partly from the ruthlessly direct and unsentimental style of his writings, and his Minute on Bharatpur showed up what he deeply felt, the shame which Barlow's desertion of the Company's friends had brought on the British name.

'It is curious, in adverting to the events of past days, to observe how our policy has operated in favor of Bhurtpore. We formed

[1] Poona Records, Alienation Office: letters 341 and 347, dated 25 October and 8 November 1811.

alliances about the same period with the states of Bhurtpore and Jyepore. Both states on the same occasion were false to their alliances, but in different degrees. Bhurtpore joined and fought with our enemy Holkar. Jyepore only hesitated to fulfil its engagements with us. The one which committed the most venial fault has suffered; the other, which sinned against us more heinously, has been befriended. With Jyepore we kept on terms during the war with Holkar, and made use of its troops against him; but after the war we abandoned it to its fate, and the country has since been overrun by the armies of Holkar and other freebooters. Bhurtpore we had to fight as the ally of Holkar, and we have ever since protected it against all enemies. Jyepore has been sinking every day since we dissolved the alliance with that state, and is now nearly annihilated. Bhurtpore has been growing in wealth, power, and consequence under our protection. Jyepore is now at our feet begging for protection and alliance. Bhurtpore refuses to admit our agent to reside at his Court.'

In exasperation he urged that an overwhelming force be sent, to storm Bharatpur without further nonsense. But his old chief Seton, who was now a member of the Governor-General's Council, wrote to him privately, that the Java war had taken all the money. All Metcalfe could do was to dismiss from his own immediate durbar at Delhi the Bharatpur agent.

Under Metcalfe's watchful eyes, the slow disintegration of Central India continued. He reports Amir Khan's predatory movements, and the intrigues stirring behind them. 'A person of respectable appearance and good manners' brings him letters from eight of the free companion's *sirdars*, offering to put themselves under his (Metcalfe's) orders. Amir Khan has lost the confidence of all, and 'a general determination prevailed not to serve him longer'. Metcalfe received the messenger, and 'informed him civilly that it would be unbecoming in me to maintain this species of clandestine intercourse'. The time was not yet ripe (though he did not say this). There was no chance of the dissidents being taken into British employment.[1]

His agents brought him news from all parts. Reports of the civil war raging in Afghanistan flit in and out of news that locusts are ravaging the territory from Delhi[2] to Bhawalpur. Herat has been attacked, but not taken, by the Persians; it is in danger. The Persian commander has sent dresses to the Khan of Khorasan, 'and has announced to them that they may consider those dresses as their shrouds'; he has come to conquer as far as Kashmir, 'and is the same Prince who has repeatedly waged successful war with

[1] Poona Records, Alienation Office: Metcalfe's letters, generally to Edmonstone: these two are dated 8 and 9 December 1811.

[2] Metcalfe always spells Dihlee.

the French and Russians'.[1] The Persian commander has been recalled from Herat.[2] Shah Suja, the fugitive ruler of Kabul, has been imprisoned by a Kashmir chieftain.[3] Three weeks later, he is confined at Attock.[4]

Metcalfe took a particular interest in his old antagonist. 'Success continues to attend Runjeet Sing's able and energetic Government.'[5] Presently Ranjit has met with a check from hill rajas 'hitherto of no note'. Sikh prisoners have been treated with savage barbarity, whereupon Ranjit has sent out his main forces, and announced that he will take the field in person, 'to wipe off this stain on the lustre of his arms'.[6] Ranjit has come into a windfall (if that is the right term), and 'is reaping a most productive harvest in consequence of the death of Sunder Jymul Sing, whose possessions were great both in land and money'.[7]

He watched closely the major freebooters. Holkar has got into difficulties against Jaipur, and has saved his artillery by surrendering five hundred hostages. Muhammad Shah Khan joined him, and perhaps enabled him to get off.[8] Jaipur has fallen again into extreme distress, and is overrun by pillagers connected with Amir Khan and Muhammad Khan. Its wretched Court has grown even unusually tyrannous in consequence.[9] It has picked up again, and is reporting to be in its turn besieging Muhammad Shah, who dare not meet its armies in the field.[10] Holkar and 'Meer Khan' and the Raja of Jodhpur have come to his assistance, and he has got away.[11] Holkar has imprisoned a Pindari (Kharim Khan), and Metcalfe has written urging him not to free his prisoner. 'It would be an unfriendly act towards all other states, as robbers and plunderers are the general enemies of all mankind.'[12] 'Our old friendship makes me confident that this will be an additional stimulus to your exertions.'[13] The Regent of Kotah has asked Metcalfe for a treaty with the British Government. 'I made the usual friendly excuse.'[14]

If there was any pre-eminence in misery, perhaps it fell to Jaipur, which was periodically the hunting-ground of Amir Khan and Muhammad Khan, and Chitu, a renowned Pindari. In 1812, the Rao Raja of Macheri took a hand in what had become a round game, and occupied a section of Jaipur territory. Metcalfe

[1] Poona Records: no. 71: 8 May 1812.
[2] *Ibid* 10 June 1812.
[3] *Ibid*: 219: 20 August 1812.
[4] *Ibid*: 253: 10 September 1812.
[5] *Ibid:* No. 47: 10 June 1812.
[6] *Ibid:* 253: 10 September 1812.
[7] *Ibid:* 221: 23 August 1812.
[8] *Ibid:* 71: 8 May 1812.
[9] *Ibid:* 213: 13 August 1812.
[10] *Ibid:* 221: 23 August 1812.
[11] *Ibid:* 253: 10 September 1812.
[12] *Ibid:* 105 and 187: 12 August and 31 July 1812.
[13] *Ibid:* 189: 31 July 1812.
[14] *Ibid:* 253: 10 September 1812.

immediately protested. But Rajasthan was outside the line of Company protectorates, and all through 1812 and 1813 the usurper stayed. Metcalfe's consciousness of baffled helplessness is in every line of the undignified remonstrance, which was the utmost he could do:

'Never, never, never will the British Government cease to demand the restoration of Doobbee and Sikrawa to the Rajah of Jyepore. . . . I perform the duty of a friend in giving you warning. If you should be ruined by not following my advice, you will not have to blame me. I have given you notice. Remember what I say.'

However, in the autumn of 1813, a new Governor-General, Lord Moira, reached India; and in November his Political Secretary, John Adam, one of the band of close friends, of whom Metcalfe was another, who had risen steadily together, wrote to apprise Metcalfe that hostilities were sanctioned. He therefore sent a force against the Rao Raja, who hastily promised amendment and reimbursed the cost of the expedition.

XXXI

THE COMPANY'S SATRAPS

I HAVE written as though the life of Metcalfe was one of strain and difficulty only. It was all this, of course. On the other hand, probably never since the world began, probably never in any other land, have men known so free and exhilarating a life as these lords of the marches on the Company's north-west border. When Hollywood has got tired of its obsession with the North-West Frontier of to-day, here is a theme full of excitements subtler and nobler, and in which imagination can have full play, without doing violence to sense or regard for Indian self-respect!

The evidence is still hidden in native records that are untranslated. But glimpses can be given, though our narrative cannot pause for a complete picture.

They lived as Princes, and were assumed to be such; were referred to as Princes were, and were known to be possessed of power and authority far above that of any of India's Princes. States kept accredited *vakils* at their courts. They were regarded as deriving position (like other Princes) from the only true fountain of honour, the King of Delhi, the Mogul Emperor, and were styled accordingly. Metcalfe was Muntazim-ud-Daula, 'Administrator of the State'; Ochterlony was Nasir-ud-Daula, 'Helper of the State' (or, if his name was used, 'Loney Akhtar'—a transposition of Ochterlony). Their work and the grandeur of their dominion and responsibility united these two in a peculiar closeness of friendship.

The man who found his place most easily, as if by manner born to it, in this region of wavering and changing regalities, was David Ochterlony. He was born at Boston, Massachusetts, and became a Canadian, his parents being Loyalists whom the Revolution expelled. At the unusually mature age of nineteen, he joined the Bengal Army, and his remaining forty-eight years, without a break, were passed in India. *Pro conscientia* a natural heathen, he shared the people's viewpoint and understood their thought. He was quickly on terms of intimacy with Ranjit Singh; to feasts and holydays, 'Loney Akhtar, the wisest of the sahebs', was constantly invited over the border. From Ludhiana, for the marriage (28 January 1812) of Ranjit's heir, Kharak Singh, he came, accompanied by lesser chieftains, the Rajas of Nabha, Jind,

Kaithal, and by request brought the gift of a galloper gun. 'The Noble Sarkar' ('Government': in this case, Ranjit Singh) 'sat on a golden chair, while the Colonel Saheb sat on a chair of silver'.[1] With extreme openness, Ranjit showed him his new battalions (about 1809, he began to drill in the British manner) and the fortifications of Lahore. In reply to protests, he answered, 'If I did not trust Loney Akhtar, why ask him over at all?'

Ranjit's amusements were not edifying. They were horses, while vigour remained to him: then (and previously) nautches, and drink, and (from 1812 onwards) pederasty. 'All the dancing girls appeared on elephants, dressed in fine garments, and began to make dancing movements, as is customary with their class. The Noble Sarkar, inviting all of them, sent for wine. He took wine and asked them to dance, which he enjoyed until noon. There is nothing else to record until that time.'[2]

As Superintendent of Sikh affairs and relations, Ochterlony took by far the largest share in the continual childish interchange of presents, elephants passing as it were from hand to hand: in the hard drinking, in the nautches and heavy prolonged meals deep into night. But others on occasion accompanied him, and frequently Metcalfe was of the party. They accepted Indian conventions, and lived by them. 'The glorious sahebs' sometimes complained that Sikh sentries had been placed too near to their harems, besmirching their honour by being where they might peep in.

Bishop Heber, who met Ochterlony in his last days, wrote of the latter's legendary grandeur with some disappointment:

'There certainly was a very considerable number of led horses, elephants, palanquins, and covered carriages, belonging chiefly, I apprehend (besides his own family), to the families of his native servants. There was an escort of two companies of infantry, a troop of regular cavalry, and I should guess forty or fifty irregulars, on horse and foot, armed with spears and matchlocks of all possible forms; the string of camels was a very long one, and the whole procession was what might pass in Europe for that of an eastern prince travelling. Still, neither in numbers nor splendour did it at all equal my expectation. Sir David himself was in a carriage and four, and civilly got out to speak to me. He is a tall and pleasing-looking old man, but was so wrapped up in shawls, kincob, fur, and a Mogul furred cap, that his face was all that was visible. I was not sorry to have even this glimpse of an old officer whose exploits in India have been so distinguished. . . . He is now considerably above seventy, infirm, and

[1] 7 February 1812. Poona Records, Alienation Office: see *Events at the Court of Ranjit Singh*, 31.

[2] 15 December 1811, *Ibid.*

has been often advised to return to England. But he has been absent from thence fifty-four years; he has there neither friend nor relation—he has been for many years habituated to eastern habits and parade, and who can wonder that he clings to the only country in the world where he can feel himself at home? Within these few days I have been reading Cox's *Life of Marlborough*, and at this moment it struck me forcibly how little it would have seemed in the compass of possibility to any of the warriors, statesmen, or divines of Queen Anne's time, that an English General and an English Bishop would ever shake hands on a desert plain in the heart of Rajpootana!'[1]

There were other things about Ochterlony that struck the English Bishop with surprise. A friend had passed the famous soldier when the latter

'was merely travelling with his own family and personal followers . . . and his retinue, including servants, escort, European and the various non-descripts of an Asiatic train, together with the apparatus of horses, elephants, and camels—the number of his tents, and the size of the enclosure hung round with red cloth . . . were what an European, or even an old Indian, whose experience had been confined to Bengal would scarcely be brought to credit.'

Ochterlony's and his daughter's private tents 'were fenced in from the eyes of the profane'. 'All this', the Bishop thought, was 'at least harmless, and so far as it suits the habits and ideas of the natives themselves, it may have a good effect'.[2]

Heber perhaps did not suspect the full extent of the old General's accommodation to Indian ideas of the way a great man should live. Tradition has preserved a picture of Ochterlony's thirteen wives on thirteen elephants, every evening taking the air in Delhi, heavily veiled—a story which almost seems to carry us across the borders of folklore.[3] His baronetcy was finally inherited by a nephew, by special remainder.

Ochterlony's friend, Charles Metcalfe, lived more discreetly, retired at Shalimar Gardens,[4] a few miles away from the dust and turmoil of Delhi. We know nothing about the Indian lady who lived with him and whose obscure life ended in 1820. I believe she was originally a near relation of Ranjit Singh—Metcalfe met her when on his memorable mission. This connection may have been without benefit of clergy but was honourable, though the second of his three sons, the only one to survive him, inherited none of his titles. The eldest died by his own hand, after a life of failure and unhappiness: one lived to be aide-de-camp to Lords Dalhousie

[1] *Narrative*, ii. 392–3. 'Fifty-four years' is an exaggeration.

[2] *Narrative*, ii. 362–3. 'An old Indian' is what was later styled an Anglo-Indian, that is, a European who had been long in India.

[3] See my *Metcalfe*, 101.

[4] *Ibid*, 149–50.

and Clyde: the youngest, a non-commissioned medical officer, was one of the thirteen killed on the snows at Gandamak, in January 1842, in the disastrous rout of Kabul and the Khyber.[1]

There were disadvantages, judging by the strictest standards, in this lordly manner of existence.[2] Metcalfe himself was honest to the edge of what less scrupulous people considered almost imbecility. But the corruption and rapacity of his personal servants was made notorious by his enemies (partly from malice, but not altogether). As to Ochterlony, his emoluments were extensive and various, 'from different sources' (reported Heber, who of course knew only what got out on hearsay, which was a small part of the whole) amounting to 'little less than 15,000 s.rupees[3] monthly, and he spends it almost all'. In Agra and Delhi,

'though Sir David is uniformly spoken of as a kind, honourable, and worthy man, I was shocked to find that the venality and corruption of the people by whom he is surrounded was a matter of exceeding scandal. Against one of his moonshees it appears that he had been frequently warned without effect, till at length, in the course of a casual conversation with the Emperor's treasurer, Sir David found to his astonishment, that his own name stood as a pensioner on the poor old sovereign's civil list, to the amount of 1000 rupees monthly! The moonshee had demanded it in his master's name; to refuse was out of the question, and delicacy had prevented the Emperor from naming the subject to the person whom, as he supposed, he was laying under an obligation!'[4]

Against the strict morality of the men of the next generation—such men as Nicholson, Herbert Edwardes, Havelock—the men of the generation of Malcolm, Metcalfe, Ochterlony, seem a speckled and ring-straked brotherhood. It was the difference between the easy manners of the Regency and the rigid living, 'as ever in my great Taskmaster's eye', of the generation whose leading educationist was Arnold of Rugby. But it was also the passing from humanism to a certainty of rectitude, of God with you and against those you were ruling—from the time of Erasmus to that of John Knox, and Erasmus is the better ruler, if the happiness of the ruled is of importance. Never have men wielded such absolute power as the men of Ochterlony's and Metcalfe's generation, with such understanding and gentleness.

[1] For this information concerning Frank Metcalfe's end, I am indebted to Colonel H. Bullock, of the Indian Army. Dr. Brydon, who had escaped by a slightly different route with a handful of well under a dozen others, was, as most people know, the only ultimate survivor.

[2] For some succinct further information, see T. G. P. Spear, *The Nabobs*, 93 and 166.

[3] Sicca rupees: sterling or Company's rupees. [4] *Narrative*, ii. 362–3.

The Position of Half-Castes

The new Governor-General, like everyone else of any intelligence visiting India for the first time, was shocked by the manners of Anglo-Indians, their aloofness and insolence to all who were outside their charmed circle. The Empire had been deeply indebted to the valour of half-caste sons of distinguished soldiers and civilians. These were now treated with a sweeping scorn[1] that astonished the English nobleman, as it was to astonish Lord William Bentinck and Lord Auckland after him. Along with this went a growing contempt for Indians.

But there was still a sprinkling of men, and these the best men in every way, who shared neither meanness. Colonel Skinner after his unique services in the war against Holkar had been treated shabbily, yet had continued to place his skill and gallantry at the Company's disposal, in the never-quite-finished simmer of petty wars. Malcolm testified to his distinction. Seton also stood his consistent friend, and when leaving Delhi assured him that he would work for him and his brother, whose career had been hardly less brilliant:

> 'Lord Minto is already well acquainted with your merits; in short, both of you stand high in the general estimation. Remember me in the kindest manner to your brother Robert, and tell him for me, that, wherever I am, he must consider me his sincere *friend* and *agent*. God bless you, my dear Skinner. Believe me ever most cordially yours,
>
> A. Seton.
>
> P.S. It is most gratifying to me to reflect, that our friend Metcalfe, who succeeds me, feels towards your brother and you exactly as I do.'

Seton's was no idle promise. These men of a century ago may seem to us to have practised crudely direct ways to power and fortune, as against the subtler and more delicate methods of our own day, and they did not talk so expansively about their own entire disinterestedness. But they were intensely and steadily loyal to others' merit when they saw it, and their correspondence is freer from jealousy and the baser sorts of intrigue than any other known to me, before or since. Seton, Metcalfe, and Ochterlony worked for the Skinners, and when Moira succeeded Minto and the campaign to exterminate the Pindaris was in preparation the last men who could be dispensed with were the gallant brothers. The Governor-General wrote to James Skinner, 25 March 1815, begging him to dissuade Robert from asking to retire. Three weeks

[1] Metcalfe's youngest son, for example, could rise only to the rank of subconductor.

later, he offered them the ranks of lieutenant-colonel and major. It could be 'qualified rank' only, for 'you are sufficiently aware of the jealousy with which the opening such a door would be regarded by the officers of the regular army': the most junior major of the line would rank above them, but field-officers of the irregular soldiery were to command all captains and subalterns in the regular services. At this unexpected kindness Skinner broke down. Lord Moira also persuaded his intimate the Prince Regent to extend the Order of the Bath to officers of the Company's service, and Skinner's claims were pressed in London by Colonel Worseley, who had been Lake's D.A.G. and shared the immense admiration and gratitude felt towards Sikander Saheb by all who had engaged in the chase of Holkar. They were pressed in vain. But Skinner had the consolation of knowing that his omission from Honours Lists caused more notice than other men's inclusion.[1] The Governor-General had done all he could, to set right a cruel wrong. His wife, Lady Loudoun, supported him, and made it known that the wives of Eurasians of high position were welcome at Government House.

In the meantime, the Company was participating in another bout of 'the great game', with woeful results. Lord Moira came to a ravaged treasury and (as he noted) the prospect of 'seven distinct wars'. The one that actually materialized burst from an unexpected quarter, in the winter of 1814.

[1] The C.B. was awarded to him at last, in 1828.

XXXII

THE GURKHA WAR

WARREN HASTINGS had waged against the Gurkhas of Nepal an exceedingly minor war. It was on too trivial a scale to teach the Company anything about these mysterious neighbours. In 1814, border raids and boundary disputes gradually led to a bigger quarrel, which for a time was 'regarded as a mere affair with a troublesome Raja of the frontier'.[1] In the upshot, however, it 'made us acquainted with a formidable power, whose military strength was previously unknown and egregiously underrated. Then, for the first time in India, we had recourse to superiority of numbers to overpower the bravery and discipline of the enemy, combined with the natural advantages of his defensive positions'.[2] Throughout 1814 and 1815, the Company had 40,000 men employed in the war; and in 1816 a force of 16,000, which included several European regiments as a spearhead, was needed for Ochterlony's thrust into the country.

Like that other major disastrous war, the Afghan War of 1839, the Gurkha War was decided on by the Government, with little encouragement either from the financiers or the men closest to the field of action. St. George Tucker eyed the new Governor-General with misgiving:

> 'There is a little of the romantic in his character, and I think he will like to take a part, if there should be any serious work on hand. . . . I already look upon our crore[3] of rupees as upon a departed spirit. . . . There are more crores in the same coffers, if we should be much at a loss; and we may repay them with the sovereignty of Nepaul, if we should succeed in conquering it. I am only surprised that any individual should prefer war to peace, after the example of the French Emperor.'[4]

Tucker glanced nervously at India behind the Army's back. 'What an opportunity for the Mahrattas, while we are knocking our heads against these mountains! But they are, I trust, in too distracted a state to avail themselves of it.' Even Ochterlony,

[1] Henry T. Prinsep, *History of the Political and Military Transactions in India during the Administration of the Marquess of Hastings, 1813-23*, i. 133.

[2] Metcalfe, 6 March 1830: Kaye, *Selections*, 186.

[3] A crore is 100 *lakhs*.

[4] 14 November 1814. Kaye, *Life of Tucker*.

though it meant for him at last promotion to the command of a division, wrote to Metcalfe, 25 August 1814:

'to set off with the idea of overthrowing a long-established Government, and for such an unprofitable purpose, appears to me the most Quixotic and the most impolitic measure we have ever attempted—setting aside all physical difficulties.'

This does not mean that there was no *casus belli*; no civilized Government worthy of the name has ever had any difficulty in finding such. There were frontier incidents, murders of police posts, encroachments. But there would probably have been no war, if the new Governor-General, with his casualness about money matters, had not regarded a mere punitive expedition with a border chieftain as something not calling for enough expenditure to justify hesitation.

Captain (presently Major) Henry Hearsey, one of the famous Anglo-Indian family of Hearsey, was the great authority on Gurkha affairs. He produced, 24 August 1814, one of the most ridiculous reports ever penned, pouring scorn on their capacity for defence. It was to this report that Ochterlony presently, scoffing at the British preparations to intercept the Gurkha leader's '*retreat*',[1] referred. Every stockade of the enemy 'has hitherto been spoken of equally contemptuously; but, under the impressions of the present moment, I feel myself necessitated to consider them as extremely formidable'—far more so than the stockades of Kalunga (where the first great repulse came). 'I am aware of the tone of despondency that prevails.' It was poetic justice when Hearsey was routed in April 1815, and wounded and taken prisoner.[2]

The war began, and for long continued, unsuccessfully. On 30 October 1814, General Gillespie tried to rush the stockaded fort of Kalunga, or Nalapani, as he had formerly rushed Vellore and Fort Cornelis, and was shot through the heart. Adored and half legendary, he was the Nikal Seyn of his day, and a young lady composed and sang extempore a dirge which moved all who heard it to tears and became an immediate favourite:

'Ye banks and braes of bonny Doon![3]
How late your scenes sae peaceful smiled!
How sweetly bloomed your mountain rose,
In spotless white sae saft and mild!
But now ensanguined be thy flower!
And fatal be thy banks, fair vale!
While sad amang the blooming braes
Resounds the soldier's mournful wail!

[1] Ochterlony's italics of derision.

[2] *I.O.R., H.M.S.*, 515, 516.

[3] Kalunga is in the Dehra Doon valley.

How lately burned our hero's soul
  In glory's fatal, bright career!
Ah, Doon! thy bosom now entombs
  The heart that never knew a fear!
Ye banks and braes of bloody Doon!
  Ah, woe the while! ye're Rollo's tomb!
But with his sacred blood imbrued
  Your glens shall know immortal bloom!'

This outstanding defeat staggered public opinion, and the war's course quickly became such that the British needed all the consolation which divine poesy could afford them. At a second assault on the Kalunga stockades, 27 November, the troops hung back and let their officers die. The two attacks cost 260 and 480 casualties respectively, a total considerably more than the whole number of the garrison.

Three days after the second repulse, close siege, combined with heavy bombardment of the confined space, resulted in Kalunga's evacuation. The Gurkha commander and seventy men, the only unwounded section of his force of nearly 600 men, slipped unnoticed through our posts. The victors found the fortress 'in a shocking state, full of the mangled remains of men and women killed by . . . our batteries . . . the stench was intolerable. Upwards of ninety bodies were collected and burnt; and the wounded sent to our hospitals'.[1]

Metcalfe, whose early exploits as Lake's 'little stormer of Dig' perhaps made him overassess his insight into martial problems, in November produced, hurriedly and in much heat, an alarmed memorandum, which has as much personal interest as political, showing plainly that his fears were rooted in unforgettable experience. He forwarded it to the Governor-General (then on tour and far away),[2] 'with much trepidation, because I am not sure that his Lordship will approve of my intruding my thoughts on his notice, on a subject not perhaps within the bounds of my official duty'. He had written 'under a conviction, probably erroneous, but working powerfully in my mind'.

There was abundant sense in the memorandum; no man ever proceeded more cautiously yet more independently to his conclusions than Metcalfe. He stressed almost to the point of wearisomeness the fact that the Company held its empire, not by the will of the people, but by the sword, 'whatever delusion may prevail in England respecting the security to be derived from the affections of our Indian subjects and a character for moderation

[1] Prinsep, i. 94.
[2] It was read by him in January 1815

and forbearance with foreign native states'. He made it plain that he thought it easy to estimate too highly the intelligence of the minds that directed our armies. There was always a lot of boisterous talk about, and those who suggested that thinking and planning had their uses were dismissed as mean-spirited chicken-hearted fellows:

'Men of sanguine dispositions give favorable reports, and anticipate unqualified victories. . . . Encouraging intelligence is always the more agreeable; and men do not like to subject themselves to the reproach of being alarmists. We are apt to despise our opponents, till from defeat we acquire an opposite sensation. Before we come to the contest, their powers of resistance are ridiculed. Their forts are said to be contemptible, and their arms are described to be useless. Yet we find on the trial, that with these useless weapons in their contemptible forts they can deal about death among their assailants, and stand to their defences, notwithstanding the skill and bravery of our army.'[1]

He urged that artillery should be taken seriously, and an abundant supply of it and of shells should be tried before storming. 'We have on our side the science of Europe, and we ought to bring it into play. Economy in this department is ruinous. We ought to be lavish of the contents of our arsenals, and saving of the lives of our men.' He concluded pessimistically, that if the British were to remain in India at all there must be a large increase of the permanent army:

'Our power in India rests upon our military superiority. It has no foundation in the affections of our subjects. It cannot derive support from the good will or good faith of our neighbours.'

The Company's rule rested on their prowess in the field. That prowess had been roughly handled, and a famous general killed.

Then he jumps to Bharatpur, a failure which he knew so well. There 'four assaults and the greatest exertions of the united armies of Bengal and Bombay' had failed 'against a straggling and extensive walled town, situated on a plain, with a dry ditch which the activity of the enemy converted into a wet one before the breach, and defended by men whom we used to call a rabble'. Metcalfe analyses the reasons for that failure, and goes on to show how they had been so little laid to heart that the same errors had been committed in subsequent sieges.

And now at Kalunga? Wavering in the absence of circumstantial information, as to whether here repulse was due more to 'the insurmountable nature of the obstacles or the determined resistance of the enemy', he decides that it was probably due to 'the united effects of both causes'. He already knew enough to be

[1] Kaye, *Selections from the Papers of Lord Metcalfe*, 85.

aware that in the Gurkhas the British had met such an opposition as India had never produced before; and he brushes aside, as irrelevant, former instances of successful assault—of what were merely 'large villages without guns' or places insignificantly defended in the popgun warfare with paltry chieftains which was all that had taken place in Lord Minto's time. There had been occasions when British troops had hung back, or, worse, had fled from 'foes who, in theory, would be considered contemptible, and who to this day are compared by some writers in England to a flock of sheep'. Either 'the gradual and imperceptible circulation of knowledge' had given India, as exemplified by the Gurkhas, better arms and methods of defence; or the Company's charm of invincibility had gone. India's fate had often depended on a single army.

> 'We have met with an enemy who shows decidedly greater bravery and greater steadiness than our troops possess; and it is impossible to say what may be the end of such a reverse of the order of things. In some instances our troops, European and Native, have been repulsed by inferior numbers with sticks and stones. In others our troops have been charged by the enemy sword in hand, and driven for miles like a flock of sheep. In a late instance of complete rout, we lost more muskets by a great number than there were killed, wounded and missing. . . . In this war, dreadful to say, we have had numbers on our side, and skill and bravery on the side of our enemy. We have had the inhabitants of the country disposed to favor us, and yet overawed, notwithstanding our presence and partial success, by the character of the army.'

Metcalfe's comprehensive scheme for the general settlement of all Central India we must consider later. But from now, until his mind after many years at last turned wearily away from warfare altogether, he continued to urge, as his *delenda est Carthago,* his conviction that the Company must be mighty with the sword, and must build more and bigger armies. It was a hard doctrine for the times. 'The Pindarrees of Leadenhall Street, with their restrictions and retrenchments, were assailing the rear of the Governor-General',[1] and trying to hamper the adequate playing of 'the great game', on the ignoble excuse of expense.

A detailed history of the war would be one of innumerable tiny engagements. As many reputations were lost, and as quickly, as in the first two years of the Mesopotamian campaign in the First World War, when two score generals were 'degummed'.[2] One army commander, in a mood of precipitate pessimism, outstripped his followers (which was perhaps not strange, as he was excellently

[1] Kaye, *Metcalfe,* i. 399.
[2] By the beginning of August 1916.

mounted), and reached the base before the retreat had begun, or, indeed, the enemy's attack that preceded it. Presently, the division which Gillespie had led out from Meerut had lost a third of its numbers. Sheer terror of a foe so mobile, so fearless, and so cloaked, as by invisibility, by his hills and forests, took hold of men's minds. His 'successes', the Governor-General noted (January 1815), 'have intimidated our troops and our generals'.[1]

The Gurkhas advanced to the sound of huge harsh stirring trumpets, matchlock in the left hand and broadsword in the right, some carrying shields—disregarding regularity, and 'like a pack of hounds in full cry'.[2] If a soldier were killed, often his widow mounted his pyre in the sight of both armies. From a foe so fearless in barbaric desperate valour, the sepoys 'turned, almost uniformly . . . before a blow had been struck, under the influence of a moral impulse'.[3] As to their stockades—which were merely piles of stones and logs and branches, looking so contemptible that a straightforward dash, such as Gillespie had thought sufficient, seemed all that was needed, without the bother and delay of effecting a breach—

'appearances were deceitful; and the Goorkhas, having a just confidence in their defences, always stood boldly to them, and made the assailants pay dearly for their temerity. The lighter artillery made little or no impression.[4]'

The Gurkhas, however, were satisfied with a successful defensive war. They pushed home no advantages, but were abundantly pleased if they could repulse an attack here, and cut off an outpost there. The latter feat became more difficult, when the British themselves erected stockades. The Company's armies, cautious at last, kept up large fires at night, at a distance of about 200 yards before their pickets, so that anyone approaching them was bewildered by the glare and became an easy target for the artillery from the outposts.[5]

When both armies were stockaded, the war became one of 'continuance, that is . . . length of the purse'; a 'war of posts' succeeded to the earlier mode. A campaign of attrition set in.

[1] *Private Journal*, i. 298.

[2] *Military Sketches of the Goorka War in India, in the Years 1814, 1815, 1816*, 13–14. The Gurkhas' ferocity became a legend. Lady Amherst, wife of the next Governor-General, wrote in her diary: 'Captain Newton . . . told us various stories of the extraordinary bravery of the Gurkhas. . . . The children are without covering of any kind; fighting is almost their only recreation' (Anne Thackeray Ritchie and Richardson Evans, *Lord Amherst*, 198–9).

[3] *Ibid*, xiv.

[4] Prinsep, i. 138.

[5] *I.O.R., H.M.S.*, 646, p. 383.

As with Lake's failures before Bharatpur, actual reverses were less important, however vexing, than their repercussions in the political field. Ranjit Singh began to mobilize, and took up an attitude of armed watchfulness. The Maratha chiefs began to dream, and to dream hopefully, of recovering independence. 'It was now that the seeds of the next Maratha War were sown.'[1]

The Company had practically never come up against patriotism, and in India might be pardoned for forgetting the possibility of its existence. They did not at first realize that one reason why the mountaineers put up such magnificent resistance was that they felt for their fastness homes as Swiss and Scots felt for theirs. Metcalfe at Delhi was ordered to conduct large scale intrigues, which failed, precisely because they were countered by patriotism.

British territory abounded in petty kings whom their own people had ejected for good enough reason. The War, running true to accepted form, opened with a comprehensive proclamation that the Company intended to restore these victims of criminal factiousness, and invited the co-operation of all right-minded persons. Having done this, Lord Moira proceeded to make inquiries, of Metcalfe mostly. Some of these projected restorations—based on rumours that the Company's better informed officers had passed on to headquarters—called for closer examination, not only on moral, but on political grounds also. For example, the Governor-General 'has for the present' (but only for the present) 'deemed it inexpedient to except the expelled Rajah of Sereenagar'[2] from the general intention of restoring the exiled Hill Chiefs to their possessions. Information concerning the Raja's family, who were understood to reside at Saharanpur, in Metcalfe's domains, was very imperfect. The Governor-General was wondering about annexing their territory, the valley from Srinagar 'to the foot of the Himaleh range', as a commercial link with Central Asia when the War had finished. Should this 'suggested appropriation' be relinquished? Could Mr. Metcalfe get any information 'calculated to throw light on that subject?'

There was said to be at Hardwar a revolutionary leader from the same district, whose influence in his former haunts was believed to be considerable. He knew the topography of the regions into which the Company's armies were thrusting. Metcalfe must get in touch with him; or, better still, inveigle him to Delhi and pump him personally.

There was also an exiled heir to Kumaon, whose restoration

[1] Thompson and Garratt, *The Rise and Fulfilment of British Rule in India*, 257.

[2] Srinagar (i.e. Kashmir).

seemed dubious policy. He was said to be detested on account of his father's cruelties, while Bum Sah, the Gurkha governor of the province, was loved for his mildness and justice. Bum Sah himself had grievances against his own Government at Khatmandu, which had executed members of his family. Metcalfe might hold out to him privately a promise to be made Raja of much of Kumaon—perhaps all of it?—if he came over to the Company.[1]

Metcalfe was warned that he was likely to get overtures from two Gurkha commanders, father and son, Amar Singh Thappa and Ranjor Singh Thappa. Other chiefs, too, were understood to be disaffected. Overtures were unlikely to be 'of a tenor which can be listened to under present circumstances' (a detached tone which was presently abandoned). But Metcalfe should receive them and send on their gist. He was also to persuade the hill people to rise in rear of the Gurkha armies, to occupy the high passes behind Dehra Doon, and especially to cut off the enemy's retreat when Ochterlony struck his anticipated blow at their communications.

These plans all went wrong. There was plenty of retreating, but it was executed by the Company's own armies. The hill people proved backward in taking up their allotted role, a shyness which it was thought proceeded from dread of Gurkha vengeance and 'the impression necessarily produced by the unfortunate affair of Kalunga'. The Governor-General presently threatened that if they did not do their duty soon he would hold himself released from his proclamation promising them liberation, and would give their territories over as a separate principality (with certain reservations) to one of the Thappas.[2] Unfortunately, these chiefs also proved blind to their interests, and took a moral line quite unproper, Ranjor Singh Thappa expressing surprise[3] that his country had been invaded. The Gurkhas, he pointed out, 'are considered Disciples of the British'—it was as if Kim had been assaulted by his own Lama! No good, he thought, could result to either party from this impious war.

Certainly no good was resulting to the Company. The Governor-General, growing anxious, gathered military control into his own hands, and looked about for agents of outstanding efficiency. He found them in Delhi, trained by Metcalfe, whose two chief assistants, Fraser and Gardner, were seconded for special separate duty, while still acting under Metcalfe's 'general authority and

[1] Letter of 30 September 1814.
[2] Letters, 22 and 26 November 1814.
[3] Metcalfe to Adam, 12 November 1814.

instructions'. Fraser was ordered forward, 27 December 1814, to settle Dehra Doon after its conquest, and Gardner was detailed to negotiate with Bum Sah in Kumaon. It was a repetition of Metcalfe's own mission to Ranjit Singh, while still in loose tutelage to Seton. The characters of his subordinates, already wayward and masterful, Fraser especially, were strengthened into yet fiercer independence.

Gardner's task was complicated by the Governor-General, who modified his generous intentions towards Bum Sah. 'Subsequent information and a more mature consideration' of Kumaon's position and resources had decided him to annex it, as compensation for the war's costs. Bum Sah could only be given a *jagir*, therefore. His present salary, as the province's Governor, had been ascertained to be Rs.12,000 a year. Metcalfe was to find out how much he wanted, and to make his offer accordingly. Possibly Bum Sah's local influence might prove such that it would be necessary to remove him from Kumaon to an estate in some other part of India. If he stood out against temptation, and would not bring over Kumaon for a price, then (the Governor-General reluctantly concluded) Kumaon would have to be conquered by arms, not by intrigue.[1] This was what actually happened. Bum Sah, brave and loyal and far-seeing, put up a strong resistance, and had to be beaten in the field, slowly and painfully.

It was feared that Ranjit Singh might take advantage of the Company's straits.[2] But he had made up his mind about their strength and his, at the time of Metcalfe's mission, and in the interim he had made friends with Ochterlony—as we have seen, a bluff neighbourly sentinel. Ochterlony, who had proceeded cautiously, winning a small victory here (capturing 95 prisoners in Nalagarh and its dependent fort, Taragarh), suffering a small defeat occasionally (at Ramgarh, 26 November 1814, the leather belts of his sepoys shrank,[3] and they had 76 casualties), managed to break the continuity of his enemies' line of defences, and was forcing them to do the attacking, at Malaon, for example. He was proving that ultimately the Company was bound to prevail. Ranjit, genuinely troubled lest certain recent movements of his

[1] Letter of Adam to Metcalfe, 23 October 1814.

[2] To Warren Hastings his constant correspondent, William Palmer, wrote, 4 November 1813: 'Our Position at Loodiahna on the Sutlege is very offensive to him'. It might well be. The Agency at Ludhiana, established in 1808, according to the Treaty made by Metcalfe was to be discontinued, and the station evacuated. This promise was broken to the end.

[3] So far as I can read the manuscript account, it implies that the sepoys could not get at their ammunition, and it ran out.

troops might be misinterpreted—and he was probably in part thinking of Metcalfe, whose distrust of him he well knew[1]—interviewed Ochterlony's news-writer and semi-official agent, and told him the contents of a letter from the Gurkha Commander-in-Chief, informing him of his Kalunga victory, and of other subsequent letters begging for help or at least mediation. Ranjit had replied (according to his own story, which seems to have been true) that he could not offer any help, being a friend of the British, and that mediation was useless. Once the British began a war, they would not rest till it was finished. Metcalfe, passing all this on to Adam (16 November 1814), was excessively suspicious. Ranjit is, and will remain, he says, *tertius gaudens*, so long as the war remains doubtful.

The Gurkhas continued to batter at Ranjit's doors for help. Metcalfe by his spies collected their overtures and passed them on. Thus, in May 1815, the Maharaja of Nepal exhorted Ranjit: 'Do not suffer yourself to be deceived by the engagements and protestations of the English. They had friendly engagements with me also, and the good faith which they display is manifest'. He offered Ranjit a fort and then money, and told him that the Nawab of Lucknow and all the Marathas and the Rampur Rohillas 'are entirely attached to me, and on hearing of your coming will all join us'. The conquest of Hindusthan and the expulsion of the foreigners would become easy. Ranjit, handing on this information, observed, 'When a man is drowning he catches with hands and feet at every straw'.

On 19 February 1815, Lieutenant Pickersgill, an alert intelligence officer, trapped 500 Gurkhas in a hollow where they were cut up by cavalry, a disaster which made their armies hurriedly withdraw to the hills where they felt safe. The Governor-General, the regular troops having failed, raised a Rohilla detachment as being more likely to meet the Gurkhas in their own fashion, and Colonel Gardner and Major Hearsey (already mentioned), two famous soldier-adventurers who had come over from service with the Marathas, were charged to make a double thrust into Kumaon. The Rohillas conducted from ridge to ridge a clever and rapid warfare. In April, Colonel Jasper Nicolls was sent up in support.

[1] Cf. Metcalfe's complaint to Edmonstone, 19 October 1811, that Ranjit's activities since his Treaty with the Company had incessantly consolidated his power. 'The successful progress of this system has already produced a most material difference to the state of the Punjab, and there is, I believe, no doubt that it is his determination to put an end to the existence of any authority but his own.' Poona MSS. Records, Alienation Office, File 61,325.

But Hearsey's Rohillas lost their leader, a wounded prisoner, at Champawat, and 'hastened back to the plains with the utmost terror and expedition'.[1] Thereafter, whenever brought to action at all, they proved inadequate.

The enemy's decisive superiority in individual quality was increased by an event due to the nervousness with which Gillespie's successor had managed to infect his whole army. Two hundred Gurkhas, surrounded at Chamalgarh by two thousand irregulars, 'seeing their situation desperate . . . adopted the resolution to die bravely together'. It proved superfluous. Their besiegers fled precipitately, and 'this unlooked-for result of their intrepidity' gave the Gurkhas 'so much confidence, that they never afterwards failed to attack a post of irregulars whenever placed within their reach; and, even when stockaded, they generally succeeded'.

The war settled down into one of watchfulness, both sides relying on strong posts, elaborately stockaded and in a condition of loose but permanent siege. But one new reputation presently emerged; and one established one survived. Colonel Jasper Nicolls did excellent work in the one solid success, the occupation of Kumaon; and General Ochterlony, his commanding officer, plodded on ('a battle was his last resort')[2] despite minor repulses. With characteristic generosity, he ascribed his progress to Lieutenant Lawtie, a brilliant and brave young engineer, 'whose youthful energy carried him to points which I could not have ascended, and whose Active and intelligent mind furnished me with the most useful Information'.[3] Lawtie's sense of position for batteries in those wild rocky mountains was unexampled. When he died of fever, at Ratangarh, the whole army went into mourning, and Ochterlony sent Metcalfe 'a very particular request':

> 'It is that you will get a slab of marble, and on it cut an inscription of your own composition for the tomb of our lamented Lawtie, at Ruttunghur. Few will read it; but I do not wish an European visitor to pass without knowing that the spot contains the remains of one so deservedly valued and lamented.'[4]

Ochterlony's advance shook the enemy, who in May 1815 opened negotiations for peace. They failed, mainly over the demand to station a British Resident at Khatmandu. An intercepted letter from the Gurkha leader Amar Singh to his Prince showed the misgivings which made him, though in a position of peril from Ochterlony, desire to risk everything rather than enter upon a course which would end in loss of independence:

[1] Prinsep, i. 152. [2] *Military Sketches, etc.*, 48.
[3] *I.O.R., H.M.S.*, 643. [4] Thompson, *Life of Metcalfe*, 163.

'Suffer the enemy to retain the low lands for a couple of years: measures can afterwards be taken to expel them. Lands transferred under a written agreement cannot again be resumed, but if they have been taken by force, force may be employed to recover them. Fear nothing, even though the Sikhs should not join us. Should you succeed now in bringing our differences to an amicable termination by the cession of territory, the enemy in the course of a few years would be in possession of Nipal, as he took possession of the country of Tipu.'

In March 1816, however, the Gurkhas accepted the Treaty of Sagauli, by which they lost Garhwal and Kumaon and much of the Terai (the swampy level between the Himalayas and India). Some of the Terai, which is valuable chiefly to the big game hunter, has been returned since, notably after the Mutiny, in acknowledgment of the services of Gurkha auxiliaries. To their intense humiliation and reluctance, the Nepal Government had also to accept a British Resident at Khatmandu.

The war was not only a terrible though interesting story in itself—standing quite apart from the 'gymkhana wars'. It had its own individual features. The Gurkhas fought from the beginning with such amenities as mark off war that is considered 'civilized' from war that is merely savage. They extorted respect, and freely gave it. Burial of the dead was 'a courtesy they never refused . . . and not the only one we experienced at their hands'.[1] The services of our surgeons won for us at least as much prestige as the skill of our generals. Moreover, they attached importance to keeping their word, as they showed eminently in the years of peace that followed, which was one reason—a minor one, perhaps, the character of their country and their own prowess being the major ones; but, nevertheless, a reason—why their independence has survived to this day.

An important result of the war was the friendly confidence which gave the Indian Army its renowned Gurkha regiments. Descendants of the men who defeated us at Kalunga and Jitgarh fought beside us at Sannaiyat and the Shumran crossing of the Tigris. Their dead and those of the Black Watch lay thickly together on the morning after the grim struggle for Istabulat, 22 April 1917. These cheerful humorous little soldiers enjoy a special popularity with all British ranks, and mix with them without any feeling of wounded nationalism on their part.

The war had political results outside India. It is often forgotten that Tibet, and in a less degree China, claim a shadowy suzerainty over Nepal, which towards the end of the eighteenth century Tibet, at any rate, occasionally managed to enforce. Nepal has

[1] Prinsep, i. 107.

been the eyes with which for a long while Central Asia, and Tibet especially, looked at India and the outside world. It was during this campaign that Tibet took stock of the dangerous and aggressive Power that had come from the sea, and resolved to shut herself off more closely from the possibility of neighbourhood to such peril.

The war left the Company with a much lowered prestige and funds that were restored only by a huge enforced loan, or rather two loans, from the Nawab of Oudh, who in return was permitted to style himself henceforward King of Oudh. His embarrassed and unhappy sovereignty lasted only until 1856, when its extinction was one of the causes that led to the outbreak of the Mutiny. It had no practical effect now, as regards Oudh, or its rulers. The state continued the prey of European adventurers, and in a condition of fantastic misgovernment. But, since the Nawab was technically nothing more than an officer of the Mogul Emperor, his assumption of the regal title offended Muhammadan sentiment, and made such old-stagers as Malcolm feel 'sick':

> 'If the King of Delhi was in fact an absurdity or a mockery (I do not admit it was either), it had its root in a wise conformance to usage, in a generous consideration of the feelings of fallen greatness. It was the veneration of a great power that had passed away; and the superstition that continued to give homage to the shrine which we had addressed to propitiate our rise, was sanctioned by the example of the wisest among nations.'[1]

The Nizam was offered the same title of King, but rejected it with indignation. As his own title showed, he claimed to be merely the chief officer of state of the Mogul Emperor, who 'was still regarded by the natives of Hindoostan as the only legitimate fountain of either honour or dominion'.[2] The Nawab's acceptance of the name of King, and from the East India Company, was considered by Moslems a disloyal action. The placing of the servant on the same plane as his helpless master further loosened the ramshackle polity of India. Another rough shake and it would fall to pieces. That shake came in the Third Anglo-Maratha War.

[1] Letter to Gerald Wellesley: *Life of Malcolm*, ii. 378.
[2] J. Monckton. *See I.O.R., H.M.S.*, 708 (L831).

XXXIII

THE PESHWA AND GANGADHAR SASTRI'S MURDER

THE THIRD ANGLO-MARATHA WAR arose partly out of the drive to sweep up and finish the Pindaris, but its real causes lay in the utter chaos in which Central India had been left and in the long-drawn-out trouble between the British and the Peshwa.

The latter cause can be dealt with first. When he had been restored in 1803, it was to what Arthur Wellesley styled (January 1, 1804) 'a dreary waste, overrun by thieves, and his Highness is incapable of conducting his Government himself'. As time passed matters improved somewhat, and the Peshwa's ambitions rose.

In 1811, Elphinstone was sent to Poona as his Resident. Thenceforward his intrigues and actions lay exposed to the coolest as well as most energetic mind in India. That mind in 1815 drew up for the Governor-General an account of his character which, like everything Elphinstone wrote, is masterly in expression and conception both.

'The character of his Highness the Peshwa has always perplexed those who have been interested in discovering his sentiments or calculating on his conduct. This is partly owing to the inconsistency of many of his inclinations with his ruling passion of fear. . . . If he were less deficient in courage, he would be ambitious, imperious, inflexible, and persevering; and his active propensities would probably overcome his love of ease and pleasure, which are now so strong, from their alliance with his timidity. As it is, he is eager for power, though he wants the boldness necessary to acquire it, and is tenacious of authority, though too indolent to exercise it. Even his indolence is broken in on by his habits of suspicion and vigilance, and there is no part of his character that is to be found unmixed and entire. His love of consequence makes him fond of the company of low dependents, where he can enjoy his superiority unresisted. With them he is haughty and overbearing, and even with others he is proud and lofty on some occasions; but when it suits his purposes, there is no meanness to which he will not descend. Though capricious and changeable in his humours, he is steady in his serious designs. Concession encourages him to persevere, and opposition only increases his obstinacy, unless it operates on his fears. He is vindictive in the extreme, he never forgets an injury, and spares no machinations to ruin the object of his resentment. . . .

To balance his vices it must be admitted that the Peshwa is by no means deficient in abilities, that he is scrupulously just in pecuniary transactions; humane, when not actuated by fear or revenge; frugal, but not parsimonious in his expenses, and at once courteous and dignified in his manners. Some other parts of the Peshwa's character must be mentioned, though they do not affect his public conduct. He is a slave to superstition; half his life is spent in fasts, prayers and pilgrimages. A large part of his revenue is consumed in magical practices, and his life is disturbed by his attention to prodigies and omens. His superstition imposes no restraint upon his pleasures, and the greater part of his time that is not occupied by religion is devoted to vicious indulgences. Though he affects great purity in his own person, scarcely a day passes that he does not spend some hours with his favourites in large assemblies of women, when he enjoys the coarsest buffoonery, and witnesses most disgusting scenes of debauchery. These parties are generally composed of women of rank, and his Highness's most implacable enmities are those which he bears towards Sirdars who refuse to allow their wives to join them.'

After the close of the Second Anglo-Maratha War, the Peshwa set himself to cut away all taller poppies and reduce his dominions to a dead level of humble dependence. He was anxious to recover his long-forfeited control over Sindhia, Holkar, the Gaekwar, and the Bhonsla Raja, originally not 'Princes' at all, but admittedly 'servants of the Peshwa', and as such 'in tolerable subordination till the murder of Narayun Rao[1] by Ragoba, the father of the present Peshwa'. He revived his claims against them, and revived also claims of *chauth* against the Nizam. He tried to revive claims to suzerainty and tribute even in Hindusthan. But he worked most persistently, and for a time with some success, against his own *jagirdars*. These were chiefs, some of them descendants of men who had been partners rather than dependents of Sivaji, founder of the Maratha empire, with land grants going back to his time. Others possessed grants of more recent date. The Peshwa included with the *jagirdars* such independent rajas as those of Kolhapur and Savantwadi, and was determined to dispossess as many as he could and to humble the rest.

Elphinstone examined the disputed tenures, and on the whole found them clear except for the 'passions which had been called into action by the prolonged struggle'[2] and by the successful strugglers' 'unwillingness to surrender possessions usurped in times of confusion'. The *jagirdars*, unlike the Peshwa, actually had authority, and they had an interest in the prosperity of their territories. They held these territories together with more success than attended the administration of some greater rulers. Several had co-operated loyally with Arthur Wellesley, in the last Anglo-Maratha War, whose upshot had been the practical dissolution of the Peshwa's authority—a result which could hardly have

[1] In 1773. [2] *Life*, i. 249.

endeared them to him and might work them harm if they were put completely under his power.

Elphinstone averted civil war by enforcing a settlement. The British Government's own gain was in the cession by the Raja of Kolhapur, by treaty, October 1812, of his port of Malvan and some of his fortresses. He surrendered all claim to external independence, promised to submit his quarrels to the Company's decision, abandoned his practice of seizing wrecked or storm-driven vessels in his ports, and gave the Company's Marine entire powers of entry and search, at the same time engaging not to employ or fit out any armed vessels himself. Ever since the earliest East India Company days, the Malabar coast had been infested with pirates, whose retreat latterly had been more and more in the dominions of such petty chiefs as possessed a seaboard. The Raja of Kolhapur was the worst of these offenders and had proved the hardest to handle.

The Raja had carried on a desultory but sometimes spirited warfare against the Peshwa, chiefly at second hand, by attacking *jagirdars* to whose allegiance the Peshwa laid claim. There were also lands which lay in dispute between the Raja and the Peshwa. The Peshwa by himself was unable to enforce his sovereignty, even over *jagirdars*, and the Kolhapur Raja was a descendant of Sivaji, with strong rights to that Maratha suzerainty which the great Peshwas had gathered into their own hands. He lay outside the Maratha confederacy, in so far as that still existed, and the British Government treated with him as with a Prince and not a dissident *jagirdar*, while compelling him to renounce the Peshwa's dependencies that he had tried to conquer.

A great name, inextricably interwoven with Indian history and that of the Marathas in especial, vanished from the scene, as the strands of the slow long process that finally sent the last Peshwa as a prisoner to exile were being gradually drawn together. Elphinstone heard, 21 September 1813, of Barry Close's death in England: 'I doubt whether such an assemblage of manly virtues remains behind him. A strong and hardy frame, a clear head and vigorous understanding, fixed principles, unshaken courage, contempt for pomp and pleasure, entire devotion to the public service, joined to the utmost modesty and simplicity . . . a character such as one would rather think imagined in ancient Rome than met with in our own age and nation.'

Elphinstone was his disciple, as we have seen. When he entered on his Indian service, as Close's junior, by his own admission he was often wild and intemperate in thought and speech. Those fires had long been damped down, and first of all because of observation of Close's own practice. 'I have long since given up the opinion that frequent anger expedites affairs . . . passion not only injures dignity and takes from the weight of just resentment, but renders a man apt to receive insults tamely, from a consciousness of his irritability . . . and tempts him often to betray his secrets out . . . I must be particularly cautious with the Peshwa and his Minister, whom it is my business to conciliate, though I have neither respect nor esteem for either of them'.[1]

The Peshwa's jealous sense of insecurity made him fly immediately to the thought of having his own British-officered force, distinct from his subsidiary force, to overawe his own feudatories. Elphinstone had instructions to encourage him, and reported (12 July 1813) that everything was going satisfactorily. 'The arrangements about pay and the establishments of the corps are all in the highest style of good sense and liberality.' He settled this and other problems; he wrote his story of the Kabul embassy, he entertained some charming people, especially the beautiful and vivacious Lady Hood (one of the most disturbing apparitions that ever flitted across India); he explored ancient temples, he hunted, he read Greek and a wide miscellany of history of all sorts, from Robert Bruce to Timur, he watched the amusing habits of the people—those who barked like dogs, because they were a local deity's hounds, and others who in pursuance of a vow rolled from one shrine to another—he encouraged the infant science of Orientalism, as here and there an enthusiast began to practise it. And all the while he kept so careful an espionage on the Peshwa that, as the latter after his downfall complained, Mr. Elphinstone knew the very dishes that were set before him every day. Mr. Elphinstone knew all this; and much more besides. Most unsettling of all, he kept a careful control of himself, as of everyone else.

The Peshwa as yet had no hostile intentions against the Company, to whom he owed all he had. But their thwarting his wishes concerning the *jagirdars* incensed him, at the same time as their bringing the latter back under his authority encouraged him to resolve to restore the old Maratha confederacy. Moreover, he had found his one real confidant, Trimbakji Danglia—a man who had been a spy and professional letter-carrier, in which capacity he had earned the Peshwa's gratitude when he fled before Yeswant Rao Holkar in 1802. In him the Peshwa found 'an instrument too low to be feared, too despicable to excite jealousy, and too servile to irritate by opposition', and his response was to 'lavish upon him

[1] 20 October 1812.

the confidence which he withheld from all the rest of mankind'.[1] Trimbakji was his Piers Gaveston, and expressed his sense of devotion by assuring Elphinstone, 'If my master order me I will kill a çow'. This we may dismiss as the flowery extravagance of a courtier. Trimbakji, however, gave an almost equal proof of devotion when he was an accessory to the killing of a hardly less sacred object, a Brahman.

The Brahman was Gangadhar Sastri, who was in effect, though not in name, the Gaekwar's Prime Minister. He came to Poona in 1814, to negotiate a matter of claims and counter-claims about lands and debts—behind which there loomed the shadow of the Peshwa's ancient claims to suzerainty over the Gaekwar. He was a clever fellow, with a gift for unconscious comedy that delighted Elphinstone. 'He affects to be quite an Englishman, walks fast, talks fast, interrupts and contradicts, and calls the Peshwa and his ministers "old fools" and "damned rascals", or rather "dam rascal" '. He was a pioneer in that common Indian custom of to-day, which jumbles English and vernacular words together, with often hilarious results. Holkar (the dead Yeswant Rao, for the present Holkar was a mere baby) he styled a 'bahut tricks walla' and 'kukhye' (cock-eyed—a reference to his famous misfortune). He behaved generally as if Poona belonged to him, lavishing money and showing off his cavalry bodyguard 'in such style as to draw the attention of the whole place'.

He was hardly *persona grata* with his host; but he considered himself safe, since the British Government, at the Gaekwar's special request, had guaranteed his protection. In this undue confidence, he accepted a proposal of marriage between his son and the Peshwa's sister-in-law, and then broke it off, in such a manner as to give some offence. He gave still more, by forbidding his wife to join in the Peshwa's family amusements, which were the reverse of reputable. Gangadhar Sastri was suddenly murdered in the open street, 14 July 1815, at Pandharpur, the most sacred of Maratha places of pilgrimage, just after he had been in friendly intercourse with the Peshwa.

Elphinstone immediately demanded the arrest and punishment of Trimbakji, which after delay the Peshwa reluctantly promised, but only after he saw British troops assembling in Poona. Elphinstone insisting on the surrender, Trimbakji, to the extreme distress of the Peshwa, was imprisoned in the fort of Tannah, on Salsette Island.

Gangadhar's murder has always been assumed to have been a

[1] Elphinstone. For a short time, Elphinstone thought well of him (*Life*, i. 278).

reprisal for what the Peshwa considered an insult, and Elphinstone's belief that Trimbakji was the procurer of the murder has been generally accepted. Yet there probably was a slight element of doubt, even in Elphinstone's mind, since from first to last (even after the accused's escape from prison) the British Government was willing to assure the Peshwa that Trimbakji would not be punished capitally. Dr. P. C. Gupta, in a valuable recent study, produces evidence that the real instigators of the crime may have been at the Gaekwar's own court, where there was a growing anti-British party, whose focus (as so often in such cases) was the ladies of the court.[1] 'There were good reasons why Elphinstone should have desired Trimbakji's imprisonment and believed in his complicity in the Sastri's murder. But that is no reason why the historian should ignore the probability' (or, at any rate, the possibility) that the Peshwa and Trimbakji were not the most guilty, though they may have afforded facilities for what was done.

Yet, against Dr. Gupta's opinion, I am going to subpoena a ghost, from the untranslated documents of the Peshwa's *daftar* (muniments office) at Poona. When the protracted coil was finished and the Peshwa was in exile, in late 1818, his wife Varanasi Bai believed herself to be possessed and would cry out repeatedly, 'I am Gangadhar Sastri! I was in vain murdered, and I would avenge my murder!' That at any rate seems to show what the Peshwa's own family believed.[2]

The Peshwa with humility, even servility, repeatedly begged for his friend's release, and that friend presently released himself, by one of the most celebrated exploits of India.[3] Trimbakji's guards were all European soldiers. A Maratha offered his services to the commandant, as a syce or groom, and was accepted. When cooling down his master's horse he used to walk him up and down under the prison windows, and to sing Marathi verses such as the following:

'Behind the bush the bowmen hide,
  The horse beneath the tree;
Where shall I find a knight will ride
  The jungle paths with me?

[1] *Baji Rao II and the East India Company*, 137 ff. Elphinstone seems to have acquitted the Peshwa, though later he sometimes wavered in opinion.

[2] The Marathi text is printed by Rai Saheb Sardesai: *Selections from the Peshwa Daftar*, 41, letter 245.

[3] The exploit was copied in an escape of a few years ago, which I am afraid cannot be made public in this generation.

There are five and fifty coursers there,
And four and fifty men;
When the fifty-fifth shall mount his steed,
The Deccan thrives again.'[1]

He sang out details of a plot, by which Trimbakji evaded his jailors (12 September 1816), apparently through a stable, *via* the lavatory.

The episode was from the first as renowned among Trimbakji's countrymen as Queen Mary's escape from Lochleven among hers, and the odium that attached to the murder of a Brahman was soon lost in glee over cunning and daring that had outwitted the *Feringhis*. For a while Trimbakji kept to wild and hilly places, but he was soon in frequent communication with the Peshwa, as Elphinstone knew, despite denials. Both the Peshwa and the Company prepared for war, which obviously awaited only a spark, and hardly even that.

[1] Heber, ii. 335.

XXXIV

THE PINDARIS AND THE CHAOS OF CENTRAL INDIA

THE SPARK was supplied by the Governor-General's measures to suppress the long-seething disorders of Central India. These came to a head in the incursions and raids of the Pindaris, who were, however, a symptom rather than a cause.

Certain sections of them had their homes inside the orbit of the Maratha chieftains, styled themselves Sindhia or Holkar Pindaris, and in some vague fashion considered themselves dependents of these families. This did not prevent them from plundering their patrons' territory when other sources of supply were drained or became closed to them. Since the political situation of Central India resembled a bog which is drying up slowly and has not yet become firm ground, even Sindhia (and still less Holkar) was hardly what we should now consider a territorial power. The Pindaris were a military convenience, moreover, to the Maratha Princes and even to the Nizam:

> 'Those sovereigns have no sensibility for the sufferings of their subjects. They only calculate the diminution which their revenue may undergo, setting against that loss the convenience of being able on the sudden to take into their pay such a swarm of light troops in case of any breach with this Government. To us the Pindarries are no eventual resource; for a stipulation in their engagements is invariably an unlimited right of plunder, an atrocity to which no extremity could make us give countenance.'[1]

Some of their leaders, notably Amir Khan—who was half a Pindari and (as we have seen) half a quasi-dependent ally of Holkar—had almost risen to be independent chiefs. They maintained regular armies which had to be fed and rewarded and cajoled.

In time of peace, there was no way of paying the Pindaris except by allowing them to forage for themselves. This they did, with dreadful results. Nagpur, in particular, was swept by them periodically. As a rule, they gave Sindhia's and Holkar's dominions a miss, to make sure of a refuge when in trouble. They raced along the Nizam's borders, and plundered inside his frontier,

[1] *The Private Journal of the Marquess of Hastings*, i. 42–3.

which like all native state frontiers was a debatable one, with considerable interlacing with other frontiers. But the Nizam was under Company protection. So there remained only the Rajput states and the Bhonsla Raja's territory. The latter, pertinaciously refusing to pay the price of a subsidiary force, was ostentatiously delivered over to Satan, who plagued Nagpur exceedingly and regularly. As for the Rajput states, as the Governor-General in January 1815 noted, they 'have assailed me with repeated petitions to take them under protection as feudatories'. Their petitions were barred by Sir George Barlow's 'inexplicable treaty', which rendered 'a step equally counselled by a generous humanity and by an unquestionable interest' 'a direct breach of public faith'.[1]

Meanwhile, Sindhia himself, who had sunk to being nothing much more than a superior Pindari, was suffering steady attrition of what he considered his resources. In December 1814, he had to acquiesce in the Nawab of Bhopal's escape into the British sphere, and could no longer exact tribute from that quarter. His quasi-ally, the Bhonsla Raja, protested (1 February 1815),[2] against cessions of territory which the Company forced on him, to their new protégé. He was under no illusions as to the purpose of this arrangement, which was obviously an occupation, one of many such, of territory that would be strategically useful to the Company in the coming Anglo-Maratha war:

'by fixing ourselves in the little principality of Bhopaul, we shall gain a fulcrum, from which we may sweep away or smash the Pindarries, and drive a subsidiary treaty down the throat of the Berar Rajah.'[3]

Sindhia was off the mark almost simultaneously (31 January), with a protest not merely against the protection of Bhopal, but against the Company's similar treaties with Jaipur, Jodhpur, Alwar, Bharatpur, and Gohad. It was stipulated in his own treaties with the Company, 'that the Muharaja may take tribute from them according to his pleasure, and that the British Government has no connection with the Country of Malwa or the Rajas of that country, and will not enter into Treaty with any of them'. Bhopal was part of Malwa, and from ancient times subject to the Peshwa, who had made over his rights of suzerainty (which in practice, and Sindhia hardly troubled to make it seem otherwise, meant pillage) to Sindhia. Technically, Sindhia had a strong case; Bhopal was his dependent, and admitted as much. But the Governor-General was now one who cared little about technicali-

[1] *Ibid*, i. 300.

[2] Poona Records, Alienation Office: Metcalfe's letter of date given in the text.

[3] H. St. G. Tucker, 12 November 1814: Kaye, *Life of Tucker*, 286.

ties, and in any case had ceased to care even as much as when he first came to India. He regarded Sindhia as the head and front of all offence and the Company's principal menace, and he was resolute to find some fairly reputable *casus belli*, to break his power once for all.

There can be no question that Lord Hastings overestimated both Sindhia's power and his hostility. It was easy enough, with the Company's efficient and ever-active system of spies and news writers, to discover from time to time evidence of the Maratha chief's intrigues with other states. These impressed the Governor-General, who had come to a conviction of Sindhia's utter dishonesty. They did not impress the Members of his Council, whose notions and knowledge of Indian conditions had been formed in Lord Wellesley's time, when Edmonstone, now the Senior Member of Council, had been that nobleman's political arm. They were aware that Sindhia cherished no affection for the British, but were aware also of how casual and desultory were the occasional feelers and inquiries which served him, as they served other chieftains, for diplomacy.

Sindhia was never a menace, he never engaged in any serious plot to overturn a Power whose tremendous strength he well knew. Moreover, he himself was often restive under the Pindaris' pillaging, and at times would even have welcomed what ultimately became his fate, his subsidence into dependent status, if pride had not made him loth to admit his impotence. These Princes, whom Hastings so distrusted, were little more than prisoners in the midst of their own pretorians, and Sindhia at any rate sometimes tried with some sincerity to control his Pindaris. Edmonstone realized this, and he and Seton and Dowdeswell all opposed the Governor-General's far-reaching schemes, which aimed at creating a kind of League of States in Northern India, independent internally but under complete Company suzerainty in all external affairs. They thought the arrangement inherited from Wellesley's time adequate—one of subsidiary States, with a core of military efficiency under British officers, and of other States which were weak and disorderly, but harmless to anyone but themselves. It is doubtful if even Lord Hastings would have proved so pertinacious, against his own Council's opposition, if it had not been for the decision and earnestness of Metcalfe, who was the first of the old Wellesley group to see that the subsidiary system—originally Edmonstone's idea—was now out of date. In 1816, however, first Seton changed his mind; then Dowdeswell, and finally Edmonstone, also came over to the Governor-General's plans.

As to Sindhia, his position was particularly unhappy. Looking round the rapidly narrowing field still open to him, he objected to the protection of Jhansi and other principalities. His expenses were heavy and were increasing. He was paying five lakhs annually for the upkeep of John Baptiste's army to keep down the Pindaris, 'solely with a view to an increase of friendship with the British Government', whose Resident was hostile and returned flat refusals to all expressions of his desires.

Sindhia's own court, during part of every year, was an armed camp, which moved round his dominions, collecting revenue by the argument of artillery. In January 1815 the Governor-General rejoiced over an episode 'equally fortunate and equally beyond calculation', which 'has been of no little benefit to us in this crisis'. Sindhia's two chief generals fought a pitched battle, in which one took many guns from the other.

In all this, his own attitude and actions and the attitude and actions of others, the Governor-General never pretended that there was any case for judgment on moral grounds. His outlook was solely 'realist' (and in a better sense than that of this much abused term to-day). A disillusioned old man, steeped in Regency intrigues and politics long before he came to India, he was singularly free from the habit of patriotic misrepresentation, either of his own or his country's doings. At the outset of his term, he had written (February 1814) of 'the wanton provocations which we have been giving on trivial subjects to all the States around us'. 'We are engaged in captious bickerings with all around us.' These States

> 'must be ready to start up into combination whenever they may see us occupied with an enemy capable of employing our forces for any time. . . . We have not simply to look to the irritation of those whom we have actually scourged with nettles. Each sovereign must have brought the case home to himself, and must have secretly sympathized with the durbars which he saw insulted and humiliated.'

The Nawab Wazir of Oudh had been made to cede a large territory as the price of independence explicitly promised, but found himself still in galling tutelage, and had been 'driven to a desperation which he proclaimed in open durbar'. The Bhonsla Raja was openly aggrieved. 'The Nizam does not disguise his absolute hatred of us, though he is in shackles whence he cannot extricate himself.' The Raja of Mysore and his Resident 'are engaged in a contest of mutual crimination'. And inside their own territories, though the Company were all-powerful, they were unloved, because of the depression to which they had brought the people and their refusal either to use them in honourable employments or to treat them with courtesy:

> 'Again and again I say that men are to be gratified not by what we think important, but by what comes home to their habitual feelings and prejudices, howsoever trifling it may appear to us. This is a policy sadly neglected by the British in this country, and the consequence is visible in the very little approach to assimilation towards which our long dominion over the country has led the natives.'

Lord Hastings had to deal with the political situation as he found it, however, and to put on one side his private convictions. The line he ultimately took was dictated partly by the necessities of the position, which he judged calmly and disinterestedly, without sentiment of any kind—the excitement and enthusiasm of the early days of the war with Napoleon, when Wellesley was Governor-General, had vanished like a dream. Reinforcing his own judgment he had Metcalfe's urgent advocacy of a policy of *Thorough*—of a strong hand that would extirpate moribund regalities and enforce a general peace and submission. The two met in November 1814; Hastings was touring the North-Western Provinces. In December, in the Governor-General's camp, Metcalfe drew up his plan for the pacification and settlement of Central India.

First, the pretensions of the Emperor, or King, as he was now styled, had to be settled. Metcalfe had repeatedly assured his Majesty that, while the Governor-General was anxious to pay him personal attentions, it was not possible to acquiesce in any ceremonial, however attenuated and symbolic, that in any degree acknowledged the suzerainty which the Emperor claimed over the British dominions. Lord Hastings concurred. 'It is dangerous to uphold for the Mussulmans a rallying-point, sanctioned by our acknowledgment that a just title to supremacy exists in the King of Delhi.' What made it particularly dangerous was the likelihood that the next King would be of very different character, the energetic Prince Jahangir:

> 'We should then find that we had invested a young vigorous man, who cherishes the deepest animosity towards us, with unquestioned right to call on the native sovereigns for support against our oppressive encroachments on his rule. We should have difficulty in making out a good case consistently with our own theory; and the practical part of the business might be no less embarrassing. The house of Timour had been put so much out of sight, that all notion of adverting to it was failing fast in India; and nothing has kept up the floating notion of a duty owed to the imperial family but our gratuitous and persevering exhibition of their pretensions—an exhibition attended

with much servile obeisance in the etiquettes imposed upon us by the ceremonial of the court.'[1]

Warren Hastings, who had enjoyed it as a kind of stately play, had written in terms of creeping humility to the Emperor. But Lord Hastings rightly saw that the time when this was innocuous had gone by. He refused to visit the King in person, since the King was unwilling to be visited except as a suzerain. The Governor-General took a further significant step in peremptorily stopping the *nazars* (token gifts of homage) hitherto presented by Residents on special occasions. 'This custom I have abrogated: considering such a public testimony of dependence and subservience as irreconcileable to any rational policy.' The King was to receive their value in one consolidated sum.

The whole drive was now towards rational, and utterly away from sentimental, policy. Metcalfe's famous paper, which exercised a profound influence for many years to come, distinguished between three kinds of Native State: (1) 'substantive states, ardently desiring our overthrow, and ambitious to aggrandise themselves'; (2) 'military powers not substantive states . . . living by plunder and devastation—the enemies of all regular governments, more especially hostile in spirit to us', 'more dangerous, perhaps', than the substantive states; (3) 'petty states . . . subject to the continual plunder and oppression of the two former classes, who in consequence look up to us for protection, and are therefore well-disposed towards us'. Delighting in political discussion, which no man ever handled more illuminatingly, he was aware that this division, like all divisions, presented confusions. His analysis of the states' characters, and his sub-division of them, showing how one class tended to rise to a higher class or sink to a lower one, and how some states partook of the particularities of more than one class, is masterly. Almost every sentence merits quotation, for sheer delight in its expressive quality; it is equally fine as an exposition of political realism, less unscrupulously machiavellian than it seems on the surface.

The substantive states had 'armies in their service capable of being converted at a moment's warning into instruments of destruction to our provinces'; these states 'only want an encouraging opportunity to strike a blow at our existence'. The military states were 'less tangible and had less to lose', but were a potential inundation liable, at any weakening of the barriers which held them back, to overrun British territory. Sindhia was the most powerful of his three substantive states, the other two, Holkar and

[1] *Journal*, 22 January 1815.

the Bhonsla, being very much on the decline, so riddled with dissension that they seemed about to break up into robber fragments. All three, however, were 'hostile in heart, and in heart confederated against us'; only necessity would force them to fly to the Company's protecting arms. The military states Metcalfe distinguished into Pindaris generally, and Amir Khan and Muhammad Khan. The last two were settling down into a double role, 'as servants of Holkar and as independent chieftains'; Amir Khan, especially, with his regular army and powerful artillery, seemed likely to emerge as a substantive state. All these organizations, 'and all others that exist by upsetting peaceful states and disturbing the general tranquillity', must be considered as enemies, since they forced the Company to take the same defensive precautions as against avowed enemies.

The 'petty states' were the Rajput ones, and those on the borders of Gujarat, 'and, generally, all states who are subject to the oppression of the military and predatory powers'. Substantive and military states should be annihilated or reduced to helplessness. 'The weak and harmless and well-disposed petty states' should be supported because of vital interest, though their protection was also 'a just and proper object of wise and liberal policy'.

Before anything else could be done, however, the Pindaris must be extirpated. It was a waste of time to try to differentiate among them. They were all equally noxious, all of them the enemies of every state, busy ravaging British territory or that of allies. No campaigning could be undertaken without the likelihood that they would seize the opportunity of doing a little looting behind the British back. 'We ought to recollect that the Pindarree is now what the Mahratta power was in the decline of the Mogul Empire.' Take warning, and escape that Empire's downfall, which was 'chiefly from the hands of the predecessors of the Pindarrees'.

It was hard to strike at an insect-cloud, such as the Pindaris were. Their reputation and power, Metcalfe pointed out, did not depend on their victories, for they never won any, and repeated defeats would merely scatter them. But this was not quite the whole truth; they did possess some forts and lands, where they kept their families. Strike at these centres, and capture their families, at the same time hunting down armed bands remorselessly, giving them no respite till destroyed. Sindhia, Holkar, and the Bhonsla Raja should be 'invited' to assist. If they consented, and co-operated 'cordially'—a possibility which he regretfully admits is unlikely—their 'acting in union with the British Government for one common interest might lay the foundation of a general confederacy of the established states of India, with the British Government as the acknowledged head'—he says, harking wistfully back to the dreams of his master Lord Wellesley and anticipating the arrangement which was made three years later and has continued as the political framework of India until this day. If Sindhia, Holkar, and the Bhonsla Raja opposed or obstructed, they must be treated ruthlessly as enemies. 'The war in this case would require greater exertions', but would bring more solid gain. Yet—so long as they behaved in the spirit of their treaty engagements—'we have no right . . . to deviate from the spirit of existing engagements, however desirable a deviation may occasionally be', though (he adds longingly) 'we ought never to forget, that as long as these, or any of these powers, are military, ambitious, and unprincipled, it is our interest to overthrow them, or bring them under our influence'. Every opportunity, consistently with good faith and justice, should be taken to bring about one of these two results. If war came with one of these powers, 'it is our interest to secure the greatest possible acquisition of territory, in order that we may maintain the greatest possible amount of force'.

The Governor-General, with his contempt for any pretence to possession of lofty political principles, did not conceal his intention to bar 'the continuance of that confederacy of Bassein' (which, apparently, he thought still in being). By that Treaty it had been intended to shut the Marathas in for ever.[1]

As to Amir Khan and Muhammad Khan, the satellites of that confederacy, they must be disposed of, either by destruction or by disbanding their troops and giving them some provision, Metcalfe advised—an alternative which showed that he had done some thinking over their proposals (which he had received in his ominously silent manner) to settle down as orthodox princes and regard their harvest of wild oats as at last adequate. Though Muntazim-ud-Daula had said nothing, he had seen that their point was well taken.

Through these years, he needed to have the hundred eyes of Argus, and ears that could catch a thousand whispers. A selection of details from his reports and letters will show the constant maddening crisscrossing of intrigue and petty warfare, that was hardly anything as dignified as even brigandage. If ever 'States' had fallen to pieces, and almost out of existence—as close to utter dematerialization as can be conceived without becoming that completely—the dominions of the Indian Princes, with few exceptions (and most of those very partial exceptions), had done this,

[1] *Private Journal of the Marquess of Hastings*, 23 March 1817.

before the British took over paramountcy and established them and picked them out of limbo.

Banswara and Udaipur (Metcalfe tells Adam) are begging for a treaty and protection, which has been in especial Udaipur's constant prayer. The Company's treaties with Sindhia and Holkar, 'exclusive of the prevailing principles of our present policy', forbade this, so he had returned his usual reply.[1] Udaipur then varied the request, into one for the Rana's reinstatement, chiefly against his barons who were in rebellion.[2] Jaipur, after buying off assailants (its constant task), in extreme distress, its Raja hard pressed, also faces rebellion. Holkar is temporarily inactive, encamped on the Chambal. Kharim Khan is at large in his own camp, a semi-prisoner, closely watched by his own men. Amir Khan too is in trouble; his unpaid troops have mutinied, and one of his chiefs asks to enter Company service. The Pindaris are raiding Kotah.[3] Jodhpur seeks an alliance, and has received the same reply as others.[4] A Bharatpur subject has committed an outrage inside British territory, and Metcalfe has sent a protest to the Raja.[5] Holkar is likely to release Kharim Khan.[6] Metcalfe is having immense bother with Bharatpur, whose agents are unwilling to leave Delhi, as ordered. Until 'the entire removal of all restraints that are inconsistent with the relations existing between our Government and Bhurtpoor and with the practise of Native States, one towards another, I have no intention of permitting the return of the Bhurtpoor Agents to Dihlee'. He is getting endless letters from the Raja; once four in one day.[7] The Raja of Macheri is now behaving well.[8] Holkar has had the kindness to warn Metcalfe against Jaipur, whose habit of intrigue has often caused trouble. 'The plunder of Jypoor has been long monopolised by Meer Khan and does not afford any direct aid to the Court of Holkar.'[9] Ranjit Singh has had a mutiny,[10] and one of his hill chiefs has forged a letter from Metcalfe, instructing him not to pay tribute to the Sikh ruler. Ranjit has shown it to Metcalfe's news-writer, and Metcalfe has sent a friendly assurance that it is not authentic. Ranjit is raising a Gurkha corps, which he expects to find useful in the hills. Amir Khan is often the prisoner of his unpaid soldiery. Muhammad Khan wants to be employed in the Company's war with Nepal (it was clear that the veteran bandits felt their sands were running out). Jodhpur and Udaipur are

[1] Poona Records: 29 March 1814. [2] *Ibid*: 3 April 1814.
[3] *Ibid*: 29 March 1814. [4] *Ibid*: 3 April. [5] *Ibid*: same date.
[6] *Ibid*: 21 February. [7] *Ibid*: 23 February. [8] *Ibid*: 15 February.
[9] *Ibid:* 28 March 1815. [10] *Ibid*: 13 April.

insistent to be given treaties, and Jaipur still more so (urging that there is no obstacle of any treaty with the Maratha chiefs).[1] The Peshwa is intriguing with the Court of Holkar.[2]

[1] *Ibid*: 21 May 1815. [2] *Ibid*: 15 July 1816.

XXXV

PRELIMINARIES OF THE PINDARI CAMPAIGN

METCALFE AT last took steps to accept the allegiance which the Rajput and other states had proferred so long. Under his instructions, in March 1815 John Wauchope, the British Resident in Bundelkhand, drew up the first draft of a treaty with Bhopal, which had been in friendly relations with the Company ever since Warren Hastings' time. The treaty became formal in the general pacification of India after the Peshwa's downfall, its actual ratification being on 26 February 1818. It will serve as an example of all these treaties of this time. Variations were slight, and do not touch their general tenor and texture.

There were fourteen open articles: (1) A permanent friendship and alliance. The friends and enemies of one were to be the friends and enemies of both. (2) The Company guaranteed the Nawab and his line, and to 'protect his rights in the same manner as its own from all enemies Whatever'. (3) The State was to receive a subsidiary force, and British troops were to be free always to use Bhopal in case of necessity. (4) Because of the devastation Bhopal had suffered, the Company agreed to forgo the cost of its subsidiary troops for one year, and to consider forgoing part of their cost for a second year. (5) Bhopal handed over a military station for the subsidiary force. (6) The Company was entitled to diminish or increase its subsidiary force, but there would be no increase of the charge for it. (7) The State would help to get cattle for British rations. (8) If the Company were at war, the State would help in hostilities, and also to get supplies. (9) There would be no internal interference by the protecting Power. (10) Bhopal would submit disputes to the protecting Power's arbitrament. (11) In case of war, the State would act under the orders of the British Government. (12) It would hold no negotiations with other States, without the Company's consent and knowledge. (13) It would employ no European or American, or any subject of another State; without the Company's sanction. (14) Ratification would be within fourteen days.

A secret article promised that the Company would try to get back for the State territory occupied by the Pindaris or taken by Sindhia and given to Pindari leaders.[1]

[1] *I.O.R., H.M.S.*, 599 (7), pp. 295–305. The same file, in its preceding section—(6)—contains letters from Lord Hastings to the Governor of Cey-

When Metcalfe took Bhopal under protection, Sagar also was taken. This gave the Company a belt of territory linking two important rivers, the Jumna and the Narbada.

Then, in 1816, the Raja of Jaipur was pinned into his capital by Amir Khan, who brought up 200 cannon. In his desperation he begged again and again for a subsidiary alliance,[1] which Metcalfe granted. A British force assembled on the Jaipur frontier, and Amir Khan hurriedly withdrew his precious guns. The Raja thereupon sent expresses to his *vakils* at Delhi, telling them not to sign the treaty. Metcalfe in response merely asked for an explicit declaration that the matter was finished, and remarked that the Raja was now left to his fate. The Governor-General was equally unimpassioned, noting (11 June) that 'the conduct of the Jyepore Rajah shows with how short a forecast these native princes act, and may explain how they have successively sunk before our steady policy'. In October, the Raja took fright again, and said his *vakils* had been mistaken, and implored to be accepted as a feudatory. Lord Hastings observed that he wanted the appearance of alliance with the Company, without the objectionable fact of subordination to them. To the Raja he replied that he could sign the treaty he had already rejected, but without further argument. The Raja procrastinated. But his actions had ceased to have any relevance. The stage was set for war and a comprehensive settlement.

This last[2] Anglo-Maratha war was unavoidable. Nevertheless, lesser factors than the inevitability of sooner or later clearing up the appalling chaos of Central India operated towards its outbreak. In April 1816 the Governor-General received the news of a Pindari incursion into British territory, the Guntur Sircar, south of Orissa.[3] They swept up the young girls along with other booty, tying them three or four, 'like calves on a horse, to be sold'. Hundreds of women drowned themselves, to escape violation. In one village the inhabitants set fire to their huts and immolated themselves. 'I am strictly forbidden by the Court of Directors', the Governor-General lamented, 'to undertake the suppression of the fiends who occasioned this heart-rending scene, lest I should provoke a war with the Mahrattas.' But in December he persuaded his Council

lon, 6 December 1814, explaining the necessity of taking over Bhopal and Sagar; and similar correspondence occurs elsewhere in this file. The settlement of India was a protracted process, practically settled from the time when Metcalfe and the Governor-General first discussed it. But they both waited and watched their time.

[1] 25 Sept. 1816. [2] The war with Gwalior in 1843 was a mere local episode.

[3] Through 1816 and 1817, they raided Madras Presidency more than once, from headquarters on the River Narbada.

to a unanimous declaration that the Pindaris must be extirpated, war or no war. He prepared for both contingencies and notified the Directors of this decision.

The general expectation was that undoubtedly a new general Maratha war must result, and it caused intense joy. 'The sportsmen of the day regarded it as a grand *battue* of the princes and chiefs of India.'[1] The 'great game' had been played unsatisfactorily against the Gurkhas; it was to be resumed under conditions which made success a certainty. Nor was expectation disappointed. The campaign which followed was undoubtedly the pleasantest and easiest which the British ever waged in India. The Marathas, who saw the attack on the Pindaris as merely a cloak and excuse to extinguish their own last vestiges of independence, were greatly alarmed.

An army of over 100,000 men, including 13,000 Europeans, with 300 guns, was launched at the Pindari haunts along the Narbada and the Sipra, in Malwa and the Vindhya mountains. This force was divided into a Northern Army, personally commanded by the Governor-General, and a Southern Army, under Sir Thomas Hislop, the Commander-in-Chief of Madras Presidency, who had with him Sir John Malcolm as his principal brigadier and also political officer.

Malcolm's joy at finding himself in high military command at last, a soldier and not a mere diplomat, was almost childlike. 'What is really delightful, from the Governor-General down to the lowest, black or white, red or brown, clothed or naked, all appear happy at my advancement.' As the Southern Army moved northward, in Mysore 'I was welcomed with horns and taumtaums, dancing girls, amildars, peons, bazaar-men; in short, by high and low, of every description. My vanity was not a little tickled to hear *Malcolm-Sahib* on every tongue'.[2] The war was not regarded as a serious one, and personal popularity could be safely indulged, allowing the best liked man in India to try his hand at strategy and tactics.

Both armies together operated as a vast net drawing closer and closer to the Pindari fastnesses. The Pindaris fell back, trusting (one surmises, not too hopefully) to secret promises of help from the Peshwa.

The only objections were those raised by the department responsible for financial supplies. H. St. G. Tucker, observing, 14 November 1814, 'We must be downright bunglers if we cannot

[1] Kaye, *Life of Malcolm*, ii. 187.
[2] 9 July 1817.

find at any moment an excuse for interfering in the affairs of Hindostan and the Dekhun', foresaw that, however far the frontier was extended, it would always have troublesome neighbours. 'Annihilate you must, in pretty round numbers, if you are determined that no soldiers of fortune shall remain in any part of India'. However, the war proved less costly than he feared, thanks to the Nawab of Oudh's assistance, both in loans and by purchase of territory taken from Nepal; and the annihilation of the Pindaris was in the end effected as nearly completely as could be expected. Lord Hastings' relations of personal friendship with the Prince Regent made him feel the political, as well as social, superior of the Directors, and he went ahead with his plans, not overmuch troubled by fear of their possible disapproval.

The Governor-General announced (6 May 1817) that he wished 'to pursue a course which will promote the stability of even Scindiah's and Holkar's Governments. Were those chiefs, however, to make common cause with the Pindarrees, either openly or by covert assistance, they would discard their character as rulers of states, and must be dealt with as predatory aggressors'. All the Maratha chiefs, accordingly, were ordered in the frankest manner to co-operate.

Holkar, who was a child, his court in 'everlasting turmoil', took no action until action was doomed to certain disaster. Sindhia sullenly thought of refusal. After the spasmodic attempts he had made to check the Pindaris[1] when they went beyond tolerable bounds, he and they had come to a kind of 'gentlemen's agreement' by which they usually spared his territory. Indolent and low-spirited, he thought that even the East India Company, this demon of restlessness which an incalculable Providence had set in the midst of India, might have let things rest and slide. In the time's chronic confusion, standards of order and comfort had sunk low, and he felt that his oppressors were fussing unnecessarily. He protested and procrastinated. But he had few friends to help him. Malcolm might have 'fallen in love with him', as Elphinstone remarked; but Elphinstone and Metcalfe, who had both served short terms at his court, loathed him, and passed their distrust on to the Governor-General. When the British demands were put before his Minister, the latter 'shrugged up his shoulders and said, "The weakest must obey the stronger" '. The Resident caught at the expression, and asked sternly if he was suggesting that the British Government were meditating any unprovoked hostility. Oh, no,

[1] Valentine Blacker, *Memoir of the Operations of the British Army in India during the Mahratta War of 1817, 1818, and 1819*, 3.

was the hurried reply; 'the customs of the British Government were too well known for anything insidious to be apprehended . . . but it was still humiliating to appear to act through constraint'. He was assured that everything possible would be done to avoid that appearance, and was grateful. The appearance was nevertheless difficult to avoid altogether, for Sindhia had to grant free passage through all parts of his dominions: to bind himself not to raise any troops during the operations or to move any division of his army from its present station: and to surrender temporarily, as security for his honesty, the forts of Hindia and Asirgarh, which, as the Governor-General noted with satisfaction, 'absolutely commanded' his territories. The arrangement 'is to render his power very unimportant ever after'.

The Army of the North moved rapidly, and by November 1817 was in control of Sindhia's State. He subscribed (5 November) 'to all the conditions which I dictated, and has swallowed a bitter drench in so doing. I should have thought myself oppressive had he not been so thoroughly false a fellow', wrote the Governor-General, resolved 'to rivet such shackles upon Scindiah and Holkar' that they would be 'impotent. In fact, the downfall of the Mahrattas is achieved'. He knew that Sindhia's self-respect would never recover[1] from having to abandon to destruction those Pindaris who had lived under his protection, and to give up his forts.

But, though it was the Company's conquests that had first broken up the polity of Central India, to drive those conquests through to a finish was now the only policy which could mitigate an appalling state of affairs. Lord Hastings' piety was of a mild and occasional kind. Unlike some who have been more fervent, however, in some degree he genuinely cared for what befell the common people. 'I trust that my soul is adequately grateful to the Almighty for allowing me to be the humble instrument of a change beneficial to so many of my fellow-creatures.' There was nothing ethical about his piety, though, as was revealed when Sindhia's acceptance of the harsh terms imposed and his unsporting refusal to put up a fight led to what has some claims to be considered the most extraordinary official pronouncement ever made in India. Sindhia could, and should, have done better and more valiantly! He had under arms 31,500 men, and had 140 light

[1] Malcolm observes that Sindhia was 'forced to abandon his cherished prospects, and to become, at the very moment he was recognized as its most powerful chief, the marked deserter of the cause of his Nation'. *Central India*, ii. 227–8.

guns.[1] The British Army were disappointed, and the Governor-General, sharing their regret, apologized to them. 'His Highness', he announced,

> 'engages to afford every facilitation to the British troops. . . . In consequence, the troops and country of His Highness are to be regarded as those of an ally. The generous confidence and animated zeal of the army may experience a shade of disappointment in the diminished prospect of serious exertion; but the Governor-General is convinced that the reflection of every officer and soldier in the army will satisfy him that the carrying every point by equity and moderation is the proudest triumph for the British character.'

It was going to be a poor war. Nevertheless, let all work to make it as good a war as possible; and let them remember, as some consolation, that they possessed what was far far better than loot or glory, the consciousness of perfect rectitude.

However, the Peshwa and the Bhonsla Raja (whose example Holkar belatedly followed) made it a somewhat more satisfactory war than at first seemed likely.

[1] In October 1817. Colonel Blacker gives for other possible enemies these figures: Holkar had 24,000 men and 107 guns: the Peshwa 41,000 men and 37 guns: the Raja of Nagpur 33,500 men and 85 guns: the Nizam about 50,000 men, a dispirited rabble, and an artillery of unknown strength: Amir Khan had (in May 1817), 12,000 cavalry and 'several indifferent battalions', and 200 to 300 guns: Muhammad Shah Khan about 12,000 infantry, 6,000 cavalry, and 112 guns. Malcolm estimated Sindhia's forces at 15,500 horse, 13,000 regular infantry, and between 300 and 400 guns: Holkar's at 15,000 horse, 10,000 infantry, and about 100 guns: Amir Khan's at 20,000 horse, 8,000 infantry, and about 200 guns.

XXXVI

ELPHINSTONE AND THE PESHWA

AFTER TRIMBAKJI'S escape, the Peshwa worked hard to restore the Maratha confederacy that had so long ago fallen into disrepair. He was not very successful, but he sent his secret messengers from court to court, and made his own preparations. He seems to have worked himself up into a state of terror and hatred of the imperturbable man who was watching him, reckless of his own safety. One night, in the spring of 1817, one of Elphinstone's assistants (John Briggs, afterwards Lieutenant-General Briggs) came to him to tell him that the Peshwa's guns were drawn up, with their transport bullocks, that Poona streets were full of armed men, and the Peshwa was in durbar discussing the question of immediate war. Elphinstone was in a large tent, 'engaged in playing a round game of cards with a party, among whom were several ladies'. He saw from Briggs' manner that he had anxious news. But he continued the game as usual, and then, 'after handing the last lady of the party into her palankeen, he came up to me rubbing his hands, and said, "Well, what is it?" ' He received Briggs' tidings calmly, and they walked together to his office, where they found the European officer of the Residency force. They decided that nothing could be done but wait. They waited accordingly, and the night passed quietly, the Peshwa shrinking back from actual war.

Next day, however, Elphinstone sent for a reinforcement and two more guns. The Governor-General at the same time wrote to the Peshwa,

> 'for the purpose of showing him that we were apprized of what he had been doing. I mentioned this kindly as an aberration of which I was sure he had not comprehended the quality, entreating that no shyness might follow the discovery, but that he would rest upon me with all his former confidence if he determined (as I doubted not would be the case) to dispel from his mind projects incompatible with the friendship between the two states.'[1]

The Peshwa replied in the same gently elegiac strain, expressing gratitude for the way in which his attempt to recover merely his old titular pre-eminence among the Marathas—an attempt he now saw was open to misconstruction—had been taken. He asked

[1] *Private Journal*, 23 May 1817.

forgiveness, repudiated his agents (who 'had gone beyond his instructions'), and threw himself unreservedly on the British Government's generosity, imploring them 'to rely implicitly on his good faith and attachment to a government to which he owed his dominions'.

He continued to assemble troops, while Elphinstone, an unsleeping silent Argus, looked on with the absorbed interest of a naturalist about to complete the study of patient years. The infatuated Peshwa pressed for the pardon of Trimbakji, who was now almost openly in high command. To Elphinstone he flung out a threat, which with contemptuous charity was passed over 'as a momentary ebullition of peevishness'. In April, the subsidiary force, assisted by a *jagirdar* whose heart was not in his nominal dependence on the Peshwa, routed Trimbakji's troops, so that he became again a fugitive.

The Governor-General now had complete proof of the Peshwa's intrigues. He knew also that Sindhia and Holkar had promised assistance in a war against the Company. This was probably not more than polite acquiescence in an earnest request; the Peshwa's stock was excessively low, and from first to last there is no sign that any State, however desperate, wanted him as an ally. But Lord Hastings hardened his heart against them, and he drew close his net:

'I deceive myself much if I leave them the power of stirring. I am satisfied that none of them, not even the Peishwa, are aware of the degree in which I have silently and gradually augmented the divisions on the southern frontiers of the Mahrattas, from a timely conception of the exigencies likely to occur. Those different bodies, in fact armies, are in positions which would allow of their acting instantaneously; and they intercept the communication between the native powers as far as regards the march of bodies of troops.'

The blow was prepared, and could be struck at any moment.

Elphinstone had just picked up from Herodotus the proverb, 'What cares Hippocleides?' and was watching what might be the approach of his death, with that perfect mixture of coolness and imagination which astonishes afresh every time the reader comes across it in his journals (which is almost on every page). The moment his mind was freed from the immediate necessity for action, it was absorbed in some new book: Southey's *Life of Nelson*, a book of travels in Greece or one on early eighteenth-century politics and discussing Swift and Arbuthnot. During a long night ride, he and a companion repeated with delight the ' "Country Churchyard", the "Allegro" and "Penseroso", and some other poetry' (14 February).

'*7 March.* Hard fagging at Trimbukjee and the Peshwa. I do not see how all this is to end. Last night the moon was nearly full, and it was cloudy. The combination gave a peculiar, romantic, and even awful light. I walked about and enjoyed it. It was a night to see a good spirit. I have something of the hot-weather-feel this evening. . . .

24 March. I have been hard at the Peshwa and Trimbukjee. The former is recruiting and putting forts in order; the latter is breaking out. Things draw to a crisis. I have sent in plans for the future, political and military. . . . The weather is hot now, but my health is not bad, and my spirits are excellent. I do not know whether to attribute it to my being busy and interested, or to the new philosophy I have taken up; but I have not for a long time felt so cheerful and easy in society as of late. I wish it were the latter cause, which is permanent, and arises from myself.

28 March. The 17th marched in. I have been reading the *Edinburgh Review* with a capital critique on Swift, and some instructive discussion about his character. Things looked very like war yesterday, but to-day have come round. . . .

31 March. The Peshwa submitted yesterday, and agreed to dismiss his troops, dismantle his garrisons, and wait the Governor-General's decision, which I have told him would be more or less severe, in proportion to the sincerity with which he acts against the rebels. I do not much think his Highness is at all sincere. Even if he is, we may have a row still. I have put tatties up to-day. The days are rather hot, and I am feverish; but the moonlight nights are cool and delightful, and on the whole there is no reason to complain yet'.

General Lionel Smith moved forward troops, in detachments and unobtrusively, till they were where a forced march would bring them all together at Poona. Then Elphinstone, laying aside his literary studies, ordered the Peshwa (30 March) to choose between immediate war and an engagement to surrender Trimbakji within one month, meanwhile handing over his three strongest fortresses (Raigarh, Singarh, Purundar) as a pledge of good faith.[1] He was given twenty-four hours to reply.

At midnight, he sent a temporizing answer to Elphinstone, who replied that his instructions left him no room to negotiate. 'He had no further function till his Highness's choice was made'. At eight next morning, the city was invested; the Peshwa submitted, and proclaimed a reward of £25,000 for the arrest of Trimbakji, who to the relief of everyone disappeared. A new treaty was signed (13 June 1817), by which the Peshwa repudiated for ever all claims to supremacy in the Maratha confederacy and declared the other chieftains independent. He engaged not to interfere with them in any way, not to maintain representatives at any other Court or to receive representatives, not to admit into his dominions any European or American without the Resident's con-

[1] He received them back in November.

sent. All contested points between him and the Gaekwar were settled in the latter's favour, and he ceded to the Company his rights in Bundelkhand and the fortress of Ahmadnagar—which was 'of extraordinary importance in keeping up the communication between the Hyderabad and the Poonah subsidiary forces'—and districts connecting Bombay Presidency and Surat and affording 'a clear revenue of thirty-four lacs of rupees' (£425,000). He lost all his territory north of the Narbada. That is, he put himself in fetters, as well as practically out of the list of ruling powers. Elphinstone expressed his belief that he was now bound to break into open hostility, if ever encouraging circumstances arose. The Governor-General agreed. Both made their silent preparations, and the Governor-General proceeded, as already related, to put shackles on Sindhia and Holkar.

XXXVII

AMIR KHAN. THE RAJPUT STATES

THERE REMAINED Amir Khan. Prinsep[1] sets out the distinction between him and the Pindaris. The latter were common robbers (except perhaps their most efficient member, Chitu); Amir Khan was a most uncommon one. They attacked individuals; he held up governments, and

'moved about with the materials of regular battles and sieges, so as to work on the fears of princes and men in power, extorting contributions and other advantages from them by such intimidation as an efficient army only could impress.'

So respectable a brigand, as Metcalfe pointed out (though not to Amir Khan himself), must be given 'some provision . . . to induce and enable him to quit his present course of life, and it is proper that it should consist of the same territories which have hitherto supported him as a pest to the peaceable part of India'. These territories he held nominally from the Holkar family. But the latter were in extreme distress, desperately embarrassed and disorganized and weak. Metcalfe, at Delhi, as superhumanly watchful and unshaken as Elphinstone at Poona, thought their refraining from asking for Company assistance

'one of the strongest proofs that could be conceived of their reluctance to be connected with us. The only idea that I can suppose to govern their councils is that of struggling, if possible, with their distresses, and retaining their independence until the arrival of the young Maharajah at manhood, in the hope that he may be able to restore the honor of the fallen state. They know that their independence must cease as soon as they come under our protection; they therefore try every expedient rather than apply to us, and even have recourse to Scindiah, their old enemy, for pecuniary assistance.'

The wolf himself at last appeared as a convinced penitent, prepared to take the cowl and vows, but a little disappointed to be given not too warm encouragement. Amir Khan represented to Metcalfe that 'because of his advanced age' he wished to show his attachment to the British, not by attacking his fellow-robbers but Sind and the countries bordering the Indus (Bhawalpur chiefly). He was nervous of pillaging Jaipur, whose Raja had forged Metcalfe's signature (which was well known and closely studied)

[1] *History of the Political and Military Transactions in India during the Administration of the Marquess of Hastings*, i. 49.

to a document with which he had frightened his persecutor. 'Affected concealment on a matter of notoriety would have been useless.' Metcalfe therefore admitted to Amir Khan's Agent that at one time the Governor-General *had* contemplated (with the friendliest intentions towards Holkar and Amir Khan) taking Jaipur under his protection, but the Raja had lost the chance by double-dealing, 'and matters were just as they were . . . with the addition of some displeasure against the Court of Jypoor for its deceitful and inconsistent conduct'.[1] This was an indication that Jaipur was to be delivered over to Satan for a while longer, till it had been taught not to blaspheme. Amir Khan's Agent retired to give his master the news, for what it was worth.

A sensation was caused at Holkar's Court, by the British advance to punish Pindaris south of the Narbada.[2] Threatened chiefs got together. The Peshwa, Sindhia, Amir Khan, and others intrigued against the Company. Metcalfe doubted if Amir Khan (whose mind he was closely watching) would openly express himself on their side, but he noted 'the spirit of malicious misrepresentation which prevails regarding our operations at Poona'.[3] There was a report that the British had demanded from Raja Chandu Lal, the Nizam's Minister, 50 lakhs in cash and land producing another 50 lakhs in revenue. The Raja had refused, so the British were advancing on Hyderabad![4] Some of the rumours agitating Central India were wild in the extreme.[5]

His world must have seemed *maya*, illusion. He was a centre of spinning eddies of dust and wind and conspiracy and legend, surrounded by childish reckless minds. Amir Khan now became a frequent suppliant, possibly (Metcalfe thought) a sincere one. He was old, and his army was often rebellious. 'He may perhaps desire rest and security for the remaining years of his life, and . . . naturally . . . some certain provision for his Family, under the Guarantee of the only Power in India in whose faith strength and stability he can have any confidence.' He offered to surrender his artillery, which he said was his own property. Metcalfe disliked and distrusted him, but was thinking things over.[6] Amir Khan was presently at odds with Sindhia, and in danger of utter ruin.[7]

Holkar's camp was in more than its usual tumult and disorder,[8] agitated by rumours of the Pindaris' rout.[9] Jodhpur? 'I believe that

[1] Poona Records: 25 September 1816. [2] *Ibid:* December 13.
[3] *Ibid*: 22 July 1817. [4] *Ibid*: 25 July.
[5] *Ibid*: see especially letters dated 24 June, 5 and 10 August 1817.
[6] *Ibid*: 22 March 1817. [7] *Ibid*: 16 April. [8] *Ibid*: 4 February.
[9] *Ibid*: 27 February.

the Raja is occasionally subject to fits of insanity, and altogether not capable of governing.'[1] Shah Suja, that Wandering Afghan, wrote asking help to reconquer his country, and offering part of it, including Multan, as a gift. Or (for these suppliants were rich in alternative suggestions) he would like help to recover just Multan, after which the rest of the land would fall to him by course of nature. Or—to take from Ranjit Singh what that redoubtable adventurer had formerly taken from him. These matters Metcalfe put by, as beyond his province, and involving our good relations with other Powers. He refused to interfere against Ranjit Singh. Shah Suja, observing 'that all our proceedings are dilatory and require "the Life of Noah and the Patience of Job" ', had written these proposals out. His Agent said he could achieve the conquests unaided, but would want assistance to keep them. So he was willing therefore to make such an arrangement as the Company had with Oudh, paying them in cash (or, if they preferred, in territory: Kashmir, Sind, or else those parts that produced good sepoys, Kabul, Kandahar and so on).[2] A most accommodating inquirer.

Finally, Amir Khan, aware that his long immunity was over, succeeded in making his peace with the Company, through Metcalfe, and became an orthodox Prince, Nawab of Tonk. Lord Hastings had at last made up his mind, and, the Company at this period being very generous, he detached from the Holkar State Amir Khan's own districts, thereby making him a gift of a region worth £125,000 to £150,000 annually, and presenting him with 'those territories which he has wrested from states with whose losses we have no concern. He becomes the feudatory of the British Government, employing his army according to our direction for the present, and disbanding it on our requisition. Scindiah must feel that this force could be instantly let loose on his back, in addition to other strength of ours, even were this division reduced by the pestilence to inertness. But there is such spirit and science in our officers, that the very chips of this division, howsoever it might be thinned, would defeat any native army which could be brought against them.'[3]

The transaction has been criticized, and Ochterlony wrote to Metcalfe that the measure was convenient but otherwise without 'propriety'. However, remarks Kaye, the Holkar State behaved badly a little later on, and so 'imparted to the treaty with Ameer Khan a sort of *ex post facto* justice'.[4] In that comment, Kaye betrays himself as the man of the next generation, one which, like Macbeth, what it would highly would also holily, would not play false and

[1] *Poona Records*: 26 April. [2] *Ibid*: same date.
[3] Hastings, *Private Journal*, 17 November 1817. [4] *Metcalfe*, i. 464.

yet would wrongly win. Hastings, Metcalfe, Ochterlony, all considered that by standards of strict political morality the action was indefensible, and defensible only as being expedient. One of the many features which make their period a pleasurable study to the historian is, as I have already observed, the almost unparalleled freedom of the actors from cant and humbug of every kind; the writer of the *D.N.B.* notice of Elphinstone comments on his complete lack of the fervent piety 'that marks other Indian heroes'. Instead, we have only—and always—perfect candour and clarity.

The defence of expediency is adequate. The chaos of Central India, however caused in its beginning, was now so great that pedantry was out of place. Also, there had always been an element of almost equality in the relations of Yeswant Rao Holkar and his chief follower, and, now that the former had given place to a mere child, to make distinctions of princely quality between the Holkar State and Amir Khan's very considerable power in his own right would have been, in Dr. Johnson's words, like settling the point of precedence between a louse and a flea. Accordingly, on 9 November 1817, Amir Khan ceased to be a bandit and became a Prince. He was assured that if he behaved well in the campaign already launched, he would be made a still bigger and better Prince. 'If he will depend on me, the narrow condition of the treaty shall not be the measure of his reward.' He behaved quite well, and the promise was kept, and overkept. Rampura (now styled Aligarh) fort and *pargana*[1] was added as a gift, and a three lakhs loan, which also later became a gift, was made to him. Amir Khan lived until 1834, when he died, highly esteemed, having well outlived his somewhat prolonged season of wild oat sowing. 'His days,' observed his biographer, two years before the veteran brigand's death, 'are spent in the enjoyment of domestic happiness, and in the performance of all religious observances, such as listening to the reading and interpretation of the Koran, or joining in social and instructive discourse with the learned and pious, who have found in his Court an asylum and honoured retreat . . . the virtues and amiable qualities which distinguish him among the Chiefs and great men of his age . . . surpass the feeble powers of his humble admirers.' With this attractive portrait we may take leave of him.

Metcalfe sent out also a circular letter to the Rajput chiefs, inviting them to become feudatories of the Company, paying to it any tribute hitherto paid to a Maratha state, 'leaving us to account for it to the party to whom it might be due'. Kotah,

[1] District.

Jodhpur, Udaipur, Bundi, Bikaner, Jaisalmir, and finally (2 April 1818) Jaipur,[1] along with other smaller Rajput states, accepted the invitation. Meanwhile, the Pindaris and every Maratha power except Sindhia and the Gaekwar had been shattered in battle.

[1] For Jaipur's unsatisfactory subsequent behaviour, see Kaye, *Life of Metcalfe*, i. 466.

XXXVIII

THE PESHWA'S OUTBREAK

ALL THROUGH the rains of 1817, when the country was unfitted for their forays, the Pindaris lay like three flocks of bustards, in three separate *durras* (bands), between Indore and Sagar, under three renowned leaders, Chitu, Kharim Khan, and Wasil Muhammad. Mutual enmities prevented a plan of campaign, though all knew they were threatened. In October, Wasil Muhammad sent a detachment to ravage behind one of the advancing British divisions, in Bundelkhand. But this was a mere flutter, checked quickly, and with it ended anything that can be called an attempt to resist their doom.

As soldiers, the Pindaris were perhaps the most despicable (and this is a high claim) that the British ever met in India. They were merely robbers on horseback, who shrank from action in the field. 'An immature civilization appears to be one cause', observes Colonel Blacker, 'of this prevalence of cavalry . . . in like manner, it is found that the young, even in civilized countries, always prefer the service of the cavalry'.[1] 'It was natural' for the Pindaris 'to avoid all contest, which could only impair their numbers without adding to their booty.'[2]

Towards the end of November, Kharim Khan and Wasil Muhammad united their *durras*. Finding themselves trapped in a restricted area near Gwalior, they turned hither and thither, losing a few men at each repulse of their efforts to break through, and others as stragglers whom the villagers cut off. The only fighting was at Jawad, 12 January 1818, where they were surprised and cut up, when preparing to march at dawn, and lost close on a thousand killed, to the British casualty list of sixty-three. One considerable section managed to escape to the south, and entered British territory in the northern Carnatic, where they were broken to pieces before the end of January. The two chieftains burnt their baggage, and with about 4,000 men fled west before their hunters. Meanwhile, Chitu, the ablest Pindari and the one who had attained nearest to independent princely status, joined Holkar's army, near Mahidpur.

But events at Poona by this time had overshadowed this Pindari

[1] Pp. 19–20. [2] *Ibid*, 61.

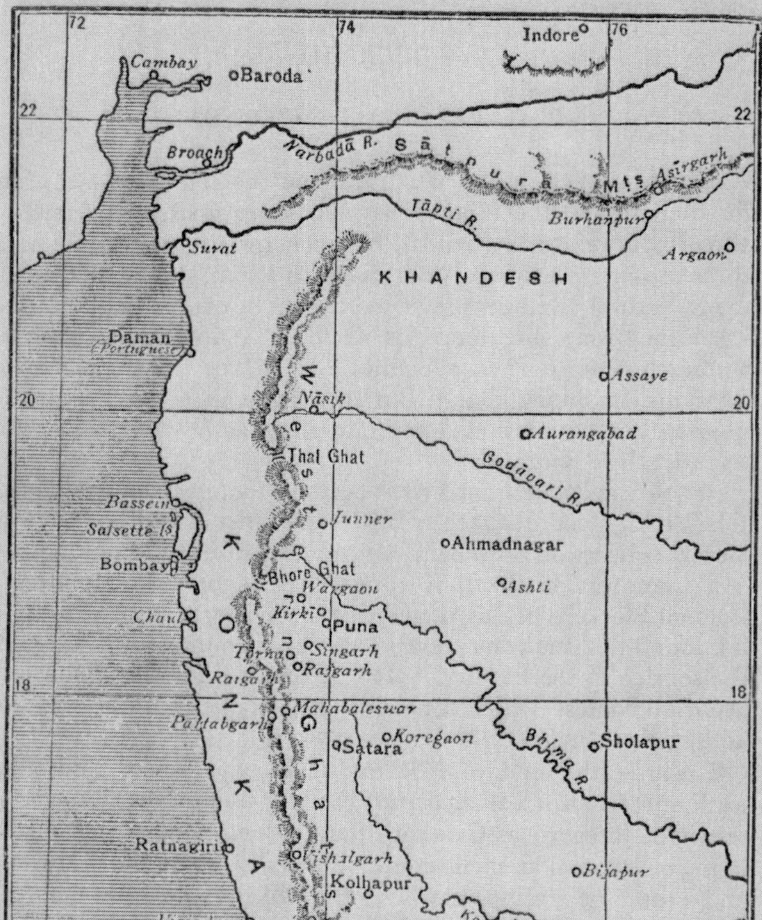

THE THIRD ANGLO-MARATHA WAR
Statute Miles
0
50
100
Indore
Cambay
Baroda
Broach
Narbadā R.
Sātpura Mts
Asirgarh
Tāpti R.
Burhanpur
Surat
Argaon
KHANDESH
Daman (Portuguese)
Assaye
Nāsik
Aurangabad
Thal Ghat
Godāvari R.
Bassein
Salsette I.
Junner
Ahmadnagar
Bombay
Bhore Ghat
Ashti
Chaul
Kirki
Puna
Singarh
Rajgarh
Raigarh
Mahabaleswar
Pattabgarh
Koregaon
Satara
Bhima R.
Sholapur
Western Ghats
KONKAN
Ratnagiri
Vishalgarh
Kolhapur
Bijapur
Krishna
Mudhol
Vingorla
Goa (Portuguese)
Dharwar
Marmagao
Karwar

business, which at best was merely a glorified police drive. Elphinstone had passed the summer troubled by unusual visitants, the blue devils of jealousy and discontent. 'It is a wretched thing in our Indian diplomatic line', he wrote (31 July), 'that we have just praise enough to stimulate ambition, without the possibility of gratifying it. This breeds bad passions and sullen reflections.' One might have thought that his career had been active and distinguished enough, in all conscience. However, so it was: Elphinstone, who had played the Peshwa so long, was now mortified that others seemed to be sent up to do the actual gaffing—Sir Thomas Hislop, with Malcolm as his Political Officer. Malcolm, as we have seen, aroused distrust in men who had not his knack of immediate and (as they thought) undignified access to native society. He was of ordinary origins, and Elphinstone at every moment of his existence was stiff with conscious aristocracy; his attitude to Malcolm had always patronage in it.

Malcolm, meanwhile, making his cheerful way across India, was spending July happily in Hyderabad—renewing old acquaintance, in his deplorably catholic fashion. He was hail-fellow-well-met with Princes and their Ministers, ready to play *holi* with them when that messy sport was seasonable. But he did not neglect humbler people, and was aware that everything does not lie in the hands of rulers and their advisers. At the Nizam's court, he reported, he

'was gratified at meeting my old friend Chandah (Maleekha), the celebrated dancing-girl. I had received several trays of fruit from this lady; she had also sent me her *picture,* with expressions of regard that were meant, she said, to revive pleasing recollections. The Court of Hyderabad is altered, and the dance and the song no longer prevail. A moody, melancholy sovereign, degraded and dejected nobles, and the impoverished retainers of a fallen Court, offer no field for the genius of Chandah; but even yet, changed as she is by eighteen years, she maintains considerable influence, and has the lion's share of all that is spent in dissipation. She has high titles, which give her rank among the first nobles, and she has the distinction of a noubut, or kettle-drum, rides on an elephant, and keeps up a good deal of state. She commands the principal sets of dancing-girls, and, now that her own bloom is past (she is above sixty), is the first monopolist in the market of beauty at the capital. She danced and she sang for upwards of an hour, but—*I know not how it is*—the *fine* tones, the *fine* acting, the faint, the recovery, the melancholy, the intoxication which she exhibited in turns, as she chanted her Hindostanee and Persian odes, did not charm me as they were wont. After all, eighteen years do make some difference in the appearance and feelings both of man and woman.'

Malika saw Malcolm again, three days later. The garland (which is what her name means) had withered round Heliodora's head, and Heliodora herself, though her dress was 'very splendid', showed signs of wear and strain. Much had happened since her Scots admirer, as a renowned soldier and diplomatist in the prime of Anglo-Indian life, had first met the Nizam's star courtesan, in 1799, when Tipu had just fallen. The Company's servants were then conscious of a World War, in which their part was something more important than a rounding up of Pindaris or degradation of a Peshwa whom everyone had for twenty years known to be unworthy of the least esteem. This new India was drab and fallen, and glamour was dying out of the world in which they moved. Malika 'looked haggard and old. Her eyes were painted overmuch, and their blackness, joined to a look of intoxication, which I fear was not feigned, made this celebrated woman an object of disgust more than of admiration'.

Malcolm left Hyderabad, and on 8 August appeared at Poona in person, 'full of good stories, good humour and good sense'. He and Elphinstone swapped hilarious yarns, they pursued and speared with great vivacity and success wild pig, and the Residency was a place where soldiers and civilians, exhilarated by the prospect of a still more exciting chase, foregathered each evening. Then Malcolm went out to his own affairs, leaving even with Elphinstone the effect of a cleansing wind:

> 'Never was anybody so frank and good-humoured. Considering his time of life, his ardour, his activity of body and mind, his inexhaustible spirits and imperturbable temper, are truly admirable, and all those qualities are accompanied with a sound judgment and a great store of knowledge, derived both from reading and observation. I remain full of anxiety to get into the thick of the bustle that is approaching.'

That bustle was again postponed; but for the last time, and a very brief space only, while Malcolm, full of even more than his usual good humour, on 11 August set off for Pandharpur, where the Peshwa was on pilgrimage. Here the two talked on the footing of old friends, or as a father advising an erring child. The Peshwa was emotional and penitent, and Malcolm returned to Poona convinced that he was not so bad at heart. He persuaded Elphinstone to send the subsidiary force northward, to the general Pindari drive, except for three sepoy battalions all below full strength. The action was decided, of course, on general grounds—the Peshwa had vacillated all his life, and had never dared to pass into open hostility, and it was unreasonable to think he would pass into it now, if all went well with the round-up of the Pindaris and the overawing of the Maratha chiefs. Both Malcolm and Elphinstone had to proceed by guesswork, and neither guessed how deep the Peshwa's angry humiliation had gone.

Elphinstone quickly awoke to it, however. The Peshwa continued to gather troops, and in reply to remonstrances said that he was merely equipping himself to do what the British Government ordered and his friend Sir John Malcolm advised, make an effective contribution to the Pindaris' suppression. Though not for a moment deceived, Elphinstone still hoped the crisis would pass without war. His spies kept him informed, and he noted, as dangerous signs of what was astir, the Peshwa's 'studied conciliation of the Raja of Sattara, to whom he has paid attention such as has not been thought of since the power of the Peshwa was first established'; and noted also that the Peshwa and his leading followers were 'careful to keep their property away from Poona'. Sindhia and the Bhonsla Raja, applied to for support, assured the Peshwa that they would give it, if he ordered them in writing. Distrustful and distrusted, he too would not commit himself.

The explosion came in such a manner as to justify Robert Orme's remark, in the earliest days of Company conquest, that 'the secrets of the princes of Indostan are very difficult to be discovered'.[1] There was nothing in it, when it came, except an utterly irrational and inefficient outburst. Night after night, Elphinstone had stood on his veranda alone or with his young assistant, Grant Duff, listening to the confusion in the Peshwa's camp in Poona. A European regiment, on its way to join the main operations in the north against the Pindaris, was expected presently to pass through the city. The Peshwa was urged to strike now or never. Elphinstone increased the Residency guard to about 700 sepoys, destroyed his most secret papers, and was 'ready for the worst'. Weather conditions made him expect this in the dark hours of 27 October:

> 'The Peshwa could not have chosen a better night for a surprise, as it is a perfect tempest of rain and wind.
>
> παννύχιος δέ σφιν κακὰ μήδετο μητιέτα Ζεύς,
> σμερδαλέα κτυπέων.'[2]

The night passed quietly, however, as did the following day. Then, 'a little before midnight of the 28th', he was told that the Maratha guns were yoked, the horses saddled, the infantry standing to. 'It was an hour of anxiety' is the exquisite understatement of his biographer. It was lived through by one who was aware of how

[1] *A History of the Military Transactions of the British Nation in Indostan*, etc., i. 59.

[2] *Iliad*, viii. 478. 'All night long Zeus resolved on evil to them' (the Trojans), 'thundering terribly.'

much depended on his decision, and was able to judge the crisis with almost superhuman impersonality, as he stood and listened, a core of brooding silence and watchfulness at the heart of confusion.

'The British cantonment and the Residency were perfectly still, and the inhabitants slept in the complete repose inspired by confidence in that profound peace to which they had been long accustomed; but in the Peishwa's camp, south of the town, all was noise and uproar. Mr. Elphinstone had as yet betrayed no suspicion of the Peishwa's treachery, and, as he now stood listening on the terrace, he probably thought that, in thus exposing the troops to be cut off without even the satisfaction of dying with their arms in their hands, he had followed the system of confidence, so strongly recommended, to a culpable extremity: but other motives influenced his conduct at this important moment. He was aware how little faith the other Mahratta princes placed in Bajee Rao, and that Sindia, who knew him well, would hesitate to engage in hostilities, until the Peishwa had fairly committed himself. Apprised of the Governor-General's secret plans and his intended movements on Gwalior, which many circumstances might have concurred to postpone, Mr. Elphinstone had studiously avoided every appearance which might affect the negotiations in Hindoostan, or by any preparation and apparent alarm on his part give Sindia's secret emissaries at Poona reason to believe that war was inevitable. To have sent to the cantonments at that hour would have occasioned considerable stir; and in the meantime, by the reports of the spies, the Peishwa was evidently deliberating; the din in the city was dying away; the night was passing; and the motives which had hitherto prevented preparation determined Mr. Elphinstone to defer it some hours longer. Major J. A. Wilson, the officer in command of the European regiment on its march from Bombay, had already been made acquainted with the critical state of affairs, and was hastening forward.'[1]

The attack did not come that night. Next day, Elphinstone sent the Peshwa a message that his troops were crowding their encampment too close to the position of the British brigade at Kirki. The message was delivered by Major Ford, an officer who had served with the Peshwa's own auxiliary force and was popular with the Marathas. Gokla (Gokhale),[2] the Peshwa's commander-in-chief, whose military career had begun under Arthur Wellesley, in the war against Tipu, saw that further procrastination was harmful, and begged to be allowed to make the attack now. But the Peshwa, dreading battle, believed that he had almost succeeded in corrupting Elphinstone's sepoys, not knowing that they had betrayed all his overtures and had taken his money only to hand it over to

[1] James Cuninghame Grant Duff, *A History of the Mahrattas*, edited by S. M. Edwardes, ii. 472–3.

[2] Gokla, the usual English spelling, is a disrespectful form: Gokhale, the plural form, is correct.

their officers as a pledge of faith. Accordingly, he spent the day in what he considered diplomacy, which Elphinstone parried in kind. On the afternoon of 30 October, the Bombay European regiment, after a forced march of thirty miles, reached the position Elphinstone and General Lionel Smith had chosen some time before, at Kirki, four miles from Poona. They were accompanied by detachments of the 65th Foot and of Bombay artillery. On 4 November, the Peshwa's Minister, Moro Pant Dixit (Dikshit), visited Major Ford, and told him that the sepoys had been bought over and that the Peshwa meant to cut the British off to a man, with the exception of Dr. Coats, a medical officer who had attended him and done many acts of gratuitous healing of other people, and had spread vaccination through the district. Moro Pant Dikshit promised to save Major Ford and his family and property, if he stood neutral. Ford, who was astonished at the news of an imminent attack, of course said he must join his own countrymen immediately. They parted affectionately, Moro Dikshit saying that in any event he would do his best to befriend Ford's family, and asking and obtaining the same pledge in return, in case the Marathas were defeated. Gokhale meanwhile had refused to entertain a proposal that Elphinstone should be assassinated. These things are pleasant to remember, even long afterwards.

Next day, 5 November, early in the afternoon a personal officer of the Peshwa came to the Residency, and demanded that the European regiment be sent away, that the Indian brigade be reduced to its usual strength, and the cantonments be removed to a place selected by the Peshwa. Elphinstone merely answered that he was unable to depart from the instructions of the Governor-General, and lamented the 'infatuation'[1] which prompted such demands. The officer departed with a menacing gesture; Elphinstone, aware that the hour had struck, abandoned the Residency and joined his tiny army. He and his escort had hardly gone when the Residency was occupied and gutted. Elphinstone, unshaken even by the spectacle of his own beloved library and papers flaming to ashes, wrote letters and watched. 'I beg you will excuse this scrawl, but all my writing implements, with everything I have except the clothes on my back, form part of the blaze of the Residency, which is now smoking in sight.'[2]

Elphinstone noted the Peshwa's 'many acts of impotent rage', of which the destruction of the Residency was one. General Smith managed presently to save Poona from general sack by his own

[1] Valentine Blacker, *Memoir of the Operation of the British Army,* etc., 66.

[2] Letter to Sir Evan Nepean.

troops, a 'success . . . attended with very important advantages, tending to maintain our general reputation, and to conciliate friends in the present contest, and as preserving a very fertile source of supply both of money and of commodities for the army'.[1]

The Peshwa's heart again failed him; he sent Gokhale an order not to fire first. Gokhale, however, did his best to make the Battle of Kirki, which followed, a whole-hearted one. Its opening stages are preserved for us in Grant Duff's marvellous picture as an eye-witness:

'Those only who have witnessed the Bore in the Gulf of Cambay, and have seen in perfection the approach of that roaring tide, can form the exact idea presented to the author at sight of the Peishwa's army. It was towards the afternoon of a very sultry day; there was a dead calm, and no sound was heard, except the rushing, the trampling and neighing of the horses, and the rumbling of the gun wheels. The effect was heightened, by seeing the peaceful peasantry flying from their work in the fields, the bullocks breaking from their yokes, the wild antelopes startled from sleep, bounding off, and then turning for a moment to gaze on this tremendous inundation, which swept all before it, levelled the hedges and standing corn, and completely overwhelmed every ordinary barrier as it moved.'

The attack proved a failure, and of such a kind as to merit little notice. A Maratha force, stated to have consisted of 18,000 horse and 8,000 foot, made so small impression on 800 Europeans and 2,000 sepoys, that the latter held their high ground easily, with only eighty-six casualties. Moro Pant Dikshit, who had been taunted by Gokhale for his anglophilism, commanded the enemy cavalry and was killed by a shot from a battery attached to his friend Ford's battalion. The British defence, having brushed away the Marathas from their front, returned to their camp at Kirki.

Gokhale intended to renew the attack, and remained at Poona for some days longer. He told Elphinstone's *munshi*,[2] who had attempted to hold out in his private house in Poona and had been persuaded to surrender:

'I have protected you because your master was an old friend of mine, though we are now enemies. The trial we have already had has not turned out as I expected, but tell him we shall persevere. We may have taken our shrouds about our heads, but we are determined to die with our swords in our hands.'

The *munshi*, and other prisoners taken in isolated posts, were allowed to join the British camp.

The Fourth Division, under General Lionel Smith, was advancing on Poona from the south. A junction between it and Elphin-

[1] *Life of Elphinstone*, ii. 4.

[2] Confidential servant and translator.

stone's escort (rather than army) was effected, 14 November, and on the 16th the Marathas vainly tried to hold the Yelura river ford. The action cost almost exactly the same casualties as the Kirki one (83, as against 86), and has just as much title to the grandiloquent name of battle. The Peshwa's resistance had hardly begun before it had crumpled up. He abandoned Poona, and became 'a heartless and desperate fugitive'.

XXXIX

THE NAGPUR OUTBREAK

MEANWHILE, THE war, complicated already by the Peshwa's irruption into what was regarded as a vast *shikar*—as when a wolf unexpectedly breaks from the bushes, into a rounding up of hares and such small game—became still more intricately confused by the accession of the Bhonsla Raja and Holkar. Both states acted with entire imbecility; they should have risen earlier, or not at all.

The Bhonsla State, until 1802, had kept itself apart from Poona and its politics, and in Clive's and Warren Hastings' time had been on friendly terms with the Company. After its defeat by Arthur Wellesley, it had rigorously refused, as we have seen, to accept a subsidiary status. But Lord Hastings obtained his chance in 1816. 'This day' (1 June) 'Nagpore in fact ranges itself as a feudatory State under our protection.' Raghoji Bhonsla, the Prince who had lost the 1803 war, had died suddenly, and his only son, Parasji, succeeded him. The new Raja had hardly been noticed until now, and the blaze of publicity flung on him caused a remarkable discovery:

'He is blind, and thence used to remain unseen in the palace, so that he was in fact unknown. He was generally understood to be of weak capacity, but when his elevation gave people the opportunity of examining him, he was discovered to be literally an idiot.'[1]

His cousin, Apa Saheb, 'an active sensible man, about twenty years of age', became actual ruler, 'with as much of assent as the Rajah could comprehend and testify'. Afraid of factions at his own court and of Sindhia's interference from outside, he 'was not difficult to be worked upon', and asked for a subsidiary force and treaty. The latter was concluded, 27 May 1816. The Governor-General ensured him against displacement by any son the titular Raja might adopt, 'by my professing to consider Pursojee incapable of the volition necessary to the act. This is most strictly true, for the poor Rajah has no will or wish beyond eating and sleeping'. Apa Saheb engaged to pay seven and a half lakhs annually for a regiment of cavalry and 6,000 infantry, and to maintain another 3,000 cavalry and 2,000 infantry. The subsidiary force by the end of the year had established Apa Saheb completely.

[1] Hastings, *Private Journal*, 1 June 1816.

He began to regret an arrangement which severed Nagpur from the rest of the Marathas, and gave the British a strong flank against Sindhia, with a base against the Pindaris. He opened up communications with the Peshwa, and as a preliminary to asserting independence had Parasji Bhonsla murdered (31 January 1817). His Resident was the Richard Jenkins who had formerly been Sindhia's prisoner-ambassador and had discussed with Elphinstone, in the intervals of settling kingdoms, such matters as Sophocles and Grotius. Jenkins, less sensitive than his friend, hardly guessed what intrigues were about him, but there came a time when it became clear that something more than the ordinary exchange of flowery messages was taking place between Apa Saheb and other chieftains. In September, the threatened Chitu had sent an emissary to discuss common action, and the proposal had been kindly received. Then came Baji Rao's attack and repulse at Kirki. Apa Saheb expressed deep indignation at such treachery. But at nightfall of 24 November he sent a messenger to inform Jenkins that the Peshwa had sent him a *khelat* and bestowed on him the title of *Senapati*.[1] He invited his Resident to witness his ceremonial acceptance of these honours next day.

Such conduct at such a time, when the Peshwa was a desperate fugitive, and such a message were a declaration of war, even if it seemed a declaration of war by a lunatic. Jenkins called in troops from their cantonments three miles west of Nagpur, and on 26 November sent an express messenger to summon General Doveton, commanding the second division of the Deccan Army, then at Jafirabad. With his own force, amounting to 1,400 sepoys, Jenkins occupied Sitabaldi, a double-crested hill with a ridge yoking its summits, separating Nagpur from the Residency, which was part of the position defended. Here he stood firm, while 18,000 men with 36 guns advanced again and again to the assault, in fighting which lasted for eighteen hours, from evening of 26 November. The defenders' losses were very severe, 367 men, or more than one in every four. The enemy, who lost about the same number, temporarily captured one of the hill-crests, whereupon Captain Fitzgerald, who was in command of the Residency, acted on his own authority and risk.

'He had repeatedly applied for permission to charge, and was as often prevented by orders from the commanding officer; but seeing the impending destruction, he made a last attempt to obtain leave. Colonel Scott's reply was, "Tell him to charge at his peril." "At my peril be it," said the gallant Fitzgerald on receiving this answer, and immediately gave the word to advance. As soon as he could form

[1] Commander-in-Chief.

clear of the enclosures, he charged the principal body of horse, drove them from two guns by which they were supported, pursued them to some distance, cut a body of infantry accompanying them to pieces, and brought back with him the captured guns. The infantry posted on the hill witnessed this exploit with loud huzzas; the greatest animation was kindled amongst them; it was proposed to storm the smaller hill . . . men and officers mingling together rushed forward. Irresistible under such an impulse, they carried everything before them, pursued the Arabs down the hill, took two of their guns, spiked them, and returned to their posts. The Arabs again assembled and evinced a determination to recover their ground; but as they were preparing to advance, a troop of cavalry, under Cornet Smith, charged round the base of the hill, took them in flank, and dispersed them. The British troops now advanced from the hills, drove the infantry from the adjoining huts, and by noon this trying conflict, only equalled during the war by the defence of Korygaom, had wholly ceased.'[1]

Apa Saheb sent *vakils* to disavow the attack and apologize for it. The Resident agreed to a suspension of hostilities, but refused to treat with him until his troops were disbanded. Reinforcements came rapidly in, and by the middle of December General Doveton's division had all reached Nagpur. On 15 December, the Resident demanded absolute surrender of the state and its ruler in person, the latter to be a hostage. He was promised terms short of annexation, if he complied. After some procrastination, Apa Saheb, who was in very imperfect control of his army, gave himself up on the morning of the sixteenth. At noon the British advanced to take over his guns, and secured the advanced battery without any opposition. But presently a desultory resistance broke out, which passed into a battle of sorts. The British loss amounted to 141 killed and wounded, chiefly from cannon fire, and the enemy's, despite his precipitate departure, was considerable. He lost his standing camp, sixty-four guns and forty elephants.

A more serious operation was the attempt to storm Nagpur fort, 24 December. This was a failure. It was held by 'Arabs', Muhammadan soldiers of fortune, and their desperate courage, rather than the place's natural strength, was responsible for what at the time was felt as a bad, though temporary, setback. To save time, which was urgently necessary, the garrison was offered generous terms and surrendered, though they had suffered hardly any loss, against the assailants' loss of over 300 men. They were escorted out of Bhonsla territory and then discharged, with a gratuity of half a lakh and their own personal property.

Meanwhile, at Jubalpur another of the confused encounters,

[1] Grant Duff, iii. 49.

bloody for the defeated but almost bloodless for the victors, took place, 29 December. The Raja's troops lost heavily, against a British total loss of twelve men and a score of horses, in two hours' fighting. Jubalpur fort and town were occupied next morning, and nine guns and military stores captured.

Nagpur territory was quickly overrun. Jenkins reinstated Apa Saheb, under terms which surrendered complete military control to the British. Apa Saheb ceded territory producing twenty-four lakhs of revenue, which included Berar itself and Gawilgarh and lands along the Narbada. Sitabaldi was to be included inside the Company's boundary, and to be fortified, to overawe his capital. This treaty the Governor-General allowed with much reluctance. 6 January 1818. It had been his intention to dethrone Apa Saheb, Like Malcolm's dealings with the Peshwa presently, Jenkins' negotiations illustrate the tremendous freedom and power of the great soldiers and politicals, a change since Lord Wellesley's time.

Metcalfe and the Rajput States

The greatest of all the satraps was simultaneously busy in gaffing the fish he had played so long. They came to land now (13 January 1818): Dungarpur, Banswara, Jaipur, Jodhpur, Bundi, Kotah, Udaipur. They lost the pretence of independent status towards the outside world, and were picked up and set in their niche in the nearly built political fabric of modern India, as tributary Princes. The Paramount Power promised to keep each dynasty in place, and to prevent encroachment on its dignity and authority, and fixed all questions of tribute and subsidiary forces and the rest. Hard cases were considered, and allowed for; for the first five years Udaipur was to pay one-quarter of its revenue as tribute, and afterwards in perpetuity three-eighths: Jaipur, which had endured annual devastation for many years, because of this was excused all tribute for the first year.

XL

THE CAMPAIGN AGAINST HOLKAR

HOLKAR'S STATE 'still commanded great resources, which his weak Government was incapable of organizing or controlling'.[1] Lord Hastings drew his own conclusions. The British Government, 'in the failure of those States whose more immediate duty it was', had been 'compelled to take the lead in the important work of destroying the Pindari powers'. The 'dissolution of Holkar's Government and its absolute incapacity to maintain the relations of peace and amity' had 'nullified' the Treaty with Yeswant Rao Holkar in January 1806, and 'absolved the British Government from any necessity for respecting the provisions of that Treaty, which is not imposed by general equity without reference to specific convention'. The Governor-General issued his orders, from his camp at Cawnpur, 1 October 1817, and Metcalfe tried to get them accepted:

'If Holkar's Government possess neither the power nor the inclination to bear its part in a duty incumbent on every substantive State in India, it must incur the consequences of its inability to discharge that duty, and must either submit to be considered as an accomplice of the freebooters, or must place its resources at the disposal of a Power which will direct them to their proper object.'

Lord Hastings demanded that the Regent, Tulasi Bai, and the young Maharaja should reside under British protection until their country had been reduced to order. Meanwhile all its resources were to be put into the general pool, to exterminate the Pindaris. Part of this proposal must be traced to Tulasi Bai herself, who had been secretly negotiating with the Company, and offering to place herself and the boy Maharaja under its protection. For a long time past, she had been restive under Amir Khan's control of the State, and perhaps did not realize that events, and that skilful brigand's perception of the approaching shadows of things to come, had already freed her from that control for the future.

The war that followed was an outbreak of patriotism, though a useless and disorganized one. Sir Thomas Hislop's army, temporarily abandoning the chase of Chitu (who on 4 December bolted into Holkar's camp), gathered to attack Holkar. Malcolm and Maratha envoys spent a week in arguments which failed; the

[1] M. S. Mehta, *Lord Hastings and the Indian States*, 113 ff.

Indore state was unwilling to shackle itself as Sindhia's had done. Tulasi Bai was taken down to the Sipra in her palanquin, on the morning of 20 December, and publicly beheaded. Next day, the British army, with Malcolm leading, exhilarated as a schoolboy ('A man may get a red ribband out of this!') at the chance of military distinction on this scale at last, crossed the river at Mahidpur, and went straight for the Maratha position. 'I ascended the bank of the river with proud feelings. I never before had such a chance of fair fame as a soldier; and if the countenances of white and black in this gallant army are to be trusted, I did not lose the opportunity afforded me.'[1] Critics said that Malcolm 'clubbed his battalions'. To this he exultantly answered, 'Well, if I did, you have to admit that I clubbed them to some purpose!'

Holkar's cavalry fled early, and his gunners and infantry lost 3,000 men, most of them in the pursuit. The victors' loss was also heavy, 778 casualties. The campaign's historian draws the conclusion 'that more victories have been gained in the field by British armies in India through the bravery of the troops, than by manœuvres of the commander'. This is true, and India has proved a costly training ground when our generals have had to operate elsewhere, against real armies. For in India recklessness has usually been opposed by generalship of a despicable kind, which has simplified the art of war to a point which professional opponents have considered amateurish enthusiasm:

> 'In fact, the armies are too small for extensive manœuvre beyond cannon range. That they are continually permitted to deploy within it shews that the enemy to be coped with are deficient in a most important part of military conduct, a deficiency which obviates the necessity of abiding by those rules and precautions which are respected in Europe.'[2]

Malcolm with a well mounted force followed the cavalry up, not unduly worrying about them. They were, he heard, 'quite broken down and broken-hearted', and he had plenty of sport on the way (and this kind of war was itself merely a more exciting sport than most). 'I have just returned from shooting and hunting all the morning. I had seven or eight fine Arabians to ride, fifty people to beat for game, and all appendages of rank.' 'When we march, I hunt on the flank. When we do not march, I rise at daybreak, and hunt over ten or twelve miles of country. I have famous horses.' 'He rode fifteen stone, and he rode hard.'

The boy Maharaja had been present at Mahidpur, mounted on

[1] Letter to Lady Malcolm.

[2] Blacker, 157.

an elephant. He burst into tears when he saw his army retreat, and fled with his cavalry. The campaign, however, was soon over. On 6 January 1818, peace was restored. Holkar accepted the agreement which made Amir Khan independent and ruler of Tonk Rampura; he transferred the Rajput States which were his tributaries to the Company's roll of tributaries, ceded territory in several places, and made the usual engagements as to employing Europeans and Americans and discharging most of his army. Chitu (who had been present at Mahidpur) vanished, and Malcolm settled down to enjoy himself in his own expansive fatherly fashion. 'The Pindarrees have gone from this quarter. I do nothing on the march but shoot and hunt.' The young prince, especially, was the jolliest boy imaginable.

'I went out to hunt with him a few days ago, and we had great fun. The little fellow, though only eleven years of age, rides beautifully. He mounted a tall bay horse, very fairly broken, and taking a blunt spear nine feet in length, tilted with two or three others in very superior style, wheeling, charging, and using his spear as well as the rest of them. He expressed grief at my going away, as he discovered that I was very fond of play and hunting.'

In the recent disturbances he had lost a small pet elephant 'that dances like a dancing-girl'. Malcolm recovered it, and set him on it.

The young Holkar, it was said, had never been known to laugh out aloud. But Malcolm caused him to lie on his back, and rock with glee.[1]

This happy finish of warfare had other amenities, not forgetting literature. Among his officers Malcolm discovered a son of Robert Burns. 'We had a grand evening, and I made him sing his father's songs. He has a modest but serious pride of being the son of the bard of his country, which quite delighted me.' As for the Marathas, no one could be nicer. 'The fellows that I was hunting like wild beasts are all now tame, and combine in declaring that I am their only friend.' Life was very pleasant.

It seemed hard when Malcolm had to go south-westward, to negotiate yet another treaty, this time with the Peshwa. That unhappy being was about to end his strange course as a ruling prince.

On his flight from Poona, he was about to leave, with more or less precipitation, the neighbourhood of Koregaon, a village on high ground above the Bhima river, when an unexpected prey appeared. He had caught a tiny force of some 800 men, all Indians except their officers and twenty-four gunners in charge of two

[1] Shipp, *Memoirs*, iii. 241.

six-pounders. They were exhausted by a long night march, but from noon until nearly nine at night, under a burning sun and far from the thin stream of water winding in the river's vast bed far below them, they held part of the village, though exposed to sniping from its roofs and to repeated desperate charges by bodies of a thousand men at a time. The artillerymen withheld their match on some occasions until a compact mass of their assailants were within a few yards of the muzzles. Twenty of the gunners became casualties, and 251 of the sepoys. The Marathas lost almost twice as many, 'and have the generosity on all occasions to do justice to the heroic defenders of Korygaom.'[1]

It is characteristic, however, of the coolly professional manner in which war was beginning to be assessed, after the prolonged instruction of Napoleon's campaigns in Europe, that at the time the stand was criticized. Men argued that to hold what should have proved an untenable position was profligate temerity; Staunton should have surrendered on terms. Against this was urged the successful, though costly, upshot of the affair, and the chance that terms might have been violated.

Elphinstone, who visited the scene of the battle not long afterwards, in his own cool fashion summed up, and came to the onclusion which history has accepted:

'Horse charged into the village, but the great damage was done by Arabs in an enclosure which could not be stormed. Our men could not be got to storm. The Europeans talked of surrendering. The native officers behaved very ill, and the men latterly could scarce be got, even by kicks and blows, to form small parties to defend themselves. They were sunk under hunger, thirst, fatigue, and despondency. Most that I have seen tried to excuse themselves, and are surprised to find they are thought to have done great action; yet an action really greater has seldom been achieved—a strong incitement never to despair.'[2]

A considerable proportion of the names on the Koregaon monument, it may be worth while recalling, are those of Mahars,[3] or leather-workers—'untouchables'. The East India Company, like the Moguls and Sivaji himself, were catholic in choice of their fighting material.

The Peshwa watched the struggle from rising ground across the

[1] Grant Duff, iii. 437.

[2] *Life*, ii. 17–18.

[3] Dr. B. R. Ambedkar, the well-known political leader of Bombay Scheduled Classes to-day, is a Mahar. The Mahar regiment was disbanded in 1892, in deference to the prejudices of the higher castes: revived for a short time in the First World War, disbanded when it finished, and again revived in the Second World War.

river. His southward choice of flight had been to get hold of the Raja of Satara, whose person he 'collected' for political reasons, much as Mahadaji Sindhia, and afterwards General Lake, had collected the Mogul Emperor. This helpless potentate saw the battle with him, and was ill-advised enough to erect a screen from the glare, which the Peshwa asked him to put down, 'or the English would put a cannon-ball through it'. Gokhale and other officers directed the attacks, to the assistance of their master's despairing taunts, and Trimbakji on one occasion forced his way into the village. Next day the discomfited Marathas still hovered about the stricken defenders, half-heartedly pondering the chances of a renewed attack. But Staunton's force opened fire on them, and they heard, moreover, of General Smith's approach. They fled therefore. Staunton, taking as many of his wounded as he could, retreated to Serur.

The Peshwa detached a corps under Gokhale, to hold off his enemy's pursuit. On 17 January 1818, they unwisely attempted the double operation of gathering in some cattle and at the same time reconnoitring a small force of British cavalry. 'To an eye unaccustomed to contemplate large bodies of native horse in solid though irregular bodies', observes Colonel Blacker, the historian of the campaign, in which he took part, 'they must appear a formidable object for the attack of a few squadrons; but a consideration of their composition removes the impression, while to an officer like Major Doveton, who had served long in India, habit had rendered such reasoning superfluous.' Doveton at once dispersed them, with a loss of three men to their hundred. On 29 January, another body of the Peshwa's cavalry was caught in a defile of the Ghats, near Lonad, between the hammer and anvil of an infantry detachment and a cavalry force, and slain or scattered. Satara fort surrendered, 10 February, with twenty-five guns. Fort after fort tumbled into British hands, while the Peshwa raced and doubled, with a celerity and hopeless misery that impressed themselves on the communal mind; to this day, the villagers remember that spectacle, of power reduced to helplessness and confusion, and the scamper of his horses' hooves is heard on the wind.

Fresh surprises awaited him as he hurried desperately still southward, into country which he supposed faithful to him and found already in British possession. This had been the work of Thomas Munro, who like Malcolm was to 'get a red ribband out of' this business. Munro had been sent from Madras to settle the districts which the Peshwa had been made to cede in 1817. When it became clear that war was likely, he was eager to have his chance at last of military distinction, and in the friendly world of that day his peers were almost equally eager that Tom Munro should be given an opportunity of adding the soldier's laurels to his other ones. He was made brigadier, and when hostilities broke out he entered on a course of quietly amassing one fort after another, with little or no bloodshed. His own force was negligible, except that in this ridiculous campaign, where the enemy was under a faithless and detested Prince, any compact body of well armed soldiers seemed able to rout the disheartened rabble which was all that was opposed to them. Munro was presently given command of a second force, under General Pritzler. He routed an army drawn up to defend Sholapur, and Pritzler overtook the fugitives seven miles away and killed some eight hundred more, 10 May 1818. Munro captured thirty-seven guns and innumerable other weapons and material, and his total loss for all operations came to just over a hundred men. He was quickly able to settle down to the work he did supremely well, the civil arrangements of the newly conquered territory.

The delight felt in the success of this deeply beloved man was expressed by Malcolm, writing to John Adam in Calcutta:

'I send you a copy of a public letter from *Tom Munro Saheb,* written for the information of Sir Thomas Hislop. If this letter makes the same impression upon you that it did on me, we shall all recede, as this extraordinary man comes forward. We use common vulgar means, and go on zealously, and actively, and courageously enough; but how different is his part in the drama! Insulated in an enemy's country, with no military means whatever (five disposable companies of sepoys were nothing), he forms the plan of subduing the country, expelling the army by which it is occupied, and collecting the revenues that are due to the enemy, through the means of the inhabitants themselves, aided and supported by a few irregular infantry, whom he invites from the neighbouring provinces for that purpose. His plan, which is at once simple and great, is successful in a degree, that a mind like his alone could have anticipated. The country comes into his hands by the most legitimate of all modes, the zealous and spirited efforts of the natives, to place themselves under his rule, and to enjoy the benefits of a Government which, when administered by a man like him, is one of the best in the world. Munro, they say, has been aided in this great work by his local reputation—but *that* adds to his title to praise. . . .

Confess, after reading the inclosed, that I have a right to exult in the eagerness with which I pressed upon you the necessity of bringing forward this *master-workman.* You had only heard of him at a distance; I had seen him near.'[1]

[1] 17 February 1818, before the Sholapur victory.

Lord Hastings privately apologized to Munro for the inadequate public acknowledgment 'of your exploits'. 'I cannot be satisfied; it may be liable to be considered as one of those official recognitions, where the phrases are not supposed to be exactly measured; and when he who offers the compliment may be suspected of exaggeration in the terms, for the sake of proving his own liberality in the estimate of his command of language. . . I may assert the formal tribute . . . to have been strictly what your conduct claimed.' In the House of Commons, Canning added: 'He went into the field with not more than five or six hundred men, of whom a very small proportion were Europeans, and marched into the Mahratta territories, to take possession of the country which had been ceded to us by the treaty of Poonah. The population, which he subjugated by arms, he managed with such address, equity, and wisdom, that he established an empire over their hearts and feelings. Nine forts were surrendered to him, or taken by assault, on his way; and at the end of a silent and scarcely observed progress he emerged from a territory heretofore hostile to the British interest with an accession instead of a diminution of force, leaving everything secure and tranquil behind him'.

'Of marauding or wanton plunder, scarcely an instance occurred during the entire course'[1] of Munro's service. The secret of his fame was simple. 'I never met such a considerate man', one of his staff testified. 'He never would allow a rude or discourteous letter to be addressed to any officer, let his rank be what it may, though he never allowed anything improper to pass unnoticed.' He always apologized for an injustice or unjust word of severity, and apologized openly. He remembered that everyone, British or Indian, had rights as an individual, and feelings that could be hurt.

What remained of the Pindaris, who never made a real stand and rarely put up what could even be considered a defence, were now fleeing like partridges on the hills. Chitu after the battle of Mahidpur found temporary refuge with a chieftain whose camp and town were presently blown open by the British for this service. Chitu had already gone when this happened, and was being chased north-westward. Doubling and redoubling on his tracks, losing men continually, as parties were surprised and cut up, he tried to make a halt near Dhar. On 25 January 1818, his *durra* was smashed near Hindia.

This finished the Pindaris as an organized menace. After this, leaders and followers alike sought only opportunities to surrender. The hillmen aborigines, Bhils and others, took up the hunt zestfully, butchering scattered groups as they tried to escape and hide.

[1] *Life*, i. 506.

Chitu remained at large. To the end he showed the Maratha courage and the Maratha skill in using the wild country's folds and coverings as a cloak; in a record of skilled guerillas that contains the names of Sivaji and Tantia Tupi he deserves a niche in memory.

The war had opened with treachery, and worse; at the time of the Peshwa's attack on the Poona Residency, two British officers, travelling to join duty, had been caught and hanged. Towards the end hostilities, which had hardly ever risen to the plane of warfare, sagged down into massacre which cannot be dignified with the name of fighting and which was accompanied by the contempt that in itself often leads to cruel deeds.

The commandant of Talneir, who had at first refused to surrender his fort, though told that these were the orders of his master Holkar, gave himself up before any loss had been caused. But while a confused and little intelligible discussion was being held with the defenders of the fifth and innermost gate an unfortunate attack was made, which cost the lives of two British officers. Sir Thomas Hislop in reprisal hanged the commandant that evening from a tree on the flagstaff tower, and gave the Maratha cause a martyr. The execution was deplored by many and defended by few, for the victim's original refusal to obey a pusillanimous decision (as it seemed to him) was such disobedience as British officers have shown on occasion, with their countrymen's applause, and he was in no way responsible for what happened after he had surrendered. Even that event was admitted to have been due to misunderstanding and not deliberate treachery. The whole garrison was put to death, only one man out of three hundred escaping, by leaping from the wall. Talneir gained a grim reputation, and is a black stain on British honour.

Through the wild and lovely Maratha country the chase went on, with zest and joy for the pursuers. 'Three fox-chases on the line of march, and one trip out with a detachment of infantry and auxiliaries. . . . We galloped after a few fellows with about twelve of our own, but to no purpose' (3 December 1817).[1] 'When all was over we had much laughing and talking over our adventures, all sensible of our past danger, and in spirits with our escape. If the enemy had behaved with tolerable spirit, or if those on the plain had supported the party opposed to us, not a man could have rejoined the line' (7 December). 'The grey haze or smoke which our camp throws over everything heightens the beauty of the hills. . . . Coats observed the wild pepper vine, which, with the

[1] Malcolm.

high trees through which we passed in the evening, renewed the memory of Malabar' (3 April 1818).

The Peshwa fought his last battle, if battle it can be called, on 20 February 1818, at Ashti. Approaching behind a hill that hid them, the British at dawn heard his drums beating. The Peshwa leapt from his palanquin, and fled on horseback; his wives, hurriedly donning male dress, galloped after him. He had made from time to time overtures for peace, and in one of these had blamed his actions entirely on to Gokhale, whom he offered to poison as a peace-offering. Finding himself now all but surrounded by British cavalry, he taunted this brave officer, who replied merely that he might be sure his escape would be guarded. In a mood of fatality, Bapu Gokhale answered suggestions of retreat with the comment, 'Whatever is to be done must be done here'. He died as he had promised, sword in hand, and, with a last gesture, in falling drew his shawl quietly about his head—the gesture of departure, which he had predicted. 'He really fought like a soldier', wrote Lionel Smith to Elphinstone. The conquerors remembered that at the Battle of Assaye the dead man who had now gone out of life with such quiet valour and dignity had ridden beside their own Duke of Wellington. For a long while his wife refused to believe in his death and continued to wear the marks of marriage.[1]

The British, with the loss of under a score of men, captured camels, elephants, baggage, and completely dispersed the Peshwa's army. The Raja of Satara and his family, whom the Peshwa had been carrying about with him like chattels, passed into their custody and protection.

'The Raja's family', General Smith reported, 'is rather a nuisance to me; they insist on my not leaving them, and I cannot keep up any useful pursuit with them.' Elphinstone hurried up accordingly, and the Raja was made over to him, and by him reinstated. 'The Raja went into Sattara in procession with the pomp of a prince and the delight of a schoolboy' (29 March 1818). 'The people here received our government with perfect submission, if not with pleasure. There is not the smallest popular feeling against us, partly no doubt from the hopelessness of resistance, partly also from the hope of good government and anxiety for peace' (16 April). Malcolm presently wrote to Elphinstone: 'The Mahrattas have been beaten and bullied into a state of considerably humility. It would be glorious (and the times are favourable

[1] Poona Records, 18 August 1818. See Sardesai, *The Last Days of the Maratha Raj*, 240.

to the experiment) to render the descendant of Sevajee the restorer of his race to habits of order and good government.'[1]

Another Indian war, which had ranged over an immense tract of territory but otherwise had been little more than a succession of skirmishes, was practically over. The total British and sepoy casualties in all operations, including the chase of the Pindaris, were 749 killed, 2,509 wounded, and sixteen missing. The remaining actions were trivial, with one exception, the siege of Asirgarh. A number of the Raja of Nagpur's fortress commandants refused to surrender, although their Prince's resistance had finished—one of these misguided men, the commandant of Mundala, was court-martialled as a rebel, but found to have acted under the Raja's orders. They made a defence of sorts, often expensive to the garrisons but never costing the besiegers more than a dozen or under a score of casualties.

Apart from Asirgarh, one other of these minor investments deserves notice, for an interesting reason. The traditional Sword of Sivaji is still worshipped at Satara, in a special shrine; it is credited with miraculous qualities, and women desirous of sons drink water through which it has been drawn, with (it is said) satisfactory results. There is nevertheless an undercurrent of doubt throughout the Maratha country as to its genuineness and I have often been asked when there if I could say where the *Bhawani Tulwar*,[2] the Sword of Kali—that is, Sivaji's true sword—now is. There is a tradition that it was taken to Windsor Castle, when the hill fort of Raigarh, in April 1818, surrendered after fourteen days' bombardment from the neighbouring spur of Kalkai. In Raigarh five lakhs of treasure were found—and also (says Maratha belief) the *Bhawani Tulwar*.

The Siege of Asirgarh

Jenkins, who learnt that Apa Saheb was meditating a fresh outbreak, arrested him, 15 March. On 3 May, the Raja was sent to Allahabad as a prisoner, but on the way escaped, disguised as a sepoy, one of a party supposed to be marching off elsewhere as a relief guard. Ten days later, he fled to the hills between the upper Narbada and his own country of Nagpur, where Chitu joined him. They gathered about them a band of broken and desperate men.

All eyes now settled on Asirgarh, the fortress where Maratha

[1] *Life*, ii. 355.

[2] Bhawani is a name of Kali, Sivaji's patroness.

independence was about to make its final effort. Lord Hastings had demanded it from Sindhia, as a pledge of compliance with the terms forced upon him, but its commandant had refused to surrender it. The Peshwa, who still had some 8,000 men, hovered uncertainly towards it, and in April 1819, when Doveton and Malcolm were besieging it, Chitu's skill enabled Apa Saheb to slip through his pursuers and reach its immediate vicinity. It is doubtful if the Bhonsla Raja ever actually entered Asirgarh, however. The fort fell, 9 April, after a twenty days' investment, mainly because its walls had been so smashed by gunfire that further defence was felt to be hopeless. The siege had been memorable because the disparity of loss was for once on the British side; the Marathas had only 138 casualties, whereas their assailants had 323. Apa Saheb found sanctuary with the Sikhs, and Trimbakji, captured in June 1818, became a life-prisoner of the British. The Maratha campaign was finished.

The Death of Chitu

Terror now took hold on Chitu, and, most of all, terror of transportation and loss of caste. Even in his troubled slumbers he raved about *kala pani*, the black water, to cross which would put him outside his own community for ever. He was tracked from refuge to refuge, by means of the prodigious hoofs of the gigantic horse that he rode, and at last even the beasts of the wilderness rose against him. His end came from them, when, starving and alone, he met a tiger, which killed and partly devoured him. His head, found in the jungle beside his mangled body, was brought to Malcolm, and acknowledged as Chitu's by his son, who was Malcolm's prisoner.

XLI

SURRENDER OF THE PESHWA

THERE REMAINED at large only the Peshwa. Malcolm had been following in pursuit of him, in an even more than usually exultant frame of mind, after his quelling and soothing of kingdoms and bandit chieftaincies:

'You will rejoice to hear all my undertakings succeed. I have just tranquillised, by beating some and petting others, the most troublesome province in Malwah; and during my operations against the few remaining Pindarrees in this quarter, though the country is covered with mountains and forests, though my detachments have marched everywhere, and through countries so infested with robbers and lawless mountaineers that our troops, from past suffering, dreaded them, I have not had a rupee's worth of value stolen, and not a follower wounded. This, my dear Charlotte, I am proud of, for it is the result of good arrangement, and of a general impression, which even the most lawless own, of my being neither unmerciful nor unjust. I am the general arbitrator and pacificator of the whole country. I support my title to these names by accessibility at all hours to the peasant as well as the prince. The labor is great, but its result is delightful. Out of forty-six villages within ten miles of this, only seven were inhabited six days ago, when I declared it was my intention to cantoon here. The rest were in complete ruins, every house roofless. The inhabitants of twenty have already returned to their homes, and are beginning to rebuild. . . . Nadir Bheel, the mountain chief, who has committed all these devastations, and is the terror of the country, has already sent his only son, a fine boy, just the age of George, and promises to come himself. I gave the young plunderer knives with six blades and a nice little Arab pony. He has taken a great affection for me, is going to settle in my camp, to hunt, shoot, and play with me, and to learn cultivation instead of plundering; and he insists that I must take a pet elk[1] that has been broken in to ride, and can run faster up a stony hill, the little fellow says, than a swift horse!'

From such exploits and pastimes, Malcolm, hoping that all fighting was over, moved reluctantly.

He nevertheless had to leave them. On 17 May, an emissary from Baji Rao came to him at Mhow, to plead for his master. Malcolm made it clear that the Peshwa's title was gone for ever. 'I shall still, however, be rejoiced to be the instrument of saving him from total ruin'; he promised that prompt and absolute submission would secure generous financial treatment. Rejecting a

[1] Sambhur.

request that he himself should visit the fugitive, Malcolm sent a confidential officer, Lieutenant John Low. Low in after-years played a very great part in Indian politics, especially as Resident at Lucknow during Lord Auckland's time. One of the staunchest of the dwindling band who carried the spirit of earlier and generous days into the annexationist régime of Lord Dalhousie, he worked hard to save Indian States from humiliation.

The Peshwa seemed fairly cornered at last, and Malcolm made all preparations to prevent his escape. There was a temporary complication, which at first sight looked serious, when Apa Saheb gave Jenkins the slip. But the Bhonsla Raja made his way to the Sikhs, to trouble British India no more. Malcolm drew his net closer, General Doveton got ready to attack.

Malcolm now rose to his greatness, and showed that he desired the pacification of wretched Central India, rather than cheap military laurels for himself. 'Look at the date', he wrote to his wife, 28 May, from 'Camp, 30 miles north of Asseerghur',

'and think of me in a murky jungle, in rather an old tent, with the thermometer above 120 degrees, a terrible land wind blowing. . . . My two assistants, Captain Low and Alexander Macdonald, are actually to-day with Badjee Row, settling for his meeting me to-morrow or the day after. We have got troops all around him, and he can only protract the war by going among the hills, and leading, for a period at least, the life of a common freebooter, and for this course neither his habits of body nor mind are adapted. . . . I have a bitter pill to offer him. He must resign both the name and power of a sovereign. After that he will enjoy comfort and affluence, and as much liberty as can be granted consistent either with his good or our safety. . . . If I can reconcile this Prince to his fate, and terminate the war, I shall be the most fortunate of men. All that I could have seen in my dreams will have occurred within a short twelvemonth.'

Three days later, Malcolm and the Peshwa met at Keyri, in the latter's camp. The Peshwa was extremely dejected, and there was no comfort for him except in the kindness of Malcolm's manner. He was told plainly that he would be Peshwa no longer, and must leave the Deccan:

'There are periods in the lives of men when great sacrifices are demanded of them. The tribe to which your Highness belongs has been celebrated in all ages for its courage. Brahmin women have burnt upon the funeral piles of their husbands. Men have thrown themselves from precipices to propitiate the deity for themselves, or to avert misfortune from their families. You are called upon for no such effort. . . . The sooner you determine your course the better.'

The Peshwa despairingly replied that he had once three friends—Arthur Wellesley, Barry Close, and John Malcolm; the first was now a great man far away, the second dead, and his only hope lay in the last-named. The interview ended, with nothing settled, and it was not until two hours before noon of 3 June—two hours before the time when Malcolm had told the Peshwa he should treat him as an enemy—that the Maratha surrendered. Having surrendered, he began to recover his complacency of mind. His life, at any rate, was now safe, and Malcolm was jesting with him as with an old friend.

Malcolm had reached what he felt was the highest peak of his career. Disappointment was intense when he learnt that in granting the Peshwa a pension of eight lakhs—equal to more than £80,000—he was considered to have been wildly generous. Lord Hastings held that the Peshwa was a helpless fugitive, with no choice but surrender. Malcolm argued that he still had 6,000 horse and 5,000 infantry; at the time he (as well as Malcolm) believed Asirgarh to be untaken, with Sindhia's commandant, who had already accepted the charge of his property, willing to receive him.

Historians have generally concurred in the Governor-General's disapproval, and the fact that the pension had to be paid for a quarter of a century, while the Peshwa unexpectedly and inconsiderately lived on, surviving both former and later excesses, and happy with his Ganges water, buffoons and dancing girls, has naturally deepened exasperation. 'I have heard the longevity of Badjee Rao spoken of as one of Malcolm's offences.'[1]

Malcolm's real defence seems to me one which he never put forward. His ideas had been formed in expansive days, when Arthur Wellesley had awarded a far less important chieftain a pension of seven lakhs.[2] Until he found himself criticized, Malcolm probably never dreamt that eight lakhs would be regarded as excessive, and it is interesting to note that his peers, such men as Munro, Elphinstone, Ochterlony, Jenkins, did not regard it as excessive. Writing to Munro, to thank him for his approbation, in language strangely recalling Waller's noble words to his friend Ralph Hopton,[3] when they had perforce become enemies in the civil war between Charles I and his Commons, Malcolm reveals

[1] *Life of Malcolm*, i. 265.

[2] Yet, as a sign of how quickly British attitude changed, note that in 1809 Lord Minto (*Minute*, 6 June: see also Kaye, *Metcalfe*, i. 350) thought it puzzling that the Directors ever sanctioned such a pension as even that granted to the King of Delhi.

[3] 'We are both upon the stage, and must act such parts as are assigned us in this tragedy. Let us do it in a way of honour and without personal animosities': 16 June 1643. There is not the slightest reason to think that Malcolm knew of this letter.

the imaginative plane on which his generation moved and acted. 'We exist on impression; and on occasions like this, where all are anxious spectators, we must play our part well or we should be hissed. . . . I well knew that the moment he submitted he would unstring a bow that he never could rebend.' He could not agree with the Governor-General's opinion that Baji Rao's distress 'would force him to submit on any conditions, and that his enormities deprived him of all right either to princely treatment or princely pension'.

All this, however, was essentially beside the point, which was that the age had not yet dawned when anyone in India (or anywhere else) was to ask if vast payments to Princes were fair to the people. All that was considered was the right of rulers to luxury, and of the Company to dispose of revenue. In this world, the only world by whose standards we should judge him, Malcolm moved magnanimously, declining to press the fallen down to the lowest and least that they would accept. Of Malcolm himself, Elphinstone, who was not in the habit of giving his admiration cheaply, wrote, 10 May 1819:

'It is melancholy to think that he is not young,[1] and that he is the last of the class of politicians to which he belongs. The later statesmen are certainly more imperious and harsher in their notions, and are inferior in wisdom, inasmuch as they reckon more on force than he does, and less on affection'.[2]

The criticisms he received from Calcutta, and from John Adam most of all, did something to damp Malcolm's spirits, for which he apologized: 'God knows, getting rid of Badjee Rao and the cholera morbus in the same week is enough to put any human being in spirits'. However, he felt he had done right, and, though to-day everyone says he did wrong, the perusal of his letters, the most temperately argued that he ever wrote, shows that he had a strong case. His eyes were on the settlement of Central India, and the reconciliation of a great and proud race to their position of subordination henceforth. He maintained that 'the liberality and the humanity' which the British Government 'had displayed on such occasions' as this 'had done more than its arms towards the firm establishment of its power. It was, in fact, a conquest over mind, and among men so riveted in their habits or prejudices as the natives of this country the effect, though unseen, was great beyond calculation'.

He was, as it happens, entirely right. Any historian who to-day will travel through the Maratha country and has the means

[1] He was fifty. [2] *Life*, ii. 66.

(which are not financial means) to get in touch with the sentiment of the people will find this; he will reject the condemnation so lightly copied from generation to generation, by historians who have never known India outside British books or British circles. To this day the Maratha nation remembers with gratitude the generosity shown in his utter ruin to the man who, however personally unworthy, was their accepted chief (for the Satara Raja had become a shadow). Even after all these years, it is a salve to the humiliation felt when they recall their dismissal from power. They are a magnanimous nation, and one that does not dwell overmuch on its own wrongs and failures; and, for the fact that, not merely in the Mutiny but through the last hundred and twenty years, on the whole they have remained unembittered against their conquerors, Malcolm's action—seen, as only a few political actions are, in a kind of eternal stillness, as of a picture: the victor of free volition granting to the fallen more than necessity enforced—in my judgment was a main reason.

Those who thought like Malcolm—and he himself more eminently than any—were about to test the validity of the principles he stated, by putting them into action in the political reconstruction of India.

XLII

THE BRITISH LEADERS AND THE COMMON SOLDIER

When the actors are themselves interesting, and move on a plane of conduct which has some nobility, history ceases to be a solely depressing record of crime and folly. The British leaders in India during the first twenty years of the nineteenth century enforced on the military and political field doctrines which in the hands of the ordinary run of conquerors would have led to utter disregard of all but power. But they happened to be humanists and not fanatics; intellectual catholicity softened, by tolerance and understanding, the impact of the changes they put through.

By a happy accident not repeated on anything like the same scale, the British leaders possessed an individuality always rare, and in their case developed by the fact that they left home before adolescence set in. Their education was in India itself, and their minds were formed by early responsibility, exercised usually in conditions of extreme isolation. Their ranks contained, of course, the self-seeking, the brutal, the shallow and self-sufficient. But their outstanding figures, who would have been remarkable in any age, were free from the conviction which in following generations was to ravage the relationship of East and West, that they represented civilization warring against savagery. Hence, even among men whom Fame has forgotten almost entirely, we repeatedly find a magnanimity that lights up the mind to recall it. For example, in General Lionel Smith. Later, under circumstances harder than any he endured in India,[1] he showed a moral courage equal to the physical courage he had long ago shown in the field, and an ability to put himself where he could see with the eyes of even men held to be below the status of man.

The French Revolution influenced them not at all. It accompanied them to India merely as a bogy of the nursery and of their own social class. Hinduism for the most part they saw as a debased idolatry, with a multiplicity of cruel and revolting practices. We need not condemn them for despising it, for it was then at its worst and lowest, and of Sanskrit and the Vedas and the Vedantist philosophy they knew hardly anything. But they did not escape

[1] He was Governor of Jamaica during years of anger and racial bitterness, the last years before slavery was abolished.

the influence and mood of the Regency or of a more spacious day which had not even yet altogether finished in the land of their adoption. The civilization which they found in India was admittedly a dying civilization, but it was one with rich colours and tragic memories. It fitted in with the mood of their own Age in Europe; and they came to Courts which, however poverty-stricken and devoid of actual power, cherished forms of careful politeness, and behind these Courts was the cultural tradition of Persia and the Persian language. Their minds turned to this language, without distaste or condescension, and found in it delight. It is strange that Persian had so little influence on English literature[1] until FitzGerald's *Omar Khayyam*, for long before that Persian poetry was the familiar study of British soldiers and administrators, not only in the period of which this book treats, but in the decade which followed, when such men as Alexander Burnes read it with pleasure and discrimination, and with a critical ability that showed how free was their judgment from European limitations. Perhaps this was because to them it was less of a dead language and literature, a solely official study, and more of a living process. They were in close touch with India's shifting North-West frontier, and through it with Central Asia and Persia generally. In the time of Burnes, travellers could pass beyond India's borders, to Bokhara and Khiva and Samarkand—not without difficulty, yet without encountering the extreme mistrust and xenophobia that later ruled outside India, from the First Afghan War to our own time.

The men who made India's political framework had, moreover, an advantage beyond their own character and abilities, in the almost unparalleled picturesqueness of the background on which they moved. The mind kindles at thought of the lion-haunted[2] hills of Rajputana and Gwalior, of Central India's thorn-studded pampas and gnarled mountains—of the poured-out bewildered turbulence of Delhi, where Majesty was dying by inches—of the new Sikh empire growing and knitting together behind its Maginot Line of mighty rivers. We see the tents pitched for some border conference of Ranjit Singh and his Sirdars, with 'Loney Akhtar, the wisest of the sahebs', and taciturn dreaded Muntazim-ud-Daula, the real 'King of Delhi'[3]—a veritable concourse of Asir and Jotuns! Malcolm, with poised spear, races along the jungle

[1] The reader will hardly expect me to allow *Lalla Rookh* as an exception.

[2] The last five were killed in 1873; four in Jodhpur and one, the last of all, in Gwalior (on Waterloo Day, too good a day for such a deed).

[3] Metcalfe's nickname among his friends.

edges beside the march of his army, or cajoles some humiliated sulking princeling into half-belief that the future may yet be good, even though his kingdom is shattered. Elphinstone gravely admonishes the Peshwa or escorts back to Satara Sivaji's puppet descendant—tolerantly noting the schoolboy glee of a kinglet returning to a kingdom that is one of show and glitter only.

To pass from the time of Malcolm and Metcalfe to that of the infinitely better known and admired men of the Mutiny period—the 'God's Englishmen' of fiction and our tribal tradition—is like passing from Erasmus and Colet to John Knox. The present writer was brought up in the school of Knox—

> 'For rigorous teachers seized my youth,
> And purged its faith and trimmed its fire'—

but has come to conviction that a world governed and guided by the other is happier and nobler:

> '*Thebes* did his green unknowing Youth ingage,
> He chuses *Athens* in his riper Age.'

To-day, when humanism is hard put to it to survive at all and when 'realist' politics and philosophies dismiss it as a by-product of weakness in will and failure in energy, it is well to remember Jenkins and Elphinstone discussing Sophocles as they rode side by side to rearrange kingdoms, and putting their official work through expeditiously, in order to have time to read more of their favourite author before night fell: Metcalfe in his distressed survey of the chaos at his doors pausing to compare Horace and Hafiz: Malcolm, the Scots farmer's son, finding that his happiness needed to rest on the poetry of Persia as well as that of Robert Burns.

Other Ranks

But what of the common soldier—who did not chase elk and boar on the edges of forward-moving battle—who conducted no embassies with distant half-legendary chieftains—of whom we have had glimpses as he went on his lawful occasions, storming walls, racing across nullas which the enemy was evacuating, ripping up bags of rupees and filling his pockets, footsore and sun-wearied as he filed to what he hoped was rest and learnt that this glint in the foreground was Sindhia's or the Bhonsla Raja's army, which he must forthwith cause to skirr away? Does he present a picture as pleasing to national pride, or as bright to the inner world of imagination, as that left by his leaders and betters?

I am afraid he does not. The discrepancy in England, between the highest and the ordinary levels of our civilization, has always been immense; I doubt if there is anything like it in any country with which we should wish to be compared, and it is a discrepancy that lessens so slowly that it often seems hardly to lessen at all. The gap between the common soldier and his leaders was the plummet's bound from Lucifer's Heaven to the Hell where he was hurled.

There was, as a first factor, discipline. This was brutal to the point of lunacy. In this respect, at least, the India we conquered had a higher civilization.

A century ago, for the death penalty (with which, in our own day, the Anzacs dispensed, without any lapse from soldierly efficiency) and for the flogging administered so prodigally, the arguments which we still hear were put forward. Unfortunately, the only evidence ever heard is that of men whose station raises them above the misery they support. Here is an exchange of question and answer, before the Commission on Military Punishments, March 1836:

Questioner. 'When Your Grace commanded the army, was it your wish, and did you endeavour, to diminish the frequency of corporal punishment as much as you could?'

The Duke of Wellington. 'As much as possible. From the time I entered the army[1] it has been the desire of every commanding officer that ever I have seen, who knew what his duty was, to diminish corporal punishment as much as possible. There is one very remarkable circumstance, which I beg the board will never lose sight of, that is, that this punishment is always inflicted in public. . . . It is done in public, and there is a security that it will not go to any excess'.

The reasoning doubtless seemed fool-proof; we can imagine the hum of satisfaction and agreement. Nevertheless, during the Peninsular War men under the Duke's own command died under the lash, or from its effects. And there was other evidence before the Commission, which made nonsense of what he said. A medical officer told how he had to be on duty when a sentence of several hundred lashes was carried out. Horrified by the sufferer's mangled back and his obvious closeness to physical collapse, he tried to stop the torture. The officer in charge turned to him. 'Do you realize, doctor, that the poor devil will only have to go through the rest of the sentence afterwards?' The doctor had no choice but to allow the flogging to proceed.

Men liable to this brutality, which from the comfort and security of commissioned rank seemed so trivial and entirely justified, have nevertheless left some record of how it appeared to the common

[1] In 1787.

soldier. Lieutenant Shipp won a commission from the ranks, a most exceptional achievement, by outstanding valour, and before he was deprived of it (by what was hard measure) served for some years in India as an officer. Shipp was a man of ordinary intelligence, sharpened by knowledge of two utterly contrasted worlds. He published his military experiences, and his testimony has the quality of a cry of misery and desperation.

A flogged man, he says, never recovered self-respect. 'I can most solemnly affirm that . . . flogging is, and always will be, the best, quickest, and most certain method that can be devised, to eradicate from the bosom of a British soldier his most loyal and laudable feelings'.[1] Blood often spirted out yards from the sufferer, whose back became so ghastly a spectacle that officers looked away.[2] Large lumps of thick callous flesh and dreadful weals formed, and a flogged man was afterwards ashamed to show his naked person. Men died in their early twenties, from the effect of thousands of lashes. Flogging depended on the caprice of the commanding officer, who often gave the choice of lashes or of a court-martial with its powers of life and death. The man wielding the lash was sometimes told to count five between strokes. The condemned might faint, and more than once—to be restored each time, and put back into punishment afresh. Shipp asks the supporters of this barbarity:

'Have they served in the ranks, and mixed and lived in social friendship with the private soldiers of our country? Have they ever sat at the bedside of a flogged man, and witnessed the agony of his heart and the destruction of his mind? Have they ever heard the unintimidated and unbiassed opinion of the soldiers in their barrack-rooms respecting the ignominious lash?'

We who recall the outburst of popular interest in the flogging of 'the Mayfair gangsters' and the furious wrath of women whom the wretchedness of social and economic conditions could not anger, when Sir Samuel Hoare as Home Secretary tried to do away by degrees with the use of 'the cat', cannot pretend that we do not know that there is always for some a titillation of the imagination, in the knowledge that some majestic horror is about to be inflicted. The two younger and least intelligent of the Misses Bennet, in *Pride and Prejudice*, felt an excited pleasure when their officer friends told them a private soldier was to be flogged. Shipp, however, who had been a private soldier, asks: 'Why can French soldiers be governed without resorting to similar punishment?' In the British

[1] *Memoirs*, iii. 162–3.

[2] *Ibid*, 187. References for the statements that follow in the text are Shipp, iii. 162–202 *passim*.

Army, even boys of thirteen were often given six or seven dozen lashes, whereas 'The French liberal system of discipline encourages the young aspirant, and infuses into the minds of the soldiers that they are a people far above the common peasantry.' Colonel Monson, not a brilliant commander but a man whose personal fearlessness was renowned throughout the army, 'was one who hated the very name of flogging . . . saying it was an evil of the greatest magnitude'. He would always avoid such a parade if he could. 'For almost all the crimes for which men, generally speaking, are first flogged, 2 or 3 hours' extra drills or duty would be an ample reparation.' Yet three out of every four men returning from foreign service had scarred backs. The often flogged became 'like spotted or diseased sheep bearing some pestilential mark'.

Flogging, however, was considered mercy, the death sentence was so common. We have records of these terrible scenes also. Soldiers were paraded to form three sides of a square, the fourth being left for the condemned and his executioners. Then from guardroom to execution a procession moved to the strains of the 'Dead March': the Provost Marshal on horseback, followed by two files of soldiers with arms reversed, the prisoner and parson, and last of all the shooting party—twelve privates, under a corporal and sergeant. After parading round the square, the procession halted beside the coffin, where the clergyman prayed, himself often weeping, the watching soldiers weeping, the sepoys usually in almost hysteria. Then the condemned man stood to attention, with his eyes bound, to hear the death warrant read again to him.

Such were executions of the more formal kind. But in the prodigality with which men's lives were spilt, and not only in battle, often there was no time for all this pageantry of wretchedness; the condemned were sent huggermugger out of life. Here is a vignette, from that Peninsular campaign which is one of England's glories:

'Eleven knelt on one grave at Ituero. It is an awful ceremony, a military execution. . . . Some prisoners were fortunate enough to be *killed*, others were only wounded, some untouched. I galloped up. An unfortunate Rifleman called to me by name—he was awfully wounded—"Oh, Mr. Smith, put me out of my misery," and I literally ordered the firing-party, when reloaded, to run up and shoot the poor wretches.'[1]

We have got rather far away from the Duke of Wellington's comfortable words to the Military Discipline Commission. Returning to that Commission, we can now perhaps understand some of the other evidence given before it.

[1] *The Autobiography of Sir Harry Smith*, i. 59–60.

'*Question.* Do you take recruits for the East India Company?

Answer. No, only for the King's service. . . . I had the son of a peer of the realm come to me within the last few months. . . . I recently had a lady who came down in her carriage with her own son to place him with me as a recruit. I asked her to tell me what was his prevailing vice, and she candidly told me that he was a robber; but from the father of the other young gentleman I never could obtain any direct information of the sort; he merely said that his son was "a finished blackguard". I certainly found him wanting in proper pride, but he has sometimes cried before me, which I thought showed not a total absence of feeling.

Question. In your opinion, which is the best description of recruit?

Answer. The common agricultural labourer.

Question. Would you prefer such to the sons of tradesmen, who have been taught to read and write, and received a certain degree of education?

Answer. By far. I have observed that the fewer men who read or write in a troop or company the better behaved they are.'

We have seen that this was also the opinion of General Lake, though not of Charles Metcalfe, his Political Officer. From all this testimony the reader may draw what conclusions he likes.

The life of the common soldier, then, was little above that of the brutes that eat and sleep and pursue and mate, and in their season die, and in some respects was far below this existence. In such glancing references as his betters give him, he is seen, as right up to our own day it has been too much the vogue to see him—as a being who must be kept always under the strictest discipline, a splendid fellow when he is launched at death and overcomes his dread of it, at other times living on a barely sentient level, amenable to animal inducements of physical pleasure and pain. This opinion is kept up by the usual conventions. When a military man is writing his memoirs, at some point sooner or later he reminds himself that he must bring in 'humour' ('Where is Moonshine? Call Moonshine'), and humour is brought in accordingly. The author chucklingly tells of an Irish soldier he once knew—or of whom he heard—and how 'Pat' or 'Mike' with a 'rich brogue' (usually reproduced, with a sprinkling of 'Begorras') said something which sent his listeners into peals of laughter, just after Pat (or Mike) had done something outrageously unlawful or was about to be sentenced to something outstandingly painful. The convention never varied—until, within our own memory 'Easter slew Connolly's men' and showed us an Irishman who was not quite the grinning forelock-pulling devil of an amusing scapegrace of Kipling (and how many writers of the pre-Kipling era) and the Irish R.M. stories. The incident related often takes up quite a lot of space on the printed page, but the reader who can recall one that afforded him a smile has been luckier than the present writer, though I think I have read reasonably widely in military literature of the period we have been considering. Generally the humour lurks in what has always seemed funny to people not readily amused by any other kind of comedy—in the poverty or ragged misery of those who look or say what is held to be funny.

We have with us still those who bring forward the old arguments for the infliction of death for loss of nerve or for giving way to sleep when the body sags down helplessly under long-continued fatigue. The mentality still persists, which considers that the fighting man should be kept at a brute level, unvexed by sharing,

'Though full of pain, this intellectual being,
These thoughts that wander through eternity.'

Now, however, the historian cannot be historian only. He must have opinions of some kind, and must sometimes, when his mind is arrested by some wretchedness of yesterday, wonder if its cause and the possibility of recurrence have even now vanished for ever —and wonder even if it was right, or necessary, or worthy of the fame of a very great nation, such as we are. On this point some of us have a right to speak, for in our youth we saw at close quarters these military executions, and we know the unimaginative stupidity that puts them through.

XLIII

REFLECTIONS: POLITICAL

'PROBABLY PEACE has never descended anywhere more gratefully than on the wasted regions of Central India.'[1] Its principal authors were aware of the boon that they were bringing, and with a complacency not altogether unjustified regarded themselves as qualified by character to bring such gifts:

'With the means we had at our command, the work of force was comparatively easy; the liberality of our Government gave grace to conquest, and men were for the moment satisfied to be at the feet of generous and humane conquerors. Wearied with a state of continued warfare and anarchy, the loss even of power was hardly regretted: halcyon days were anticipated, and men prostrated themselves in hopes of elevation. All these impressions, made by the combined effects of power, humanity, and fortune, were improved to the utmost by the character of our first measures. The agents of Government were generally individuals who had acquired a name in the scene where they were employed: they were unfettered by rules and their acts were adapted to soothe the passions, and accord with the habits and prejudices of those whom they had to conciliate or to reduce to obedience.'[2]

There was in all India one Power, and one Power only.

'Rich and poor, princes and sepoys, fear the *Koompanny Bahador* (the Honourable Company), and the resident, as its representative. To them this Koompanny Bahador is a terrible myth, that awes and terrifies. Amongst the very ignorant in India, it is no uncommon impression that the Koompanny is a frightful monster of portentous power and energy, dwelling in a far-off land, but able to see all that takes place in India—whether man or angel or devil, they cannot say, but something awful and frightful unquestionably.'[3]

The representatives of this man-eating demon now set the Princes in their positions, lifting them out of the chaos in which they were submerged. When thus picked up and re-established, 'the Princes' were as completely helpless and derelict as any powers since the beginning of the world. Had the British Government not intervened, nothing but extinction lay before the Rajput States, and disintegration before the Maratha States. As for such States as Oudh and the Nizam's dominions, their very existence was

[1] Thompson and Garratt, *The Rise and Fulfilment of British Rule in India*, 280.
[2] Malcolm, *Central India*, ii. 264–5.
[3] *The Private Life of an Eastern King*, 192.

bogus; they were kept in a semblance of life, only by means of the breath blown through them by the Protecting Power.

The deed was done in a good-humoured mood, that was generous with gestures. It had the tolerance that often goes with cynicism and makes cynicism (despite the moralists) sometimes so attractive a quality. The 'Princes' would be useful as buffers; and also as cesspits, into which the accumulating miseries of the rest of India could seep and, like warring germs, prey on each other. Elphinstone, in evidence before the Committee of the House of Commons on Indian Affairs, 1832, put this with characteristic clearness:

'It appears to me to be our interest as well as our duty to use every means to preserve the allied Governments: it is also our interest to keep up the number of independent powers. Their territories afford a refuge to all those whose habits of war, intrigue, or depredation make them incapable of remaining quiet in ours; and the contrast of their government has a favourable effect on our subjects, who, while they feel the evils they are actually exposed to, are apt to forget the greater ones from which they have been delivered. If the existence of independent powers gives occasional employment to our armies, it is far from being a disadvantage.'[1]

Long after he had left India, when a quarter of a century of rapid annexations had brought about the Mutiny, he did not conceal his pleasure that the later policy had proved to be mistaken. The States, even though in some the people themselves were restive or actually rose, had stood as breakwaters, saving alien rulers from submergence, at least for a time:

'I think the ardour for the consolidation of territory, concentration of authority, and uniformity of administration which was lately so powerful, must have been a good deal damped by recent events. Where should we have been now, if Sindia, the Nizam, the Sikh chiefs, &c., had been *annexed*, the subordinate presidencies abolished, the whole army thrown into one, and the revenue system brought into one mould?'[2]

A 'realist', Elphinstone expressed himself not dissimilarly to Malcolm, when the disturbances were just over. 'We have never seized a whole country at once, but have always left an independent state remaining, under which those who were discontented with our government might find a refuge' (3 May 1818). 'We must have some sink to receive all the corrupt matter that abounds in India, unless we are willing to taint our own system by stopping the discharge of it' (11 July 1818).

That some such safety-valve as the States was necessary, and not for the ignobler elements of the Indian population only, was

[1] *Life*, ii. 315.

[2] 20 December 1857. *Life*, ii. 400.

admitted. No doubt British rule brought peace and a large measure of security for person and property, but it brought also depression down to a condition of dependence and insignificance. Elphinstone, in 1819, wrote to Metcalfe:

'It must be owned our Government labours under natural disadvantages . . . both as to the means of rendering our instruments conspicuous, and of attaching them to our cause. All places of trust and honour must be filled by Europeans. We have no regular army to afford honourable employment to persons incapable of being admitted to a share of the government, and no court to make up by honours and empty favour for the absence of the other more solid objects of ambition.'

Malcolm, at the close of the wars, remarked, 'Our present condition is one of apparent repose, but full of danger'. He added:

'There are many causes which operate to make a period like this one of short duration; and the change to a colder system of policy, and the introduction of our laws and regulations into countries immediately dependent upon us, naturally excite agitation and alarm. It is the hour in which men awake from a dream. Disgust and discontent succeed to terror and admiration; and the princes, the chiefs, and all who had enjoyed rank or influence, see nothing but a system dooming them to immediate decline and ultimate annihilation. . .

The establishment of the British authority over Central India, though recognized at first by almost all classes as a real blessing, because it relieved them from intolerable evils, begins already to be regarded by the princes, the chiefs, and military portion of the community, with very mixed sentiments, among which serious apprehensions as to the permanence of their present condition are predominant. . . .

The same classes of men do not fill the same places in society, under our government, as they did under a Native prince; nor are men actuated by similar motives. Our administration, though just, is cold and rigid. If it creates no alarm, it inspires little, if any, emulation. The people are protected, but not animated or attached. It is rare that any native of India living under it can suffer injury or wrong; but still more rare that he can be encouraged or elevated by favour or distinction. Our rules and regulations constitute a despotic power, which is alike imperative upon the governors and the governed. Its character impels it to generalize, and its forms, as well as principles, are unyielding.'

All these considerations were to exist throughout the next century and still longer, and they should explain what is a perplexity to many good people, India's apparent lack of gratitude for 'all that we have done for them'. Perhaps no alien rule was ever more uniformly consistent with the rulers' own sense of justice; but no alien rule, set over a people far advanced in civilization, ever so reluctantly, and by such maddeningly calculated instalments, relinquished its absolute authority.

In British India, for even the ablest Indians, there was nothing except employment of a mean sort. Lord Hastings in his dispassionate manner noted this in his *Journal*, *passim*, as he noted also the discourteous carriage of the British in general, to those they so despised. As a matter of fact, over close on a century and a half, in India we have shocked everyone who came to us from outside—a statement which the reader can check for himself, by studying the witness of the successive Governors-General, men conservative enough as a rule but accustomed to a theory that other men had souls and personalities of a kind. It was probably in part reaction, that Lord Hastings turned so readily and trustfully to the more generous of the eager spirits who were working, not in Calcutta but in the lonely responsibilities of Native India, where they must find their amenities in good relations with the men they ruled or negotiated with. He gave them power and authority *plenis manibus*, as no Governor-General had done before him.

These men felt the faults of their countrymen and their system even more strongly than he did; they ventured to press their opinions on him, in a way they would never have dared to press them on Lord Wellesley. With Minto and Hastings, stiff though the latter was in formal intercourse and on public occasions, an easing of tension entered Indian affairs. Munro was able to send Lord Hastings his long and often quoted memorandum, 12 August 1817:

'The strength of the British Government enables it to put down every rebellion, to repel every foreign invasion, and to give to its subjects a degree of protection which those of no Native power enjoy. Its laws and institutions also afford them a security from domestic oppression, unknown in those states; but these advantages are dearly bought. They are purchased by the sacrifice of independence, of national character, and of whatever renders a people respectable. The Natives of the British provinces may, without fear, pursue their different occupations . . . and enjoy the fruits of their labor in tranquillity; but none of them can aspire to anything beyond this mere animal state of thriving in peace—none of them can look forward to any share in the legislation or civil or military government of their country. It is from men who either hold, or are eligible to public office, that Natives take their character; where no such men exist, there can be no energy in any other class of the community. The effect of this state of things is observable in all the British provinces, whose inhabitants are certainly the most abject race in India. No elevation of character can be expected among men who, in the military line, cannot attain to any rank above that of subahdar, where they are as much below an ensign as an ensign is below the commander-in-chief, and who, in the civil line, can hope for nothing beyond some petty judicial or revenue office, in which they may, by corrupt means, make up for their slender salary.

The consequence, therefore, of the conquest of India by the British arms would be, in place of raising, to debase the whole people. There is perhaps no example of any conquest in which the Natives have been so completely excluded from all share of the government of their country as in British India.

Among all the disorders of the Native states, the field is open for every man to raise himself; and hence among them there is a spirit of emulation, of restless enterprise and independence, far preferable to the servility of our Indian subjects. The existence of independent Native states is also useful in drawing off the turbulent and disaffected among our Native troops.'

This approach not being snubbed, Munro returned to the argument, writing to the same correspondent, 12 November 1818:

'Foreign conquerors have treated the natives with violence, and often with great cruelty, but none has treated them with so much scorn as we; none have stigmatized the whole people as unworthy of trust, as incapable of honesty, and as fit to be employed only where we cannot do without them. It seems to be not only ungenerous, but impolitic, to debase the character of a people fallen under our dominion. . . .'

'Their exclusion from offices of trust and emolument has become a part of our system of government, and has been productive of no good. Whenever, from this cause, the public business falls into arrear, it is said to be owing to the want of a sufficient number of Europeans; and more European agency is recommended as a cure for every evil. Such agency is too expensive; and, even if it was not, it ought to be abridged rather than enlarged, because it is, in many cases, much less efficient than that of the natives. For the discharge of all subordinate duties, but especially in the judicial line, the natives are infinitely better qualified than Europeans. I have never seen any European whom I thought competent, from his knowledge of the language and the people, to ascertain the value of the evidence given before him. The proceedings in our courts of judicature, which in our reports make a grave and respectable appearance, are, I know, frequently the subject of derision among the natives.'

Munro is often quoted as if he stood alone in such opinions. But, as we have seen, this is not so. To John Adam, Malcolm deplored 'the vexatious and expensive litigation' that had followed every successful war except the conquest of Mysore (when the Duke of Wellington—who looked on lawyers generally as a criminal tribe—and those who were associated with him took special pains to keep civilians out). It completed the impoverishment and enslavement spread by the sword. 'I am quite assured that in nine cases out of ten this has been caused by an unwise precipitation in the process of amalgamating our new countries with our old.'[1]

[1] Elphinstone styles the High Court and its adjuncts 'the much-dreaded

Malcolm admitted to another correspondent that the lawyers and their allies were doubtless excellent persons. He pleaded, nevertheless, that Indian rule and methods should be kept alive:

'The men who, with their new systems and improvements, proceeded to the demolition of the most ancient, I might almost say sacred, institutions of India, were virtuous and able; but in acting without local and minute experience, in venturing to legislate for millions of human beings and countries with whom they were imperfectly acquainted, they showed both ignorance and presumption. Bold in personal rectitude, and proud of superior light to other public servants, they forgot, in their conscientious hurry to give their Government the full benefit of their purity and wisdom, every principle by which a sensible man proceeding in such a great task should regulate his proceedings, and what with their simplifications and generalizations they have precipitated us into a fine mess'.

Malcolm himself preferred 'the cautious diffidence of knowledge' to the spirit of ruthless 'improvement' into the system of British courts and their organized manipulation of truth, which passed for law. There was

'no one act of my friend Sir Thomas Munro that I admire so much as his sweeping Madras of all the young gentlemen, who had fixed themselves in garden-houses, as the inheritors elect of the future offices of secretaries, councillors, &c. They must now, thank God, go through country work, and learn from personal observation the men, and their habits, for whom they are to legislate'.

To yet another correspondent (J. Young), Malcolm replied:

'I regret as deeply as you, or any man can, that there is no opening for natives. The system of depression becomes more alarming as our power extends . . . we must, or we cannot last, contrive to associate the natives with us in the task of rule, and in the benefits and gratifications which accrue from it . . . the shoals of prejudice, ignorance, and jealousy that exist in what the Persians call the Sea of Power—England.'

To Elphinstone, he wrote:

'The fault I find with what you term the younger politicians (counting yourself a *Reish Suffeid*, or greybeard) is not so much that they despise the Natives and Native Governments, but that they are impatient of abuses, and too eager for reform. I do not think they know so well as we old ones what a valuable gentleman Time is; how much better work is done, when it does itself, than when done by the best of us.

There cannot be a severer trial to an active, humane, and just mind, than to condemn it to associate with those who govern Native States. It requires all the lessons of long experience, combined with

Adawluts'. The reader will remember that when Lake was marching up country, in 1803, it was said that villages fled in mass, not because they feared the soldiery, but because they understood that the High Court demon was accompanying it.

a constant recollection of what is good for our general policy, not our local interests, to stand such a trial. . . .'

Elphinstone's answer to this was one that expressed alarm: 'The picture you draw of the state of India, as it is likely to be for the next four or five years, makes me regret that you are likely so soon to leave it. It has sometimes struck me that the fault of our younger politicians—who have never seen the Indian states in the days of their power—is a contempt for the natives, and an inclination to carry everything with a high hand.'[1]

All this is now a finished controversy. Since India is on the threshold of self-government, it has a historical interest only. But it has that interest.

[1] 24 May 1819. Malcolm, as it happened, did not leave India so soon as was expected; he stayed till 1830.

XLIV

STATUS OF THE PRINCES. THE KING OF DELHI

In brief, what these men envisaged was a period when the British would do little more than preserve internal and external peace, a kind of pre-Dominion status for India. Even Metcalfe, who was prejudiced against the rule of Native States, as Malcolm and Munro and Elphinstone were not, accepted it that the work of his own people was to educate India for freedom, and to hasten on that day. Their attitude was worlds away from that of the generation beginning to enter India, and they were troubled by awareness of impending change. They themselves with complete equanimity contemplated the gradual passing of British control into the background:

'It has always been a favourite notion of mine that our object ought to be to place ourselves in the same relation to the natives as the Tartars are in to the Chinese; retaining the government and military power, but gradually relinquishing all share in the civil administration, except that degree of control which is necessary to give the whole an impulse and direction. This operation must be so gradual that it need not even alarm the Directors (as you suppose) for their civil patronage; but it ought to be kept in mind, and all our measures ought to tend to that object. The first steps are to commence a systematic education of the natives for civil offices, to make over to them at once a larger share of judicial business, to increase their emoluments generally, and to open a few high prizes for the most able and honest among them. The period when they may be admitted into Council (as you propose) seems to be distant, but they might very safely be consulted on all topics not political, and where there were no secrets to keep, and no places to dispose of. . . . With regard to the native princes here, you may leave them to their natural fate. Every Indian government (perhaps every Asiatic one) expires after a very short existence. . . . Where there is a stable government, such as Europeans alone can found, it must necessarily swallow up all the ephemeral governments around it; and to this, not to the subsidiary system, we may ascribe what has happened already, and what is still in progress.'[1]

Lord Hastings himself, though, as Dr. Mehta points out in his excellent monograph, he made more treaties than any other Governor-General (and inevitably these treaties put one of the parties engaged into a subordinate position), was not annexation-

[1] Letter to Henry Ellis, 30 October 1826: *Life of Elphinstone*, ii. 186–7.

ist. He was 'imperialistic in his outlook, without being of a predatory mentality . . . essentially a militarist . . . at the same time there was in him a conciliatory spirit, which did not make him a ruthless conqueror'.[1] He said repeatedly what was said repeatedly after his time, that the British Government had no right, no claim, no desire, to interfere in the States' internal affairs. Even where the gross misgovernment of Oudh was under discussion, Lord Hastings wrote: 'What is that to us? One must lament to see any portion of the human race under oppressive sway. But we are not charged with the quixotic obligation of vindicating the rights of all mankind.'[2]

Nevertheless, it is hard for the historian to see the States as the independent administrations that their propagandists to-day claim they were when Lord Hastings decided their external status.

Their political status was never in doubt. By title and admission, the leading Prince, the Nizam, was a representative of the Mogul Emperor, as the founder of his dynasty[3] had been in fact when his career began. We have seen how the Nizam was offended by the impropriety with which Oudh's Nawab Wazir (another title implying subordination) accepted the title of 'King', with its connotation of sovereignty. There was only one King in India, 'the King of Delhi'.

Of that King's Court, the Rajput Princes, as also the Maratha chieftains, were admittedly also officers. Two South Indian States, Mysore and Travancore, which might have claimed an independent derivation of their authority, had been brought by conquest under the Company's suzerainty, and in Mysore the former Hindu line restored. Kutch lingered on, outside the sphere where the Company was active, until it was conquered in 1819, and 'caught in the wide sweep of the net of treaties'.[4] Sind was conquered and annexed in 1843. But Sind was hardly a 'State'.

In 1819, then, there were only two independent States—Nepal, which is still outside the Indian political system, and the Punjab. In the latter, Ranjit Singh was alarmed by the growth of a Power that had now completely overrun the wild and vast regions which had kept his and its territories apart, except for the point where they impinged in the Delhi enclave and Ludhiana, that enclave's outpost. In 1822 he engaged his first foreign commanders,

[1] *Lord Hastings and the Indian States*, 261.

[2] *Minute*, 3 April: Bengal Secret Consultations, No. 4, 21 June 1814.

[3] Asaf Jah.

[4] *Oxford History of India*, 639. It had been caught earlier, in 1809, and again, in 1816.

the two Italians, Ventura and Allard, who had been colonels of infantry and cavalry respectively in Napoleon's army. But while he lived he never indulged the slightest dream of measuring his strength against that of the Company, and after his death some regard for him lived on in the British also, as having been a faithful friend and sometimes almost ally. It was not until the two hard-fought campaigns of 1846 and 1848–9, which extinguished the last independent State in India, that the Sikh Power went down.

If the Princes' political status was plain, and such as to make any claim to 'sovereign rights' in the full sense untenable, if based on an appeal to history, their actual condition of abject misery and weakness was still more obvious.

The King of Delhi

The King of Delhi was what Warren Hastings had termed his predecessor, nearly half a century earlier, an empty pageant. But he and his nominal subjects were discontented pageants. How much the still considerable pomp and prestige of the pre-Mutiny Delhi meant to Indian, and in particular Mussulman, pride and self-respect, the British have never realized.[1] Hatred crept and lurked in the festering streets, whose misery depressed Bishop Heber when he rode through them. His own compatriots were aware of the hatred, and when the final assault was made on still unconquered Bharatpur[2] they admitted 'that, should our army fail again, few events would go so near to fulfil the shouts of the mob a few months back in the streets of Delhi—"Company ka raj ko guia!" (The rule of the Company is at an end!)[3]

India's allegiance still went out to the King. This opinion affected many of the British themselves: a tradition grew up quickly, that Metcalfe as Resident had treated him harshly and discourteously. Metcalfe was aware of this, and resented it; he held to his opinion that from the first, and all along, the King had been too much deferred to. This opinion he gradually imposed on successive Governors-General.

Lord Minto (whose opinions Metcalfe did much to form) disliked the steady flow of complimentary gifts to Delhi, from Princes who still turned towards the Mogul sun, even though that

[1] For a sympathetic and impressive picture of pre-Mutiny Delhi from the accounts of survivors from that time, see C. F. Andrews' *Zaka Ullah of Delhi*.

[2] It was stormed, Metcalfe deciding on the campaign and directing it, in 1825. For an account of the campaign, from previously unused documents, I refer the reader to my *Metcalfe*, 241 ff.

[3] Heber, *Journey*, iii. 369.

sun had all but sunk below the horizon. This dislike Lord Hastings took over. When he went up country, and the King refused to meet him on a basis of equality, he instructed Adam to tell Metcalfe to dismiss all expectation of any meeting at all. 'Have the goodness, with your accustomed diplomatic ability, to reconcile the King to the impracticability of a meeting.'[1] When Lord Amherst, the next Governor-General, visited Delhi, by a trick a ceremonial was imposed on him, which in Indian eyes was an admission of the King's suzerainty. Yet even Metcalfe, looking back on this incident from Lord William Bentinck's time, tolerantly allowed it as 'not amiss, because the superiority of the King is acknowledged and the motive of the acknowledgment cannot be mistaken',[2] even while he regretted 'to see that the King is assuming more than he did' and that Bentinck had given way, though ever so little. 'We have on the whole behaved generously towards the King from the first; and I never found him unreasonable or assuming . . . I should think it our best policy in future to let him sink into insignificance, instead of upholding our dignity as we have done.'[3] He was vexed at the manner in which the Princes, while cool towards distinctions offered by the Paramount Power, eagerly sought them from the King of Delhi; for example, in 1832 the King, who had been at last forbidden to grant titles outside his own family, sold one to the Raja of Bikaner.[4]

This universal esteem made it necessary for the British Government to proceed with extreme care. 'Aware of the ghosts of former reverence still existing in the immense shadows that make up Indian opinion, ghosts still active and for the most part malignant to the British',[5] Metcalfe 'recommended a moderate and cautious use of the Supreme Government's right' as the fountain of honour, 'until opinion grew used to it'.[5] 'The same Princes who would submit to it as an Honor, even now, at the Court of Dihlee, would think it a degradation at the Hands of The Governor-General.' All that the latter could do, as late as 1832, was to insist that the King's exchange of presents with the Princes should be regulated by him. It was an immense embarrassment when in 1831 the King appealed to the Directors over the head of the Indian Government, with a threat to appeal to the King of England if the Directors proved unsatisfactory, and sent the celebrated Rammohan Roy as his representative to London. Metcalfe was angry at charges that his own actions as Resident in

[1] Thompson, *Metcalfe*, 154. [2] *Ibid*, 281: 13 November 1831.
[3] *Ibid*, 286: 26 April 1832. [4] *Ibid*, 287 ff: 9 May 1832. [5] *Ibid*.

Delhi had given additional legal basis to the King's claims to suzerainty. 'I have renounced my former allegiance to the Throne of Dihlee.' He could not recollect having done what he was alleged to have done, 'but I cannot at this time say that I never did, for when there was no appearance of presumption on the part of the King, I was disposed to be a dutiful subject. I should now think it impolitic to honour him in such pretensions, & desirable to let him down quietly, as far as possible, into insignificance, without doing anything offensive'. 'The Authorities at Home ought to decline negotiations with Ram Mohun Rae, and refer the King to the Authorities in India'. But the Company's own actions and admissions over many years put them in a difficult position, as Metcalfe's own statements abundantly indicate.[1]

The Company, then, could not deny that it had originally given sufficient, and far more than sufficient, grounds for the belief that it acknowledged its own title as held from the descendant of the Mogul Emperor. Occasions for implementing this acknowledgment came with increasing rarity and consistent inconsistency, but they came. Until 1835, the Company coined in the name of Shah Alam, the blind old man whom Lake had found seated under a tattered canopy when he entered Delhi. Since Shah Alam died in 1806, 'The Government seems to have entertained a confused notion that it safeguarded its status of independence by using the dead monarch's authority, instead of that of his successors'.[2] When the question was brought up by Rammohan Roy's mission, in 1831, it was not much use for the man who knew most about the matter, Major E. W. Cunninghame, to protest that the King's position in 1805 'you must perceive was merely given as a plaything'. Even Cunninghame had to admit, 'it must be confessed there was a laxity in the early stages of his being under our protection that has been the Basis of all the intrigue and misconception'.[3]

The question has some historical importance. In the first place, there has been unnecessary lack of understanding of the fact that the Mutiny of 1857 at once found a focus in the Court of Delhi. Secondly, there has been a good deal of literature justifying the trial and condemnation, for rebellion, after the Mutiny was crushed, of the last King of Delhi, Bahadur Shah II. The events which caused his disappearance from the land where his ancestors

[1] I am sorry to refer to my own *Metcalfe* so much, but a study of Rammohan Roy's mission from manuscript sources is in this book, 286 ff, and I must refer the reader to it for fuller knowledge.

[2] *Ibid*, 137.

[3] *I.O.R., H.M.S.*, 708, is a file that contains the history of thirty years, from Lake's capture of Delhi onwards.

played so tremendous and imposing a part are summed up discreetly in standard works,[1] but the trial was one of those events which show, beyond the possibility of confusion, the differences between generations. We need not trouble to discuss the opposite extreme of opinion, though it has found support, that it was the Company that was guilty of 'rebellion'; it is too grotesque for examination. But that the titular King of Delhi could be brought to trial as a rebel would have angered every man of first rank, who had served in India before 1835. As to the trial, it was a piece of politics, not of justice; and, as unpublished letters of John Lawrence, giving instructions that the King should be found guilty, show, was a waste of time.[2]

The King, then, was nothing in himself, but in his claims an embarrassment. Until this relict of the Mogul Empire had gone, in the body politic of India there existed a constant irritant. Or we may say, changing the metaphor, the political framework was not complete, despite the extent and overwhelming character of the British victories, while the King lived in Delhi.

The last Emperor died in Rangoon, in exile, 1862. Two of his sons, as everyone knows, were summarily executed outside Humayan's tomb, by Major Hodson, in 1858. Another son, Ferozshah, escaped from India after the Mutiny (in which he bore a gallant and chivalrous part), and was last heard of about 1864, as a beggar by the wayside, near Mecca. Yet another son, Fakr-ud-Din, acted as a spy on a British officer, disguised as his servant, was discovered and shot through the knees and left for dead, recovered, and for many years after the Mutiny lived as a crippled faquir in Delhi, dying at the beginning of this century, his identity unknown to the British, but known to, and deeply reverenced by, many Hindus and Moslems. There are still descendants of the House of Timur in Delhi. One is said to have been accidentally hurt by the Duke of Connaught's car, when plying a *tikka ghari*.[3]

[1] 'In January 1858 he was brought to trial, and after two months' investigation was condemned to exile': *Oxford History of India*, 723.

'Bahadur Shah was tried for rebellion, condemned, and removed a prisoner to Rangoon': *Cambridge Shorter History of India*, 757.

[2] I have read these letters, and can put my hands on them again.

[3] A *tikka ghari* is a tat-drawn carriage plying for hire. I have heard that the Duke visited the man in hospital, but do not know if this is true.

XLV

THE DOCTRINE OF PARAMOUNTCY

PARAMOUNTCY IS now a question to be decided by the lawyers and politicians, and by the course of future events. Its historical origin and growth have been made clear, but a few pages of summary are called for.

Lord Wellesley acted, and always felt, as the Paramount Power, and his immediate subordinates adopted his attitude. Of the East India Company, Metcalfe wrote, 1806 ('granting, without discussion, the full justice of all the lamentations which are uttered on this subject by many worthy directors and proprietors'), 'Sovereigns you are, and as such must act'. He and his friends, while awaiting the assumption of paramountcy in the fullness of time, consistently so acted whenever they could. The idea came as no abrupt inspiration, although its first clear expression as a doctrine is in Ochterlony's letter to Metcalfe, 21 March 1820.[1] Metcalfe's letter to his father, from which I have quoted, shows that it had then been long familiar to him and his circle—this belief, constantly talked over, that the British Government had rights overruling the rights of all other Governments in India. Ochterlony himself, in 1812, deposed the Raja of Patiala (and was wounded by a man who disapproved of this proceeding).

The term 'paramountcy' was frequently used by Lord Hastings, who picked it up from his own great officers. Subsequent events, however, had submerged the thoughts and attitude of Lord Wellesley's time, and even Metcalfe, as we have seen, like the rest of his countrymen in India had to recede from his belief. 'Paramountcy' sank back into shadow, and the Princes' position became uncertain, especially since the Company still acknowledged 'the King of Delhi' as India's real suzerain. It was set back further by the third major war of these twenty years, 1799–1819, that against the Gurkhas of Nepal. This war, chequered and in many episodes inglorious, aroused doubts, and not in Indians only, of the Company's ability and strength. It directly encouraged the Peshwa to his attempt to break free. But in the end the Peshwa's dismissal,

[1] Now in the Parasnis MSS. Collection, at Satara. 'I hope His Lordship will in Virtue of his Power & Paramountcy forbid all future Invasions of Surhoie & fix himself a Sum which the Rajah *must take*'.

after desultory fighting that was a disturbance rather than a campaign, and the binding down, without actual war, of his chief subordinate chiefs (who to-day are 'Ruling Princes'), left the Company in a pre-eminence so plain that all could see that the alleged suzerain in Delhi was, even more than when Warren Hastings used the phrase, 'a mere pageant'.

During this process of half-forgetfulness and slow recovery, the doctrine of paramountcy came back by degrees to the wisest and most experienced of the British officers, such men as Malcolm, Munro, Metcalfe, Elphinstone, Jenkins, and Ochterlony. Of these, only Metcalfe and Ochterlony were from the first prepared to proclaim it and act on it. It was these two, in their long years of vigil in and above the confusion of Central India, who formally evolved the full doctrine, in a form indistinguishable from that held by Lord Reading, in his two letters to the Nizam. The classical document is Metcalfe's Minute, August 1825, by which he justified his decision to carry the Company's quarrel with Bharatpur to the conquest of that State. He speaks of the *fact*[1] of paramountcy, by which the British Government had its 'duty as supreme guardians of general tranquillity, law, and right, to maintain the legal succession'.[2] The Directors, after Bharatpur had fallen, marked their rejection, and indeed resentment, of this doctrine. Their 'high sense' of 'the ability and services' of Sir Charles Metcalfe made it 'only the more necessary that we should distinctly express our dissent from his opinions' and his endeavour 'to establish the necessity and propriety of British interference in the succession and internal concerns of independent native powers'. 'The extension of our power by the events of the years 1817–18' had not 'in any degree extended our right of interference'. Whatever happened, as to succession or anything else inside a State, 'we have neither the right nor the duty to act as "Supreme Guardians of Law and Right", and as such to constitute ourselves judges of the validity of the person who exercises the functions of Government'.

This reply, which was dated 26 March 1826, was clear in its terms. But meanwhile Bharatpur, about which the Directors were arguing, had fallen, with tremendous slaughter, 18 January 1826, eight thousand of the defenders lying dead in a confined area. All India had heard the cannon and exploding mines, which spoke louder than the Directors' chidings. No communication therefore ever fell more dead. The Company was paramount, not only in

[1] Metcalfe's italics.

[2] See Thompson, *Life of Lord Metcalfe*, 242 ff., pages based mainly on unpublished and previously unexamined letters.

power but by the decision of its representatives on the spot, and from now onward it acted as such.

But of course the decision, which Wellesley had anticipated and Minto had kept in abeyance, had been finally taken by Lord Hastings, in the settlement of 1818 and 1819. Unless the Company had been the Paramount Power, he had no right to compel Sindhia to forsake his own suzerain, the Peshwa. It is against all historical fact for the Princes to argue to-day, as they do:

'States like Baroda, Gwalior, Udaipur, Alwar, Nawanagar or Tripura existed already as full-powered States when they first accepted British paramountcy. Their sovereignty was their own, not granted to them by the British. Indeed they were the donors and the Crown the donee. For paramountcy was created by their cession of certain sovereign rights to the Crown.'[1]

Every one of the States there mentioned acknowledged the Mogul as overlord, not one of them then claimed 'sovereignty'. What the States 'granted' was taken by the Company without too much permission being thought necessary, and was increased whenever the Company thought its own exigencies and occasions called for extension. In all essentials, the political framework of India was finished in 1819. 'The relative positions of the parties had changed too decidedly to be governed merely by the written words of the treaties'.[2]

Nevertheless, it is true that, although in 1819 the States which now exist finally ceased to be independent, the conquerors assiduously rebuilt their internal independence and gave back a great deal, and for the next fifteen years even showed a desire to give back still more. The Paramount Power on many occasions explicitly acknowledged that Sindhia and Holkar (for example) were completely independent in internal affairs. Lord Hastings, said Elphinstone (who ought to know, if anyone did), made the States acknowledge British supremacy, but he claimed no control over them internally or over their successions (control over successions was arrogated later without legal right). The object 'was to secure the political supremacy . . . and to obtain the *subordinate co-operation* of the native prince as an ally, not his subjection as a vassal'. The Company was supreme

'in all transactions with foreign States; but all internal affairs were to be regulated as before by the law and usage of the territory, free from any interference of the British Government. The succession, I conceive, was an internal affair.'

[1] *The British Crown and Indian States*, 78, 82. This statement is understood to have been largely the work of Mr. Rushbrooke Williams.

[2] Mehta, 242.

Earlier in the same letter, Elphinstone testified:

'Our relations with the principal states (the Nizam, the Peshwa, Sindia, Holkar, and Raja of Berar, &c.) were those of independent equal Powers, and we possessed no right to interfere in their successions, except such as were derived from our treaties with them, or our situation as a neighbouring state.'[1]

By the strict letter of their treaties, then, the sense of grievance widely felt by the Princes to-day is justified. There has been all along abundant interference in internal affairs. The presence and authority of the Political Officers are resented. One great Maharaja, whose services had been Imperial as well as Indian, told me he himself had had only one Resident whom he did not dislike.

This does not mean that all interference has been unjustified, even if not according to treaty stipulations. The wars did not clear up all India's confusion. Reckless and adventurous spirits were driven into confined areas or into underground activities. Thuggee, in my opinion, was discovered largely because it had known a great increase after the Pindaris were extirpated. In Bentinck's campaign against it, the States—Hyderabad, Oudh, Gwalior in particular, since they were infected regions—co-operated with a readiness in contrast with their reluctance against the Pindaris.

In the last hundred years are numerous instances of major interference by the Paramount Power. One ruler of Baroda has been made to go, and one ruler of Indore also (another was coaxed or trapped into going). Alwar, Nabha, are other States which in recent memory have had their rulers dismissed. The Paramount Power has come down heavily sometimes on barbaric punishments. One Prince during the last century chopped off a thief's hand and foot: another cut off a slave's nose and ears: a third flogged two jailors to death: a fourth impaled an offender: a fifth publicly tortured a criminal: a sixth 'committed an outrage of too shocking and disgusting a character to bear repetition'.[2]

In 1857, the States justified Colonel Sleeman's prediction, that they would one day act as 'breakwaters'. Nationalist India to-day bears them no affection for their services then, which are often cited against them. In 1858, Queen Victoria's Proclamation promised: 'We shall respect the rights, dignity, and honour of native princes as our own'. Annexations ceased, and have not been repeated. In 1861, *sanads*[3] were issued, that defined and guaranteed the Princes' status and rights.

[1] Letter to Colebrooke, 13 February 1850: *Life*, ii. 392.

[2] Sir William Lee-Warner, *The Protected Princes of India*, 306.

[3] Documents granting or guaranteeing status or possessions.

Conclusion

The reader, then, cannot have failed to notice that the men who made the settlements of 1818 and 1819 held in common a body of political doctrine, which they had worked out over a course of many years. Unlike the men of Lord Wellesley's time, they were not opportunists—no men of action ever were less so. They knew their way and had a very fair guess as to its termination and goal. They built wittingly and deliberately, where both their predecessors and immediate successors did it by sheer accident of forceful blows.

Out of prolonged and growing confusion an empire had crystallized. Men who were realists, yet also humanists, found themselves grappling with a system—or lack of system—as unreal as Prester John's fantastic lordship of wilderness. The Mogul Empire was little more than a mist which obscured the forces that were alive in the land. Those forces, Maratha, Gurkha, Sikh, the chieftain, the Pindaris, the war-lords and soldiers of fortune, had to be reckoned with, brushed aside where possible or desirable, acknowledged when necessary. The *Minutes* and letters of the period reflect the eighteenth century's absorption in and grasp of constitutional and political issues, but after Wellesley had gone the British officers who were framing a new world saw that European kingdoms were misleading as models. Therefore, although in their task these men found full scope for exercise of their legal and political acumen, their function was not to provide a flawless political constitution and framework, but to precipitate (in the chemical sense of that word) out of chaos a form that would admit of freer action, undisturbed by a succession of wars. Their philosophy was pragmatic, guided by the principle of workability and also by a sense of justice, often flawed and imperfectly followed out, but nevertheless present. Bitterness came later, in abundant measure and with frequent justification. But perhaps no conquest on such a scale was ever put through with so little of bitterness at the time, and little of bitterness clings to its memory. The work they achieved was to stand the test of over a century, and when all empire and dominion at last are finished their work will still win toleration and sympathy, and not in their own land only.

BIBLIOGRAPHY

THERE IS a lack of good monographs on the leading figures of British-Indian history, but a number of useful books exist, such as Lord Hastings' *Private Journal*, an excellent mirror of his dry and honest, even if limited, intelligence and one that sets down concisely what was thought by the men who influenced him most. There are also some accounts of campaigns by men who took part in them. The same personal and contemporary quality is in the really excellent *Histories* written before 1865: such writers as Marshman, Thornton, Beveridge (whose *History*, 1872, is rather later), Montgomery Martin, have never had adequate recognition of their merits. They had this advantage, that they had only a public of their own people to consider, and did not have to keep glancing over their shoulder, to see if frankness and truthfulness would be overheard and have an adverse political effect. Another flaw in British-Indian historical writing is the way in which our want of interest in anything Indian has allowed such interest as we have felt occasionally to concentrate on one or two episodes, notably the Mutiny, to the almost complete neglect of other events. The outstanding example of this is the War with Nepal. Apart from one practically contemporary account, published in 1822, and the account embedded in Prinsep's book on the Administration of Lord Hastings, I know of nothing that deals with this war, certainly one of the two greatest campaigns in British-Indian history.

My own chapter on it, far the longest in this book, has been written almost entirely from manuscript sources.

MSS. SOURCES

India Office Records, *Home Miscellaneous Series*: referred to in text as I.O.R., H.M.S.: Files 455a, 506, 506a (Metcalfe's 1805 Memoir of Hindusthan West of the Jumna), 511 (pp. 33–87 are concerned with the Ranjit Singh Mission), 512 (Elphinstone's Mission to Kabul), 515–16a (mainly on the Nepal and Pindari-Maratha Wars), 518–22 (mainly Central Indian affairs, in Lord Hastings' time), 542 (2), 542a, 558–61 (Maratha affairs, in Lord Wellesley's time), 578–82 (the same), 591, 592–5 (Mission to Ranjit Singh), 595a–604 (Pindaris, etc.), 616–27 (Maratha and Hyderabad affairs, in Lord Wellesley's time), 636–41 (many treaties, etc., between 1781 and 1830), 643–56 (the Nepal War), 657–9 (Elphinstone's Kabul Mission), 708 (affairs of the King of Delhi, and Rammohan Roy's Mission to London), 724, 733–7 (Malcolm's papers), 738, 776 (district reports, including Metcalfe's on Delhi), 777.

Clive Bayley MSS: letters from Sir Charles Metcalfe to his sister, Georgiana Smyth, beginning in October 1819: 136 letters, with a few of Mrs. Smyth's replies.

Bentinck MSS: 150 letters from Sir Charles Metcalfe to Lord William Bentinck, with some of the latter's answers.

Bombay: Government of Bombay Records.

Calcutta: Imperial Government of India Records.

Lahore: Sohan Lal's *Umdut-ut-Twarikh.*

Poona: Peshwa's *daftar.*
Alienation Office English and Persian Records.

Pondichéry: French records in the Bibliothèque Nationale.

Printed Sources

Acworth, Harry Arbuthnot, *Ballads of the Marathas* (Longmans, 1894).

Aitchison, C. U., *A Collection of Treaties, Engagements and Sunnuds relating to India and Neighbouring Countries*, 7 vols. (Calcutta, 1862 and 1876).

Amir Khan: *see* Busawan Lal.

Army Historical Research, The Journal of, January 1932 (Battle of Delhi, 1803).

Asiastic Annual Register, The, for 1801: *see* Tone, W. H.

Banaji: *see* Gense.

Bennet, Lieutenant: *see* Shah Sooja.

Beveridge, Henry, *A Comprehensive History of India . . . from The First Landing of the English to the Suppression of the Sepoy Revolt*, 3 vols. (London, 1872).

Blacker, Valentine, *Memoir of the Operations . . . during the Mahratta War of 1817, 1818, and 1819* (London, 1821).

Blakiston, J., *Twelve Years' Military Adventures in Three Quarters of the Globe*, 2 vols., 1803–1814 (London, 1829).

Brief Remarks on the Mahratta War and on the Rise and Progress of the French Government in Hindostan under Generals De Boigne and Perron (London, 1804).

Briggs, Lieut.-Colonel John, *An Autobiographical Memoir of the Early Life of Nana Farnavis*, translated by. *See* Macdonald, A.

Broughton, T. D., *Letters written in a Mahratta Camp in the Year 1809:* new edition with introduction by the Right Hon. Sir M. G. Grant Duff (Constable, 1892).

Buckland, C. E., *Dictionary of Indian Biography* (London, 1906).

Burton, Lieut.-Colonel R. S., *The Mahratta and Pindari War.* Compiled for the General Staff, India (Simla, 1910).

Busawan Lal, *Memoirs of the Pathan Soldier of Fortune the Nuwab Ameer-ood-Doulah Mohummud Ameer Khan* (Calcutta, 1832).

Bute, Marchioness of: *see* Hastings, Lord.

Cadell, Sir Patrick, *History of the Bombay Army* (Longmans, 1938).

Cambridge History of India, The, vols. v and vi (Cambridge University Press, 1932).

Cardew, Sir Alexander, *The White Mutiny* (London, 1929).

Cardew, F. G., *A Sketch of the Services of the Bengal Native Army* (Calcutta, 1903).

Carpenter, Mary, *A Review of the Labours, Opinions and Character of Rajah Rammohun Roy* (London and Bristol, 1833).

Chopra, G. L.: *see* Garrett, H. L. O.

Colebrooke, Sir T. E., *Life of the Honourable Mountstuart Elphinstone*, 2 vols. (London, 1884).

Compton, H., *A Particular Account of the European Military Adventurers of Hindustan, from 1784 to 1803* (Fisher Unwin, 1892).

Cunningham, J. D., *A History of the Sikhs* (2nd edition, London, 1853).

Delhi Residency and Agency, Records of the (Lahore: Punjab Government Publications, 1911).

Dodwell E., and Miles, *Alphabetical List of the Hon'ble East India Company's Bengal Civil Servants*, 1780–1803 (London, 1839).

Doss, Ramchunder (under direction of the Hon'ble H. T. Prinsep), *A General Register of the Hon'ble East India Company's Civil Servants of the Bengal Establishment, from 1790 to 1842* (Calcutta, 1844).

Douglas, James, *Bombay and Western India*, 2 vols. (London, 1893).

Dowson, J.: *see* Elliot.

Duff, James Grant, *A History of the Mahrattas*, 3 vols. (London, 1826). Revised by S. M. Edwardes, 2 vols. (Oxford University Press, 1921).

East India Military Calendar, The: containing the Services of General and Field Officers of the Indian Army, 2 vols. (London, 1823).

East India Register and Directory for 1820, The, (London).

East India United Service Journal, The, vol. ii ('A Military Autobiography'); No. V, Part I ('The Pindarry Chief').

Elliot, Sir H. M., and Dowson, J., *The History of India as told by its own Historians* (London, 1877), vol. viii, for story of Bharatpur siege.

Elphinstone, The Honourable Mountstuart, *An Account of the Kingdom of Caubul*, etc. (London, 1815; 2 vols., 1839).

Essays by the Students of the College of Fort William in Bengal, 1802 (Calcutta, 1802).

Fanshawe, H. C., *Delhi Past and Present* (Murray, 1902).

Forrest, Sir G. W., *Selections from Letters, Despatches, etc., in the Bombay Secretariat:* Maratha series (Bombay, 1885).
Selections from State Papers, etc., 2 vols. (Bombay, 1885).
Selections from the State Papers of the Governors-General of India, Warren Hastings, 2 vols. (Oxford, Blackwell: and London, Constable, 1910).

Foster, Sir William, *A Guide to the India Office Records* (London, 1919.)

Francklin, W., *Military Memoirs of George Thomas* (Calcutta, 1803).

Fraser, J. B., *Military Memoir of Lieutenant-Colonel James Skinner, C.B.* (London, 1851).

Furber, Holden, *Henry Dundas, First Viscount Melville, 1742–1811* (Oxford University Press, 1931).

Garratt, G. T., and Thompson, E., *The Rise and Fulfilment of British Rule in India* (Macmillans, 1934).

Garrett, H. L. O., and Chopra, G. L., *Events at the Court of Ranjit Singh, 1810–1817: translated from papers in the Alienation Office, Poona* (Lahore, 1939). *See* Grey.

Gense, J. H. and D. R. Banaji, *The Third English Embassy to Poona* (Mostyn's Diary and Letters): (Bombay, 1934).

Gleig, the Rev. G. R., *The Life of Sir Thomas Munro*, 2 vols. (London, 1830).

The one-volume edition of the same (Murray, London, 1849), contains interesting material omitted from the longer *Life*.

Grey, C., and Garrett, H. L. O., *European Adventurers of Northern India, 1785 to 1849* (Lahore, 1929).

Griffin, Sir Lepel, *Ranjit Singh* ('Rulers of India' series: Clarendon Press, 1893).

Gupta, P. C., *Baji Rao II and the East India Company 1796–1818* (Oxford University Press, 1939).

Gurwood, J., *The Despatches of . . . the Duke of Wellington*, 12 vols. (London, 1834–8). Reissues and revisions (8 vols. 1844–7, and supplementary volumes, at later dates).

Hastings, Lord, the Private Journal of, edited by the Marchioness of Bute, 2 vols. (London, 1858).

Heber, Reginald, *Narrative of a Journey through the Upper Provinces of India, from Calcutta to Bombay, 1824–5, etc.* (John Murray, 1829).

Indian Historical Records Commission, vol. viii (Government of India, 1926).

Innes, P. P., *The History of the Bengal European Regiment, now the Royal Munster Fusiliers, and How It Helped to Win India* (London, 1885).

Jacquemont, Victor, *Letters from India, 1829–32* (London, 1834: and translated with introduction by Catherine Alison Phillips, Macmillan, 1936).

Kaye, Sir John William: *The Administration of the East India Company: a history of Indian Progress* (London, 1853).

Lives of Indian Officers, 3 vols. (London, 1883).

The Life and Correspondence of Major-General Sir John Malcolm, G.C.B., 2 vols. (London, 1856).

The Life and Correspondence of Charles, Lord Metcalfe, 2 vols. (London, 1854: second edition, considerably changed, 1858).

Selections from the Papers of Lord Metcalfe (London, 1855).

The Life of H. St. George Tucker (London, 1864).

Keene, H. G., *History of India from the Earliest Times to the End of the Nineteenth Century*, 2 vols. (Edinburgh, 1906).

Keith, Arthur Berriedale, *A Constitutional History of India* (Methuen, 1936).

Kincaid, C. A., and Parasnis, D. B., *History of the Maratha People*, 3 vols. (Oxford University Press, 1931).

Kindersley, H. F., *A Handbook of the Bombay Government Records* (Bombay, 1921).

Knighton, W., *The Private Life of an Eastern King:* reprinted, with Introduction and Notes by S. B. Smith (Oxford University Press, 1921).

Lee-Warner, Sir William, *The Protected Princes of India* (London, 1894).

Low, Ursula, *Fifty Years with John Company* (Murray, 1936). (The Life of Sir John Low).

Macdonald, A., *Memoir of the Life of the late Nana Furnawees* (1851). Reprinted, together with Briggs' Memoir, and edited, H. G. Rawlinson (Oxford University Press, 1927).

Malcolm, Sir John, *Memoir of Central India, including Malwa and Adjoining Provinces*, 2 vols. (London, 1823: 2nd edition, 1824).

A Mission to Persia (London, 1818).
A Sketch of the Political History of India, from the Introduction of Mr. Pitt's Bill, 1784 to 1823, 2 vols. (London, 1826).
A Sketch of the Sikhs; a Singular Nation, who inhabit the Provinces of the Penjab (London, 1812).
Marsh, Charles, *Review of some Important Passages in the Late Administration of Sir G. H. Barlow at Madras* (London, 1813).
Marshman, J. C., *A History of India*, 3 vols. (London, 1867): abridged one vol. (London, 1876).
Martin, R. Montgomery, *Despatches, Minutes and Correspondence of the Marquess Wellesley, K.G., during his Administration in India*, 5 vols. (London, 1833–7).
The Indian Empire, 5 vols. (London, 1857).
Mehta, M. S., *Lord Hastings and the Indian States* (Taraporevala, Bombay, 1930).
Metcalfe, Charles Theophilus: *see* Essays by Students of Fort William College, *and* Selections from State Papers of, Kaye.
Miles, Captain R. H.: *see East Indian United Service Journal.*
Military Sketches of the Goorka War in India, in the Years 1814, 1815, 1816 (printed by J. Loder, Woodbridge, 1822).
Mill, James, *The History of British India* (with H. H. Wilson's continuation), 9 vols. (London, 1840–6).
Minto, The Countess of, *Life and Letters of Gilbert Elliott, First Earl of, from 1807 to 1814* (Longmans Green, 1880).
Morris, Henry, *The Life of Charles Grant* (John Murray, 1904).
Murray, William: *see* Prinsep, H. T., *Origin of the Sikh Power.*
Nazim, M., *Selections from the Peshwa's Daftar, Miscellaneous Papers* (Bombay Government, 1933). *N.B.* These are in Persian, and deal chiefly with periods earlier and later than this book.
Osborne, the Hon. W. G., *The Court and Camp of Runjeet Singh* (1842).
Owen, Sidney J., *A Selection from the despatches, treaties and other papers of the Marquess of Wellesley during his government of India* (Clarendon Press, 1877).
A Selection from the Despatches . . . relating to India, of Field-Marshal the Duke of Wellington, K.G. (Clarendon Press, 1880).
Parasnis, *see* Kincaid.
Pearse, Colonel Hugh, *Memoir of the Life and Military Services of Viscount Lake* (Blackwood, 1908).
Phillips, Catherine Alison: *see* Jacquemont, Victor.
Press Lists of Old Records in the Punjab Secretariat, 2 vols. (Lahore, 1915).
Prinsep, H. T., *History of the Political and Military Transactions in India during the Administration of the Marquess of Hastings, 1813–23* (London, 1825).
Origin of the Sikh Power in the Punjaub, and Life of Muharaja Runjeet Singh, etc. (Calcutta, 1834).
Punjab Historical Society, Journal of the (Lahore, 1911 onwards).
Rawlinson, H. G., *see* Briggs, also Macdonald.
Raymond, G. M., *Memoires du Comte de Boigne* (Chambéry, 1830).
Roberts, P. E., *History of British India* (Clarendon Press, 1923).
India under Wellesley (Macmillan, 1929).
Ross, Williamson, *The Correspondence of Lord Cornwallis* (London, 1859).

Saint-Genis, Victor de, *Le Général de Boigne* (Poitiers, 1873).
Salt, H., *see* Valentia, Viscount.
Sardesai, Rai Saheb Govind Sakharam, *Handbook to the Records in the Alienation Office* (Bombay Government, 1933).
Malet's Embassy, 1786–97 (Bombay Government, 1936).
The Main Currents of Maratha History (Bombay, 1933).
Marathi Risayats or the History of the Marathas, vols. vii and viii (Bombay, 1938).
Selections from the Peshwa Daftar, esp. vols. 32, *The Private Life of the Later Peshwas*, and 41, *The Last Days of the Maratha Raj, 1779–1818* (Bombay Government, 1933 and 1934). *N.B.* These, and the *Risayats*, are in Marathi and as yet untranslated.
Letters of Mahadji Sindhia (5 vols., Swalior, 1937).
Sarkar, Sir Jadunath, *Mahadji Sindhia and North Indian Affairs, 1785–94* (Bombay Government, 1936).
Poona Residency Correspondence, 4 vols. (Bombay, 1936–7). *See also Malet's Embassy*, Sardesai, S. G. S.
Sen, Surendranath, *Administrative System of the Marathas* (University of Calcutta, 1925).
Military System of the Marathas (Calcutta, 1928).
Studies in Indian History (University of Calcutta, 1930).
Shah Sooja, *Biographical Sketches of, written by Himself at Loôdianah, in 1826–7:* translated by Lieutenant Bennet (*Calcutta Monthly Journal*, 1839).
Shipp, J., *Memoirs of the Extraordinary Military Career of, Late a Lieutenant in His Majesty's 87th Regiment, written by Himself*, 3 vols. (London, 1829).
Smith, Sir Harry, The Autobiography of (London, 1901).
Smith, Vincent A., *The Oxford History of India* (Clarendon Press, 1919).
Sutherland, Captain J., *Sketches of the Relations subsisting between the British Government and the Different Native States* (Calcutta, 1833).
Thompson, Edward, *Life of Lord Metcalfe* (Faber, 1937); (with G. T. Garratt) *The Rise and Fulfilment of British Rule in India* (Macmillan, 1934).
Thorn, Major William, *Memoir of the War in India, etc. 1803 to 1806* (London, 1818).
Thornton, Edward, *The History of the British Empire in India*, 6 vols. (London, 1841 and 1845).
Tikekar, Shripad R., *Sardesai Commemoration Volume* (essays by various hands, many on Maratha history: Dhawale, Bombay, 1938).
Tod, James, *Annals and Antiquities of Rajst'han*, 2 vols. (London, 1829).
Tone, William Henry, *Illustrations of some Institutions of the Mahratta People* (*see Asiatic Annual Register for 1799*, Debrett, 1801).
Valentia, Viscount, and Salt, H., *Voyages and Travels to India and the adjoining countries . . . in the years 1802–1806*, 3 vols. (London, 1809).
Wade, Sir Claude, *A Narrative of the Services, Military and Political of, from the date of his Appointment to India . . . etc., with an Appendix of Official Documents* (Ryde, Isle of Wight: no date, but published, 1847).
Wareham, Eric, *The Bravest Soldier* (Life of General Gillespie: Blackwood, 1937).
Wellesley, The Marquess of, *Notes Relative to the Late Transactions in the*

Mahratta Empire, with an Appendix of Official Documents (London, 1804).
Williams, L. F. Rushbrooke, *The British Crown and the Indian States* (London, 1929).
Wilson, W. J., *History of the Madras Army*, 4 vols. (Madras, 1882).

There are also many contemporary pamphlets, of which a good example is *Review of the Affairs of India from The Year 1798, to the Year 1806, comprehending A Summary Account of the Principal Transactions during that Eventful Period* (London, 1807). These are often annotated by someone obviously possessing firsthand knowledge and able sometimes to correct the text; the habit of annotation of an author was then far commoner than it is now. The copy of the *Review* which I consulted is marked in this manner, as 'By Mr. Welsley', which I take to mean that the Governor-General's brother Henry Wellesley was responsible for it.

INDEX